Pelican Books
The Pelican Guide to Modern Theology
Editor: R. P. C. Hanson

Volume 3
Biblical Criticism

Robert Davidson, M.A., B.D., was born at Markinch, Fife, in
1927. He graduated from the University of St Andrews with
first class honours in classics in 1949 and distinction in Old
Testament studies in 1952. He then lectured in the Department
of Biblical Studies in the University of Aberdeen until 1960,
and from 1961 to 1967 in Hebrew and Old Testament studies
at St Mary's College, University of St Andrews, after which
he became lecturer in Old Testament Literature and Theology,
New College, University of Edinburgh. He has twice been a
visiting professor in the U.S.A. Robert Davidson has
contributed articles to several periodicals and has written *The
Old Testament* and *The Bible Speaks*, which was an American
Religious Book Club choice and has been translated into
French. He is married, with five children, and his recreations
are gardening and music.

A. R. C. Leaney was educated at King Edward's School,
Birmingham, and at Hertford College and Ripon Hall,
Oxford. He entered the ministry of the Church of England in
1933 and held various parochial appointments until 1952, with
an intervening period as a chaplain in the army during the
war. He has also worked on the staff of Ripon Hall, and from
1956 he has been teaching in the Department of Theology at
Nottingham University, where he has been awarded a
personal chair with the title of 'Professor of New Testament
Studies'. He is a D.D. of Oxford University, and Secretary of
the international Studiorum Novi Testamenti Societas. In 1966
he was Selwyn Lecturer in New Zealand and in 1968 Manson
Memorial Lecturer at Manchester. Professor Leaney's books
include *A Commentary on the Gospel of St Luke* and *The Rule
of Qumran and its Meaning*. He is married, with one son and
three grandchildren. Recreations are music, gardening and
philately.

Robert Davidson
A. R. C. Leaney

Biblical Criticism

Penguin Books

Penguin Books Ltd, Harmondsworth,
Middlesex, England
Penguin Books Inc., 7110 Ambassador Road,
Baltimore, Maryland 21207, U.S.A.
Penguin Books Australia Ltd, Ringwood,
Victoria, Australia

First published 1970
Reprinted 1972
Copyright © Robert Davidson, A. R. C. Leaney, 1970

Made and printed in Great Britain by
Hazell Watson & Viney Ltd, Aylesbury, Bucks
Set in Monotype Times

Contents

Theology used to claim to be able to give authoritative information about all the phenomena in the universe, or at the least to share this privilege with philosophy. Now through the vicissitudes of the history of thought theology usually occupies a lowly place in those institutions which exist to train men and women in all the important intellectual disciplines, and in some it does not appear at all. And its sister, philosophy, has fared little better. Theology has been chastened by adversity, by discovering that its claims were disputable, and in many cases manifestly false. The brash confidence sometimes displayed by the newer disciplines may encounter a similar experience. In consequence of this development it is thought by some that theology is dying: theology is the scientific study of religion, and religion is dying. The answer to this suggestion is simply that theology is not dying as long as there are people who believe it worth while to practise it. There are still plenty of people interested enough in theology to study it and to contribute to it.

Theology is the science of thinking about God. It has to cover a vast field, including ancient history, ancient languages, church history, philosophy of religion, literary criticism (including textual criticism of two or three different types), the history of Christian thought and comparative religion. Men have always thought about God, often passionately; some of the best minds in history have been devoted to thought about God. Theology has therefore behind it a long, varied and fascinating history.

But what and how is God? This is one of the first questions handled by *The Pelican Guide to Modern Theology*. A guide of this sort should explain how people today think and in the past have thought about God. And as this is a Christian country (or at least a post-Christian one) this guide has thought it right to explain how Christians think about God. This has involved devoting a volume to the philosophy of religion (the interaction of Christian thought and philosophy), a volume to the Bible, describing how it is studied today, and a volume to historical theology, demonstrating in three different fields how scholars today handle the tradition which Christianity has formed in the course of its journey through history. We have not covered the whole field; we have had to omit, for instance, a treatment of the medieval period and we have made no reference to comparative religion. But this series will have done enough if it causes its readers to understand how it is that some people find theology the most attractive, the most exacting and the most satisfying intellectual pursuit of all.

R. P. C. HANSON

Introduction to Volume 3

The series called *The Pelican Guide to Modern Theology* appears
to be coming out backwards. First the volume called *Philosophical
Theology* was published, tracing the development of the relation
between Christian doctrine and philosophy from the eighteenth
century up to our own day. Then there came out the volume
called *Historical Theology*, giving a description of how three
separate theological disciplines are carried on, an account which
in its own way spanned the time from the primitive Church,
through the Middle Ages, up to the recent history of the Church.
Now the third volume has appeared, presenting to the reader a
survey of the work which has been done and which is being done
on the analysis of the Bible; it takes him back as far as the third
millennium before Christ, but in the other direction comes no
nearer our own times than the first century A.D. There is nothing
incorrect or absurd about this procedure. It simply means that if
the reader has followed all three volumes he will have been led
gradually back to those documents upon which all Christian
theology depends and made more aware of the importance of
understanding their true nature and function. Like a pantomime
boy in the last act, the study of the Bible has delayed its entry into
the reader's view, only to emphasize its pre-eminence. Christian
theologizing and Christian doctrine, Christian history and
Christian worship, would all be impossible without the Bible.

What are we to make of the Bible today? It has been the subject
of an intellectual revolution, and this revolution has affected all
branches of theology. Only one hundred years ago, most Christians of all traditions would have been quite content to describe
the Bible as inerrant, infallible, and inspired equally in every
part. The books which purported to be historical, even the book

9

of Esther and the book of Daniel, were regarded as straight-forward reportage of events which really happened just as they were described there. The book of Genesis was included in this simple assessment. As the author of the first modern novel, Samuel Butler, said in *The Way of All Flesh*, Mr Pontifex assumed that God had put Adam to sleep, as it might be in the gardenhouse at the bottom of Mr Pontifex's garden, removed one of his ribs, and made it into a woman, in a straightforward, matter-of-fact way. Newman, viewing the publication of the book *Essays and Reviews* (1860), which made many concessions to the advancing tide of historical criticism, could remark from his retreat in the Oratory at Birmingham with a certain grim satisfaction that once the inerrancy of the Bible was abandoned the basis of Protestantism would be removed, and Protestantism would simply collapse and disappear. When Lord Shaftesbury read Seely's very mildly critical account of the life of Jesus called *Ecce Homo* (1865), he described the book as 'vomited from the jaws of Hell'. When Liddon, canon of St Paul's, London, and a leader of the early Anglo-Catholic movement, learnt that Charles Gore, then the rising hope of the Anglo-Catholics, had admitted, under the influence of historical criticism, that the human know-ledge of Jesus was limited, he is said to have turned his face to the wall and died. J. C. Ryle, bishop of Liverpool (1880–1900), the leader of the Evangelicals in the Church of England, main-tained the inerrancy and full inspiration of the Bible to his dying day, and was shocked to find his son compromising on the subject.

But in spite of shocked churchmen, horrified canons and protesting Evangelicals, the revolution moved inexorably on. It consisted in the simple but far-reaching discovery that the docu-ments of the Bible were entirely conditioned by the circumstances of the period in which they were produced. The results of this discovery will become evident to those who read the pages of this volume. It meant that the books of the Bible were hence-forward open to being treated precisely as all other ancient documents are treated by historians of the ancient world. No sanctity, no peculiar authority, no special immunity to objective and unsparing investigation according to the most rigorous standards and methods of scholarship, could ever again be permitted to reserve the Bible from the curious eyes of scholars. The Bible might well in future be approached by scholars with presuppositions about it in their minds, but not the presupposition that this book is a sacrosanct preserve whose historical accuracy and literal truth must be maintained intact.

The results of this revolution were startling. The story of Adam and Eve, upon which most people believed the Christian doctrine of original sin to depend, could no longer be regarded as historical. The early chapters of Genesis, which were generally taken to be an authentic account of the origin of the human race, and of civilization, and of the activities of some outstanding personalities early in the history of the Jewish people, were dissolved into a medley of legends, folk-myths, primitive sagas and remnants of early cults comparable to similar material observable in other cultures. David and Solomon were cut down from figures of almost super-human wisdom and piety to petty princelings exhibiting the characteristics to be expected of Levantine despots of the eleventh century B.C. David was deprived of the authorship of the Psalms, Moses of the authorship of the Pentateuch, Isaiah of the authorship of most of the book attributed to him. It became impossible to believe in the miracles recorded in the Old Testament. The prophets were transformed from being mysterious predictors of the life of Jesus Christ and the early Church into political commentators upon the events of their own day. Daniel became a legendary figure and his visions a series of comments by a contemporary upon the events of the mid second century B.C. in Palestine. The New Testament was not left intact. It became obvious that whatever else Jesus of Nazareth was or was not, he certainly appeared to his contemporaries as a man of their own day, the period which we now call Late Ancient Judaism, imbued with all its ideas and fitting exactly into its background. The historical reliability of the Fourth Gospel, and its apostolic authorship, were put in grave doubt. A vast and complex debate about the possibility of discerning with confidence any of the historical lineaments of Jesus was begun. The theology of the epistles of the New Testament, and especially those of Paul, was rigorously scrutinized and the question was raised sharply as to whether the great classical dogmas of the Church – the doctrine of the Trinity, of the Incarnation and of the Atonement – could honestly be based upon the witness of the New Testament. The Pastoral Epistles were denied to St Paul, the Catholic Epistles to St John, St James and St Jude, St Peter was deprived of his Second Epistle and his authorship of the First was impugned. In short, the whole question of the authority of the Bible was raised anew and forced upon the attention of thinking people in the most radical fashion.

Different Christian traditions reacted to this new state of affairs in different ways. On the Continent, the Protestant communions on the whole accepted this revolution and tried to absorb it and to adjust themselves to it. In Britain there was a period of shocked outrage, of calls for condemnation of scholars who accepted this revolution, during which some victims were unjustly deprived of office or of livelihood and some regrettable resolutions were passed by official bodies. But fairly soon scholars almost everywhere began to turn their attention to the task of living with this new state of affairs. In the Roman Catholic Church, however, both on the Continent and in Britain, the acceptance of the revolution was much more slowly achieved. This communion first made a violent effort to suppress the revolution entirely by the use of sheer arbitrary authority, by the tactics of condemnation, delation, anti-Modernist oaths, 'witch-hunting' and even excommunication. Many fine scholars were suppressed, penalized or restricted in their activities. Official statements were made by Popes or by Commissions, which are now bitterly regretted. But, as an earlier victim of Roman Catholic obscurantism remarked, *eppur si muove*. Not even the despotic power of Communist governments can prevent people thinking, and the Roman Catholic Church in the nineteenth and twentieth centuries never disposed of the resources open to Communist governments. Today scholars of the Roman Catholic Church can accept the conclusions and use the techniques of historical criticism with complete freedom. At least in Western Christianity, in spite of the existence of dissident groups and parties who still speak with alarm and despondency about 'Modernism', the battle for the acceptance of historical criticism as applied to the Bible has been won.

One of the results of the arrival of this revolution in biblical study was the creation of a new world of international scholarship. Readers of this volume will get glimpses of it as they come across references to books and papers by scholars of many different nationalities, communions and even creeds. Today at the international conferences organized by the Society for Old Testament Studies, the Society for the Study of the New Testament, and similar bodies, scholars from all over Europe, from the Americas, and now increasingly from India and Africa and from the Far East, meet to read each others papers and to exchange ideas. A vast industry has grown up round the Bible. Hundreds of theses are written every year on the Old Testament, thousands on the New. An enormous and endless stream of books and articles is published. Every conceivable source of knowledge about the Bible is ransacked: literary, linguistic, archaeological. Every relevant ancient language is studied: Greek, Latin, Hebrew, Syriac, Aramaic, Coptic, Georgian, Babylonian, Egyptian. Every possible theory is advanced, criticized, emended, demolished or absorbed. The study of the Bible is an arduous and demanding discipline but also a most enjoyable one. It launches its devotees into a world of its own, with its own laws and conventions, its own rewards and penalties. The pleasantest side of it is that it introduces its students into a kind of international brotherhood or freemasonry of scholarship. The drawback to it is that it never relaxes its demands. Scholarship has never finished. One can never read all the books, articles and reviews. And it never gives final results nor absolutely secure conclusions. The course of biblical study does indeed move. It shifts its attention from one set of problems to another. In the nineteen-twenties scholars were greatly exercised about the relation of Paul's thought to that of the Greek mystery-religions. Now they are concerned about its relation to Gnosticism. In the early part of this century Old Testament scholars regarded the prophets as opponents of the cult and of sacrifice; now they tend to associate them with cult-centres. Earlier New Testament scholars tried strenuously to reconstruct the moral ideals of Jesus. In the nineteen-fifties and sixties they have found it almost impossible to determine what was his teaching on any point at all. The study of the Bible deepens, intensifies, moves now to this pole, now to that. There is no sign at all of its slacking nor reaching saturation point. On its fringes hang the philosophers of religion and the systematic theologians, attempting to integrate its findings into larger wholes.

The scholars, then, have absorbed this revolution. But the revolution has not reached the grass roots of Christianity. Between the average man in the pulpit and the average man or woman in the pew on the one hand and on the other the theologians and the scholars a great gulf is still fixed. The ordinary sermon of the ordinary parson is still quite uncritical and is usually quite untheological as well, in England and the U.S.A. at any rate. 'Theology' in these circles is indeed placed mentally in inverted commas and is regarded as a recondite and unnecessary pursuit indulged in by over-intellectual academics living in some Cloud-Cuckoo-Land remote from the real world, to which the 'Simple Gospel', uncluttered by theology and theories, can be applied. This contempt for the ignorance of theology is shown in a number of ways in this country. For instance, when the B.B.C. wants to consult somebody about a point of doctrine or theology, it seldom seems to think of consulting a professional theologian, as it would in similar circumstances consult a professional scientist or lawyer. It interviews an archdeacon or a canon, and sometimes even a bishop. It is most unlikely that any of these will ever have been professional theologians, not even if they have been heads of Anglican theological colleges. Again, the recent debate about the union scheme for the Church of England and the Methodist Church was conducted very largely in sublime ignorance of the facts and the evidence which professional theologians, and not least biblical scholars, would have at once recognized as relevant. When clergy and laity were asked to give their view upon the subject, as they were at many meetings all over the country over a period of at least two years, their ignorance of this historical revolution became distressingly apparent, though they were quite unaware of this deficiency themselves. Biblical criticism has not penetrated to the grass roots of Christianity. The gulf between the scholar and the ordinary believer is still dangerously wide.

The readers of this volume will be able to see the debate about the Bible taking place. They will be able to learn its methods, understand much of its uncertainties and some of its conclusions. They can form for themselves an impression of the stage which study of the Bible has reached, though they will not find the problems presented by the Bible solved here. Biblical theology and study today is *in via*, in a state of movement and flux, like every other department of theology, or rather every other department of theology is in a fluid state because biblical theology is. The Bible is in a peculiar way the foundation of all theology, of all thinking about Christianity. No form of Christianity can afford to dispense with the Bible. There have been times when theologians have made the desperate attempt to do so; for instance, Newman's reaction to the publication of *Essays and Reviews*, mentioned above, was to declare that while the Protestants depend absolutely upon the Bible, the Catholic Church could, if necessary, do without the Bible. But almost all scholars would now regard this as an argument of desperation, and no more. It is disturbing, unsettling and even exasperating to have to admit the indecisive state of scholarship about what is in fact the foundation document of the Christian faith, and it is perhaps understandable that the ordinary Christian believer should dismiss the world of scholarship with impatience or contempt. But in fact he cannot do without this world of scholarship. There is no other source to which he can go, no other tribunal to which he can appeal, for reliable information about the Bible, for well-informed views about its meaning and its nature. Neither the authority of the Church alone nor the experience of the individual alone are of any serious use here. The ordinary Christians must take notice of the experts here, or they will find themselves, as they often have in the past, walking in the very Cloud-Cuckoo-

Land which they accuse the professional theologians of inhabiting. Three simple examples may be taken to underline this point. In the Authorised Version of the Bible and in the Latin Vulgate the doctrine of the Trinity is set out in a concise fashion in the seventh verse of the fifth chapter of the first Epistle of John, and at times this verse has been a great stand-by to defenders of the traditional doctrine of the Trinity. But experts in the history of the text are quite certain that these words represent a very late interpolation into the text of the Epistle and are not original. There can be no appeal beyond this decision, and all modern versions of the New Testament (including the Jerusalem Bible) have dropped these words from the text. Next, the doctrine of the apostolic succession of bishops is very dear to the hearts of Roman Catholics, Eastern Orthodox and Anglicans. It is however impossible to justify this theory by an impartial investigation of the historical evidence. This doctrine is in fact an appeal to history; and in the view of most experts this particular appeal cannot be upheld. Christian believers have no alternative but to accept this judgement. They cannot invent an alternative history. Finally, belief in a 'Scriptural' ministry, i.e. a form of the ministry which is set out and approved in Scripture as the right form, or as a right form, for the Church, is widespread among Protestants. Historical research is tending to show that no such thing existed in the early Church, no form or forms of the ministry regarded as the only proper form, or as the permanent form, in such a way as to authenticate as peculiarly 'Scriptural' any existing form of the Christian ministry. Here once again, believers will have to accept the verdict of the professional theologians, and to admit that their researches can, and indeed must, have important effects upon the individual Christian's belief. To shut one's eyes to the development of scholarship is not to render it irrelevant.

It would, however, be quite wrong to represent the application of historical criticism to the Bible as an unmitigated disaster for sound Christian doctrine and traditional Christian theology. Quite apart from the fact that it represents in one sense a scientific discovery of truth, it has brought with it solid gain for the understanding of the Christian faith and for the advancement of

Christian theology. We will examine two examples of this gain, one which particularly affects the Old Testament and one which is concerned with the New.

The historical criticism of the Old Testament has introduced a quite new appreciation of the relation of God to history and his revelation within it. Before the advent of this historical revolution the Old Testament must have appeared to inquiring Christian minds either largely irrelevant or largely opaque. Two large tracts of it in particular had puzzled Christians for centuries, the Law and the Prophets. Almost everybody up to the nineteenth century had assumed that the Pentateuch – the books of Genesis, Exodus, Leviticus, Numbers and Deuteronomy – had flowed almost exactly as they now appear from the pen of one man at one period of history, from Moses during the period of the wandering of the people of Israel in the wilderness at some point in the second millennium before Christ. Some dissentient views, ascribing different origins to parts of the Pentateuch, can be faintly discerned in Christian antiquity, but they were not widespread and had little influence. This ascription of all the Law to Moses, and most of it to Moses writing directly at the dictation of God, posed considerable problems for Christian theologians of all past ages. It was difficult enough for the Jews to see the relevance of much of this legislation. But for the Christians the question of its relevance seemed a baffling one. As the great Christian theologian, Origen, remarked, writing in the middle of the third century, 'Are we to imagine that Almighty God, who was giving answers to Moses from heaven, made regulations about an oven, a frying-pan and a baking-pan?' In the end an unhappy compromise was reached by the medieval Church and inherited more or less untouched by the Church of later centuries. The Law was partly accepted as binding literally and as such incorporated into the legal systems of most European countries, where parts of it still remain in force today. Partly it was treated as allegory so that it could be induced to witness to and support Christian doctrine of one sort or another. This was, of course, a system so subjective and unscientific that it has virtually been rejected by every modern scholar. Those parts of the legal books that were not susceptible of either interpretation were relegated to a reverent neglect. The works of the prophets also created considerable difficulty for Christians of past ages. Formally they had to be regarded as predictions *in toto* of the coming of Christ, the incarnation, his death and resurrection, the coming of the Holy Spirit, the origin and growth of the Church, the activities of the apostles, the life of the Christian in the Spirit, the sacraments, the ministry, and so on. Actually it was extremely difficult to envisage all of the prophetic literature as prediction of this sort. Allegory of the most speculative type was necessary before the prophets' words could be expounded for these purposes. In fact the works of the prophets have been largely a closed book during most of the time that the Christian Church has existed, whatever the theologians might claim about them.

To the Law books and the books of the prophets historical criticism has brought new life, new meaning and new relevance. The Pentateuch was revealed not as the work of one man at one period but as a fascinating record of innumerable traditions extending over a vast period of time from the third millennium to the third century before Christ, as a kaleidoscopic compendium of the traditions, ideas, cultures and cults with which the people of Israel had come in contact, ranging from very primitive practices and notions to exalted and noble concepts of God. It proved to be a mirror of the historical experience of the Israelites, far richer, more complex and more informative than any mere law-code produced at one time. Again, the prophets' utterances were entirely transformed by the work of historical criticism. They too came alive and took on relevance and reality. Instead of being mysterious and recondite oracles relating to a time far in the future when they were uttered, they were shown to be comments made by men who were deeply concerned with the politics and the social affairs of their own day and their own country. Often the prophets could be shown to be people of great insight, of passionate integrity, sometimes gifted with great poetical talent and rhetorical power, speaking to the situations in which they found themselves with striking force and persuasiveness. The rediscovery of the significance of these two large tracts of the Bible under the influence of historical criticism not only brought new life, vividness and interest to the book but exposed in a new and impressive way the manner in which the Jewish people's understanding of its choice by God had illuminated, infused and bound together its history, using and transforming the most primitive elements in its tradition and the most unsuccessful as well as the most glorious periods of its history. Many scholars felt as they followed this process that they were discovering in a new way the activity of God in history, finding a dimension of his presence with his people which had been only dimly apprehended before.

The other gain brought about by the advent of historical criticism which can be mentioned here is the intense concentration upon the historical life of Jesus. Never in the history of civilization has so much concentration of scholarship been brought to bear on any documents as has played during the last century and a half on the Synoptic Gospels. Not only every verse, but every sentence, every word, has been analysed. The scholarly pursuit has followed up the literary sources of these three gospels and has been brought by this search to the oral sources which lie behind them. These oral sources have been analysed by the technique of Form Criticism and this in its turn has led to the analysis of the motives of the evangelists and their predecessors in arranging and modifying the oral material, a type of analysis which has been given the name of Redaction Criticism. Much reference to these techniques will be encountered in the second part of this volume. For a long period, from about 1880 till about 1920, the scholarly search was directed towards finding 'the real Jesus', the Jesus of history, in contrast to and by way of corrective of the Jesus of the Church's faith and the Church's theological elaboration. Then the tide of scholarship set in the other direction. It was the Jesus of the Church's faith who was declared to be significant. The Jesus of history was either uninteresting or irrecoverable, because in the gospels the original facts about what Jesus said and did were indistinguishably fused and confused with the Church's interpretation, modification and elaboration of what Jesus had done and said. A great readiness to believe in the

possibility of reconstructing the life of Jesus was succeeded by a
scepticism which found it hard to accept any detail as authentic.
The view began to be put forward and to be accepted in many
places that not only was it impossible to know what the Jesus of
history was like, but that it was for several reasons theologically
undesirable to do so. In recent years, however, there has been a
clearly discernible movement towards a more central position,
both on the Continent and in this country. Scholars have realized
more and more clearly that to abolish either the Jesus of history
or the Christ of the Church's faith implies ultimately a kind of
academic suicide for New Testament scholarship as well as for
systematic theology, that the Church's interpretation of Jesus is
inexplicable if we can know nothing about the historical Jesus
and that the significance of the historical Jesus is irrecoverable if
we reject the Church's interpretation of him. Scientific history
does not like being reduced to the inexplicable and the irrecoverable. The long-term prospects are good for a theology based
upon both a real historical Jesus and the Church's interpretation
of that Jesus. But no good is achieved without struggle and
difficulty, and the long debate about the Jesus of history and the
Jesus of the Church's faith, little though it may have influenced
the ideas of the man in the pulpit and the man in the pew, has
advanced the understanding of the Christian faith and has
thrown up in its path all sorts of useful and interesting discoveries,
some of which are referred to in this volume.

We have come a long way from the traditional description of
the Bible as inerrant, as, in the Reformation phrase, 'the lively
oracles of God', from the attitude which put the Bible on a
pedestal and found in it all wisdom and infallible guidance.
Instead we have found it a book teeming with contradictions,
errors and imperfections, but also teeming with life. The Bible
has in all ages possessed this capacity for communicating to each
generation the life to which it witnesses, often managing to
overcome the most resolute prejudices and misunderstandings in
the process. In the last century and a half it has stepped down
from the pedestal upon which it has been mistakenly placed and

has cast away from it the blanket of oracular mysteriousness with which it has been enveloped, and has thereby brought home to those who study it in quite a new way its witness to the life of God among men and women in all sorts of different periods and situations from Abraham to Paul. Contemporary biblical scholarship has certainly not succeeded in solving all the problems raised by the Bible. It would be deceiving the reader to pretend that the pages of this volume will neatly answer all historical and theological questions in the field of biblical study. But it is hoped that they will succeed in conveying to the reader the sense of liveliness, of liveliness reflecting a living message, which the labours of scholars have disclosed within the pages of the Bible.

R. P. C. HANSON.

The Old Testament
by Robert Davidson

Introduction

To many people today the Old Testament is either an embarrassment or a largely unopened book. To lose one's bearing in the mass of varied material within it is all too easy; to be offended by some of its contents is even easier. A humanist will point to primitive, barbaric images of God, subhuman ethics and a perverse religious nationalism. Many a Christian will think of the relationships between Old and New Testaments largely in terms of contrast rather than continuity. To be sure it has its quota of memorable stories – Joseph, the baby Moses, David and Goliath. Suitably edited, they can be a useful part of any child's education. It has passages worthy of inclusion in any anthology from the world's great religions – Genesis i–iii, Psalm xxiii, Isaiah xlff. and many others. The overall picture, however, is blurred and unattractive. It may come as a surprise to be told that over the past generation no field of scholarship has been more exciting, and none of greater relevance to fundamental questions of faith than the Old Testament. This survey is an attempt to share this excitement and to communicate something of this relevance.

The Old Testament comes to us out of the past, out of what for most of us in the West is an essentially alien culture. Whether we think of the language in which it is written, the society which it reflects or the faith to which it bears witness, the Old Testament is meaningful today only as part of the wider world of the Ancient Near East. Many scholarly disciplines dealing with various facets of that world have therefore contributed and are increasingly contributing to our understanding of the Old Testament – Hittite, Sumerian, Akkadian, Canaanite, Egyptian, Aramaic and Arabic studies. Each of these disciplines has its self-appointed tasks and self-chosen aims. We shall draw on them only in so far as their work impinges directly on the Old Testament.

The justification for much work in the Old Testament field, however, during the past generation must stand or fall with the conviction that the Old Testament is not only part of an ancient culture. In 1938, an article on 'The Present State of Old Testament Studies'[1] could survey the entire field without once using the word 'theology'. If this was myopic in 1938, it is impossible today. Increasingly, and particularly in Germany, where the anti-Semitic character of the Nazi régime led to deep heart-searching, the place and value of the Old Testament in the Christian Church and in Jewish tradition has been vigorously debated. Is there a witness to God of lasting validity in the Old Testament? If so, where is it to be found amid the rich diversity of documents and thought patterns within the Old Testament? What is meant by speaking of the Old Testament as 'prophecy' which finds its 'fulfilment' in the New Testament or in Judaism, or as the 'old covenant' which looks forward to the 'new covenant'? The answers are 'not yet'; perhaps we have still to learn how to formulate the questions properly. That the high priests of orthodoxy and the apostles of secular Christianity (see Harvey Cox, *The Secular City*, 1965) can both appeal to the Old Testament is witness to the fact that the Old Testament lies close to the heart of the contemporary theological ferment.

Although no generation of scholarship ever stands, or would wish to stand, in isolation from the work of its predecessors, the Second World War provides in certain respects a natural watershed. During the years of conflict, archaeological work in Palestine and in the Near East in general was discontinued. In many respects this proved a blessing in disguise. It provided a welcome breathing space during which the immense amount of new material unearthed prior to 1939 could be assimilated and its significance assessed. Writing in 1938, W. F. Albright, the doyen of modern biblical archaeologists, could say, 'One of the most encouraging aspects of Syro-Palestinian archaeology is the speed with which old problems are being solved and new ones introduced into the foreground. We can hardly be far wrong in predicting that the next ten years will see a more rapid substitution of new problems for old than any decade which has preceded. The day of diminishing returns is far from having arrived.'[2] Although war delayed its fulfilment, this prediction has been brilliantly vindicated in the post-war years.

The years 1939–45, moreover, saw the disruption, and in many cases the complete severance, of the normal channels of communication upon which international cooperation in scholarship depends. Many of the most important periodicals, particularly on the Continent, operated on a severely restricted basis or were temporarily discontinued. In the post-war years, not only have the traditional channels been re-opened, but new links have been forged both through international organizations and through learned journals. In 1950, on the initiative of the Dutch Old Testament Society, there came into being an international Organization for the Study of the Old Testament which sponsors at three-yearly intervals an international congress; the sixth congress met in Rome in 1968. Since January 1951 it has promoted a quarterly journal *Vetus Testamentum*, and a series of occasional *Supplements* to *Vetus Testamentum* which have contained not only congress transactions, but important monographs. Among other new periodicals devoted entirely or in part to Old Testament studies which have appeared since 1940 are *Oudtestamentische Studien* published by the Dutch Old Testament Society, *The Journal of Semitic Studies* (Manchester, 1956), *Abr. Naharaim* (Melbourne, 1959/60), *Textus* (Jerusalem, 1960), *Israel Exploration Fund Journal* (Jerusalem, 1951), *Annual of the Swedish Theological Institute* (Jerusalem, 1958), *Annual of the Leeds Oriental Society* (Leeds, 1959), *Revue de Qumrân* (Paris, 1963).

If Old Testament scholarship is truly international, it is also now happily interdenominational. From the content of many a book on the Old Testament it would be impossible to tell whether its author were Jew or Christian, Protestant or Roman Catholic. All share a common critical concern and use similar critical tools. One of the notable features of the period under review has been a renaissance in Roman Catholic critical scholarship, a renaissance which owes much to the 1943 Papal Encyclical *Divino Afflante Spiritu*. Both the major Roman Catholic biblical periodicals, *Biblica* and The *Catholic Biblical Quarterly* are indispensable tools in the hands of all Old Testament scholars.

To attempt to analyse the work of a generation of scholarship in a discipline as swiftly changing and as richly creative as Old Testament studies is difficult; to pretend competence in all or even most branches of this discipline would be impertinence. Inevitably this must be a highly subjective report. It reflects, perhaps even more than the author himself realizes, personal interests and personal prejudices.

I am indebted to Mrs E. M. Paterson, New College, for the typing of the final copy and to Mr Alistair Symington M.A. for careful proof-reading.

New College, Edinburgh, 1969

One

Widening Horizons –
The Contribution
of Archaeology

Archaeology has become one of the most important disciplines in the development of Old Testament studies; it is also one of the most commonly misunderstood. The misunderstanding is well illustrated in the introduction to *The Bible as History*, by W. Keller (English translation by William Neil). 'In view', he writes, 'of the overwhelming mass of authentic and well attested evidence now available, as I thought of the sceptical criticism which, from the eighteenth century onwards, would fain have demolished the Bible altogether, there kept hammering in my brain this one sentence, "The Bible is right after all".' The mass of authentic and well attested evidence to which he appeals is that provided by archaeology. But what is meant by this highly ambiguous sentence 'The Bible is right after all'; 'right' in what sense?

Let us take two examples. Genesis xii records how Abram left North Mesopotamia and travelled westwards with his family to Canaan to become the pilgrim father of the Hebrew people. If we say of this story 'The Bible is right', what do we mean? A tribal migration westward fits in well with what we now know of the history of the Ancient Near East between 2000 and 1400 B.C. For this we have a mass of interlocking archaeological evidence to thank (cf. pp. 39ff). But what evidence confirms that a man called Abram was part of this migration? Why indeed does the narrative focus on Abram? The story of this Abram is presented to us in Genesis xiiff. as the story of a man who responds in faith to a call from God. This is the sole reason why the story has significance for the Old Testament. What kind of archaeological data will prove, or disprove, that this all-important faith dimension in the narrative is 'right after all'?

Consider the story of the Flood as recorded in Genesis vi, 5 to

29

viii. In spite of repeated statements to the contrary there is no archaeological evidence to authenticate the story of a flood of such dimensions that 'the waters prevailed so mightily upon the earth that all the high mountains under the whole heaven were covered; the waters prevailed above the mountains covering them fifteen cubits deep' (Genesis vii, 19–20). What archaeology does provide is evidence for more or less severe local flooding of several city states in southern Mesopotamia, flooding which occurred at different times in different cities. In any case, the attempt to call in archaeology to bolster up the fabric of the Genesis flood story assumes that this story is handed down to us as historical fact. But if, as there are good grounds for believing, it is narrated as 'myth' or 'religious parable', then the problem of its historicity becomes irrelevant, and any attempt to use archaeology to prove that it is 'right after all', merely ludicrous.

It cannot be too strongly emphasized that the archaeologist sets out neither to prove nor to disprove the Old Testament; but to discover what still remains in the protecting earth of cities and civilizations which have long since perished. In this respect, the major break-through in Palestinian archaeology came with the recognition that many of the *Tells* or mounds dotted across the Palestinian landscape were not natural hills but the accumulated debris of cities and villages which had been built, destroyed and re-built many times on the same site. As a trained archaeologist digs down through the successive layers or strata of such a *Tell*, what does he expect to find? Palestinian sites have been remarkably frugal in the preservation of long hidden documents or inscriptions. The scrolls from the caves overlooking the north-west end of the Dead Sea are a notable exception. The archaeologist is on the look-out for the remains of ruined city gates and city walls, private houses, public buildings and temples, and tombs which record burial customs and sometimes contain rich deposits of commonly used objects and utensils. Above all, everywhere he finds broken pottery, countless fragments of that fragile but essentially indestructible artifact. It was Sir W. Flinders Petrie, towards the end of the nineteenth century, who first realized that pottery, with its changing materials and methods of manufacture, style and decoration, provides us with the essential alphabet of archaeology in any attempt to write the history and chronology of buried cities.

The steady accumulation of pottery from many sites in Palestine and in the larger world of the Ancient Near East enabled G. Ernest Wright to produce in 1937 *The Pottery of Palestine from the Earliest Times to the End of the Early Bronze Age*. Wright's work has been developed, adjusted and extended by many subsequent studies, notably in recent years from his fellow American Paul W. Lapp. We now possess a reliable ceramic index covering the whole Old Testament period. Until the appearance of datable coins during the Persian period (fifth century B.C.) pottery remains our surest guide to the dating of different occupation levels at ancient sites.

It is not always easy to identify correctly an ancient site. Sometimes the modern Arabic name for a village may retain the basic elements of an Old Testament name; for example, modern El Jib is Old Testament Gibeon. Once a site has been identified there can take place a fruitful dialogue between the evidence uncovered by the archaeologist and such written records as we possess both in the Bible and in other documents from the Ancient Near East. It is, however, a dialogue which must be entered upon with due caution, for it may often have to be content with probabilities rather than certainties. It may leave many unanswered and perhaps unanswerable questions.

Let us take two examples. Joshua x, 28–39 describes how the invading Israelites under Joshua in the course of a southern campaign captured the towns of Makkedah, Libnah, Lachish, Eglon, Hebron and Debir; while another strand in the conquest tradition states that Debir formerly called Kiriathsepher fell to the Kenazite allies of the Israelites (cf. Joshua xv, 17, Judges i, 13). Excavations directed by W. F. Albright in 1926–32 at Tell Beit Mirsim, which Albright identified with Debir – an identification which has not gone undisputed – provided clear evidence that the Late Bronze age settlement was violently destroyed circa 1225 B.C. Likewise at Tell el Duweir (ancient Lachish), some eight miles away to the north-west, destruction befell the city towards

the end of the thirteenth century B.C. The archaeological evidence
for destruction in both cases is indisputable, but by whom were
these towns destroyed? To cast the Israelites under Joshua, or
even their allies, in the role of the destroyers is tempting, indeed
plausible in the light of the Old Testament tradition, but it is not
the only possibility. The victory stele of the Egyptian Pharaoh
Merneptah, dated 1223 B.C., speaks of an Egyptian plundering
of parts of Canaan in this general region; and by the end of the
thirteenth century B.C. the 'Sea Peoples' from across the Mediterranean, among whom were the Philistines, were settling in force
on the coastal plain of Canaan. Although it may be hypercritical
at this point to separate the archaeological evidence and the Old
Testament tradition in order to cast doubt on that tradition,
nevertheless if we did not possess the Old Testament record the
temptation to attribute the destruction of Debir and Lachish of
this period to either the Egyptians or the Sea Peoples would be
very strong.

Here is a case where archaeology has provided us with documentary evidence. A stele, or monument, of the Egyptian
Emperor Seti I dated circa 1318 B.C. was recovered from the
important Canaanite-Egyptian city of Bethshean. It speaks of
troubled conditions in the countryside around. An attempt made
to seize the city itself is forestalled apparently by Seti's energetic
troops dispositions. Both Joshua xvii, 11 ff. and Judges i, 27 tell
us that the tribe of Manasseh failed to drive out the inhabitants
of Bethshean and its surrounding villages. Do we have here two
different versions of one and the same set of events? If so, then
we would have a firm date for the push into northern Canaan of
one group of Israelites. It is possible to make this link between
the Bethshean stele and the Old Testament narrative; but we are
not compelled so to do. The latter half of the fourteenth century
B.C. was a period of general instability and confusion in Canaan;
there are several other possible candidates for the role of the
troublemakers at Bethshean.

It is wrong always to expect firm conclusions to emerge from
the dialogue between archaeological evidence and the Old
Testament literary tradition; often the dialogue will be tentative

and exploratory. An interesting recent example of such an attempted dialogue is to be found in G. Ernest Wright's book *Shechem*, the account of the Drew–McCormack expedition at Shechem between 1956 and 1962.

What then is the contribution which archaeology has been making to our understanding of the Old Testament in the past two or three decades? In many respects the period has been so productive that it is impossible to do more than to indicate in very general terms the overall pattern, and thereafter to be highly selective in discussing points at which recent work seems to have an important direct or indirect bearing on the Old Testament. An abundance of evidence has come to us from excavations at many important Palestinian sites including Jericho, Ai, Lachish, Khirbet Kerak, Dothan, Hazor, Gibeon, Gezer, Tell el Far'ah, Jerusalem, Shechem.

THE HISTORICAL BACKGROUND

Increasingly, there is emerging before our eyes in broad yet firm outline a connected historical picture of life in Canaan and in the wider world of the Ancient Near East, and that from the earliest times long before any written records are available. The horizons of history are being pushed progressively backwards. In this respect the excavations carried out in 1955–8 at Tell el Sultan (ancient Jericho), by the British School of Archaeology, under the direction of Miss Kathleen Kenyon, have made a significant contribution and provided a model for other digs into pre-history.[1] At Jericho we have evidence of man, the wandering hunter and food-gatherer, making the transition to becoming a member of a settled community with a developed social organization. Circa 7800 B.C. we find the earliest evidence of life at ancient Jericho in the shape of a clay platform, probably part of a sanctuary established by Mesolithic hunters encamped near the Jericho spring. All finds associated with this level link it with the culture known previously from the caves of Mount Carmel and the Wadi en Natuf, hence the name Natufian by which this culture is often identified. By circa 7000 B.C., however, there is a change to a society with larger many-roomed houses of rectangular plan and a self-sufficient farming economy with domesticated animals, goats certainly, and in all probability sheep, pigs and cows as well. Ancestor worship seems to have played a part in the religion of this community since human skulls, separated from the body, were carefully preserved, their lower part covered in plaster moulded into the likeness of human features. Further evidence of the same culture has recently come from excavations directed by Diana Kirkbride in the 'Arabah area of Southern Jordan in 1961, 1963, and 1966, where an early Neolithic village was unearthed at Beidha, and surface exploration produced signs of other sites of similar age in the region.[2] Only Jericho, however, has produced an early Neolithic fortified town. In the later Neolithic period, characterized by the first appearance of pottery, crude and rough at first yet gradually improving in technique, Jericho seems to have entered into a period of decline, the fortified town becoming a small drab village by the fifth millennium B.C.

About the middle of the fifth millennium B.C. copper makes its first appearance in Palestine. Our best evidence for this Chalcolithic period comes from a site in the Jordan valley, north-east of the Dead Sea, Teleilat el Ghazzul, excavated by Jesuit Fathers between 1929 and 1938. Here we find well-constructed houses of mud bricks with stone foundations. Some of their walls are covered with fresco paintings of intricate polychrome, geometric design, the most outstanding example being an eight-pointed star. This period also witnesses the first settlement at Tell el Far'ah, biblical Tirzah. More recently, further evidence of Chalcolithic settlement has come from Nelson Glueck's surface explorations in the northern and central Negev from 1951 to 1959, and from the excavation directed by Jean Perrot at Tell Abu Matar.

Towards the end of the fourth millennium B.C., a period of widespread cultural diffusion in the Ancient Near East, a new immigrant culture appears in Palestine, its presence indicated, *inter alia*, by distinctive pottery and by mass burials in rock cut tombs or natural caves. From such immigrant settlements there emerge gradually the independent city states of the Early Bronze Age. Such city states were to be the basic political unit of life in Canaan until David led the Hebrew tribes into the short-lived united Hebrew kingdom circa 1000 B.C. Four distinct pottery phases are usually assigned to this Early Bronze period. Early Bronze Age Jericho was a flourishing city of substantial solidly built houses. It had a somewhat chequered history, the consequence either of earthquakes, which are common enough in the Jordan Rift, or of enemy assaults. At the southern end of the *Tell* the town wall of this period reached a thickness of seventeen feet. The Early Bronze age is also well represented at Tell el Far'ah with three occupation levels between 3100 and 2800 B.C. Among the most interesting finds from this period is a potter's kiln, the earliest example so far found in Canaan. Not only was pottery now being properly fired in a kiln but increasing use was being made of the potter's wheel, especially in shaping the rims of vessels. Circa 2800 B.C. sees the first major city wall at Tell el Far'ah, a wall which survived for some two centuries. Many important Biblical sites, including Megiddo, Lachish and Hazor, spring to life during this 'the great boom age of Palestine', as it has been aptly termed. From this period come the first signs of settlement on Mount Ophel, later to become a Jebusite fortress which in turn gave way to the Davidic town of Jerusalem.

After the boom came the crash. Nomadic invaders, commonly called the Amorites, swarmed into Palestine from the north during what Miss Kenyon calls the Intermediate Early Bronze and Middle Bronze period, circa 2300–1900 B.C. The latest Early Bronze age wall at Jericho is violently destroyed by fire. The invaders settle in the region of Jericho. Their presence is marked by tombs of varying type characterized by single, occasionally double, as opposed to the preceding mass burial; but they do not build a city wall. Tombs of basically similar type have recently (1965) been discovered by Miss Kenyon near Jerusalem on the Mount of Olives. Site after site tells the same story. At Tell el Far'ah the last Early Bronze age settlement ends circa 2500 B.C. and the site is then deserted until the nineteenth century B.C.; at Megiddo there is no evidence of occupation between circa 2500 and 2000 B.C.; at Hazor only meagre remains are to be found between the well-fortified Early Bronze age city in the twenty-fourth century B.C. and the foundation of the larger Middle Bronze age city circa 1750 B.C. Similar upheavals are found during this period in Syria and Mesopotamia, while in Egypt the Old Kingdom, whose crowning glory was the pyramids, comes to a violent end at the hands of Asiatic invaders in the twenty-third century B.C. Interestingly, as confusion spreads in the great empires of the Ancient Near East and the city states of Palestine go into decline, village communities of semi-nomadic peoples begin to appear in southern Transjordan and in the Negev.

Gradually out of this dark and confused age there begin to emerge from circa 1900 B.C. onwards the prosperous Canaanite city states of the Middle Bronze Age. It is probably in this age that the patriarchal forefathers of the Hebrew race first came to Canaan. On the basis of changing pottery styles, this Middle Bronze age is usually divided into four phases, Middle Bronze I, Middle Bronze IIA, IIB, and IIC. At Jericho settlement developed slowly in the early Middle Bronze period and at first only on the east side of the mound which slopes down to the all-important spring which provided the community with its water supply. At Megiddo by circa 1850 B.C. there was an important city, probably under Egyptian control, with interesting examples of well-designed temples. At Hazor we have to wait until the second half of the eighteenth century B.C. before the impressively large city covering approximately one hundred and eighty acres comes into being. Not only did these and other sites spring into renewed life during the first two phases of the Middle Bronze age, but new sites achieved prominence. Notable in this respect is Shechem, modern Tell el Balatah. Although there is scattered evidence of encampment in the Chalcolithic period, the earliest major building activity so far discovered at Shechem comes from circa 1800 B.C.

Many of these Canaanite cities were to reach their zenith structurally and culturally during the last two phases of the Middle Bronze period, when they fell into the hands of invaders from the north. These invaders, called by the Egyptians, whom they conquered circa 1720 B.C., the Hyksos, i.e. 'rulers of foreign lands', introduced into Canaan the horse-drawn chariot and a new type of fortification in depth, examples of which have been found as far north as Qatna and Carchemish in Syria, throughout Palestine and as far south as the Nile Delta. Hazor, Shechem and Jericho provide us with our clearest examples in Palestine of such Hyksos fortifications. Their characteristic feature is the 'glacis' or steeply sloped bank leading up to the city walls at the top of the mound. At first such a 'glacis' was made of layer upon layer of beaten earth, clay, gravel and limestone, its surface covered with a layer of clay to ensure that it was smooth and slippery. In time this type of glaciś gave way to one made entirely of stone forming what is called a battered wall. The foot of the glacis was sometimes guarded by a moat. The fortifications of the Middle Bronze II city of Hazor were surrounded by such a moat eighty metres wide and reaching a depth of fifteen metres. The presence of the Hyksos is also indicated by a new style of entrance gate into a city. Earlier gate entrances tended to be L-shaped. This forced an attacker to execute a sharp turn and thus expose his unprotected flank to the city defenders. The new style is a straight, but deep entrance. It narrows at three points and is guarded on either side by large towers. The approach to such a gate, as the Hazor excavations have made clear, was by means of a roadway of gentle gradient sloping up from the right hand side. Thus any attacker had still to turn as he approached the gate.

What led to this new type of glacis defence and city gate? Since the Hyksos were responsible for the introduction of the chariot into Canaan, it was for a time believed that this was the defensive response to the use of chariotry in warfare. Chariots, however, were never used to storm cities, nor is such a glacis a more effective chariot deterrent than a perpendicular wall. The offensive weapon against which the glacis defence was constructed seems to have been the battering ram, mention of which we find in documents of the eighteenth century B.C. from Mari in North Mesopotamia and from the Hittite Kingdom. The difficulty of dragging a heavy battering ram up, or operating it effectively on, such a glacis is evident. The straight city entrance gate was probably designed to allow the chariots of the defenders swift exit from the city.

If the Hyksos thought that such laboriously constructed defences would guarantee them lasting security, they were soon to be disillusioned. Resurgent nationalism saw the rise to power of the eighteenth Egyptian dynasty circa 1580 B.C. and with it the expulsion of the Hyksos. Egyptian expeditionary forces, their activities well documented from Egyptian texts, were soon operating in Canaan. With this Egyptian activity in the mid sixteenth century B.C. we enter the Late Bronze age in Canaan. At the Jericho of this period there is evidence of violent destruction. Only stumps of buildings of the late Middle Bronze period survive among fallen debris. Everywhere there are traces of fire. The uncertain conditions of the time are well documented by the east gate at Shechem which within a period of fifty years at the end of the Middle Bronze age was destroyed and rebuilt three times. Megiddo, which provided the first pottery evidence for this period, surrendered, as we know from Egyptian texts, to Thutmoses III in 1468 B.C. during a campaign which established effective Egyptian control over Palestine for nearly a century. Hazor, undoubtedly the largest and the most powerful of the Canaanite cities, seems most successfully to have weathered the storms of political change, since there is evidence of continuous occupation of the site at Hazor from the Middle Bronze age to the beginning of the thirteenth century B.C.

The Late Bronze age in Palestine which lasted until 1150 B.C. is usually divided circa 1350 B.C. into two distinct phases – Late Bronze I and Late Bronze II. It was a period of confusion and uncertainty, as pressure from nomadic invaders built up against the city states. The chronic inability of weak Egyptian dynasties to exercise effective control over, or to provide needed protection for, their subject cities in Canaan in the face of such pressure is vividly illustrated for the fourteenth century B.C. by the archives of the Egyptian foreign office discovered in 1908 at Tell el Amarna. Evidence for widespread destruction in all but the strongest Canaanite cities is well attested archaeologically during Late Bronze II. The Israelites, under Joshua in all likelihood, formed one element in this nomadic infiltration which led, in Canaan, to a period of economic and cultural decline.

Thus archaeology gives us a picture of the historical and cultural background to the emergence of the nation of Israel. Undoubtedly this picture will have to be modified as the result of further discoveries and the reassessment of present information. This much, however, is clear: the Israelites on entering Canaan became heirs to a long tradition of settled life which we can trace as far back in Jericho as the seventh millennium B.C. They inherited a culture which for good and for ill profoundly influenced their history. Nor did this culture exist in isolation. It has been claimed that 'Greek and Hebrew civilizations are parallel structures built on the same East Mediterranean foundation' (H. Gordon, *Before the Bible*, Collins, 1962, p. 9; compare M. C. Astour, *Hellenosemitica*, Brill, Leiden, second edition 1967). Although some of the literary parallels adduced as proof of this thesis – for example between Homer and the Old Testament – may be questioned, it must be granted that much evidence remains of cultural, linguistic and trade links between the Ancient Near East and the Greek world. Many of these links come from a period prior to the emergence of the Hebrews as a nation on the stage of human history. The horizons of Old Testament research are ever widening.

So far we have been concerned solely with the overall picture of life and culture in the land of Canaan prior to the Hebrew settlement. We must now take a closer look at the way in which archaeological discoveries have shed light in recent years on particular chapters or incidents within the Old Testament story. Here, above all, limitations of space force us to confine ourselves to a representative sample of the available evidence.

THE PATRIARCHAL PERIOD

Until comparatively recently, the world of the Ancient Near East in the first half of the second millennium B.C. was virtually an unknown blank to the historian. Thus, it was possible to regard with extreme scepticism the narratives in Genesis concerning the patriarchal ancestors of the Hebrew people. Abraham, Isaac and Jacob disappeared into the mists of an unknown antiquity. The narratives preserved fossilized relics of primitivism, but otherwise were important sociologically, culturally and religiously because they reflected the much later customs and ideas of the period when this patriarchal tradition was put into written form. Such scepticism is now unwarranted. Whatever else the patriarchal narratives may be, they are not the romanticizing fabrications of later writers blissfully ignorant of life in the Ancient Near East between circa 2000 and 1500 B.C. This conclusion depends upon an interlocking mass of material from many different places. From Kultepe in Asia Minor to Nuzi on the eastern fringe of the Mesopotamian valley, from Alalakh on the Syrian coast to Mari in North Mesopotamia, from Ugarit (Ras Shamra) in North Syria to numerous sites in Canaan, evidence has been accumulating. Two of these sites claim special significance for our immediate purpose.

Towards the end of the third millennium B.C. nomads began to spill out from the Arabian desert to overrun the city states of the Mesopotamian valley. These uncouth western (Amorite) barbarians – for so they seemed to the cultured inhabitants of the city states – soon established powerful communities, one of the most important of which in the eighteenth century B.C. was the Kingdom of Mari. It reached its zenith under Zimri-lim, a contemporary of the great Hammurabi of Babylon. Another centre of Amorite, or, as some scholars prefer to say, Proto-Aramaean power was Haran in North Mesopotamia, whence Old Testament tradition traces the migration of Abram westwards to Canaan (Genesis xi, 31–32). Since 1935 the distinguished French archaeologist André Parrot has conducted a series of excavations at Tell el Harari on the middle Euphrates, ancient Mari. Thirteen volumes of documentary material from the royal archives at Mari have been published since 1946. Volumes XI (1963) and XII (1964) alone contain over a thousand administrative texts which shed light on the economic and fiscal system of the Kingdom of Mari.

When we examine Amorite personal names and social customs numerous points of contact with the Old Testament patriarchal tradition are evident. Thus we find references to certain 'banu-iamina', 'Benjamites', at Mari.

I have gathered together the chiefs of the towns of the Benjamites. (*Archives Royales de Mari II*, 92)

The Benjamites have revolted to a man. They have gone to the towns from the high (country). (*Archives Royales de Mari III*, 12)

The name 'Benjamite' simply means 'son of the right hand', i.e. the south. It is not suggested that the 'banu-iamina' at Mari be equated with the later Hebrew tribe of Benjamin, but the identity of name form across the centuries points to a degree of cultural continuity. Likewise the verbal root which lies behind the name Jacob (probably originally Jacob-el, God protects) is found at Mari. Although the name Abram (the father? god is lofty) does not occur at Mari, names of similar type are frequent. Nor are the links confined to name forms. The narrative in Genesis xxxi which describes the ambivalent contacts between Jacob and the inhabitants of Shechem makes reference to a worthy called Hamor and refers to the people of Shechem as 'the sons of Hamor' (Genesis xxxiii, 19). *Hamor* in Hebrew means 'ass', hardly a complimentary or likely personal name even in those days. The Mari texts may well throw light on these 'sons of the ass' since more than once there occurs the phrase 'killing an ass' as part of the ritual involved in drawing up a covenant or peace treaty. Most probably the 'sons of the ass' were a group of people bound together by treaty, confederates. The purpose and method of census taking in Mari are also remarkably similar to those in early Israel. Several of the Mari texts introduce us to a messenger of the god, usually the god Dagan, who appears un-summoned before king or important official with a message which claims to be divinely given. Sometimes the message relates to cultic matters, sometimes to political events; for example there are messages of doom against the enemies of Mari.[3] These Mari messengers provide us with the closest parallels so far in the world of the Ancient Near East to the status and function of the prophetic movement in the Old Testament. In the light of such evidence there is therefore nothing unreasonable in the assumption that ethnically speaking the patriarchs of Genesis belong to one or other of the Amorite or proto-Aramean peoples whom we encounter in the Mari texts. As the ancient Hebrew cultic credo preserved in Deuteronomy xxvi, 5 ff. declares, 'A wandering Aramaean was my father'.

The middle of the second millennium B.C. saw the north Euphrates valley in the general area of Haran dominated by the Kingdom of Mitanni, a power strong enough to control Assyria and to need very careful diplomatic handling by the Egyptians. This kingdom was founded by a people called the Hurrians who spoke a strange non-Semitic language, evidence for which is found widespread throughout the Ancient Near East at this period. Of over two thousand names known to us from Alalakh in North Syria of the eighteenth to fifteenth centuries B.C. the vast majority are Hurrian or contain an admixture of Hurrian and West Semitic elements.[4] One such Hurrian community was Nuzi, modern Yoghlan Tepe, some 180 miles north of Baghdad. Nuzi was excavated between 1925 and 1931 by a joint expedition sponsored by the American School of Oriental Research in Baghdad and Harvard University. Several thousand cuneiform texts from both public and private archives at Nuzi, together with a few from neighbouring Arrapkha (modern Kirkuk) provide us, *inter alia,* with some fascinating parallels to certain social customs in the Patriarchal narratives. These customs are not so closely paralleled elsewhere and find no warrant or explanation in later biblical custom and law. Four illustrations will suffice:

Three times in the Genesis narrative (xii, 10–20; xx, 1–18; xxvi, 6–11) we find the wife of a patriarch being introduced as his sister, an act of apparent deception which has puzzled and troubled many commentators. It may indeed have been equally puzzling to the writer or writers of Genesis. The background to such incidents, however, becomes clearer in the light of the practice in Hurrian society, as evidenced in the Nuzi texts. There a man, on marrying, might proceed to adopt his wife as his sister.

This 'wife–sister' marriage was the most sacrosanct relationship in the eyes of the law. It may well reflect an underlying fratriar-chal type of society where a brother had greater legal authority than a husband. The links with Haran in the Abraham and Isaac traditions give us good grounds for believing that both the Abraham–Sarah and Isaac–Rebekah marriages may originally have been of the wife–sister type. Such a relationship was not known in later Hebrew society.

In that superbly vivid, if somewhat dubiously ethical saga of the relationship between Jacob and his father-in-law Laban, we are informed that when eventually Jacob flees from his father-in-law's household, his wife Rachel 'stole her father's household gods' (Genesis xxxi, 19). It has long been a puzzle as to why Rachel took with her such images, and why Laban was so anxious to recover them. The Nuzi texts help us to see Rachel's action not as an example of piety, but of true wifely shrewdness. In certain circumstances in Hurrian society family property might pass not to the eldest son in the family, but to a daughter's husband. Legal proof of such a transaction was the handing over to the son-in-law of the family household gods. Rachel was trying to ensure that her husband Jacob had due legal claim to a share in Laban's property.

According to Genesis xv, 1–3, Abraham, while still childless, recognized as his heir a certain Eleezer of Damascus, a slave born in his household. Two types of heir are clearly distinguished in the Nuzi texts, the direct heir *aplu*, and the indirect heir *ewirru*. One text speaks of a slave being adopted as an *ewirru* in return for certain services; another makes it clear that such an *ewirru* has no longer any legal rights if later an *aplu* is born into the family. This seems precisely the situation in the Genesis narrative, Eleezer is the slave *ewirru* so long as Abraham is childless, but disappears from the narrative as soon as Isaac is born to be the *aplu*.

In the narrative of Genesis xvi, 1–2, Sarah, having failed to fulfil her wifely duty to provide Abraham with offspring, gives him her Egyptian maid Hagar, saying 'it may be that I shall obtain children by her'. A text from Nuzi prohibits a husband from marrying again if there are children of the marriage, but stipulates that, should the wife be barren, she must provide her husband with a concubine on the understanding that she has full legal rights to any child born by this concubine.

An isolated example of social custom may be dismissed as coincidence, but when examples are numerous – and more could be cited – we are entitled to look for some historical interconnexion. Again it is to this general area of North Mesopotamia, where a proto-Aramaean population was subordinated to a conquering Hurrian element, that we are directed for the most significant links with the Patriarchal tradition in Genesis.

Both Mari and Nuzi have thrown further light on the mysterious Habiru whose presence is vouched for in the Ancient Near East during the third and second millennia B.C. in texts as far apart as southern Mesopotamia, Ugarit on the coast of North Syria (where the cuneiform ideograph SA-Gaz is equivalent to Habiru) and from Egyptian sources including the Tell el Amarna documents – in Egyptian texts they are called Apiru. It is not uncommon in the Nuzi texts to find a Habiru seeking social security by joining a wealthy household as a slave. At Mari the Habiru appear sometimes as mercenary troops, but more frequently as hostile independent bands causing the local authorities considerable trouble. Amid much that is still conjecture this much seems clear; Habiru is not the description of a racial group, but a reference to the social status of certain groups. They have been varyingly described as the 'outsiders', the 'refugees', the 'donkey caravaners' of the age. In spite of certain linguistic and historical difficulties, it still seems probable that there is some connexion between the Habiru and the Hebrews of Old Testament tradition. With one exception (Jonah i,9), all occurrences of the word Hebrew in the Old Testament are in narratives or law codes which refer to incidents prior to 1000 B.C. Abram the Hebrew, heading a band of 318 retainers (Genesis xiv, 14 ff.) seems not far removed in type from a certain Izinobi, an Ismutabulaean whom we encounter at Mari, 'thirty Ismutabulaeans, Habiru, march under his command'.

On the basis of present archaeological evidence we can say

with confidence that historically, socially and culturally the patriarchal narratives fit meaningfully into the world of the Ancient Near East circa 2000–1500 B.C. and into no other milieu earlier or later.

THE SETTLEMENT IN CANAAN

The story of the Hebrew settlement in Canaan is beset with problems. They spring in part from the nature of the traditions preserved in Joshua and Judges, which have probably gone a long way towards smoothing out and unifying a complicated and disjointed series of events. Some of the difficulties inherent in an attempt to dovetail archaeological evidence and the biblical tradition of this period have already been indicated (cf. pp. 29 ff). Two other pieces of evidence, one positive and one negative, may now be considered.

Any decision as to the date of the coming into Canaan of a group of Hebrews under Joshua is linked up with the probable date of the Exodus from Egypt and the period of subsequent wandering in the wilderness. Numbers xx, 14 ff. states that Moses sent messengers to the King of Edom requesting permission to travel peacefully along the 'King's Highway', one of the recognized caravan routes running through Edomite territory. Permission was peremptorily refused. The whole tenor of the narrative with its reference to fields and vineyards (v. 17) presupposes extensive Edomite settlement in the area south and south east of the Dead Sea. Nelson Glueck's surface explorations in Transjordan, graphically described in *The Other Side of Jordan* (1946), revealed few traces of life and no important settled communities in this entire area from the end of Middle Bronze I, circa nineteenth century B.C., until the thirteenth and twelfth centuries B.C. This seems to carry with it the implication that the Hebrews under Moses could not have traversed this part of Transjordan during this period. Any pre-thirteenth century B.C. date for the settlement in Canaan is, therefore, ruled out. A late thirteenth-century B.C. date, however, would be consistent with this evidence and also with one interpretation of the destruction of southern

45

Canaanite cities, such as Lachish and Debir, at this period (see p. 32).

According to Joshua vi, Jericho was the first major Canaanite fortress to fall to the invaders. Certain assumptions in that vivid narrative, which culminates in the walls of the city falling flat and the city being burned with fire, are obviously incapable of archaeological investigation. Ruined city walls, however, and the remains of fire-charred buildings are precisely the kind of material on which we may expect light from archaeological work. In the 1920s the site of ancient Jericho was excavated by a British expedition led by John Garstang. According to the expedition reports, the outer and inner defensive walls of the Late Bronze age city and their associated buildings came to a violent end. The outer wall fell down the slope of the Tell, the inner wall was largely in ruins and everywhere on buildings of the period traces of intense fire were to be seen. As to date, 'The evidence all points ... towards the year 1400 B.C. for the fall of Jericho'.[5] This conclusion, which did not go uncontested by other archaeologists, would inevitably carry with it a fifteenth-century date for the Exodus from Egypt and would conveniently link the Hebrew intrusion into Canaan with the Habiru mentioned in the Tell el Amaran documents. From 1955-8, however, further work on the site by the British School of Archaeology, directed by Kathleen Kenyon, has nullified any appeal to evidence from Jericho in the solution of chronological problems surrounding the settlement period. The walls and associated buildings which Garstang attributed to the Late Bronze age are now known to have belonged to the Early Bronze age, perhaps some 1500 years earlier. Of Late Bronze age Jericho very little has been found. After the violent destruction of the Middle Bronze age city, probably by the Egyptians towards the middle of the sixteenth century B.C., no meaningful continuous picture of extensive settlement emerges. This may be partly explained by the extent to which erosion has destroyed evidence, but at least we must say that what was once confidently claimed as a key site archaeologically for the chronology of the Hebrew settlement in Canaan no longer provides us with any clear answers. The advancing frontiers of archaeological knowledge are not always describable in terms of the confirmation of biblical tradition.

THE RELIGION OF CANAAN

Old Testament tradition views the settlement in Canaan as a period of religious crisis. This was the time when the people 'forsook Yahweh,[6] the God of their fathers who had brought them out of the land of Egypt; they went after other gods from among the gods of the people who were round about them and bowed down to them; and they provoked Yahweh to anger. They forsook Yahweh and served the Baals and the Ashtaroth' (Judges ii, 12–13). It was to be a continuing crisis. Some five hundred years later the prophet Hosea protests over the faithlessness of Israel, the bride of Yahweh who 'did not know that it was I who gave her the grain and the wine and the oil, and who lavished upon her silver and gold which they used for Baal' (Hosea ii, 8: cf. xi, 2). Many religious practices abhorrent to the prophets but widely practised in the community, for example cult prostitution, are traced to the insidious influence of the Canaanite worship of Baal (cf. Amos ii, 7; Hosea iv, 13–14). Indeed, even when worship was officially offered in the name of Yahweh, the god of Israel, it seems often to have been but a thinly disguised form of the worship of Baal.

Information concerning Baal and the type of religion centring on his worship was, until comparatively recently, second-hand and from obviously hostile sources. In March 1928 a Syrian peasant ploughing his land struck a stone which, on competent examination, was found to be part of a grave. In April 1929 at a near-by mound systematic excavations were begun by the French under the direction of Claud F. A. Schaeffer. They have continued, with interruptions, ever since. In May 1929 the first clay tablets were unearthed, soon to be followed by others from a library attached to a temple of Baal. In the course of 1930 the clue to the decipherment of these tablets written in a hitherto unknown language in alphabetic cuneiform was found, thanks to the brillliant work of Hans Bauer in Germany and Édouard

47

Dhorme in France. There is no doubt as to the identity of this site on the Syrian coast, almost due east of the tip of Cyprus. It is the ancient city of Ugarit, settled from the Neolithic age until the time of its destruction by the 'Sea Peoples' towards the end of the thirteenth or the early twelfth century B.C. The majority of the texts uncovered in the early stages of the excavations from the library of the Baal temple were of a religious and mythological character. These texts date from circa 1400 B.C., though they undoubtedly reflect religious and social practices current for centuries at Ugarit. More recently, attention has been concentrated on the palace complex and from its muniments room has come a rich store of tablets, letters, documents legal and financial, as well as the oldest known alphabet. Some of the texts are in Ugaritic, some in Akkadian, some in Hurrian. The way in which the Ugaritic material has increased in volume and importance may be seen in the publications of C. H. Gordon. From the slim *Ugaritic Grammar* in 1940 there has developed the massive 1965 *Ugaritic Textbook*, 547 pages of grammar and texts in translation. Like the comparable material from Mari, these texts throw a flood of light on the history of the period, revealing long and close relationships between Ugarit, the Hittite Empire to the north and the Egyptian Empire to the south.

The palace texts may in the long run be of greater importance than the mythological and religious texts for our understanding of the world of the Ancient Near East. We shall limit our discussion to the religious and mythological texts, however, because of their immediate relevance to the Old Testament. These texts reveal to us a pantheon of gods presided over by an aged and perhaps ailing figure *'El*, the 'Father of Man', the 'Kindly and Merciful'. 'El's consort is the goddess *Athirat*, mother of two of the most vigorous deities in the Ugaritic pantheon, *Baal* and his sister virgin *'Anat*. Baal appears frequently in the Old Testament, both as the name of an active Canaanite deity, and in compound name forms e.g. Baal peor (Numbers xxv, 3; Deuteronomy iv, 3), Baal berith (Judges viii, 33; ix, 4), Baal Zebul (2 Kings i, 2, 3, 6), Eshbaal (1 Chronicles viii, 33) and Jerubaal (Judges vii, 1). In the Ugaritic texts he is the god of rain and fertility, Baal the 'Strong',

Baal 'who mounts the clouds', to give him two of his most common titles. The virgin 'Anat is goddess of love, fertility and war, who ferociously strikes down the enemies of Baal.

> She plunged both knees
> in the blood of the guards, her skirts in the gore
>   of the warriors.

In many respects the most interesting feature of these Ugaritic texts is the series of conflicts in which Baal plays a leading role. They touch on mythological themes which we can document from elsewhere in the Ancient Near East and which are frequently echoed in the Old Testament. Two major conflict themes are prominent, though the relationship between them and indeed the reconstruction of them are matters of considerable dispute, involving delicate problems in the ordering of fragmentary tablets.

The first theme centres upon how Baal, with the help of weapons fashioned by the divine craftsmen Khathir and Khasis, 'Skilful' and 'Clever', crushes his enemies, Prince Sea and Judge River. This seems to be the Canaanite form of the familiar conflict between the champion of the gods and the power of chaos symbolized by the unruly waters, Marduk against Tiamat in the Babylonian version of the Mesopotamian Creation Epic. In the Babylonian version, once Marduk has triumphed, the other gods build him his temple Esagila. In the Ugaritic texts we find Baal complaining that he has no palace. After some dubious divine diplomacy, and arguments over the architectural features of the proposed palace, Baal has his mountain mansion built and dedicated amid general feasting and rejoicing. The most commonly advanced explanation of this myth is to see it as part of the liturgy of the Canaanite New Year Festival in which the kingship of the Baal, giver of life and order, and his victory over all the forces of chaos were dramatically re-enacted, thus guaranteeing the security and well-being of the community throughout the coming year.

The second conflict theme concerns Baal and his adversary Mot, i.e. Death. In this cycle Baal dies and descends into the earth, vanquished by Mot. After 'El and 'Anat have performed elaborate mourning rites, 'Anat goes in search of her dead brother. Meanwhile all nature languishes,

> The luminary of the gods Shapash [i.e. the sun] was blazing hot with no rain from heaven because of Mot, the son of 'El.

'Anat seizes Mot, slays him, winnows him in a sieve, burns him, grinds him between two mill stones and sows him in a field where the birds peck the pieces. Amid general rejoicing, Baal then comes to life. Again this myth has been related to the seasonal religious ritual of the Syrian peasant farmer, the annual conflict between the powers of fertility and sterility in nature.

This interpretation of the Baal poems, however, in terms of seasonal myth has not gone unchallenged. In particular, C. H. Gordon and G. R. Driver[7] have pointed out that nowhere in the texts is it explicitly stated that the death and resurrection of Baal are an annual event. Indeed at one fragmentary point in the text, a drought of seven years is said to follow the death of Baal. Driver would interpret the conflict between Baal and Prince Sea and Judge River as a struggle between gods representative of differing forms of irrigation to succeed to the vacant throne as viceroy of ageing 'El. Thus the cycle depicts how Baal, the fertilizing rain, defeats the rival powers of seas and rivers and ultimately vanquishes his arch-enemy Mot, death or drought.

Among other texts of importance from Ugarit is the so-called Legend of Keret, recounting the misfortunes and victories of King Keret. This document may contain a nucleus of historical fact, though many allusions in the text, which were once believed to have contained references to people and places mentioned in the Old Testament, are now known to have been misinterpreted. It is perhaps of greatest interest as a social document, throwing light on Canaanite customs, not least on the conventions and expectations centring upon kingship.

What then is the importance of such texts for our understanding of the Old Testament?

The texts have presented Old Testament and Semitic scholars with a rich store of additional linguistic material, both lexicographical and grammatical. Words hitherto almost unintelligible become meaningful in the light of Ugaritic usage. Other words are seen to possess an unexpected range of meaning. This helps to clarify certain difficult Old Testament passages. Naturally, since most of the Ugaritic texts are in the form of epic poetry and mythology, it is in the poetic strands of the Old Testament that help has been most readily forthcoming, notably in the Psalms, Proverbs and Ecclesiastes. For example, in Proverbs vi,11; xxiv,34 the Revised Standard Version reads:

and poverty shall come upon you like a vagabond, and want like an armed man.

The translation 'armed man', however, is doubtful. Elsewhere in the Old Testament Hebrew *mgn*, translated here as 'armed', means 'shield' either in a literal or metaphorical sense. Further, 'armed man' does not make very good sense in context. We would expect rather a word parallel in meaning to vagabond. In Ugaritic the root *mgn* is found with the meaning 'beg'. We may thus render:

and poverty shall come upon you like a vagabond, and want like a beggar.[8]

The way in which such new lexicographical information may be utilized in Old Testament studies is seen at its most fascinating and challenging in the recent Anchor Bible commentaries on the Psalms by M. Dahood. There is, however, a real danger that in the flush of enthusiasm more is being demanded from this Ugaritic material than we have a right to expect, and conclusions being drawn which may not stand the test of time.

In the Ugaritic texts we are in direct touch with a liturgical and mythological tradition of which there are many echoes in the Old Testament, particularly in the prophetic books and in the Psalms. Thus Isaiah xxvii,1 speaks of God's triumph:

In that day Yahweh with his hard and great and strong sword will punish Leviathan, the fleeing serpent, Leviathan the twisting serpent, and he will slay the dragon that is in the sea (cf. Psalm lxxiv,12–14).

The Ugaritic texts speak of Baal defeating his chaos adversary Sea in the following terms,

> Thou didst smite Ltn the slippery serpent
> annihilate the crooked serpent
> the cursed? one of seven heads.

One of the standard Ugaritic descriptions of Baal in his function as god of the fertilizing rain is *rkb rpt*, 'he who mounts the clouds'. In Psalm lxviii, 4 a slight emendation to the Hebrew text gives the reading

> Sing to God, praise his name, lift up a song to him who rides upon the clouds (*rkb brbt*, cf. v. 33 and Psalm civ, 3).

Certain hitherto unsuspected mythological allusions in the Psalms now become clear. In Psalm xlviii, 2 Jerusalem and the temple mount are spoken of as

> Mount Zion in the far north, the city of the great king.

'In the far north' as a description of Mt Zion has always been something of a geographical absurdity. The Hebrew *spn*, north, however, has its equivalent in the Ugaritic texts where the abode of the gods, the Canaanite equivalent of Mt Olympus, the seat of Baal's triumph, is *spn*. When the Hebrew took over traditional Canaanite cult centres – and Jerusalem was one of them – it was natural that some of the traditional liturgical language should be naturalized in Hebrew worship. Thus Mt Zion, the abode of Yahweh, is *spn*.

Not only the language content but also the form of Hebrew liturgical poetry draws from Canaanite tradition. Hebrew poetry employs parallelism to achieve its effect, one line usually echoing by way of repetition or contrast the preceding line. Occasionally, however, we find a tricolon or three line unit,

> For lo thy enemies O LORD
> for lo thy enemies shall perish,
> all evildoers shall be scattered. (Psalm xcii, 9)

Both in form and content this is an echo of lines from the Baal cycle,

> Behold thine enemy O Baal
> Behold thine enemy thou shalt smite
> Behold thou shalt subdue thine adversary.

The Psalms abound in imagery and language drawn from Canaanite liturgical tradition as that is now revealed to us in the Ugaritic texts. It is particularly evident in psalms which speak of the kingship of God and his triumphs over the floods and the waters of chaos, for example Psalms xciii and xcviii. Psalm xxix may very well have been originally a hymn to Baal which has had to be but slightly adapted for use in Hebrew worship.

Can we go further? If such Ugaritic texts come from the liturgy of an annual Canaanite autumnal New Year festival, can we say that some at least of the Old Testament Psalms are part of the liturgy of a comparable Hebrew New Year festival celebrated at the Jerusalem temple, a festival in which, through cultic act and word, Yahweh, the God of the Hebrews, triumphed over all his enemies and was re-enthroned for the coming year? This has been one of the most creative and hotly disputed questions in the interpretation of the Psalms and in the understanding of the Hebrew religion in recent years (cf. pp. 117ff. for fuller discussion).

JERUSALEM, CITY OF DAVID

In 2 Samuel v, 6 ff. there is the account of how David captured the Jebusite fortress of Jerusalem and rebuilt it into the capital of his kingdom. For the archaeologist Jerusalem presents almost intractable problems. Instead of a deserted Tell, he faces a site continuously occupied since Old Testament times, a city built and rebuilt many times, dominated by what was once the site of Herodian and earlier temples, and is now the Moslem Haram with the Dome of the Rock. The city of Jerusalem in New Testament times lay well within the limits of present-day Jerusalem, as has been amply demonstrated by excavations in the region of the pool of Bethesda, and more recently at the Damascus Gate;

but where precisely was the ancient Jebusite fortress of Jerusalem and what were the limits of the city of David?

Since 1961 excavations in Jerusalem have endeavoured to clarify the topography of the earliest settlements. The excavations, directed by Kathleen Kenyon, have been concentrated outside the present walls of the city, on one of the two south facing spurs of Mt Ophel.[9] The earliest evidence of settlement in the area comes from the third millennium B.C., when nomadic invaders left evidence of their presence in tombs on the slopes of the Mount of Olives. There is, however, as yet no evidence to show that the Amorites of the intermediate Early Bronze–Middle Bronze age (2300–1900 B.C.) contributed anything to the history of the city. By the Middle Bronze Age, settlement on the eastern slope of Mt Ophel is certain. Substantial walls of a pre-Israelite, presumably Jebusite, settlement at Jerusalem have been uncovered well down the slopes of Mt Ophel. Although David rebuilt this Jebusite fortress he does not seem, on the basis of present evidence, to have extended it to any degree. The line of the north wall of the city of David is far from clear, but present archaeological evidence suggests that it was not until the time of Solomon, David's son and successor, that the city advanced northwards into the area now occupied by the Haram. In other words, the city of David lies on Mt Ophel, entirely outside the present walls of the city. A complex pattern of walls and rebuilding representative of the main phases of pre-exilic settlement has been uncovered on the eastern slopes of Mt Ophel. It was not until the time of Nehemiah, circa 460 B.C., that this eastern slope of Mt Ophel was finally abandoned and the wall of the city began to follow the crest of the hill.

SOLOMON

Archaeological evidence for Solomon's major building activity in Jerusalem lies sealed under the area of continuous occupation in Jerusalem. I Kings ix, 15, however, informs us that in addition to this Jerusalem activity, Solomon built 'Hazor and Megiddo and Gezer'. From all of these sites there is evidence from the Solomonic period. The interplay of evidence from the different sites is an instructive example of the way in which accumulating inter-locking evidence may lead to the revision of earlier conclusions. The Megiddo excavations (1925–39) had identified the fourth occupation level (stratum iv) as the Solomonic city. This city, enclosed by a solid stone wall averaging twelve feet thick with 'offsets' and 'insets' was entered by a magnificent gateway flanked by two towers, similar in plan to the east gate into the temple enclosure as described in Ezekiel xl, 5–16. Within the city were numerous buildings including a palace which was presumably the residence of the local Solomonic governor. Four large buildings complete with posts and mangers were identified as stables capable of housing 480 horses. Since biblical tradition informs us that 'Solomon . . . had forty thousand stalls of horses for his chariots and twelve thousand horsemen' (I Kings iv, 26), these 'Solomonic stables' at Megiddo seemed to be a classic illustration of archaeology confirming biblical tradition.

Recent excavations at Hazor and Gezer, however, have necessitated a reinterpretation both of this evidence from Megiddo and of evidence obtained from the earlier excavation of Gezer in 1912. At Hazor there came to light in a stratum, assign-able on grounds of pottery and other evidence, to the age of Solomon, a gateway similar in design to that at Solomonic Megiddo. Strangely, however, this Hazor gateway was associated with a city wall, not of the solid 'offset-inset' type but of the casement type. Re-perusing the 1912 reports on Gezer, Y. Yadin, who directed the Israeli 'dig' at Hazor from 1955–8, noted a structure of similar design to the Megiddo and Hazor gates which had been designated as a 'Maccabaean Castle' (i.e. second century B.C.). This so-called Maccabaean Castle was part of a wall of the casement type. Confirmation has been forthcoming from the current digs at Gezer that this 'Maccabaean Castle' is in fact the gate into the Solomonic city.[10] But why then should the Solomonic city of Megiddo have an entirely different type of fortification from its contemporaries at Hazor and Gezer? This puzzle led Yadin to re-examine the Megiddo reports and also to make further trial soundings at Megiddo. The results were remarkable. Beneath the solid 'offset-inset' wall were clear traces of a casement type wall similar to those at Hazor and Gezer. Since *inter alia* certain buildings associated with this wall lay partly under the stables level, our picture of Solomonic Megiddo needs to be revised. Stratum iv with its stables must now be re-dated to the post-Solomonic period; it may be the city which arose after Megiddo was destroyed by a punitive Egyptian force in the time of Solomon's son and successor Rehoboam (cf. I Kings xiv, 25 f.; 2 Chronicles xii). The so-called Solomonic stables probably date from the time of Ahab, who, as we know from the annals of the Assyrian Emperor Shalmaneser III[11] contributed 2000 chariots to the allied forces who opposed the Assyrians at Karkar in 853 B.C. That there were stables at Megiddo in Solomon's day we need not doubt, but as yet there is no archaeological evidence of them.

Solomon's stables at Megiddo have proved somewhat elusive. The same must be said of the picture, so vividly drawn by Nelson Glueck, of Solomon as a prototype Andrew Carnegie, 'a great copper king' with his port of Ezion-Geber at the head of the Gulf of Aqabah as the 'Pittsburg of Palestine'. As a result of explorations in the Wadi ʿArabah in the mid-thirties and excavations at Tell el Kheleifah (Ezion-Geber), Glueck[12] drew a picture of extensive mining and smelting operations in the Timna area of the Wadi ʿArabah from the twelfth to the sixth centuries B.C. Several buildings which he interpreted as prison camps pointed to use of slave labour. Imported oak wood was used as fuel for stone furnaces. The centre of this copper industry was Ezion-Geber. It had an important smelting refinery, complete with flues so located as to make maximum use of the strongest winds in the region, and an associated industrial area with foundry and factory rooms. Solomon thus solved his balance of payments problem by exporting the copper products of this industrial complex in the ships of Tarshish which brought to Israel the wealth of nations: gold, silver, ivory, apes and peacocks (cf. I Kings x, 22).[13]

More recent excavations in the area by B. Rothenberg suggest that this picture must be considerably modified.[14] Certainly there was in the time of Solomon an extensive copper industry employing hundreds of workmen in the Timna area of the Wadi 'Arabah, but it seems to have been of short duration. All pottery in the area is datable to the tenth, or at the latest the early ninth century B.C. There is no evidence for stone furnace or prison blocks for slave labour; nor was anything other than local acacia wood used in the charcoal for firing. There is no evidence that the industry ever produced enough to contribute to the export trade. The copper may well have been produced solely for Solomon's building projects in Jerusalem, notable the Temple. Meteorological investigations do not substantiate the claim that the so-called smelting refinery at Tell el Kheleifah was located on the site of maximum local wind. There is, moreover, a conspicuous lack of slag heaps which would be the inevitable accompaniment of such a major copper industry. Glueck's 'Pittsburg of Palestine' on reinvestigation has become a Solomonic caravanserai; its smelting refinery a large storehouse, capable of providing the local military garrison and passing caravans with needed provisions.

Such re-evaluation of archaeological evidence, which has been used to supplement the biblical traditions concerning Solomon, is a salutary reminder of the necessarily subjective element even in a discipline like archaeology which employs scientific method and technique.

THE CAPITALS OF THE NORTHERN KINGDOM

David and Solomon founded a dynasty which survived the breakdown of the united Hebrew kingdom (925 B.C.) and bequeathed to Judah, the southern and smaller fragment of the disruption, a permanent royal capital in Jerusalem. It was not so in the northern kingdom of Israel. Not only was the military *coup d'état* a recurring feature in the politics of the northern kingdom, but in the course of its two hundred years of independence the capital moved from Shechem to Tirzah, and from Tirzah to Samaria. Archaeological data has been accumulating from all these three northern capitals. According to I Kings xii, 25

Jeroboam, the first king of the dissident northern tribes, 'built Shechem in the hill country of Ephraim'. Both biblical tradition elsewhere and archaeological evidence make it clear that he was rebuilding and refortifying a site which had long associations with Hebrew life, and indeed had flourished long before the Hebrews came to Canaan.[15] Why the northern capital moved to Tirzah is unknown. Shechem, however, is not an easily defensible site. It lies in a valley flanked by Mt Ebal to the north and Mt Gerizim to the south. Perhaps the Egyptian Pharaoh Sheshak's raid in 918 B.C., evidence for which may be seen in a layer of burnt debris above stratum x at Shechem, underlined this military weakness.

Tirzah (modern Tell el Far'ah, some fourteen miles to the north east of Shechem) was excavated by a French expedition directed by Père Roland de Vaux beginning in 1946.[16] From the beginning of the Chalcolithic age in the fourth millennium B.C. until roughly 600 B.C. the site was occupied. The many gaps in its history may owe as much to the malarial character of the neighbourhood as to the vicissitudes of history. Tirzah of the tenth and ninth centuries B.C. is well documented archaeologically with abundant pottery and the remains of houses constructed in orderly lines along well marked streets. 'Each represents the home of an Israelite family and the very uniformity of the dwellings shows that there was no great social inequality among its inhabitants. This corresponds excellently with the social conditions of the period of David and Solomon and the first kings of the northern dynasty.'[17] This socially homogeneous Tirzah ended in violent destruction, presumably the victim of Omri's *coup d'état* described in I Kings xvi, 17–18. Rebuilding, superior in construction and design, took place, but was apparently never completed. There is a break in the archaeological history of Tirzah at precisely the time when the archaeological history of Samaria begins to be significant. This corresponds well with the biblical tradition that Omri, after six years in Tirzah, transferred his capital to a new site, Samaria (I Kings xvi, 23–24). The reasons for Omri's move seem clear. Tirzah was very much an eastern outpost looking towards the Jordan valley. Samaria, on the other hand, astride the north-south route along the Palestinian watershed, faced westward towards the main lines of communication on the coastal plain. It provided Omri, one of the greatest kings of Israel, with a far better strategic site and far easier access to his north western Phoenician allies.

Samaria[18] survived as the capital of the northern kingdom until its collapse in 721 B.C., its natural defensive qualities being amply demonstrated during the final protracted Assyrian siege. Whether Omri built his new capital on a virgin site, or on a hill which had an already existing small village, the earliest extensive buildings date to the period of the dynasty of Omri. At that time the summit of the hill was enclosed by a superbly built wall some five feet thick. This enclosed a royal acropolis, on its western side a royal palace, and to the north a building which has been called the 'house of ivory'. The acropolis increased in size, probably during the reign of Omri's successor, Ahab. Its fortifications were strengthened by a casement type wall. Most of the population seem to have lived outside this government preserve, further down the slope. I Kings xxii, 39 speaks of the 'ivory house' which Ahab built (cf. Amos iii, 15). Among the most interesting finds at Samaria were numerous fragments of ivory. These ivory inlays, exquisitely carved, and often enriched with gold foil and glass insets, belong artistically to a group of Phoenician and Syrian ivories of the ninth and eighth centuries B.C., artistic confirmation of powerful Phoenician influence in Samaria. The vivid narratives about Elijah (cf. I Kings xviii) describe the clash between the prophetic champions of Israel's traditional way of life and the new theology and ethics which looked to Phoenician influence at court for their inspiration. Archaeological evidence for a complete cultural break in life at Samaria circa 721 B.C. is decisive, the entire acropolis area being burned and pillaged. A thick layer of debris with charred fragments of ivory, bears eloquent witness to the *coup de grâce* which Assyrian imperialism delivered to the northern kingdom.

We have drawn upon documents from Mari and Nuzi to illuminate our understanding of the Patriarchal period. Nothing, however, has yet been said about *written evidence* unearthed from Palestinian sites or from sites outside Palestine which had Jewish settlers. While for the Old Testament period there has been nothing as sensational as the Dead Sea Scrolls (see pp. 172ff), there has been a steadily increasing amount of documentary material. Its value is considerable both for the study of the historical development of Hebrew writing and for additional information which it provides about specific episodes in Hebrew life and culture.

THE OSTRACA FROM SAMARIA

The Harvard University expedition (1908–10) found on the site of Samaria over one hundred ostraca, i.e. inscribed potsherds. Sixty-five of them had more or less legible inscriptions, many of them labels or invoices sent with oil or wine from royal estates. Although these inscriptions are brief they were of considerable interest from the standpoint of Hebrew script. They also added to our knowledge of Hebrew personal names. In addition to names already known to us from the biblical records, e.g. Ahaz, Elisha, Meribaal, new names appear. Many of them are names such as Abibaal, Shemaryau, Gaddiyau, which contain as their basic element Baal, the Canaanite fertility god, or Yau, a shortened form of Yahweh, the god of Israel. The location of these ostraca led to their being attributed, on archaeological grounds, to the time of Ahab, i.e. mid ninth century B.C. Clarification of the stratigraphy of the site by excavators in 1931–5 indicates that a more likely date for this first group of ostraca is the time of King Jeroboam II, i.e. the first half of the eighth century B.C. In addition, eleven new ostraca of similar type were discovered. Their script suggested a date somewhat later in the eighth century B.C. The longest of these, three lines of writing incised on the rim of a shallow saucer-type bowl, has been variously interpreted; for example –

> Greetings, Shallum
> Baruch 2; the one with the straw
> Imnah: barley 13?
>
> (S. Birnbaum in *Samaria-Sebaste*, III, p. 11)

> Baruch (son of) Shallum
> O Baruch, pay attention and (give?)
> to the son of Yimnah barley
> to the amount of two (or three?) measures.

> (W. F. Albright in *A.N.E.T.*, p. 321)

Several potsherds with Aramaic script lettering were also discovered. They are even more fragmentary and debatable than the Hebrew ostraca. Most of them, however, may be dated on epigraphical grounds to the fourth century B.C.[19]

HEBREW SEALS

Seals were commonly used in Ancient Israel to authenticate a document or letter or to indicate ownership of objects such as jars. Hundreds of such seals, inscribed with Hebrew names and sometimes decorated with animal or floral motifs, have come to light.[20] They range in date from the ninth to the fourth century B.C. From Tell el Kheleifeh (Ezion-geber) comes a copper seal inscribed '(belonging) to Jotham'. It is just possible that this is a royal seal belonging to King Jotham of Judah (742–735 B.C., cf. 2 Chronicles xxvi, 2). From Lachish of the sixth century B.C. comes a clay seal inscribed '(belonging' to Gedaliah who is over the household'. This may refer to Gedaliah son of Ahikam who was appointed by Nebuchadnezzar of Babylon as puppet governor of Judah after the capture of Jerusalem in 587 B.C. From El Jib (Gibeon) come a number of seals inscribed '(belonging) to the king', followed by one of four place names, Hebron, Socah, Ziph or Memshath (the last name an enigma). Such seals have also been found at other sites, e.g. Gezer. They may be the trademark either of royal potteries at such places, or of jars made specifically for wine from royal vineyards.[21] One recently discovered seal from the eighth or seventh century B.C. has the figure of a locust on it, and above that the inscription 'belonging to Azaryaw (son of) Haggobeb'. Since Haggobeb is closely related to one of the Hebrew words for locust it looks as if the locust in this case was the family emblem. Insects as family names are not unknown elsewhere in the Old Testament, cf. Ezra ii,45; x,25; Nehemiah vii,48.[22]

THE LACHISH LETTERS

In 1935 J. L. Starkey found eighteen ostraca in what was probably the guardroom between the two gateways into the Judean city of Lachish. In 1938 three more, short and very fragmentary, came to light. Most of these ostraca were in the form of letters, the first examples discovered of personal correspondence from pre-exilic Hebrew life. Apart from their linguistic and philological interest, they provide us with a contemporary witness to the confused situation in Judah as the Babylonian army closed in to sound the death knell of the independent Judaean state early in the sixth century B.C. Two of these ostraca are of particular interest for Old Testament studies.

Ostracon III

Thy servant Hoshayahu hath sent to inform my lord, May Yahweh bring thee peaceful tidings! And now (thou has sent a letter, but my lord did not) enlighten thy servant concerning the letter which my lord sent to thy servant yesterday. For the heart of the servant hath been sick since thou didst send to thy servant. And now when my lord saith 'Thou dost not know how to read a letter', as Yahweh liveth, no one has ever tried to read a letter to me, and indeed any letter which may have come to me, I have certainly not read it . . . at all.

And thy servant hath been informed saying 'The commander of the army, Konyahu son of Elnathan, hath gone down on his way to Egypt, and Hodawyahu son of Ahiyahu and his men hath he sent to obtain . . .

And as for the letter of Tobyahu, servant of the king, which came to Shallum son of Yaddua, through the instrumentality of the prophet, saying 'Take care', thy servant hath sent it to my lord.[23]

The 'Hoshayahu' of this ostracon seems to have been the commander of a small Judean outpost. He is anxiously disclaiming all knowledge of a letter sent to him by his immediate superior Yoash, commander of the Lachish garrison. What this lost letter contained we do not know. It may have been military orders with which Hoshayahu had failed to comply. The reference to 'Konyahu son of Elnathon . . . on his way to Egypt' is consistent with what we know from the book of Jeremiah of a strong pro-Egyptian party in Judean politics at this time. Many Judean emissaries must have taken the road to Egypt as the Babylonian threat increased. There is, however, no reason for equating this reference with the incident recorded in Jeremiah xxvi, 20 f. which describes how Jehoiakim, King of Judah, sent emissaries to Egypt to secure the extradition of a troublesome prophet called Uriah. It is 'the prophet' mentioned in the second last line of the ostracon who has caused the greatest interest and dispute. He is essentially a shadowy figure. There are no other certain references to a prophet in the ostraca, though such references were at first claimed.[24] By some, he has been identified with the martyred Uriah (Jeremiah xxvi, 20 f.) or with Jeremiah himself. Any such identification goes well beyond the evidence. There were many prophets at this period. Some, both named and unnamed, appear in the book of Jeremiah. All that we know of this Lachish prophet is that he delivers a letter and caps it with a word of warning.

The concluding section of Ostracon IV *reads*

And (my lord) will know that we are watching for the signals of Lachish according to all the signs which my lord hath given, for we cannot see Azekah.[25]

Jeremiah vi, 1 mentions 'fire signals' and uses the same Hebrew word. Jeremiah xxxiv, 7 speaks of a stage in the Babylonian onslaught on Judah 'when the army of the king of Babylon was fighting against Jerusalem and against all the cities of Judah that were left, Lachish and Azekah; for these were the only fortified cities of Judah that remained'. If we could assume that the absence of the fire signals from Azekah meant that Azekah had fallen to the enemy then *Ostracon IV* could be dated shortly after the incident recorded in Jeremiah xxxiv. There are other reasons, of course, e.g. weather conditions, which might have been preventing the writer of *Ostracon IV* from seeing the signals from Azekah.

Again we must be on our guard against asserting too confidently direct links between such extra-biblical material and the biblical narrative; but as a contemporary witness to the political situation in Judah in the latter period of Jeremiah's ministry these Lachish letters are invaluable.

THE TELL ʿARAD OSTRACA

The most recently discovered Hebrew ostraca, seventeen in all, nine of which are reasonably well preserved, come from the southern Judean fortress of ʿArad. Discovered during excavations there in 1965, they consist of administrative documents probably from the period immediately prior to the destruction of the fortress in either 598 or 587 B.C. Most of them are addressed to a certain Eliashib. He seems to have been responsible for issuing rations to military personnel. The best preserved of the ostraca has been translated as

To Eliashib and now; give the Kittim 3(?) baths of wine and write the name of the day. And from the rest of the first flour let 1 ephah(?) of flour be mixed (?) to make bread for them. From the wine of the basins give.[26]

The 'Kittim' may well be Greek mercenaries acting as garrison troops in Judean fortresses. The presence of Egyptian mercenaries in ʿArad at a slightly earlier period is probably attested by another ostracon from the same site.[27] As the Babylonian threat to Judah's security increased, Judah had to strengthen her military effectiveness by all possible means.

THE LETTER OF ADON

In 1942 there was discovered at Saqqara (Memphis) in Egypt a letter in Aramaic. It was written by a certain Adon, a loyal Palestinian or Syrian vassal of Egypt, to plead for Pharaoh's help against the advancing Babylonians. Although the name of the city ruled over by Adon is not preserved in the letter – the text being tantalizingly broken at this point – it is a reasonable assumption that it was Ashkelon, one of the traditional five Philistine cities of the coastal plain. Faced with a Babylonian thrust as far as Aphek, probably the Aphek in the plain of Sharon (Joshua xii, 18; 1 Samuel iv, 1), Adon makes this plea:

... For Lord of Kings, Pharaoh, knows that (thy) servant (cannot stand alone against the king of Babylon. May it therefore please him) to send an army to rescue me. Do not abandon (me. For thy servant is loyal to my lord) and thy servant has safeguarded his property, and this region (is my lord's possession. But if the king of Babylon takes it, he will set up) a governor in the land and . . .[28]

The letter should probably be dated 603/2 B.C., though a slightly earlier date is by no means impossible. This provides us with contemporary documentation for the period covered by the narrative of 2 Kings xxiii–xxiv. Not only is the letter of historical interest, but the very fact that towards the end of the seventh century B.C. a letter written from a Palestinian king to his Egyptian overlord should be written in Aramaic proves that Aramaic was well on the way to becoming the *lingua franca* of Near Eastern diplomacy at a much earlier date than was once thought.

THE BABYLONIAN CHRONICLE

For some time it has been possible to check the biblical records of the history of the divided Hebrew kingdoms against information available from both Assyrian and Babylonian sources. The latest addition to our information from such sources came with the publication in 1956 by D. J. Wiseman of *Chronicles of Chaldean Kings (626–556 B.C.) in the British Museum*. It contained four hitherto unpublished manuscripts (B.M. 25125, 22047, 21946, 25124) and a re-editing of one manuscript (B.M. 21901) previously published by C. J. Gadd in *The Fall of Nineveh*, 1923. We can now handle with greater certainty the chronology of the closing years of the Judean state. B.M. 21946 begins by describing the decisive battle of Carchemish which guaranteed Babylonian suzerainty over Syria–Palestine, and fixes its date at 605 B.C. probably in May–June. Nebuchadnezzar, crown prince of Babylon, then commander–in–chief at Carchemish, succeeded to the

Babylonian throne on 6/7 September 605 B.C. The Chronicle claims that in the first year of his reign, he marched unopposed into Hatti territory until the month of Kislev.

'All the kings of the Hatti land came before him and he received their heavy tribute.' Allowing for an element of modest exaggeration in this Babylonian communiqué, it seems nevertheless likely that among those kings was Jehoiakim of Judah. The narrative in 2 Kings xxiv informs us that 'Nebuchadnezzar king of Babylon came up and Jehoiakim became his servant three years' (i.e. 604–601 B.C.). Thereafter Nebuchadnezzar launched yearly campaigns in strength into Hatti land, no doubt to make certain of loyalty and tribute. The siege and capture of Jerusalem is described in the Chronicle as follows:

> In the seventh month, the month of Kislev, the Babylonian king mustered his troops, marched to Hatti land and encamped against the city of Judah, and on the second day of the month of Adar he took the city and captured the king. He appointed therein a king of his own choice, received its heavy tribute and sent (them) to Babylon.

This is the Babylonian counterpart to 2 Kings xxiv, 10 ff. It provides us with a fixed date, 16 March 597 B.C. for the first Babylonian capture of Jerusalem, and thus helps to fix other dates in the closing years of the Judean state. Not all the chronological difficulties of the period are resolved, however, since there is unfortunately a gap in the Babylonian Chronicle from 594 to 556 B.C., a gap which included the last crucial years of Judean independence and the final destruction of Jerusalem.[29]

ARAMAIC DOCUMENTS FROM EGYPT

In the closing decade of last century and the opening decade of this century, there came to light a series of Aramaic papyri which opened up the life of a colony of Jewish mercenary troops stationed at Elephantine (ancient Yeb), an island in the Nile opposite Assuan (ancient Syene) on the southern borders of Egypt. The documents, which dealt with family, social and religious matters, spanned the fifth century B.C. They contained surprises. For one thing, this colony had a temple of Yahu (Yahweh); yet it had been generally believed that, after the religious reformation in Judah of 621 B.C. (2 Kings xxii–xxiii) the temple at Jerusalem had been the sole legitimate centre of Jewish worship. For another, the religious outlook of this colony seems to have left room for the worship of more than one deity. A list of contributions for the cult of Yahu reveals monetary gifts offered to other deities, Ishum bethel and 'Anath bethel. Elsewhere we find mention of Herembethel and 'Anath yahu; the latter by all analogy should mean "'Anath the female consort of Yahu'. An edition of the available texts was published in 1923 by A. E. Cowley, *Aramaic Papyri of the Fifth Century B.C.*

Life for this colony of Jewish mercenaries in the pay of the Persians was not all plain sailing. Texts 30 and 31 in Cowley's edition describe how an Egyptian mob, aided and abetted apparently by the local Persian garrison commander Widrang, destroyed the temple of Yahu. In a letter sent to the Persian governor of Judah, the colonists appeal for help. They are careful to point out that the incident happened while Arsam the Persian Satrap of Egypt was absent from the country, presumably enjoying a well-earned leave. From scattered references in the papyri it is likely that Arsam was out of Egypt from 410 to 408 B.C. His firm hand seems to have been badly missed, to judge from a new series of thirteen letters, written on leather, first published by G. R. Driver in 1954. A revised abbreviated edition of these letters, all of which are of an official or semi-official nature, appeared in *Aramaic Documents of the Fifth Century B.C.* in 1957. Ten of these letters were sent by Arsam. Letter IV deals with a typical case of insubordination.

From Arsam to Arampi the officer (who is in Egypt) concerning Psamseki's saying (The troop which is under me does not obey me).
From Arsam to Arampi
And now Psamek my officer has sent (word) to me (and) said thus: 'Arampi with the troop which is under him does not obey me in my lord's affairs, on which I am instructing them.'
Now Arsam says thus
(In regard to) this affair of my estate on which Psamek will instruct thee and that troop which is under thee – obey him and do (what he says).

Thus shall it be known to thee: if hereafter Psamek sends me (any) complaint of thee, thou wilt be strictly called to account and reprimanded.

Bagasoni is cognizant of this order; Ah-pipi is the scribe.

Further light has also been forthcoming on the internal affairs of the Jewish colony at Elephantine. It is one of the ironies of scholarship that the earliest Aramaic papyri recovered in Egypt – they were purchased by an American C. E. Wilbur in 1893 – were among the last to be published. They remained unknown until 1947 when Wilbur's daughter bequeathed some of her father's possessions to the Brooklyn Museum. They were published in 1953 in *The Brooklyn Museum Aramaic Papyri* edited by E. G. Kraeling. Some of the personnel of the colony, known already from the other texts, reappear including Yedoniah ben Gemariah, the head of the community. New names also appear, notably one family group, Ananiah ben Azariah, his wife Tamut, his daughter Yehoyishma and his son-in-law Ananiah ben Haggai. The Brooklyn papyri, sixteen in all, some well preserved, some very fragmentary, deal with family affairs, legal documents relating to marriage, slavery, deeds of sale of property. Two of the new papyri, numbers 2 and 7, are marriage contracts. Like the similar contract in Cowley's edition, number 15, they make it clear that, contrary to normal Hebrew practice, or indeed legal custom over a large part of the Ancient Near East, the initiative in divorce proceedings can be taken by the wife as well as by the husband. It is possible that Egyptian influence is reflected here.[30] These new papyri provide further information concerning Persian administrative problems in Egypt, increase our knowledge of life in this Jewish colony at Elephantine, and are of priceless value, philologically and linguistically, for Aramaic and kindred studies.

THE SAMARITAN PAPYRI

In the spring of 1962 news reached Jerusalem of the discovery by Ta'amerah tribesmen of documents in a cave in the Wadi

Daliyah, a remote area some eight or nine miles north of ancient Jericho. By the end of 1962 the first papyrus fragments were being studied. In all, some forty documents are now known, more than half of them only brief fragments. In addition to the documents, over one hundred seals, some seventy of them in good condition with either Persian or Attic motifs, have come to light, as well as a homogeneous collection of fourth century B.C. pottery and a large number of skeletons, male and female, young and old. All of the papyri seem to have been written in Samaria; this is stated whenever the opening or concluding formulae survive on the documents. They span a period of some forty years from 375 to 335 B.C. and are in the nature of legal and administrative documents dealing with slavery, manumission, real estate transactions and conveyancy. All the documents seem to have come from a group of Samaritans who rose in revolt against Alexander the Great. They fled from Samaria only to be tracked down and massacred by Macedonian troops in the cave where they had sought refuge.

Although much work still remains to be done on these documents, their importance is clear. Names of a type well known from the biblical records appear. There is, for example, a certain slave called Nehemiah. Most of the names contain an element derived from the Hebrew god Yahweh, but there are also names compounded of the pagan gods, Baal, Nabu (Babylonian) and Kemosh (Moabite). Of great interest is the reference to Sanballat as governor of Samaria. This cannot be the Sanballat known to us from Nehemiah's memoirs as governor of Samaria in the latter part of the fifth century B.C. (cf. Nehemiah iv ff.). It looks as if under the Persians more than one Sanballat held office as governor of Samaria. The name was probably, as in common practice, handed down from grandfather to grandson. This must lead to a revision of the sceptical attitude towards statements in the Jewish writer Josephus concerning a Sanballat as governor of Samaria when Alexander the Great invaded Syria (cf. *Antiquities*, XI, 302 f.). Palaeographically the papyri are of great significance since they provide the first fixed dates for Aramaic cursive writing of the fourth century B.C. Historically they are to be welcomed, since the fourth century B.C. is one of the least well known periods in Palestinian history.[31]

Archaeology is also enabling our picture of everyday life in Old Testament times to come more sharply into focus. Much information has been gleaned from tombs which have preserved cosmetics and jewellery, cooking utensils and weapons, amulets and figurines, tables and chairs as well as the ubiquitous pottery. Let El Jib, ancient Gibeon, provide us with two illustrations of a somewhat different kind.

Gibeon dramatically illustrates a community's need for adequate water supply. The problem was particularly acute in time of war when the local spring, located at or near the foot of the *Tell*, might be outside the defensive wall. From bed-rock just inside the wall on the north east of the city, there was hewn out a large shaft thirty-seven feet in diameter. It had a five-foot-wide spiral staircase leading down thirty-five feet. Then it sloped off into a tunnel which, forty-five feet below the surface, opened out into a roughly shaped chamber, presumably a reservoir. Probably constructed in the twelfth or eleventh century B.C. this reservoir seems to have proved inadequate since it was soon to be supplemented by a tunnel, 172 steps in all, cut from the top of the hill. This led down to meet a deeper tunnel cut back into the hillside some hundred and twelve feet from a cave which contained the local spring. Access to the cave from the outside was, in time of trouble, sealed off by a massive stone barricade.[32] Similar constructions serving a similar purpose are known at Megiddo and Gezer.

But what of the economy of Gibeon? If J. B. Pritchard is correct in his interpretation of the evidence, Gibeon was the Bordeaux of ancient Palestine. On the surface of the *Tell*, grouped in certain areas, were over sixty round openings, three feet in diameter, each with an appropriate stone seal. These openings led into underground chambers some six or seven feet deep and wide. They may very well have been vats, capable of storing twenty-five thousand gallons of liquid in jars stacked in double layers. The temperature in these 'vats' is a constant 65°F., precisely the temperature at which wine is stored today in the Trappist colony at Latrum which is not far distant. Thus one small site reveals long hidden secrets of its life in war and peace.

The sheer volume of evidence now available is daunting. And the end is not yet. Any report on archaeology and new sources of information is inevitably not only a highly selective, but also an interim report, in danger of being out of date as soon as it is written. It has been calculated that properly directed excavations have been carried through at only two per cent of potentially significant Palestinian sites. Given reasonable political stability in the Middle East, we may look forward confidently to new sources of information which will fill in gaps in our present knowledge and force us to revaluate what we already know.[33]

Two

New Ways of
Handling the
Literature

'Stalemate' was one of the words used by G. von Rad in 1938 to describe the situation in the study of the Old Testament traditions contained within the books from Genesis to Joshua. 'So far as the analysis of the source documents is concerned', he wrote, 'there are signs that the road has come to an end. Some would say we have already gone too far.'[1] This is but one witness to a widespread feeling that the methods of literary criticism which had been so fruitful in the nineteenth and early twentieth centuries had reached the point of diminishing returns. Literary criticism had worked on the basis of certain more or less unquestioned assumptions, among them the following:

(1) From a very early age in Israel, as in most modern cultures, *written* documents were the normal method of fixing, preserving, and handing on information, traditions, teaching, stories, etc.

(2) Much time and energy was therefore spent in trying to discover the 'authors' of such documents. Who wrote it? When was it written? Why was it written? Such were the questions to ask of any Old Testament book.

(3) If there were inconsistencies of thought or differences of style within one book, they were to be explained as the work of different authors or of later editors working over the text of the original author.

It was in the study of the first five books of the Old Testament, the Pentateuch (Genesis–Deuteronomy), that such literary criticism led to exciting and apparently assured results. These five books in their present form were regarded as the end product of the joining together of four originally independent written documents. The earliest of these documents, probably tenth century

B.C., was the J document, emanating from southern Judean circles. E, a more or less parallel northern tradition, was dated some two centuries later. The legislative kernel of our present book of Deuteronomy, chapters xii–xxvi, was the third, D, document. It had been the basis of an attempted radical religious reformation in Judah under King Josiah in the year 621 B.C. The fourth document was P, a priestly document of post-exilic date, probably fifth century B.C. D was the fixed chronological point in what is known as the Graf–Wellhausen hypothesis after two nineteenth-century German scholars who were largely responsible for its final formulation. It was generally agreed that J and E preceded D in date, while P followed it. Although many attempts have been made on literary critical grounds to attack this four-document hypothesis at its Achilles' heel, the date of Deuteronomy, either by pushing D forward to the period of the early monarchy[2] or holding it back to the exilic or post-exilic period,[3] the link with Josiah's reformation has stood the test of critical assault, and with it the four documents, J, E, D and P in that chronological order.

Literary criticism had used certain criteria to isolate the documents. Different divine names are found in the narratives; God (*'elohim*) in Genesis i–ii,4a, LORD God (*Yahweh 'elohim*) in Genesis ii,4b–iii. Another clear example is the flood tradition in Genesis vi–ix which oscillates between *Yahweh* and *'elohim*. There are alternative names for people and places; the mountain of God being called Sinai in Exodus xix,11, 18, but Horeb in Exodus iii,1, xvii,6 and throughout Deuteronomy. There are narratives which look suspiciously similar; compare Genesis xii,10–xiii,1 with xx,1–18 and xxvi,6–11. Contradictions are also evident in the narratives. Exodus vi,3 claims that God was not known to the patriarchs by his name Yahweh; yet this is precisely the name under which he reveals himself to Abraham in Genesis xv,7.

If such inconsistencies and apparent contradictions are used to isolate different documents, how far can they be pushed? Similar criteria were soon to be used to raise awkward questions about the four documents. Thus O. Eissfeldt isolated from J in Genesis and Exodus an earlier L or 'lay' source at the opposite end of the spectrum from the P or priestly source. It contained the crudest and most primitive elements in the tradition.[4] J. Morgenstern proposed in Exodus a K (Kenite) source, and R. H. Pfeiffer found in Genesis an S (Southern or Seir) source. Others found it necessary to operate with an increasingly complex set of source symbols, J^1 J^2 J^3 P^a P^b etc. Parallel with this atomizing process there has been a questioning of the relationship between J and E, which are usually regarded as two more or less parallel narratives. The need to isolate E as a separate document has been called into question.[5] If a reputed author, such as the author of the J document, is fragmented into several distinct personalities, and one of his confrères, E, is regarded as otiose in certain quarters, what then becomes of the Graf–Wellhausen theory in its classical form? Is it merely an illusion rooted perhaps in the mistaken application of modern western criteria of literary criticism to ancient Near Eastern texts? If not an illusion, has the theory not been pushed beyond the bounds within which it may legitimately operate? At this point two kinds of questions call for clarification.

Assuming the existence of documents such as J, E, D and P, what lies behind them? What kind of material was available to the authors or editors of such documents? When did the material circulate in ancient Israel, and in what form?

Do we need to operate with the hypothesis of written documents in ancient Israel? Would it not be truer to assume that, until the time of the breakdown of the normal structure of the nation's life in the exile of the sixth century B.C., the accepted method of transmitting material was not by way of written documents, but by a living process of oral tradition, material passed on by word of mouth from generation to generation, shaped and reshaped in what we may describe as 'traditionist circles'?

It is here that the focus of interest in the study of Old Testament literature in the period under review has tended to swing from literary criticism to form criticism (*Gattungsgeschichte* or *Formgeschichte*) and tradition history (*Traditionshistorie*)[6]. Literary criticism had employed an analytical method in its search for such individual characteristics as provide clues to the author, authors or editors of a particular piece of literature. Form criticism assumes that the literature of an ancient community reflects the life of that community in its entirety. It looks for separate units of material within that literature and seeks to classify them according to type (*Gattung*). It concerns itself with the conventional, the typical rather than the individual, and it does so on the basis of a catholic understanding of the various types of literature that emerge in human society. Thus form criticism classifies material into types such as 'myth', 'saga', 'cult legend', 'dirge', 'priestly instruction', 'prophetic oracle', 'hymn', 'royal psalm', 'national lament', to take a few examples from the Old Testament. For the impact of form criticism on New Testament studies see pp. 246ff.

Each type has its distinctive fixed forms of expression; compare our typical fairy tale with its 'once upon a time . . . and they all lived happily ever after', or a letter beginning 'Dear Sir' and ending 'Yours faithfully'. Further each type has its own *Sitz im Leben*; that is to say it originally springs out of, and is closely tied to, a particular situation in the life of the community. Thus the dirge, e.g. 2 Samuel i, 19–27, has its *Sitz im Leben* in the customary mourning rites of the community; the Psalms of national lament e.g. Psalm xliv; lx; lxxiv, have their *Sitz im Leben* in the liturgy of a day of national penitence. In this way form criticism seeks to take us back beyond the Old Testament documents to the life of Ancient Israel and to the immediate circumstances in the life of this community in which this or that particular passage was spoken or narrated. It found its first truly great exponent in the biblical field in Hermann Gunkel who creatively applied its methods in his commentaries on Genesis in 1901 (fifth edition 1922) and on the Psalms (fourth edition 1926).

Tradition history seeks to show how these individual units, isolated by form criticism and traced back to their original *Sitz im Leben*, have been handed down largely in oral form, within the community. It examines how, in the process, they have been shaped and reshaped until they eventually reached the form in which they now lie before us in the literature of the Old Testament.

The Old Testament

Let us take note of some of the ways in which form criticism and tradition history have made an impact on the study of the different kinds of literature within the Old Testament.

THE PENTATEUCH

The Laws in the Pentateuch

In a stimulating essay, 'Die Ursprünge des israelitischen Rechts', 1934 (English translation 'The Origins of Israelite Law', in *Essays on Old Testament History and Religion*, 1966, pp. 101–72), A. Alt pointed out the limitations of any literary critical approach to the various codes of law within the Pentateuch. 'We must give full attention to the possibility that the very oldest compilations of laws are separated from the real origins of the law by a considerable period in which the law was developed and handed down orally' (op. cit., p. 110). Not only so, but in this oral stage it had already received fixed forms which reflect tensions at work in the formulation of Israelite law. Two such forms are clearly distinguishable:

(a) *Casuistic law* in which the main case is introduced by 'when' or 'supposing that' (Hebrew *ki*), and subsidiary cases introduced by 'if' (Hebrew *'im*). For example 'When a man strikes his slave, male or female, with a rod, and the slave dies under his hand, he shall be punished. But if the slave survives a day or two, he is not to be punished; for the slave is his money' (Exodus xxi, 20 f.). The basic form of such laws is almost always in the third person. This is the normal form of secular jurisdiction throughout the Ancient Near East. We find it reflected in Assyrian, Babylonian and Hittite law codes. There is nothing specifically Israelite in this type of law. The real source of such law in Israel was probably Canaanite law adapted by the Israelites after their entry into Canaan, but before the foundation of the Hebrew monarchy, in the twelfth and eleventh centuries B.C.

(b) *Apodeictic law*. Woven into the so-called 'Book of the Covenant', Exodus xx, 22 – xxiii, 33, which contains in the main casuistic law, there is another type of law totally distinct in form and also in origin, e.g. Exodus xxi, 12, 'Whoever strikes a man so that he dies shall be put to death'. In Hebrew, this is a terse rhythmic five-word statement, not casuistic in form and wholly unconditional in content. Here we are dealing with 'the implacable will of the national god instead of secular legislation' (op. cit., p. 131). Closely allied in type to such laws is the series of curses found in Deuteronomy xxvii, 15–26, all of them concerned with crimes committed in secret and having as their penalty a curse upon the evildoer which means his exclusion from the religious community. The classic example of such apodeictic law, however, is the Decalogue (Exodus xx, 2–17; Deuteronomy v, 6–21) in its original form. Each of its commands was probably brief, with the regulations concerning the Sabbath and parents originally as categorical prohibitions, 'Thou shalt not . . .' like the other regulations. The *Sitz im Leben* of this type of law, according to Alt, is 'cultic'; that is to say, its natural home is the community gathered for worship, gathered to speak certain words and to perform certain ritual acts. 'The apodeictic law provides the central text for a sacral action involving the whole nation, and those who proclaim it are the mouthpiece of Yahweh, the levitical priests, whose task in the assembly of the whole nation was by no means only to conduct the worship of Yahweh, but who also carried out the function, at least equally important, of making his demands known to Israel' (op. cit., p. 161). The particular sacral or cultic occasion for the proclamation of such law was the Feast of the Tabernacles at which the covenant between Yahweh and Israel was regularly renewed. Such law, claimed Alt, is distinctively Israelite and emanates from the formative period of Israel's life, before settlement in Canaan. Much of the tension in Israel's religious life, from the time of the settlement in Canaan onwards, is seen in the interaction of these two different types of law. The Canaanite casuistic type remains basically secular; the apodeictic, being aggressively religious, more and more claims the whole of life for Yahweh.

Alt's essay brilliantly illustrates the method and techniques of form criticism. There is the recognition of the need to go back beyond the literary tradition, the classifying of material on the basis of form, the positing of a specific *Sitz im Leben* for each of the forms and, in the case of the casuistic type of law, the use of comparative material from the wider world of Ancient Near Eastern culture.

Although Alt had clearly isolated apodeictic law and stressed its distinctively Israelite and cultic character, he left many questions concerning this type of law unanswered. Comparative material was apparently lacking here. The Decalogue, on grounds of form, he regarded as stemming from a fairly late period, there being no proof that it was in any way the prototype of apodeictic law. The next significant step was taken by G. E. Mendenhall in *Law and Covenant in Israel and the Ancient Near East*, 1955. Hittite treaty documents of the fourteenth and thirteenth centuries B.C. had long been known: it was left to Mendenhall to direct attention to their form, and to draw from this certain conclusions of relevance to the Decalogue. The Hittite treaty documents contained certain common recurring elements.

(1) A prologue identifying the great king of the Hittite empire and giving his titles.

(2) A statement of the past gracious acts of the king towards his vassals.

(3) A statement of the conditions upon which the treaty is made, prominent among them a prohibition on any trafficking with the king's enemies.

(4) The provision that the treaty document be deposited in a temple and regularly read to the community.

(5) A list of the gods cited as witnesses to the treaty.

(6) Blessings and curses consequent upon the keeping or violation of the treaty.

The Decalogue, which Old Testament tradition claims to be the character of the covenant between Yahweh and his people at Mt Sinai, probably in the thirteenth century B.C., is remarkably similar to such treaties in form.

(1) There is a prologue identifying this god and giving his title, 'I am Yahweh your god'.

(2) There is a statement of his past gracious act: 'who brought you out of the land of Egypt, out of the house of bondage'.

(3) There is a statement of the conditions inherent in this covenant headed by 'you shall have no other gods before me'.

(4) The cultic *Sitz im Leben* of this type of law had been stressed by Alt, and everything points to the Decalogue having been read in Israel at some regular covenant renewal ceremony.

(5) Deuteronomy xxvii-xxviii has a series of curses and blessings connected with the people's disobedience or obedience to the commandments.

The exclusiveness of Yahweh in Hebrew tradition naturally prevented any direct parallel to gods being cited as witnesses.[7]

Mendenhall concluded that the Decalogue must be described as a formal treaty covenant regulating the relationship between Yahweh and his vassal people, and further that it must come from the same general period as the Hittite treaties. The discussion has since been broadened to take account of later Assyrian treaty documents, particularly with reference to the form of the Book of Deuteronomy.[8] Although Mendenhall's conclusions have been challenged, his and subsequent studies have breathed new life into discussions concerning the concept of the covenant and the place which it occupies in Israel's religious traditions. At the very least, the evidence he adduced is consistent with an early date for the Decalogue as the basic charter for such a covenant.[9]

The Early History of Israel

Old Testament tradition presents us with a unified picture of Israel's early history. It begins with the coming of Abraham from the east to settle in Canaan. A period of enslavement in Egypt ends in the miracle of deliverance and the subsequent covenant at Mt Sinai or Horeb. Thereafter the Hebrew tribes invade and conquer Canaan. Each stage in this story is directly and causally related to the preceding stage. But what happens to this picture when its narrative sources are subjected to form criticism? In 'The Form-Critical Problem of the Pentateuch' (*The Problem of the Pentateuch and other Essays*, 1966, pp. 1–78, an essay first published in German in 1938), G. von Rad argued that in Deuteronomy xxvi, 5b–9, 'A wandering Aramean was my father . . .', we have what is probably the earliest recognizable example of a creed in the Old Testament. In this creed, in similar credal statements in Deuteronomy vi, 20–24, Joshua xxiv, 2b–13 and in free poetic embellishments of such creeds in the Psalms and elsewhere (e.g. Psalms lxxviii; cxxxv; cxxxvi; Exodus xv), there is one remarkable fact: the total absence of any reference to the Sinai covenant story which features so prominently in the narrative sections of Exodus. This tradition, which he designated the 'Settlement tradition', was to be thought of as a cult legend which enabled the Israelites to appropriate for their own use a Canaanite agricultural festival at a time when ownership of the land of Canaan was still a living issue between the incoming Hebrews and the indigenous population. Its original *Sitz im Leben* was the Feast of Weeks celebrated at the Gilgal sanctuary near Jericho (cf. Joshua iii ff.).

The 'Sinai tradition' in Exodus is quite distinct. It too is reflected in free poetic variations, e.g. Deuteronomy xxxiii, Judges v, Habakkuk iii. It is most fully developed in the body of the book of Deuteronomy. Central to this tradition are theophany (God's appearing to the people) and a covenant-making ceremony. It has its own place in the religious life of Israel, namely at the Feast of Booths, a distinctively Israelite New Year Festival celebrated at the sanctuary at Shechem (cf. Joshua viii).

The joining of these two traditions, according to von Rad, was the literary work of 'J', who found them already detached from their original cultic *Sitz im Leben*. The basis of 'J's' work is the 'Settlement tradition', but on to this he has grafted the 'Sinai tradition'. He has developed the theological relationship between the stories of the Patriarchs coming to Canaan and the post-Exodus conquest of Canaan in terms of promise and fulfilment, and prefixed to the whole the primeval traditions of Genesis i–xi which serve to link the history of Israel to God's purposes for the entire human race.

Von Rad emphasizes that the cult at Shechem did not invent the Sinai tradition. Indeed the legend precedes the cult and provides the authority for it; but beyond that general statement we must adopt an attitude of historical agnosticism. The real question concerning such a tradition 'is not whether it is historically credible, but what particular place and function it has in religious life, i.e. its situation in life. Such material cannot, on principle, be teased out in order to serve as sources for the reconstruction of the historical course of events' (op. cit., p. 20).

This atomizing of the tradition, with a consequent radical revision of, or agnosticism towards, the history of Israel prior to the settlement in Canaan, has been carried a stage further by M. Noth in *Überlieferungsgeschichte des Pentateuch*, 1948, the results of which are utilized and summarized in *The History of Israel* (1958, second edition E.T.). The early Old Testament traditions are presented to us as the traditions of Israel; but, says Noth, 'Israel' as a nation did not exist prior to the settlement in the land of Canaan. The traditions which go back beyond the settlement, therefore, once existed separately as the traditions of different tribes or groups of tribes which only later coalesced into the national entity 'Israel'. We can isolate one from another several major traditions, – 'Deliverance from Egypt', 'The Patriarchs', 'The Covenant at Sinai'. Nor are these traditions, even when thus isolated, homogeneous. Thus the 'Deliverance from Egypt' tradition has been grafted on to a Passover legend. Passover was originally nothing but a religious rite practised by nomadic shepherds. It had no link with the story of the Exodus from Egypt. In particular, the Patriarchal traditions in Genesis present us with a mosaic of material, much of which once had nothing to do with the Hebrew patriarchs. Examples of this are the aetiological story of the destruction of the cities of the plain (Genesis xviii–xix), the cult legends of the sanctuary in the land of Moriah (Genesis xxii, 1–19) or of the night demon at the ford Jabbok (Genesis xxxii, 24–32). Such stories were native to the land and religion of Canaan long before the coming of Abram. Noth believed that these separate traditions had already been gathered together in much of their present form and interrelatedness by oral tradition, before they achieved literary status in the earliest of the written Pentateuch sources, J.

In terms of such an approach, a considerable rewriting of the early history and religion of Israel is necessary. For example, the figure of Moses dominates the Pentateuch from Exodus onwards, and has been decisive for all later Jewish thought. Since, however, the Pentateuch has been compiled step by step from a series of originally independent traditions, the inevitable question arises: in which of the traditions was Moses originally at home? On Noth's thesis, this question is extraordinarily difficult to answer. Indeed the most positive attitude he can adopt is a negative one, i.e. that Moses was not originally connected with the Sinai covenant tradition.[10] Others have argued that the Moses of tradition represents an institution or profession, that of 'law preacher' which existed in Israel from an early period. The methodology lying behind Noth's approach to the Pentateuch tradition has been radically, if somewhat extremely, criticized by John Bright in *Early Israel in Recent History Writing*, 1956, and an alternative approach adhering much more closely to the present Old Testament narrative is presented in his *A History of Israel*, 1960.

The Radical Rejection of Literary Criticism

Both von Rad and Noth work on the assumption that a period when material was being transmitted in oral form in Israel was succeeded, or at least supplemented at a fairly early date – say tenth century B.C., with the appearance of J – by a period when the tradition was handed down definitively in written form. On this view, form criticism is a convenient tool to take us back beyond early written documents, a supplement rather than an alternative to literary criticism. A much more radical theory has been advanced by the so-called Uppsala school, and in particular by I. Engnell.[11] Engnell has expressed dissatisfaction with the Graf–Wellhausen hypothesis on several grounds. Recent archaeological work has taught us, he claims, to treat the Old Testament narratives with greater respect. The four-document hypothesis rests on certain no longer acceptable evolutionary assumptions in the study of religion. Above all, it fails to realize the importance of oral tradition as the normal method of transmitting material in Israel and in the Ancient Orient in general. Only a typically modern, Western, logic-chopping type of literary criticism could ever assent to the theory of four separate written documents in the Pentateuch. Many of the repetitions and so-called inconsistencies in the narratives are merely the marks of a tradition which has gradually been built up and handed down in oral form. Far from the flowering of national self-consciousness under David and Solomon in the tenth century B.C. providing the stimulus towards a written record of Israel's history, it is only in an age of crisis and breakdown of the normal patterns of communication, i.e. the exile of the sixth century B.C., that there comes a need to replace the living stream of oral tradition by a written record. Although some of the material in Genesis–Deuteronomy, e.g. laws, may have been fixed in writing at an early date, the theory of four documents is not only unnecessary, but it prevents us from truly understanding the form in which the material has come down to us, and therefore blinds us to its true religious significance.

Instead of J, E, D and P as written documents, Engnell works with two major blocks of tradition originally independent of each other. The one, Genesis–Numbers, the nucleus of which is the Passover legend in Exodus i–xv, he terms the P work. In it, old traditions from many sources have been shaped and reshaped into their present form by a traditionist circle centred on Jerusalem. The basic outlook of this tradition is similar to that of the reputed author of the P document in terms of literary critical analysis. The other tradition, the D work, runs from Deuteronomy to 2 Kings.[12] It draws on ancient oral traditions, many of them of northern Israelite origin, which have been shaped by a circle sharing the standpoint of the great reforming prophets of the eighth and seventh centuries B.C. Like the P work this D work in its present form is post-exilic, probably fifth century B.C.

Wherein lies the basic difference between this traditio-historical approach to the Pentateuch and the literary critical documentary hypothesis? No one today seriously doubts that the Pentateuch is composite, the product of many hands and many periods. Both approaches recognize that there are differences in emphasis, and indeed contradictions, within the material as we now have it.

For example, in terms of the literary critical approach, the opening chapters of Genesis are said to contain two different creation stories. The later, more theologically sophisticated account in Genesis i–ii,4a is attributed to P, the earlier, more naïve J account begins at Genesis ii,4b. Note the change in the divine name from God (*'elohim*) in Genesis i to LORD God (*Yahweh 'elohim*) in Genesis ii,4b. Engnell, refusing to accept these documents, and seeing in Genesis–Numbers one great tradition work for his 'P' circle, nonetheless admits that Genesis ii,4b ff. contains tradition material from other than his P circle.[13] The crucial dividing question is whether the admitted differences so belong together in constants as to demand the hypothesis of written documents of different date and authorship. May they not simply reflect disparate traditions which had long been circulating orally side by side in different circles within Israel? Such separate traditions would gradually assimilate to one another in oral transmission even before achieving written form.

Engnell and others have been justified in drawing attention to the important part that oral tradition must have played in the transmission of Israel's early historical record. It is, however, highly questionable whether they have sounded the death knell of literary criticism. It is not demonstrable, and indeed highly unlikely in the light of material such as the Ras Shamra texts from Canaan of the fourteenth century B.C., that oral tradition was the sole or even the main method of transmitting Israel's historical consciousness until the time of the exile. On the whole the documentary hypothesis, though battle-scarred, and with the distinction between J and E much less assured than once was thought, still holds the field, and will continue to do so until some other theory explains, with equal or greater cogency, the evidence of the texts.[14]

THE PSALMS

Nowhere has the influence of form criticism been more decisive or more creative than in the study of the Psalms. R. H. Pfeiffer in his *Introduction to the Old Testament*, written in 1948, but representing a point of view indifferent to the form critical approach, could say of the Psalms that only xxiv and xlv were definitely pre-exilic, i.e. earlier than the sixth century B.C.; Engnell, *per contra*, could claim in *Studies in Divine Kingship in the Ancient Near East*, written in 1943, that there was only one psalm in the whole Psalter of which he was convinced that it was post-exilic, Psalm cxxxvii. Both are extreme statements; but while Pfeiffer would have been granted a respectable hearing in the 1870s, Engnell stands on this side of a revolution in the study of the Psalms which has been gathering momentum over the past forty years.

The nature of this revolution may be seen by comparing the introductory comments to Psalm lxxv in two commentaries on the Psalms, both of which first appeared in German and then in English translation. F. Delitzsch in *Commentary on the Psalms*, volume 2, 1871 (English translation of second German edition), assigns the psalm to the period when Assyrian power was threatening Jerusalem, at the end of the eighth century B.C. It is, he says, 'the lyrical companion of the prophecies which Isaiah uttered in the presence of the ruin which threatened from Assyria'. He notes another view which would date the psalm to the period of Judas Maccabaeus in the second century B.C., and thinks it would also be possible to place it earlier than the time of Isaiah to the reign of Jehoshaphat, mid ninth century B.C. A. Weiser in *The Psalms*, 1962 (English translation of the fifth German edition) describes Psalm lxxv as 'part of a cultic liturgy which has been preceded by a testimony of the congregation'. The testimony (verse 1) 'briefly recapitulates what has taken place in the divine service immediately before; God has appeared and is near to them in the sanctuary . . .'. No longer is any attempt made to locate the precise historical situation in the life of the community which gave birth to the psalm. The *Sitz im Leben* of the psalm is now recognized to be a recurring congregational situation. It is part of the liturgy of an act of worship, practised in pre-exilic Israel, probably in the Jerusalem temple.

One man, more than any other, was responsible for giving this new direction to the study of the Psalms; Hermann Gunkel. In a series of studies culminating in his commentary *Die Psalmen*, 1926, he made brilliant use of insights gleaned from comparative Babylonian and Egyptian material, to substitute for a purely personal and individual approach to the Psalms the attempt to classify them according to types (*Gattungen*). Within the Psalms he recognized five main types each with its own *Sitz im Leben*.

(1) *Hymns*, of which there were more than twenty, including Psalms viii; xix; xxix; xxxiii; lxv. They give voice to the praise of God and were originally intended for choral or solo use in an act of worship. The opening and closing verses of Psalm viii clearly indicate the dominant mood of such hymns,

> 'O LORD, our Lord,
> how majestic is thy name in all the earth'.

Closely related to such hymns he recognized two special categories,

(a) *The Songs of Sion*: Psalms xlvi; xlviii; lxxvi; lxxxvii, centring on the praise of Jerusalem and its temple mount.

(b) *Enthronement Songs*: Psalms xlvii; xciii; xcvi, 10 ff.; xcvii; xcviii; xcix, composed to celebrate the enthronement of Yahweh as universal king. Such 'Songs' have a strongly eschatological flavour, i.e. they point forward to the future, ultimate triumph of Israel's god.

(2) *Communal Laments*: e.g. Psalms xliv; lxxiv; lxxix; lxxx; lxxxiii. In such laments, the community assembled at the sanctuary gives voice to grief and penitence in face of some community disaster.

(3) *Royal Psalms*: Psalms ii; xviii; xx; xxi; xlv; lxxii; ci; cx; cxxxii. All of them are related to various aspects of the life and function of the monarchy in pre-exilic Israel. Thus Psalms ii, ci and cx find their *Sitz im Leben* in the religious ceremonies surrounding the king's enthronement, while Psalm xlv celebrates a royal wedding.

(4) *Individual Laments*: the most common type of all, e.g. Psalms iii; v; vi; vii; xiii. In them the plight of a Psalmist, often threatened by enemies or 'workers of iniquity' is graphically described and an appeal for vindication made to God.

(5) *Individual Songs of Thanksgiving:* these are the personal counterpart to the hymns. In them God is praised for some act of personal deliverance experienced by the worshipper, e.g. Psalms xviii; lxxxv; xli.

As well as these five major types, there were four minor types, *Songs of Pilgrimage* (Pss. lxxxiv; cxxii ff.), *Communal Songs of Thanksgiving*, composed for special occasions (Psalms lxvii; cxxiv), *Wisdom Psalms* (Psalms i; xxxvii; xlix; lxxiii; cii; cxxvii; cxxviii; cxxxiii), and *Liturgies* characterized by an antiphonal element and dialogue form (Psalms xii; xv; xxiv; lxxv; lxxxv; cxxvi). Certain other psalms could only be described as mixed types. Gunkel further clearly saw that such Psalm types were not merely confined to the Psalter. Exodus xv, the triumphant song of the Sea, celebrating the victory over Pharaoh and his chariots, and 1 Samuel ii, 1–10, the Song of Hannah, belong to the *Hymn* category. Isaiah xxxviii, 10–20, Hezekiah's prayer, and Jonah ii, 3–10 are *Individual Songs of Thanksgiving*.

Gunkel recognized that most of these types had their original *Sitz im Leben* in the cult. Some of them continued to be organically related to worship, particularly the *Individual Songs* of *Thanksgiving* which often accompanied a sacrifice of thanksgiving offered to Yahweh in response to experienced deliverance. He was, however, convinced that many of them, particularly the *Hymns* and *Individual Laments*, had been loosed, as it were, from their cultic moorings to become spiritual imitations of cultic prototypes, expressions of purely personal adoration of spiritual travail. They could thus be dated fairly late in the sixth and fifth centuries B.C.

It was left to Sigmund Mowinckel, the great Norwegian Old Testament scholar, acknowledging his dependence on Gunkel, to take the next decisive step. In a series of studies on the Psalms, *Psalmenstudien I–IV*, 1921–4, developed and modified in *Offersang og Sangoffer*, 1951, of which a revised English translation, *The Psalms in Israel's Worship*, vols. I–II, appeared in 1962, Mowinckel argued that the great majority of the Psalms, far from being merely imitations of cultic prototypes were in fact composed specifically for use in worship. Their true significance only becomes apparent when their original cultic *Sitz im Leben* is recognized and reconstructed. In most cases this takes us back to the pre-exilic ritual of the Jerusalem temple. Mowinckel's work, supported by a wealth of evidence drawn from primitive anthropology and psychology, comparative Ancient Near Eastern religion, and later Jewish rabbinic traditions, has been brilliantly creative not least in the dissent which it has provoked. There is space to touch only on two topics which have been the centre of much subsequent discussion.

In Psalm v,6 (English versions verse 5), and in many other *Individual Laments*, there is a reference to the Psalmist's enemies as 'workers of iniquity' (R.S.V. 'evildoers'). Arguing that the word translated 'iniquity' (Hebrew *'awen*) means power in the sense of magical power or sorcery, Mowinckel in *Psalmenstudien I* saw in these 'workers of iniquity' 'sorcerers and their demonic allies' who had cast evil spells upon the worshipper. The Psalms in question were therefore cultic compositions suitable for use by or on behalf of the believer as he underwent certain purificatory rites designed to annul such spells. This thesis, rooted in primitive ideas of the power residing in a word, has had few followers. Mowinckel himself later admitted that it was one-sided.[15] It did, however, stimulate new interest in the attempt to prove the identity of such enemies in the Psalms. 'False accusers',[16] with some of the Psalms of Lament being interpreted as cultic protestations of innocence in oath form, and 'foreigners'[17] have been suggested. The latter view is of particular interest since it carried with it the suggestion that the 'I' who speaks in such Psalms may have been in certain cases the king in pre-exilic Israel. The role of the king in the religious life of Israel has been a much debated topic in the period under review (cf. Chapter 4, pp. 121 ff). The various attempts to draft the enemies who appear in these Psalms into one category probably prove that no one category is likely to be adequate to cover the very varied situations to which these Laments of the Individual are directed. Recent discussions, however, are united in rejecting the view once commonly held that such Psalms are late, and the 'enemies' in them evidence for party strife in post-exilic Judaism.

The importance of the cultic *Sitz im Leben* of the Psalms for Mowinckel is seen at its clearest in his handling of that group of Psalms designated by Gunkel as 'Enthronement Songs'. Instead of pointing forward to some future universal triumph of Israel's god, such Psalms, he claimed, were part of the liturgy of an annual New Year Festival in ancient Israel, the Israelite equivalent of Babylonian and Canaanite New Year festivals. This festival, celebrated in the Jerusalem temple in the autumn and known to us elsewhere in the Old Testament as the Feast of Tabernacles, has roots which go back to a pre-Israelite cult in Jerusalem. The key phrase in such Psalms is 'Yahweh malakh' (Psalms xlvii, 8; xciii, 1; xcvi, 10; xcvii, 1; xcix, 1; R.S.V. 'the LORD reigns'). On the analogy of coronation rites in Israel, this must mean 'Yahweh has become king', not merely 'Yahweh reigns' or 'is king'. The ritual of this festival annually celebrated Yahweh's epiphany as king of creation, victor over all the forces of chaos which threatened the created order, supreme over all other gods. He is also lord of all history, repeating his mighty acts of deliverance, crushing the nations who oppose his purposes. He chooses Israel to be his own people, renews his covenant with the nation and with the royal house of David and guarantees fullness of life to the community throughout the coming year. This reliving in the 'now' of cultic experience of some of the fundamental assertions of Israel's faith corresponds to the way in which the Christian will, at Easter, relive the Resurrection experience and declare his faith in hymns such as 'Jesus Christ is risen *today*'. Into the net of this Israelite New Year enthronement festival, Mowinckel gathered not only Gunkel's Enthronement Songs, but also his Songs of Sion and many other Psalms including Psalms viii; xv; xxiv; xxxiii; lxviii; lxxv; lxxxi; lxxxii; lxxxiv; xcv; xciv; cxlix.[18]

There is no doubt that the language of many of these Psalms can be interpreted in the light of such a New Year enthronement festival in pre-exilic Israel. Mowinckel failed to prove, however, that they *must* be so interpreted. 'Yahweh malakh' may mean 'Yahweh has become king', but it may equally well mean 'Yahweh reigns' or 'It is *Yahweh* who reigns'. To those who have accused him of inventing a new and otherwise unattested festival in ancient Israel, Mowinckel has rightly replied that he is dealing with the old harvest and New Year festival known in the Old Testament as the Feast of Tabernacles (Booths). What is at stake, however, is not the existence of this festival, but its character. Apart from the interpretation of the language of the Psalms in question, there is little evidence within the Old Testament that the Feast of Tabernacles is an enthronement festival of the kind he posits. The jump from the language of the Psalms to the festival is only plausible in the light of comparative Ancient Near Eastern material. The extent to which inferences may legitimately be drawn from such comparative material to shed light on the religion of Israel is one of the major bones of contention in contemporary Old Testament scholarship (cf. Chapter 4, pp. 117 ff).

Other scholars, while rejecting Mowinckel's thesis in the form in which he stated it, have nevertheless followed him in positing specific religious festivals as the *Sitz im Leben* of many of the Psalms. A. Weiser in *The Psalms* remains within the framework of what he believes to be more strictly Israelite traditions. He finds the original *Sitz im Leben* of the vast majority of Psalms of all types to be an annual Covenant Festival of Yahweh, celebrated at the autumnal New Year, first by the tribal confederacy in the early years of the settlement in Canaan and later under the monarchy in the Jerusalem temple. Central to this festival was a theophany, Yahweh's self-revelation to his assembled people. This theophany was closely linked with the Ark, the cultic symbol of Yahweh's presence in the midst of his people. Associated with this theophany was the declaration of the nature of Yahweh through the recapitulation of his mighty deeds in his people's history. There was also the proclamation of Yahweh's will in the form of commandments to which the people had to assent before the act of covenant renewal could take place. This basic Covenant Festival tradition gathered to itself ideas associated with the kingship of Yahweh and with creation mythology. It is hard to resist the conclusion that Weiser's Covenant Festival is a convenient umbrella of somewhat uncertain shape under which shelters a mass of material which may have been very diverse not only in origin, but in history.

H. J. Kraus in *Die Konigsherrschaft Jahwes*, 1951, argued that from the time of David and Solomon there had been celebrated in the Jerusalem temple a Royal Zion Festival centring on the twin themes of Yahweh's covenant with the Davidic royal family and the choice of the Jerusalem sanctuary on Mt Zion as his true cult centre. This festival was the *Sitz im Leben* of certain Psalms, e.g. cxxxii. Only when this human kingship of the house of David had lost its rationale with the disappearance of the Judean state at the exile did the concept of the kingship of Yahweh emerge. Thus all the enthronement Psalms are post-exilic. They depend in fact upon the theology of the great anonymous poet–prophet of the exilic period who wrote Isaiah xl–lv. Mowinckel had argued, *per contra*, that the teaching of Isaiah xl–lv was dependent upon the pre-exilic enthronement Psalms.[19]

When such diverse conclusions as to the nature of the cult in pre-exilic Israel are possible it must be evident that a considerable element of doubt surrounds any attempt to spell out the precise cultic *Sitz im Leben* of many of the Psalms.

Although the cultic interpretation of the Psalms on form critical grounds has dominated the period under review, it has not been without its critics. Claus Westermann in *The Praise of God in the Psalms*, 1965 (English translation of the second edition of *Loben Gottes in den Psalmen*, 1962) suggests that the whole attempt to explain the Psalms in the light of the ideology of some festival or other has produced meagre results. No such thing as 'the cult' – a confused and vague expression, he claims – existed in the Old Testament period. There was only worship, very varied in form, time, place and personnel, worship which developed gradually in the course of Israel's history. His plea is for a return to Gunkel's approach before it becomes side-tracked along what, in his opinion, were so many festival dead ends. All the Psalms spring for him out of two basic modes of addressing God, praise and petition. Whether his approach is in the long run acceptable or not, he has raised questions which demand an answer and has shown that it is possible to have a fruitful form critical approach to the Psalms without being committed to any particular cult thesis.

PROPHETIC LITERATURE

'The words of Jeremiah . . . to whom the word of Yahweh came.' So an editor introduces what now lies before us in the Old Testament as 'The Book of Jeremiah', fifty-two chapters in all. Immediately several questions arise. What is the relationship between 'the words of Jeremiah' and that 'word of Yahweh' which came to him? Are they identical, wholly dissimilar or do they partly overlap? Within the present book of Jeremiah certain passages are clearly introduced by phrases which indicate that this is a word of Yahweh – 'The word of Yahweh came to me saying', e.g. i,4, 11; ii,1 or 'Thus says Yahweh', e.g. vi,6, 9, 16, 22; others again have as their concluding phrase 'oracle of Yahweh' (R.S.V. 'says the LORD'), e.g. i,8, 19; ii,3, 9. Numerous passages, however, are not so indicated, e.g. iii,21 f.; iv,23 f. Within chapters xi–xx, a series of passages usually called Jeremiah's Confessions are in the form of words, often very bitter words, from Jeremiah to Yahweh, not vice versa. Even if we assume that the 'words of Jeremiah' is intended to be a more inclusive term than 'the word of Yahweh' it is still far from being an adequate indication of the contents of our present book. In it we find a considerable amount of biographical material describing the prophet's activity e.g. xx; xxiv ff., as well as a concluding chapter which is an excerpt from 2 Kings describing the last days of the kingdom of Judah.

Anyone who tries to read consecutively through the book soon discovers that, in its present form, it cannot possibly be a document written according to a logical plan by one man. Some of the biographical material is badly arranged from a chronological standpoint. Chapter xxxii is dated to the tenth year of King Zedekiah while chapters xxxv and xxxvi are dated to the reign of his predecessor, King Jehoiakim. It is extremely difficult to see any logical connection between certain sections of the book. At other points we find blocks of material of similar theme probably gathered together by an editor, since material within such blocks often appears elsewhere, isolated and scattered throughout the book. Thus chapter xxiii, 9 ff. is headed 'Concerning the Prophets'. Chapters xxx, xxxi and xxxiii form what has been called a 'Book of Consolation', a collection of oracles of hope for the community. Within this collection, xxx, 10–11 is found elsewhere at xlvi, 27–28 and xxxiii, 14–16 with minor variations at xxiii, 5–6. All of this raises the question: what is the book of Jeremiah – or that of any other prophet? What is the basic raw material out of which it is built, and how did this material reach its present form? Much recent study of prophetic literature has attempted to clarify these issues.

If we look first at the basic raw material of a prophetic book, the period under review has seen the continuation and development of a form-critical approach which, as in the case of the Psalms, owes much to pioneer work by Hermann Gunkel.[20] It begins with the recognition that the basic unit of prophecy is not a written document, or even a lengthy sermon or discourse, but a short rhythmic saying, the prophetic oracle, e.g.

> Yahweh roars from Zion
>   and utters his voice from Jerusalem,
> the pastures of the shepherds mourn
>   and the top of Carmel withers. (Amos i, 2)

> Hear, O heavens, and give ear, O earth
>   for Yahweh has spoken
> Sons have I reared and brought up
>   but they have rebelled against me.

> The ox knows its owner,
>   and the ass its master's crib
> but Israel does not know
>   my people does not understand.   (Isaiah i, 2–3)

Collections of such sayings, which originally existed more or less independently, are the basic ingredients in any prophetic book. Public oracles, which contain the prophet's teaching to the community, are usually introduced by 'Thus says Yahweh' or some similar phrase. R.B.Y. Scott in an essay entitled 'The

Literary Structure of Israel's Oracles' in *Studies in Old Testament Prophecy*, 1950, pp. 175–86 (see further his introduction to Isaiah i–xxxix in the *Interpreter's Bible*, Vol. V, 1956), distinguishes four types of such public oracles; the *reproach*, very often introduced by a word like 'Woe' or 'Ah' e.g. Isaiah i, 4; v, 8; the *threat* linked sometimes to the reproach by 'therefore' e.g. Isaiah v, 24, or existing independently in oath form e.g. Isaiah xiv, 24 f.; the *promise* heralded frequently by a phrase such as 'On that day' e.g. Isaiah vii, 18 ff; and, least common, the *exhortation* e.g. Isaiah i, 16–17. In addition to such public oracles, Scott finds within the book of Isaiah *private oracles* in which God speaks solely to the prophet e.g. Isaiah xxii, 14, 15 f.; xxx, 8 f.; *autobiographical narratives* which often contain oracles within them, e.g. Isaiah vi, 1–13; and *biographical narratives* of a primary, e.g. Isaiah vii, 1–7, and a secondary kind, e.g. Isaiah xxxvi–xxxix. There are many other possible ways of classifying the material. Claus Westermann in *Basic Forms of Prophetic Speech*, 1967 (English translation of *Grundformen prophetischer Rede*, 1964)[21] distinguishes between

(1) *accounts* which cover visions, biographical narratives etc.

(2) *prophetic speeches*, which are either judgement speeches or salvation speeches.

(3) *utterances from man to God*, either in the form of praise, e.g. the doxologies in Amos, iv, 13; v, 8–9; ix, 5–6, or laments, e.g. the Confessions of Jeremiah.

Prophets likewise in their speaking made use of many fixed forms borrowed from other areas of Israel's life, for example the funeral dirge (Amos v, 1–3; Jeremiah ix, 17–19), the law suit (Micah vi, 1–5; Isaiah iii, 13–15; Malachi iii, 5), the parable (2 Samuel xii, 1–4; Isaiah v, 1–7).

Amid this almost embarrassingly rich diversity of material found in prophetic literature is there any one type to which we can point and say, this is of the very essence of prophecy *qua* prophecy? After many a twist and turn into what have proved to be dead ends, form criticism now seems to be pointing more or less steadily in one direction.

Two studies[22] published independently in the 1920s pointed the way to what has been the most influential approach to the basic unit in prophetic literature, an approach which may now be seen at its clearest in Claus Westermann (op. cit.). Its starting point is the fact that both in the prophetic books in the Old Testament and in narratives concerning prophets in the historical books, e.g. 1 Kings xxi, 18–19; 2 Kings i, 3–4, the characteristic prophetic statement is brief, easily memorized and prefaced by the words 'Thus says Yahweh'. If we look for parallels to this type of statement, they are found within Old Testament tradition in, for example, Genesis xxxii, 4–5, where Jacob sends messengers to his brother Esau with a brief message prefaced by the words 'Thus says your servant Jacob'. In the wider world of the Ancient Near East we find parallels in numerous examples of secular correspondence, now known to us from Babylonian, Canaanite and other sources. When the prophet therefore stands before his people and declares 'Thus says Yahweh', his character is that of a messenger, duly commissioned by God to deliver a message from God to the community.

This description of prophetic speech as basically 'messenger speech' has been powerfully supported by some of the material from Mari in which prophets, closely associated with the cult, appear as messengers of the gods, particularly to the king (cf. p. 41). This pattern is repeated over and over again in the Old Testament, in the narratives in Samuel and Kings; Samuel, God's messenger to Saul, Nathan to David, Elijah to Ahab, Micaiah ben Imlah to Ahab. There may be a world of difference between the searing moral realism of Isaiah of Jerusalem and the content of the message delivered by a prophet at Mari, but both appear as messengers of God, and their words bear the formal character- istics of a message delivered by word of mouth by a man com- missioned by higher authority. Again it is important to note that a form-critical approach to the literature not only provides us with a method of evaluating the literature *qua* literature, but has important wider consequences. In this case, it sheds light on the nature and function of prophecy in Ancient Israel.

The more we analyse the prophetic books of the Old Testament into numerous small units, the more we need to answer the question, how then did the prophetic books as we know them come into existence? At this point emphasis in recent studies has been placed on two factors.

There is a strong presumption that the initial way in which the teaching of the prophets was handed down was by oral transmission. The very fact that the messenger speeches are brief and easily memorized corresponds to their need to be transmitted accurately by word of mouth.

In the case of the prophets, the people responsible for this process of oral transmission were groups of disciples who gathered round a creative prophetic personality. Positive evidence for this is to be found in Isaiah viii, 16 where the prophet talks of 'binding up the testimony and sealing the teaching among my disciples'. Such prophetic disciple groups may or may not be related to the so-called cultic prophets who have figured prominently in recent research into prophecy (see Chapter 4, pp. 127 ff.). They must not be regarded merely as automatic transmitters of their master's teaching. They were part of a living *creative* tradition, preserving their master's words but at the same time adapting them and transforming them to make them more immediately relevant to ever changing historical circumstances. Thus if we ask what the Book of Amos is, we must say that it is the final literary deposit of an Amos tradition. It contains within it original sayings of Amos, sayings of Amos which have been adapted and modified by his prophetic disciples and sayings which emanate solely from such disciples. In certain cases it may be extremely difficult to differentiate between these different categories. The nearer the disciples are to the mind of the master, the more difficult it becomes.

Consider the Book of Isaiah. Literary criticism has usually analysed it into three separate sections: (a) i–xxxix, coming in the main from Isaiah of Jerusalem towards the end of the eighth century B.C.; (b) xl–lv, from an unknown poet of the sixth century exilic period, called for want of a more convenient term Deutero or Second Isaiah; (c) lvi ff., Trito Isaiah, from the period after the return from exile. But why should these three sections, so clearly different in terms of authorship and historical background, have ever been gathered into the one Book of Isaiah? The answer in traditio-historical terms is that they all stem from an Isaianic circle of tradition: Chapters i–xxxix are, in the main, the tradition of the teaching of Isaiah of Jerusalem mediated to us by the group or groups of disciples called into being by his ministry; xl–lv the work of one creative personality who steps forth from the same continuing tradition circle in the sixth century B.C., and lvi ff., which are less coherent than xl–lv, a series of oracles probably of different authorship, but from within this same tradition at a later stage.[23]

In its more extreme form, as represented by certain Scandinavian scholars, notably H. S. Nyberg, H. Birkeland and I. Engnell,[24] who appealed *inter alia* to the place of oral tradition in pre-Islamic and early Islamic literature, these two factors tended to harden into the following thesis:

All our present prophetic books in their literary form are the product of the post-exilic period, the mere literary fixation of an already stable oral tradition. Literary criticism is therefore a wholly inadequate tool for dealing with their contents. Engnell, in response to criticism from Mowinckel and G. Widengren[25] modified his view to the extent of distinguishing between two different types of prophetic books, what he called the *diwan type* e.g. Amos, Isaiah i–xxxix, transmitted orally from the beginning, and the *liturgy type*, e.g. Nahum, Habakkuk, Joel, Deutero-Isaiah, which had existed in written form from the beginning. This distinction, however, is far from easy to maintain in certain cases.

Since the prophetic books are the product of a living developing tradition, it is virtually impossible to get behind the tradition as we now have it. In other words, any attempt to work back to the *ipsissima verba* of Amos or Isaiah or Jeremiah is doomed to failure at the outset. Even if we grant the formative place of oral tradition, it is difficult to see why we need to accept this conclusion. Inasmuch as the material in, say, the books of Hosea, Amos, Isaiah and Jeremiah can be distinguished one from the other stylistically and theologically as well as historically, it would seem reasonable to suppose that these differences go back to the creative personalities who stand behind the respective traditions. Provided we understand the factors operative in oral transmission the attempt to discover the *ipsissima verba* of such prophets, or something closely akin to their *ipsissima verba*, need not be self-defeating.[26]

As in the case of the Pentateuch, so in the case of the prophetic books, oral transmission may have played a far more important role than was once realized, but it is extremely unlikely that form criticism and tradition history will be regarded by most scholars as a substitute for literary criticism.

THE WISDOM LITERATURE

'Wisdom' is a many faceted phenomenon in the Old Testament. It ranges all the way from the brief, shrewd comments on life and conduct collected within the Book of Proverbs, through the type of judicial wisdom for which Solomon is lauded in 1 Kings iii, to the penetrating scepticism of Ecclesiastes and Job's passionate wrestling with the enigma of unmerited suffering in a God-ruled world. Some of the material within these 'documents of Israel's humanism'[27] is far from being distinctively Hebraic in outlook. This is particularly true of Proverbs. The sages of many cultures dealt with basically the same problems of human conduct, observed the same follies, and advocated the same prudential behaviour. We can document a continuous tradition of the sayings of the wise in Egypt from the middle of the third millennium B.C. (*The Instructions of Ptah–hotep*) to the Persian and Greek periods (*Papyrus Insinger*).

Since the work of A. Erman in 1926[28] it has been generally accepted that one part of the Book of Proverbs, xxii, 17–xxiii, 11 with its thirty sayings, is a free adaptation of the Egyptian *Wisdom of Amen-em-ope* with its thirty sections. Attempts to prove that both Amen-em-ope and this section of Proverbs draw on a now lost Hebrew wisdom book which circulated in a Jewish–Egyptian settlement have not proved convincing. More recently it has been argued that the nucleus of Proverbs i–ix is ten discourses, each with an introductory formula of a common pattern, which formed a 'lesson book designated for use in scribal schools and closely modelled on Egyptian prototypes.'[29] The major advance in our knowledge of comparative material in the period under review has come from the field of Sumerian studies. Thanks largely to the work of S. N. Kramer, we now have at our disposal an extensive collection of Sumerian proverbs and related material.[30] While no collection of Canaanite wisdom sayings has yet come to light, Canaanite influence on the content, style, form and vocabulary of Hebrew wisdom sayings has been strongly urged.[31]

In the light of the accumulation of such comparative material, much of it of a very early date, the tendency to date most of the material in Proverbs to the post-exilic period, fifth century B.C. onwards, has now been largely abandoned. Many, some would say all, of the sayings in Proverbs must go back to the pre-exilic period, even if their final literary form is later. Oral tradition may well have been the vehicle of their preservation and transmission for several centuries. But when and where did such material originate in the life of Israel, and among whom did it circulate? A tradition preserved in the narrative in 1 Kings v, 9–14, in the headings to some of the collections within Proverbs (i, 1; x, 1; xxv, 5), in the introduction to the Song of Songs (i, 1) and in Jewish interpretation of Ecclesiastes, attributes such wisdom to King Solomon. Although some of this is literary fiction, similar to the way in which many of the Psalms were attributed to David, the tradition in essence is probably sound. Egyptian influence was strong at Solomon's court. Much Egyptian wisdom was concerned with the education of the young of the upper ruling class. The court and royal patronage, therefore, provided the natural *Sitz im Leben* for the emergence of a special class of sages within Israel, and such sages in turn exercised an important influence on political policy.[32] Even those who reject this Solomonic tradition as entirely fictitious still wish to retain the link between the sages and the monarchy. In R. B. Y. Scott's view, for example, Hebrew wisdom received the first real impetus in King Hezekiah's attempt towards the end of the eighth century B.C., to revive the glories of Solomon's reign.[33]

Although wisdom may have flourished in Israel, as elsewhere, in court circles, it is extremely questionable whether such circles are the original *Sitz im Leben* of many of the wisdom sayings in Proverbs. Few of such sayings are concerned with court life, royal etiquette or kingly responsibility. Recent form critical studies have opened anew the whole question of the origins of Israel's wisdom tradition.

In a stimulating study E. Gerstenberger[34] has compared the prohibitions in Hebrew law codes with wisdom teaching. Just as the religious context of law codes such as Exodus xxii, 22–xxiii, 9 is a later framework superimposed upon what was originally secular, customary law, so much of the wisdom material must be taken out of its present royal setting and traced back to the ethos of the early tribal and family structure in Israel. Many of the wisdom sayings have their *Sitz im Leben* in the kind of instruction for which the head of the group was responsible. Both through prohibition and admonition he sought to ensure that all the members of the group were aware of what was expected of them in their relationship with one another, if any orderly social life were to be maintained. Thus questions of sex, justice and charity figure prominently in such teaching. W. Richter[35], while agreeing in the main with this thesis, argues that from an early date, there must have existed 'schools' in which such traditional teaching was formulated and discussed. Increasingly such schools came to reflect not the legal standards of the tribal group, but the ethos of the ruling and official classes. However much the sages may have flourished in the cosmopolitan, city-orientated culture of Israel, which took its tone from the court, we are led back beyond the monarchy, beyond city life, in our search for the original *Sitz im Leben* of the wisdom material. If in its present form it owes much to international contacts, in its origin it is more homely.

Form criticism has also been directing attention to the way in which wisdom-type material is to be found outside the broad main stream of the wisdom literature. The Joseph story (Genesis xxxvii ff.) is very different in character from the other patriarchal sagas in Genesis. It has been well described as an example of early wisdom writing. It is intentionally didactic and draws heavily on Egyptian sources both for its ethical and educational ideals and for its theological emphasis.[36] Some of the Psalms are either in their entirety wisdom poems or have strong wisdom elements in them; for example Psalms i; xxiv; xlix; lxxviii. Passages in many of the prophetic books look as if they had been written by men trained in the wisdom schools.[37] It has been claimed that the source of much of Amos' teaching is the oral tradition of ancient Israelite tribal wisdom. The origins of the wisdom tradition in Israel are thus being pushed back in time, and its influence seen to be much more pervasive than was once thought.

Our preoccupation with new ways of handling the literature must not be allowed to give the impression that the literary critical work of a previous generation has been superseded or has come to an end. Far from it. A glance at any of the recent 'Introductions' to the literature of the Old Testament – for example, that of O. Eissfeldt – will show clearly the way in which, in the case of every book in the Old Testament, the work of literary criticism has been consolidated and directed to the answering of new questions. Form criticism and tradition history have claimed our attention, partly because they are comparatively new in their application to the literature of the Old Testament, partly because, as with historical and literary critical methods in the nineteenth century, new methods pose new questions in the field of the history and religion of Israel. The form critical approach to the Decalogue and the covenant tradition in the Pentateuch has evoked new interest in the question of whether, and in what sense, the idea of the covenant is central to the early religious traditions of Israel. M. Noth's analysis of the historical traditions has forced us to ask what we mean by the history of Israel prior to the monarchy. The new approach to the Psalms has led to much debate on the character of the autumnal New Year festival in pre-exilic Israel. The delineation of the basic form of prophetic speech as 'messenger speech' takes us into the realm of prophetic psychology and religion. The work of Old Testament scholarship is one, the various disciplines acting and reacting on one another.

Three

The Text

Any responsible handling of the literature of the Old Testament depends upon our possessing a text, based on sound critical principles, which will represent the earliest form of the tradition which it is possible for us to reconstruct. Until recently, for example, the text of Jeremiah had been handed down to us in two main forms, the one represented by a Hebrew tradition to which our earliest witness was a tenth-century manuscript, the other represented by a Greek tradition to which our earliest witness is a fourth-century Greek manuscript. We were left wondering whether the one or the other or both were current in Palestine in the pre-Christian era. To have texts of Jeremiah from Palestine of the pre-Christian era, as we now have, thanks to the Dead Sea Scrolls (for a description of the discovery and significance of these scrolls see the N.T. section), helps us to answer such questions. Even such scrolls are separated by several centuries from the original scroll of the book of Jeremiah, but at least they enable us to trace the history of the text of Jeremiah back to a much earlier date than was hitherto possible.

THE HEBREW TRADITION

Until 1936, all printed Hebrew Bibles depended upon a textual tradition which went back at the earliest to the fourteenth century when there emerged in Hebrew manuscripts a *Textus Receptus* or standard text, the result of the conflation of different manuscript traditions. This standard text was first published in 1524–5 in the second Rabbinic Bible edited by Jacob ben Chayyim. Although Jacob ben Chayyim made strenuous efforts to trace Hebrew manuscripts, especially those provided with Massorah (the traditional comment on the text written in the margin and at the end of the various books of the Old Testament), the manuscripts at his disposal were on the whole late and poor. Nor does he seem to have followed any one textual tradition. He used his editorial right to print an eclectic text, i.e. one which he himself reconstructed from different manuscript traditions. What principles guided him in his selection of material is largely unknown. This ben Chayyim text was the basis of all printed Hebrew Bibles up to and including the second edition of Kittel's *Biblia Hebraica* of 1912. 'Thus, during the most important period in the history of the Old Testament in the Christian Church, when it was being translated into the various languages of the west, the one text regarded as normative in spite of its deficiencies, was that of ben Chayyim, and in effect it has been the basis of every commentary and translation from the time of its creation.' (B. J. Roberts, *The Old Testament Text and Versions*, p. 90.)

The first decisive break with this tradition came with the publication in 1936 of the third edition of Kittel's *Biblia Hebraica*.[1] Behind this lay some of the most fruitful and sustained research work ever done on the history of Hebrew text, Paul Kahle's investigations into the work of the Massoretes, Jewish scholars who from about the beginning of the sixth century A.D. concerned themselves with giving definitive form to the tradition (Massorah) of the Hebrew text they had inherited. Kahle's researches, published in numerous articles and books e.g. *Masoreten des Ostens*, 1913, *Masoreten des Westens* (vol. I 1917, vol. II 1930), and conveniently summarized in his Schweich Lectures *The Cairo Geniza* (1947, revised edition 1959), involved the investigation of hundreds of Hebrew manuscripts, scattered in libraries throughout the world, notably Oxford, Cambridge, the British Museum, Leningrad and the Jewish Seminary in New York. Many of these manuscripts were once part of the treasure of the storehouse (*geniza*) of a Jewish synagogue in Cairo.

As well as providing the text with certain critical notes, those in the side margins called *Massorah parva*, those at the foot of the text *Massorah magna*, the Massoretes endeavoured to fix the pronunciation of what had been hitherto basically a consonantal text by the use of certain signs indicative of the various vowel sounds. Two major centres of Massoretic activity, the one in Babylon, the other in Palestine, produced different systems. The Babylonian system was supralinear, i.e. the vowels were indicated by signs inserted above the consonantal letters. The earliest Palestinian system which was likewise supralinear gave way in the course of the eighth century to the sublinear Tiberian system (in which vowels are indicated by signs written below the consonants). This tradition was standardized in the tenth century through the work of two Massoretic families, that of ben Asher and ben Naphtali, the ben Asher tradition eventually becoming normative. For the first time, the 1936 third edition of Kittel's *Biblia Hebraica* went back beyond the conflate ben Chayyim medieval text to the ben Asher tradition as represented by the earliest then available complete text, that of Leningrad manuscript B 19^A, copied in A.D. 1008. This was printed together with an accompanying Massorah. An earlier tenth-century codex by ben Asher in the synagogue at Aleppo was known to Kahle, but permission to use it was not forthcoming. The new edition of the British and Foreign Bible Society Hebrew Bible edited by N. H. Snaith (1958) likewise returns to the ben Asher tradition as it is preserved in the original hand of British Museum manuscript Or 2626–8, written in Lisbon in 1482, and in manuscript Or 2375.

Kahle's work put the study of the Hebrew textual tradition on a much firmer foundation, not only by making available an authentic Massoretic tradition centuries older than the ben Chayyim text, but by making us aware of considerable variety within the Massoretic tradition itself. But questions remained. What, for example, was the relationship between the standard Tiberian Massoretic text of the tenth century A.D. and the text of the Old Testament in pre-Christian times? Could we assume that this Massoretic tradition represented an authentic pre-Christian textual tradition and was this the only tradition? This latter question is of particular importance since the Septuagint, essentially a pre-Christian Greek translation of the Old Testament, produced to meet the needs of the Jewish settlement in Alexandria, preserves an Old Testament text which differs markedly at points from the Massoretic tradition. A notable example is the book of Jeremiah, where the Septuagint is not only shorter than the Massoretic text but is differently ordered. It is here that the Dead Sea Scrolls have made a significant contribution to Old Testament studies.

THE DEAD SEA SCROLLS

In addition to the many extra-biblical documents found in the region of Qumran (for a description of the discovery, extent and significance of the finds see the New Testament section pp. 172 ff.), there have come to light manuscripts, some of them very fragmentary, representing every book in the Old Testament with the exception of Esther. When the first Isaiah scrolls were examined it was seen that they stood in the main within the tradition represented by the Massoretic text, known to us hitherto from manuscripts the earliest of which belonged to the tenth century A.D. In particular they did not generally support the Greek tradition when that differed substantially from the Hebrew. Although there were differences, and differences indeed between the two major Isaiah scrolls from Qumran, it could be confidently affirmed that the Massoretic tradition was witness to a type of text current in Palestine in the pre-Christian era. Subsequent discoveries, however, revealed a much more complex situation. Among the numerous fragmentary texts from Cave IV, one Hebrew text of Jeremiah (4 Q Jer.[a], dated on palaeographic grounds circa 200 B.C.) reflected the Massoretic tradition, but another Hebrew text of Jeremiah (4 Q Jer.[b], somewhat later in the second century B.C.) reflected the shorter Jeremianic text known hitherto only from the Septuagint. Similarly, fragments of a Hebrew text of Samuel – another Old Testament book where there is wide divergence between the traditional Greek and Hebrew texts – stand within the tradition represented by the Septuagint, not that represented by the Massoretic text. The books of Exodus and Numbers are also represented by two fragments (4 Q palae Ex. and 4 Q Num.[b]) which represent the textual tradition known previously only from the Samaritan version of the Pentateuch.

Although much editorial work still remains to be done, and many issues need further clarification, two things seem clear: the scrolls from Qumran are witness to a rich diversity of textual traditions current in Palestine in the centuries immediately preceding the Christian era; and all the biblical texts discovered fall into one or other of the main textual traditions already known to us, either the Massoretic or Septuagint traditions, or the Samaritan Pentateuch.

Is it possible to go further and clarify the history and inter-relatedness of these different textual traditions in pre-Christian times? Frank M. Cross[2] believes that between the fifth and the first centuries B.C. there developed in the main centres of Jewish life three distinct textual families based on different traditions:

(1) A Palestinian family with an 'expansionist' type of text, that is to say, a text characterized by glosses and scribal additions. From this family the Samaritan Pentateuch split.

(2) An Egyptian family, closely related to the Palestinian, but divergent from it to a different degree in different books of the Old Testament, and furthest removed from it in the case of Jeremiah.

(3) A Babylonian family, extant only in the Pentateuch and the Former Prophets (i.e. Judges – 2 Kings), extremely conservative, preserving a short text form badly corrupt in the case of the Former Prophets.

On this view the dominant Massoretic text preserves the Babylonian tradition in the Pentateuch and the Former Prophets and the Palestinian tradition in the rest of the Old Testament. That such different textual traditions existed seems clear. Whether, however, they developed in the kind of geographical separateness implied by this theory is an assumption that not all scholars are prepared to accept.[3]

No sweeping generalizations can be made about the text of the Old Testament. The textual traditions for each book must be examined in their own right, and the inter-relatedness of the different traditions assessed. Even those who insist that the Massoretic tradition is the main current flowing in the period

prior to the destruction of the Jewish state by the Romans in
A.D. 70 admit that 'there are rivulets flowing side by side with it,
and investigation has already shown that it is sometimes there
that the pure water flows'.[4]

THE SEPTUAGINT

The most important of such rivulets is the textual tradition represented by the Greek version of the Old Testament, the Septuagint
(LXX) so called because, according to a tradition preserved in the
Letter of Aristeas, it was translated by seventy, to be precise
seventy-two, Jewish scholars, brought from Jerusalem to Alexandria for this purpose. The Septuagint has been much used and
much abused in the textual criticism of the Old Testament. Towards the end of the last century and in the earlier part of this
century many scholars used the Septuagint with almost reckless
abandon to emend the Massoretic text. The fruits of this still
appear in the *apparatus criticus* of the third edition of Kittel's
Biblia Hebraica. Commenting on one chapter in the book of Job
where twenty-three emendations are listed, G. R. Driver[5] says,
'I thought one necessary and two or three plausible, while the
rest were clearly unwarranted or nonsense' – but many of these
emendations claimed support from the Septuagint. Reaction was
inevitable. It is seen at its most extreme in H. S. Nyberg's *Hoseabuch*, 1936. Nyberg defends the Massoretic text with an ingenuity
which sometimes falls short of conviction against all attempts to
emend it on the basis of the Septuagint and other versions.

Before the Septuagint can be used responsibly, two conditions
must be met. We must possess a reliable critical edition of the
Septuagint which takes fully into account the history of our present manuscripts of the Septuagint, and we must have an understanding of the translation technique employed by the various
translators whose work is preserved in the Septuagint. Steady
progress has been made in both these fields. Two major projects
centring on Cambridge and Göttingen have been concerned with
the provision of a critical edition of the Septuagint, both have
produced a smaller edition, in Cambridge that of H. B. Swete,

The Old Testament in Greek (3 volumes 1887–91); in Göttingen that of A. Rahlfs (1935); and both have essayed a larger edition with a more complete *apparatus criticus*, the Cambridge edition edited by A. E. Brooke, N. McLean, H. St J. Thackeray, Volume 1, 1906 (regrettably incomplete as only half of the Old Testament had appeared by 1940), and the larger Göttingen edition under the editorship of J. Ziegler. A different critical approach underlies these two editions. The Cambridge Septuagint prints the text of Codex Vaticanus (B), one of the great fourth-century manuscripts while the Göttingen Septuagint reconstructs a critical text on the basis of the major manuscripts Codex Vaticanus (B), Codex Sinaiticus (א) also of the fourth century, Codex Alexandrinus (A) of the fifth century, and other manuscripts. It is widely recognized that the larger Göttingen Septuagint provides us with the most accurate citation of evidence concerning the Septuagint tradition.

The Göttingen approach presupposes that it is possible to group all the available evidence for the Greek text of the Old Testament into well defined textual traditions, and that by critically comparing these traditions it is possible to work back to a Greek textual tradition from which all our available evidence ultimately derives. But what in fact is the Septuagint? The *Letter of Aristeas* is evidence for the translation into Greek not of the Old Testament but only of that part of it which was supremely authoritative for the Jewish community, *Torah* (the Law), the five books of Moses, Genesis – Deuteronomy. Outside *Torah*, the Septuagint displays a wide variety of different translation styles and techniques, the differences appearing even within one and the same Old Testament book. H. St J. Thackeray, in *The Septuagint and Jewish Worship*, (1921), argued that the real impetus towards the rendering of the rest of the Old Testament into Greek came from worship in the synagogue and the growth of a Jewish lectionary system. In addition to a reading from *Torah* which was fundamental to synagogue worship, there grew up the custom of having a 'second lesson', related in theme to the *Torah* lesson and drawn usually from the prophetic books. Outside *Torah*, therefore, the earliest sections of the Old Testament translated into

Greek were these 'second lessons', particularly those appropriate to the great festive occasions of the Jewish religious year. Such translations were later incorporated into what became a translation of the Old Testament as a whole.

Undoubtedly the needs of a Greek-speaking Jewish community and its worship lies behind the present Septuagint. It may be that originally passages from the Hebrew Bible were sometimes not translated but simply transliterated into Greek so the Greek-speaking Jew could pronounce the sacred text. A German scholar, Francis Xavier Wutz, in a series of publications between 1925 and 1938, propounded the thesis that behind the entire Septuagint lay such a transliteration into Greek letters of the Hebrew text. In this extreme form the thesis met with no lasting acceptance, and Wutz himself eventually severely modified it.

A formidable attack on the critical principles guiding the Göttingen Septuagint was mounted by P. Kahle in a series of studies beginning in 1915 and culminating in his chapter on the Septuagint in *The Cairo Geniza* (second revised edition 1959, pp. 212 ff.). Kahle notes the very diverse character of the textual tradition not only in the manuscripts of the Septuagint but also in quotations from the Greek Old Testament in the New Testament, in Jewish writers such as Josephus and Philo, and in early Christian writers. He concludes that from the beginning there existed a wide variety of Greek Old Testament texts in the Jewish community, just as there was initially a very wide variety of Aramaic Targums or translations. The attempt, a not wholly successful attempt, to standardize the text came later, as it did in the case of the Aramaic Targums. The so-called *Letter of Aristeas* – neither a letter, nor written as it claims by Aristeas in the third century B.C., but an example of second-century B.C. Jewish apologetic literature – is propaganda for an official version of *Torah* sponsored by Alexandrian Judaism towards the end of the second century B.C. to replace an existing, extremely confused and fluid textual situation. It follows that any attempt to find an original Septuagint behind the current mass of variant texts is doomed to failure, because there never was such an original.

Kahle's view, although supported by a wealth of evidence, has not met with acceptance by most specialists in the field of Septuagint studies. P. Katz, for example, has described Kahle's chapter on the Septuagint in *The Cairo Geniza* as 'a mass of uncoordinated information'. The wealth of variants, he declares, are perplexing 'only so long as they are neither grouped nor analysed ... most of them including the indirect quotations derive from well known secondary recensions and are neither LXX nor early'.[6] Nor have the Dead Sea Scrolls done anything to strengthen Kahle's case. All the Septuagint-type texts discovered so far fit into the textual traditions which we already know from the major Greek manuscripts of the fourth and fifth centuries.

Increasing attention has been paid in recent years not only to the problems of reconstructing a Septuagint text, but also to the character of the Septuagint as a translation. The Greek of the Septuagint is neither classical Greek nor the *koine*, the commonly spoken Greek of the Hellenistic world. It has characteristics and peculiarities of its own which can only be explained by the fact that it is translation Greek, preserving in Greek form many of the idioms, constructions and word meanings of the Hebrew which lies behind it. It is perhaps best at this point to speak of Biblical Greek since the Greek of the New Testament shares certain of the characteristics of the Septuagint. Many detailed studies have appeared in recent years of sections of the Septuagint from the linguistic standpoint.[7] Although we possess an admirable *Concordance to the Septuagint* by Hatch and Redpath, first published in Oxford in 1897, of which an Austrian photocopy reissue appeared in 1954, a pre-requisite for further study in this field, important both for New and Old Testament studies, is a dictionary of Biblical Greek.

Important research work continues in the field of all the other versions of the Old Testament text. There is space merely to note the results most directly related to Old Testament textual criticism. The Peshitto Institute at Leiden under the direction of P. A. H. de Boer is fulfilling a long felt need by producing a soundly based critical edition of the Syriac text. Aramaic studies, stimulated by the research work of Paul Kahle and Matthew Black, have gained momentum through the discovery in the

Vatican library of a hitherto unknown Aramaic Targum tradition, Codex Neofiti. In *The Bible in Aramaic*, A. Sperber has crowned a lifetime's work in a new critical edition of the main Targumic tradition. Study of the Vulgate, the Latin translation from the Hebrew produced by Jerome between A.D. 390 and 405, has also been put on a much sounder footing by the new critical edition produced by the Benedictines.

THE HEBREW UNIVERSITY BIBLE PROJECT

We return where we began, to the Hebrew text. In spite of the major step forward which it took in relationship to the Massoretic tradition, Kittel's *Biblia Hebraica* in its third and subsequent editions, remains a thoroughly unsatisfactory critical edition, particularly in terms of its *apparatus criticus*. Its citation and handling of the evidence of the versions, notably the Septuagint, but likewise the Vulgate, is highly suspect. J. Ziegler, the editor of the larger Göttingen Septuagint, has claimed that all references to the Septuagint in the *apparatus criticus* of the third edition of *Biblia Hebraica* need to be carefully rechecked. No one who has done such rechecking has much confidence in the principles followed. Not only do we now have better editions of some of the versions than were available to the editors of *Biblia Hebraica*, but the Dead Sea Scrolls have provided us with a wealth of new material of immediate relevance for the text of the Old Testament. Although some of the evidence of the Dead Sea Scrolls Isaiah texts is cited in the most recent editions of *Biblia Hebraica* it can hardly claim to have been done systematically or on sound critical principles. A new edition of *Biblia Hebraica* under the editorship of D. W. Thomas has just begun to appear (1968). It goes a long way towards meeting criticisms of the *apparatus criticus* in earlier editions.

The most ambitious project towards the production of a new critical edition of the Hebrew text is that sponsored by the Hebrew University of Jerusalem under the general editorship of M. H. Goshen-Gottstein. The periodical *Textus*, of which six volumes have appeared between 1960 and 1968, provides a

111

convenient forum for the explanation and discussion of the methodology lying behind the project and topics of related interest in the field of textual criticism. In 1965, a sample four chapters of the book of Isaiah (chapters ii, v, xi and li) were published together with an explanatory introduction. The text with accompanying Massorah is that of the tenth-century Aleppo Codex, known to, but unavailable to P. Kahle, the earliest surviving and the most faithful representative of the ben Asher tradition. The *apparatus criticus* is divided into four sections:

(i) the evidence of the non-Hebrew versions of the Old Testament, including the Septuagint, Peshitto, Vulgate, Arabic and the Aramaic Targums, pride of place being given to the Septuagint;

(ii) non-Massoretic Hebrew texts, in particular texts of such a type among the Dead Sea Scroll material and later Rabbinic literature;

(iii) readings in Bible manuscripts from the period after the fixing of the Massoretic tradition, particularly the Medieval Bible manuscripts. These are of great interest from the point of view of the evolution of the biblical text and occasionally preserve a genuine non-Massoretic reading;

(iv) minor variations in spelling, accents, vowels etc.

In many respects this project is an important advance on *Biblia Hebraica*, particularly in the *apparatus criticus*. The versions, notably the Septuagint, have been given a far more extensive and careful collation. No less important, no attempt has been made to introduce dubious conjectural emendations claiming the support of the versions. The new material from the Dead Sea Scrolls has been fully taken into account, and material not hitherto easily accessible, from Rabbinic sources, has been made available. Some of the critical assumptions lying behind the project have been and will continue to be a matter of contention, but it may be safely said that once this project is brought to fulfilment it will furnish the scholarly world with by far the most accurate and extensive corpus of material upon which to base the textual criticism of the Old Testament.

The period under review has been one of steady progress,

especially in the provision of more reliable tools for the student of the text. If today we are somewhat less sanguine than scholars have sometimes been of our ability to recover 'the original text', we are at least in a far better position to understand the history behind the form in which the text has come down to us. We are thus more able to assess the comparative value of the different textual traditions.

Four

The Religion
of Israel

We have already had occasion to note the way in which archaeological discoveries and new methods of handling the literary
sources may have important, though often disputed, consequences for our interpretation of the religious traditions within
the Old Testament. In any attempt to describe the religion of
Israel, however, there is one fundamental question which has
been increasingly recognized in recent study, or which when not
recognized has been the source of no little confusion. What do we
mean by the religion of Israel? It is one of these deceptively
simple questions which become increasingly complex the more
closely they are examined. It is a question forced upon us by the
very nature of the literary documents which must constitute
our primary source material in any study of the religion of
Israel.

The documents dealing with the early religious traditions of
Israel come to us through the hands of the post-exilic Jewish community, and reflect a process of selection, editing, and to some
extent deliberate censorship in the light of what had become religious orthodoxy for that community. To what extent did such a
thing as orthodoxy exist in pre-exilic Israel and where was it
located? The Jerusalem temple was the national shrine of the
southern kingdom of Judah from the tenth century onwards;
Bethel was an important sanctuary, politically within the orbit of
the northern kingdom of Israel. Were the religious practices and
beliefs in these two centres identical? Is the religion of Israel in the
mid eighth century B.C. to be equated with the teaching of the
prophet Amos, with his passionate insistence on the absolute
ethical sovereignty of Yahweh, or is it to be located in the popular
religion and cultic practices which he so bitterly attacks – or is it

both? What is the relationship between the Book of Deuteronomy, with its reiterated demand for a nation pledged to an exclusive loyalty to one god, Yahweh, and the religious attitude of the Jewish colonists at Elephantine in Egypt who seem to have brought with them from their homeland a form of religious syncretism which provided this Yahweh with, among other things, a female consort, in much the same way as 'El and Baal in the Ras Shamra texts are provided with appropriate goddesses (see Chapter 1, pp. 48ff.)? It has long been recognized that we must allow for historical development within the religion of Israel, even if it does not conform to a simple evolutionist pattern; but must we not equally face the fact that several different religions seem to have co-existed in Israel certainly until the time of the exile? Would it not thus be better to speak of the religions of Israel or is there within this mass of heterogeneous material some 'vital seed' or 'essence' to which we can point and say, *this* is the religion of Israel which we can clearly differentiate as such from the religion of Canaan, or Egypt, or Babylon?[1]

There is a further difficulty. Any sympathetic understanding of the religious life of Ancient Israel demands that we discard, as far as possible, twentieth century Western European presuppositions about man, his ways of thinking and the social patterns which are natural to him. We must try to come to terms with thought forms and social patterns native to Ancient Israel and the wider cultural context of the Ancient Near East to which she belonged. Fortunately this is becoming increasingly possible. R. de Vaux, *Ancient Israel* (English translation 1961) contains a masterly and indispensable survey of Israel's political, social and religious institutions. There is much of value for our understanding of Hebrew psychology and thought patterns, though it needs careful critical handling, in J. Pedersen, *Israel 1, its Life and Culture* (volumes 1–2, second edition 1959; volumes 3–4, second edition 1959), and in the monographs of A. R. Johnson, *The Vitality of the Individual in the Thought of Ancient Israel* (second edition 1964) and *The One and the Many in the Israelite Conception of God* (second edition 1961). All such studies draw heavily upon current theories in the field of comparative religion and social anthropology, particularly in their evaluation of the so-called 'primitive mentality', and may need to be modified in important respects in the light of advancing knowledge in these fields.

It is impossible even to touch upon all of the many issues within the general field of the religion of Israel which have been under discussion in recent years. Nor is it necessary to do so. Several recent books survey the field admirably, in particular H. Ringgren, *Israelite Religion*, 1966, a translation of a work first published in German in 1963, and Th. C. Vriezen, *The Religion of Ancient Israel*, 1967, which first appeared in Dutch in 1963.[2] One central interest, however, has provided a frame of reference within which much of the debate in the period under review has taken place, and it is an interest which contrasts sharply with what tended previously to occupy the centre of the stage.

In the late nineteenth and early twentieth centuries there was widespread agreement, particularly in Protestant Old Testament scholarship, that the truly significant feature of the religion of Israel was to be found in the canonical prophets. These prophets, beginning with Amos in the mid eighth century B.C., were the heralds of ethical monotheism. In this they differed not only from the earlier religious traditions of Israel, but also from the representatives of the official religion of their own day. In particular they were opposed to the priesthood and bitterly critical of, if not hostile in principle to, the entire cultic system of Israel.[3] It was this prophetic element alone which carried the vital seed of Israel's religion. Increasingly over the past thirty to forty years this assumption has been called into question. There has been a rediscovery of the positive significance and meaning of worship in Israel, and a consequent blurring of some of the over-sharp distinctions previously drawn between the prophetic and other elements in the religious life of Israel. Two useful pointers to this new interest are H. J. Kraus, *Worship in Israel*, 1966, first published in German in 1962, and H. H. Rowley, *Worship in Ancient Israel*, 1967.[4]

MYTH AND RITUAL

Reference has already been made (see pp. 87ff.) to Sigmund
Mowinckel's pioneer work on the Psalms in which he postulated a
cultic *Sitz im Leben* for many of the Psalms. Those associated with
the Kingship of Yahweh he placed in the context of the Feast of
Tabernacles which he interpreted as an annual New Year enthronement festival. Mowinckel's use of comparative Near Eastern
– in his case mainly Babylonian – material was to be taken up in-
dustriously by other Scandinavian scholars, and in Britain by
what has come to be known as the *Myth and Ritual* school.
'School' is probably a misnomer. What we are dealing with is a
common basic approach to certain problems. The approach may
lead to very diverse conclusions. Mowinckel himself has been
highly critical of some of the more extreme conclusions which
have been drawn.[5]

The approach is well illustrated in three volumes of essays
edited by S. H. Hooke, *Myth and Ritual*, 1933, *The Labyrinth*,
1935, and *Myth, Ritual and Kingship*, 1958. It draws on studies in
the field of comparative religion and in particular upon a new
understanding of the word 'myth'.[6] Myth, as used in this context,
is neither stories about the gods nor primitive pre-scientific
attempts to explain the origin and meaning of the world and
various phenomena within the world. It is the spoken word which
accompanies those ritual acts through which man endeavours to
control the unpredictable forces which surround him, particularly
the forces of nature. 'In the ritual the myth told the story of what
was being enacted; it described a situation; but the story was not
told to amuse an audience; it was a word of power. The repetition
of the right words had power to bring about or to recreate the
situation which they described.'[7] Although varying from culture
to culture, there was, so it was claimed, a common basic pattern
of ritual, with accompanying myth, discernible in many parts of
the world of the Ancient Near East, in Babylon, Egypt and Canaan in particular. It contained the following elements:

(1) the dramatic representation of the death and resurrection of
the god,

(2) the recitation or symbolic representation of the drama of creation,

(3) the ritual combat in which the god triumphed over all his foes, particularly the forces of chaos, which were ever threatening to engulf the established order in the world,

(4) the sacred marriage which guaranteed the continuance of fertility,

(5) the triumphal procession leading to the re-enthronement of the god.

It was recognized that not all of this myth-ritual pattern need appear in any given context. Indeed parts of it could appear in an adapted form with changed meaning in different cultural contexts. Further, myths loosed, as it were, from their original ritual moorings could float around and exist purely as literature in cultures which had never or no longer accepted the myth-ritual pattern.

To what extent was such a myth-ritual pattern, either in whole or in part, ever a living reality in the religious life of Ancient Israel? It has been argued that the creation narrative in Genesis i was originally part of the myth-ritual complex associated with the Feast of Tabernacles. The seven days of creation correspond to the seven days of the Festival. The parallel Babylonian creation myth was part of the Babylonian New Year *Akitu* festival.[8] The Song of Songs has been interpreted as a collection of liturgical songs which have as their *Sitz im Leben* the sacred marriage.[9] Above all, it has been claimed that, working from Ancient Near Eastern parallels, there is sufficient evidence within the Old Testament itself to enable us to reconstruct the ritual of the Israelite New Year festival, the Feast of Tabernacles. It included the removal of Yahweh and his consort ʿAnat from the temple to a sacred booth in a vineyard; the celebration of the victory of Yahweh over all the powers of chaos that threatened his rule; the consummation of the sacred marriage in this booth; the death of Yahweh, and, after a period of mourning, his subsequent restoration to life to be led in triumph again to his temple. The sacred ark, the symbol of Yahweh's presence, probably had a prominent role in the ritual processions. In the temple, Yahweh reigned until the changing seasons once again led to the re-enactment of the ritual.[10] While any acceptance or rejection of this kind of reconstruction of Israelite cultic practice must, in the last analysis, depend on a detailed study of key passages in the Old Testament, certain general comments on methodology may be permitted.

Any sound methodology must work from the Old Testament outwards into the world of the Ancient Near East, and not vice versa. At this point due allowance must be made for the fact that the Hebrews, however much they belonged to the world of the Ancient Near East, were different, and different precisely in this, that for them God was located not primarily in the recurring pattern of nature, but in certain decisive, once for all, historical events interpreted as the saving and judging acts of their God. Any straightforward transference of thought patterns, therefore, from a nature-dominated myth-ritual complex to the religion of Israel must be treated with caution. All religions, particularly at a popular level, tend to become syncretistic, accepting beliefs and practices from other religions. It would, therefore, be surprising if there were no traces of myth-ritual concepts in the Old Testament, but this leaves unanswered the question as to what constitutes the essence of Hebrew religion.

The meaning clustering round particular words or phrases depends heavily on context. The same or similar words in different cultural contexts may mean very different things. Hanoi and Washington would have difficulty in reaching a mutually acceptable definition of democracy. The kingship of Marduk may be prominent in Babylonian texts, the kingship of Baal in the Ras Shamra texts, the kingship of Yahweh in the Psalms, but this does not necessarily mean that this idea has a common meaning in Babylonian, Canaanite and Israelite religious circles. Nor does it follow that such phrases need a common, cultic *Sitz im Leben* to explain them. Furthermore, the extent to which religious language may be allusive, symbolic, metaphorical and traditional must never be forgotten. Thus from the fact that in the Psalms we find the cry, Yahweh 'lives' (Psalm xviii, 46), the exhortation of Yahweh to 'awake' (Psalm xxxv, 23; xliv, 23) and the description of Yahweh as being 'asleep' and 'drunk' (Psalm lxxviii, 65) – all phrases which occur in the Babylonian Tammuz cult of the dying and rising god – we are not entitled to assume that Yahweh was a typical dying and rising god, particularly since in Psalm lxxviii the reference throughout is to Yahweh's mighty deeds in Israel's past history, in painful contrast to his present apparent inactivity.

It is still not at all certain to what extent the myth-ritual pattern was common to the culture of the Ancient Near East. The interpretation of some of the material which has figured prominently in the discussion is still open to dispute. To take but one example: to one scholar the chief value of the religious texts from Ras Shamra, is that they 'clearly exhibit the ritual aspects of myth',[11] while to another, writing in the same volume of essays, the whole thesis that these texts are basically cultic in origin is pure hypothesis, unsupported by any close examination of the texts.[12] Until such issues are clarified, any appeal to a common myth-ritual pattern must be treated with some reserve.

In general it may be claimed that, while there are many passages in the Old Testament, notably in the prophetic books (e.g. Amos ii, 7; Hosea ii; Jeremiah ii, 20 ff.) which clearly indicate that popular religion in pre-exilic Israel was very often a form of religious syncretism, drawing heavily upon Canaanite fertility cult practices, there is no clear evidence that the main stream of Hebrew religion ever thought of Yahweh as a dying and rising god, or as participating in the sacred marriage. Hebrew religious vocabulary was enriched, and the development of certain doctrines, notably the doctrine of creation, stimulated, by close contact with such fertility cults. From the time of the Exodus from Egypt onwards, however, or at least from the time of the theological traditions which reflected on the meaning of this event, there was within Israel a vital religious seed which germinated in soil other than that provided by the myth-ritual pattern, and produced very different fruit.

KINGSHIP

There is general agreement that wherever the myth-ritual pattern is found, the king plays a central role in the cult. Indeed the ritual pattern has been described as 'the things that were done to and by the king in order to secure the prosperity of the community in every sense for the coming year'.[13] In Ancient Egypt, the ruling Pharaoh is not merely god-like, but the god incarnate. Elsewhere, for example in Mesopotamia, the king is regarded as the chosen servant or steward of the god, rather than divine. He is none the less identified with the god to the extent of playing the role of the god in various cultic actions, including the sacred marriage and rites of cultic humiliation which symbolize death and resurrection. Although sweeping generalizations have sometimes been falsely made concerning the relationship between the king and the fertility or high god in the Ancient Near East, the evidence is clear that the king is everywhere an important sacral person by virtue of his office.[14]

To what extent was this true in Ancient Israel? In *Kingship and the Gods: a Study of Ancient Near Eastern Religions as the Integration of Society and Nature*, 1948, H. Frankfort pointed to three different concepts of kingship in the Ancient Near East: the god incarnate of Egypt, the chosen servant of the gods who ruled in Mesopotamia and the leader whose authority depended upon ties of kinship. Hebrew kingship, he argued, was basically 'the odd man out' in this world of kingship. The relationship between king and people in Israel was 'as nearly secular as is possible in a society wherein religion is a living force' (op. cit., p. 361). Both political and religious evidence may be adduced in support of this verdict. The advent of kingship to Israel is documented in the narratives in 1 Samuel as basically a political expediency. It replaces the old tribal federation which had failed to respond adequately to the threat of Philistine imperialism. Further, it is a piece of political expediency which, in at least one of the strands which make up the complex historical tradition in 1 Samuel, is regarded as rebellion against the kingship of Yahweh (1 Samuel viii; x, 17 ff.).[15] Indeed Hebrew tradition always remembered that the formative period in the religion of Israel, the period of the Exodus and the covenant between Yahweh and the nation at Mt Sinai, had been before kingship as an institution existed in Israel. The king therefore could not be an indispensable figure in the nation's religious life, and was certainly never regarded as divine.

Strangely, Frankfort ignored that part of the Old Testament to which the strongest appeal had been, and was increasingly to be, made in support of the thesis of the essentially sacral nature of kingship in Israel – the language and interpretation of many of the Psalms. This thesis at its most persuasive, and backed by a wealth of exegetical insight, is presented in A. R. Johnson, *Sacral Kingship in Ancient Israel*, first edition 1955, second revised edition 1967.[16] Following in the footsteps of S. Mowinckel, he accepts the great autumnal festival, Tabernacles, in preexilic Israel, as the cultic *Sitz im Leben* of the Psalms of Kingship of Yahweh, but he denies that these psalms were merely cultic in orientation. If this festival 'ever had its roots in a complex of myth and ritual which was primarily concerned with the cycle of the years and an annual attempt to secure a renewal of life for a specific social unit, this had been refashioned in terms of the Hebrew experience of Yahweh's activity on the plane of history and the thought in question was really the creation of a new world order and the introduction of an age of universal righteousness and peace' (op. cit., second edition, p. 61, n. 1). Thus the festival and its associated psalms were always pointing forward to the ultimate triumph of Yahweh's righteous kingly purposes in the world. The ritual of the festival included Yahweh's triumph over the primeval forces of darkness represented by the waters of chaos, his enthronement in the assembly of the gods, his creation of the habitable world, and his re-creative work. Through ritual drama, the worshippers were given assurance of final victory over death and all Yahweh's foes, and were summoned to renew their faith in Yahweh and his purposes, to the end that Yahweh's universal rule of righteousness and peace might be realized.

What of the role of the human king in all this? Some of the so-called Royal Psalms, e.g. Psalm lxxii, point clearly to the belief that the nation's prosperity, social and material, depends upon the behaviour of society as a whole. This, in turn, depends upon the character of the king whose function it was to maintain law and order. In Hebrew thought the king could only effectively maintain a just order because of his peculiar relationship to Yahweh, a relationship reflected in the tradition of the covenant between Yahweh and the royal Davidic house (e.g. Psalm cxxxii, cf. 2 Samuel vii; xxiii). There is a close association between this Davidic royal family and the Jerusalem cultus (e.g. Psalm cx), an association which probably has its roots in pre-Israelite Jerusalem traditions (cf. Genesis xv). In the coronation ritual the king becomes Yahweh's adopted son, his anointed i.e. Messiah, his servant endowed with his spirit (Psalms ii; lxxxix; cx, etc.).

Not only was the total well-being of the community linked to the life of the king and his relationship to Yahweh, but, so it is argued, there is evidence in some of the Psalms that an essential element of the ritual drama was the defeat and humiliation of the king, from which he emerges victorious by having his loyalty to Yahweh vindicated. The king may be God's servant, but at the autumnal festival he is ritually 'a suffering Servant, he is the Messiah of Yahweh, but on this occasion at least he is a humble Messiah. What we see, however, is a ritual humiliation which is in principle not unlike that suffered by the Babylonian king in the analogous New Year Festival' (op. cit., p. 113). The Psalms in which this may be seen at its clearest are Psalms xviii; lxxxix; ci; cxviii. The final stage in the dramatic ritual is the promise of ultimate supremacy, to be realised in the person of a descendant and ideal successor from the Davidic family, the true future Messiah of David (Psalms ii; xxi; cx).

This is a balanced and fairly restrained statement of an approach which has been pushed much further by certain other scholars.[17] It is a far cry from the basically secular nature of kingship in Israel advocated by Frankfort. It looks almost as if we are being presented with two irreconcilable portraits of the king in Israel, drawn from two different strands of evidence within the Old Testament.

Care must be exercised in any attempt to generalize about kingship, not only in the Ancient Near East, but even within the more limited field of the Old Testament. It is doubtful whether there was ever one generally accepted pattern of kingship in Ancient Israel. Certainly there was no such pattern once the united monarchy broke into two separate kingdoms under Solomon's successor Rehoboam. There is a clear distinction between the type of kingship which survived in the southern kingdom of Judah – a comparatively stable Davidic dynasty, always closely linked to the nation's worship in the Jerusalem temple – and the chronically unstable dynasties of the northern kingdom of Israel, many of them born in military *coups d'état* and following one another often in rapid succession.

The historical traditions concerning the advent of kingship to Israel, and the persistent and radical prophetic criticism of abuse of the kingly power (e.g. 2 Samuel xii, 1–15; 1 Kings xxi; Jeremiah xxii, 13–19), effectively prevented any attempt to deify the king in Israel's religion. Much of the fulsome, oriental court-style language applied to Hebrew monarchs must be handled cautiously in the light of this. If the king was neither divine nor the *sine qua non* of the nation's religious life, nevertheless the king of the royal Davidic family was an important religious figure by virtue of his office, particularly in the Jerusalem cult tradition. It is this which is reflected pre-eminently in the Psalms. We are hardly justified in using the expression 'Divine Kingship' in Israel, but it is difficult to see how we can avoid using 'Sacral Kingship'. The importance of the king *qua* king in the religious traditions of the Old Testament is unquestionable. What is not so certain is the precise part played by the king in the ritual of the Jerusalem Temple.

The problem of the cultic humiliation and suffering of the king illustrates the kind of questions that are involved. Apart from the weight given to extra-biblical evidence, in this case Babylonian royal humiliation rites, a decision for or against depends on two factors.

(a) The first factor is the extent to which we are prepared to classify certain Psalms as 'Royal Psalms'. For example, Psalm lxxxviii which has been cited by Engnell as clear proof of royal cultic suffering, is certainly on form critical grounds a typical Individual Lament. It graphically describes the psalmist's plight – full of troubles, as good as dead, forsaken, an object of revulsion, overwhelmed by tragedy and a sense of alienation from God. Only on the thesis that the 'I' of such Psalms *must* be the king or the leaders of the community, however, are we committed to describing such suffering and humiliation as 'royal'. There is nothing within the body of this particular psalm which demands such a royal interpretation.

(b) In psalms which do specifically refer to the king and speak of humiliation and suffering – Psalms xviii, lxxxix, ci and cxviii used by Johnson come into this category – must we interpret this humiliation and suffering in cultic terms? It is equally possible that the heavily stylized language of such psalms may refer either to some particular situation of national crisis in the first instance, and thereafter to every such situation, or to real personal illness, physical and spiritual. We are not compelled merely on the basis of the language of these psalms to infer a cultic situation in the light of which the language must be interpreted. It is true that our interpretation of the psalms needs to be imaginative rather than dully prosaic – they are religious poetry – but unless our imaginative approach is controlled by positive evidence from within the Old Testament rather than from general Ancient Near Eastern analogies, it may very well lead us astray.

However many questions remain unresolved, recent discussion of kingship ideology in Ancient Israel has given new depth and dimension to the interpretation of many Old Testament passages both within and without the Psalms. Not least has it provided us with the essential background for evaluating the form and meaning of the Old Testament hope of a future king (Messiah), a subject which has received classic treatment by S. Mowinckel in *He that Cometh*, 1954 (English translation by G.W. Anderson)[18].

THE DAY OF YAHWEH

Just as kingship ideology is the foundation of Israel's hope of the future ideal Messiah, so other elements in Israel's hope for the future have been traced back to cultic origins. This is so in the case of the concept of the 'day of Yahweh', which we first meet with as a well established popular hope, bitterly attacked and radically re-interpreted by the prophet Amos.

> Woe to you who desire the day of Yahweh!
> Why would you have the day of Yahweh?
> It is darkness and not light.
> Is not the day of Yahweh darkness and not light
>   and gloom with no brightness in it?
>
> (Amos v,18 and 20, cf. Zephaniah i,7,14 ff).

S. Mowinckel, in his work on the Psalms,[19] equated this 'day of Yahweh' with what is described in Hosea ix,5 as 'the day of the appointed festival, the day of the feast of Yahweh'. The 'day of Yahweh' was originally the day of Yahweh's appearance and enthronement in the New Year festival. This 'day' therefore carried with it the thought of the fulfilment of all the expectations which were present in the minds of the worshippers on such an occasion – the guarantee of material blessings to the community, the demonstration of the kingly rule of Yahweh, and the renewal of his covenant with his people for the coming year. As well as being a joyous harvest festival of thanksgiving for what the past year had brought, the festival therefore always pointed in hope towards the future. Promise was of the very essence of this festival liturgy. Thus it is not surprising that, in any situation of crisis in the life of Israel, this idea of the 'day of Yahweh', taken out of its cultic setting, would live in the minds of the people as a powerful symbol of the moment when Yahweh would intervene to right wrongs and renew the life of his people. It is motifs taken from this New Year festival and its attendant mythology of creation, in conflict with opposing forces of evil, kingship and covenant, which form the substance of Old Testament eschatology – that is to say, its beliefs concerning the end of the present world order and the inauguration of a new age. Such beliefs emphasize a new creation, the ultimate defeat of all forces of evil, Yahweh's universal kingship, and the new covenant. Out of hope dramatically presented in the ritual of the annual festival, and repeatedly called into question by events, was born ultimate hope. Others, notably in studies on the Book of Amos, have followed Mowinckel, with many a variation in detail, in positing a cultic origin and background for the day of Yahweh.[20]

This thesis has not gone unchallenged. If we accept the kind of New Year festival that Mowinckel posits, then it is strange that in the Old Testament passages which refer to the day of Yahweh there is never any mention of the kingship of Yahweh which was central to such an enthronement festival. G. von Rad has argued that the origin of the idea of the day of Yahweh is to be found not in the liturgy of the New Year festival, but in the early Hebrew traditions of the 'holy war' in which Yahweh led his people into battle and granted them the victory. The people may well have gone into battle with the cry 'the day of Yahweh' on their lips. There would thus be, right from the beginning, a heavily nationalistic flavour about the concept. With this the prophets took issue.[21] It is doubtful whether at this stage we can hope to trace with any degree of certainty the specific origin of this belief in the 'day of Yahweh'. Perhaps it had no one such origin, but was merely a convenient summation in popular belief of many strands in the traditional religious heritage of Israel which encouraged a mood of superficial religious optimism in the community.

THE PROPHETS AND THE CULT

It was again S. Mowinckel's creative work on the Psalms which led to the calling into question of the radical distinction between prophecy and the cult which had characterized much earlier scholarship. *Cult Prophecy and Prophetic Psalms* (*Kultusprophetie und Psalmen*) was the title of the third volume of his *Psalmenstudien*, published in 1923. Within the Psalms there are many passages in which God speaks, directly addressing either his chosen representative such as the king (e.g. Psalms ii,7; cx) or the congregation as a whole (e.g. Psalms lx,6; lxxv,2–5). Who spoke such words of God within the context of an act of worship? Mowinckel argued that, in addition to the priests, there were prophets who had a recognized function in the worship of ancient

Israel. Such prophets were responsible for many of the Psalms. They acted as the mouthpiece of such oracular words of God.

Within the historical traditions of the Old Testament there is a good deal of evidence which may be interpreted as providing support for the thesis that there were in Israel, from the time of the settlement in Canaan down to the destruction of the Jerusalem temple in 587 B.C., people whom we may call 'cult prophets'. In the traditions of the emergence of the monarchy we meet with groups of prophets characterized by ecstatic behaviour which is sometimes deliberately induced by well-known techniques. Such groups of prophets are closely associated with sanctuaries (e.g. 1 Samuel x, 5–12). Samuel himself, in the tradition preserved in 1 Samuel ix, 6–x, 4 is described as a 'seer' and a 'man of God'. He is consulted on matters of difficulty. He is, moreover, a cultic figure of some importance. The community waits for his coming before sharing in a sacrificial meal. An editorial note in 1 Samuel ix, 9 informs us 'he who is now called a prophet was formerly called a seer'. The same features – prophetic groups, consultation and close cultic connexions – appear equally prominently in the traditions concerning the prophets Elijah and Elisha in 1 Kings xviii – 2 Kings xiii. It might be claimed that such prophetic groups were an early aberration in Israel's religious history, a borrowing of a Canaanite phenomenon – witness the prophets of Baal on Mt Carmel, 1 Kings xviii. As such they were never part of the authentic Hebrew religious ethos; nor did they long survive in that religion.

A. R. Johnson, however, in a well-documented monograph, *The Cultic Prophet in Ancient Israel* (first edition 1949, second edition 1962) has argued that throughout the period of the monarchy – and the evidence is particularly strong for the Jerusalem temple in the closing era of the Judean state – prophets were recognized members of the Temple personnel in much the same way as the priests. Such cultic prophets had a dual role in furthering the well-being of the community. On the one hand they were the spokesmen of Yahweh, on the other they represented the people before Yahweh, particularly in offering prayer on behalf of the community. Such prophets lost prestige when their optimistic message was falsified by the collapse of the Judean state and the exile to Babylon. They never fully recovered, but found a new role in the restored post-exilic temple as temple singers. The repeated linking of priests and prophets in the canonical prophets from Hosea onwards, and the fact that with one exception, Hosea iv, 4 ff., all such references have as their background the Jerusalem temple, are strong points in Johnson's argument.

Even if the balance of evidence does seem to point to the existence of such cultic prophets, there are still many unsolved problems. Apart from chance references, usually of a condemnatory nature, in the prophetic books of the Old Testament, we have little information about such prophets. This is in marked contrast to the priests, whose origins, qualifications and functions are well documented, although the date and character of the sources make it difficult to write a reliable historical account even of the priesthood. What, for example, were the qualifications for admission to the ranks of such cultic prophets? – heredity, training, evidence of charismatic gifts? We do not know.

One question above all needs to be clarified. What was the relationship – or lack of it – between these cultic prophets and the tradition of prophecy we find in men like Amos, Hosea, Micah, Isaiah, Jeremiah and Ezekiel? The fact that the same Hebrew word '*nabi*', prophet, does duty both for Jeremiah and the prophets, cultic or otherwise, whom he bitterly attacks forces us to ask this question. Various answers have been given. They range all the way from complete identity at the one extreme[22] to the denial of any relationship at all at the other.[23]

In the editorial introduction to the Book of Amos, the prophet is described as one of 'the shepherds of Tekoa' (Amos i, 1). The word translated 'shepherds', '*noqᵉdim*', occurs only once elsewhere in the Old Testament. In 2 Kings iii, 4 it describes Mesha, King of Moab, and is translated 'sheep-breeder' in the R.S.V. In the Ras Shamra texts, however, the phrase 'chief of the *noqᵉdim*' occurs in parallelism with 'chief of the priests'. It has therefore been argued that the word must refer to some cultic or temple official, and Amos becomes by profession a cultic prophet.

Even if the meaning of the word in the Ras Shamra texts was certain, however (and this is debatable), this is not necessarily decisive for the usage of the word in Hebrew. Both the occurrence in 2 Kings iii, 4, and what we otherwise know of Amos would be consistent with the word in Hebrew meaning something like 'sheep-breeder'. Similarly, it may be true, as I. Engnell has argued in *The Call of Isaiah*, 1949, that the prophet's call experience described in Isaiah vi mirrors living cultic traditions, central to which is divine kingship; this, however, is very far from proving that Isaiah of Jerusalem was a cultic prophet.

There is no proof that any of the major prophetic figures of the Old Testament were cultic officials, and there is at least one factor which clearly differentiates them as prophets from such officials: that is to say their 'call' experience (e.g. Amos vii, 14 f.; Isaiah vi; Jeremiah i; Ezekiel i–ii). Such men were prophets because they were burdened by a commission which they had not chosen, gripped by a self-authenticating religious experience. They were confronted by a word of God which shattered the previous pattern of their life, including their religious life. It could be argued that such a 'call' might have been the means through which they later entered an official religious order, in much the same way as an experience of conversion may lead a man to enter the ministry or the priesthood. But there is little evidence that this was the case for any of these men.

What then of the attitude of such major prophetic figures to the cult? The divine word they pronounce against it is often extreme.

> I hate, I despise your feasts,
>   and I take no delight in your solemn assemblies.
> Even though you offer me your burnt offerings
>   and cereal offerings
>
> I will not accept them
>   and the peace offerings of your fatted beasts
>   I will not look upon.
>
> But let justice roll down like waters
>   and righteousness like an everlasting stream.
>
> (Amos v, 21–24; cf. Amos iv, 4; Hosea vi, 4–6;
> Isaiah i, 10–17; Jeremiah vii, 4 ff.)

The following verdict used to be typical: in almost every one of these prophets 'you can read the flat rejection of the cultus'; it was 'the chief hindrance and stumbling block to right fellowship with God' (K. Marti, *The Religion of the Old Testament*, 1907, p. 148, 152). Very few scholars today would accept that what we hear in such prophetic statements is the rejection in principle of the entire cultic system. This outruns the evidence. The cult of the day was meaningless to such men because it was a cult practised by people whose conduct was a living denial of that righteousness and justice which was the *sine qua non* of the nation's response to Yahweh. Isaiah is equally scathing of prayer, prayer offered by people whose hands are full of blood (Isaiah i, 15).[24] There is nothing to suggest that in different circumstances such prophets might not have welcomed the cult as a genuine means of grace. The prophets were critical of the cult because the cult was failing to elicit from the community a genuine religious response.[25] They were critical of the priests, not *qua* priests, but because the priests of their day failed to fulfil their function, the giving of true *torah*, i.e. instruction, to the community (cf. Jeremiah ii, 8).

Thus far we have been looking at the relationship between the prophetic movement and the cult from the standpoint of the criticism of cultic practice that is found in prophetic teaching. An attempt has also been made to build a bridge between these two aspects of Israel's religious life from the other end. Is there not evidence within the prophetic books themselves, that the major prophetic figures in Israel not only knew and were deeply influenced by cultic traditions, but delivered their message in a liturgical context or, at the very least, used liturgical forms in their teaching?

In support of his thesis that cultic prophets were responsible for material in the Psalms, Mowinckel drew attention to the character of certain of the prophetic books, in particular Joel and Habakkuk. Habakkuk iii is an obvious point of departure since it contains the same kind of cultic rubrics which are to be found in the Psalms – rubrics whose interpretation is still in many cases a matter of dispute. There is a heading 'A prayer of Habakkuk the prophet, according to Shigionoth' (v. i); the periodic call 'Selah' (vv. 3, 9, 13); and a closing rubric of the kind usually found in the heading to the Psalms 'To the choirmaster: with stringed instruments' (v. 19). If this chapter had appeared as one of the Old Testament Psalms, it would have occasioned no surprise. P. Humbert in *Problèmes du livre d'Habaccuc*, 1944, argued that the entire book was a liturgy prepared for a festival in the Jerusalem temple in the year 602–601 B.C. The background to the liturgy is the threatened Babylonian attack on the city. It contains two elements – a call for a realistic faith in the face of this crisis, and an attack on the despotic ruler of Judah, Jehoiakim, who in the prophet's eyes was everything that the true Messiah of Yahweh ought not to be (cf. Jeremiah xxii, 13–19). Habakkuk is thus an interesting example of a prophet using the cult and cultic forms to attack one who ought to have been one of the most important religious functionaries in the nation's life.[26]

A detailed study of Joel from this general standpoint was made by A. S. Kapelrud in *Joel Studies*, 1948. He attributes the book to a cultic prophet who has drawn material from two main sources, the festival of the enthronement of Yahweh and the fertility cult pattern of the Ancient Near East, particularly in the Canaanite form in which we now know it from the Ras Shamra texts. Kapelrud did not claim that Joel was ever used liturgically, but he did argue strongly for it being composed in imitation liturgical style.

The book of Nahum has always presented something of a problem in the corpus of prophetic writings. In its entirety its theme is judgement upon Israel's enemy, in this case Assyria (cf. Obadiah), and salvation for Israel. This is precisely the kind of nationalistic fervour that prophets like Amos and Jeremiah violently attack. It fits in well however with the message of the prophets who opposed Jeremiah. If, as A. R. Johnson argued, they were part of the personnel of the Jerusalem temple, then there is much to be said for the Book of Nahum as the product of some cultic prophet or group of prophets utilizing familiar liturgical material. Nineveh, the capital of the Assyrian Empire, fell to the Babylonians in the year 612 B.C., though the writing had already been on the wall for several decades. P. Humbert and others[27] have argued that the Book of Nahum is a prophetic liturgy composed for the autumnal festival in Jerusalem a few months after the downfall of Nineveh. A. Halder, however, in *Studies in the Book of Nahum*, 1947, argued that it was the work of a cultic prophet prior to the fall of Nineveh, probably circa 614 B.C.; a good example of religio-political propaganda. It utilizes expressions and motifs drawn from the circle of ideas associated with the mythological conflict between Yahweh and his foes, ideas which echo material found in the wider circle of Ancient Near Eastern mythology. The Book of Jonah also contains within it in chapter ii, 3–10 (English versions ii, 2–9) a Psalm which is a typical Psalm of Thanksgiving, probably of cultic origin.[28]

A topic which has probably received more critical discussion than any other in the Old Testament is the figure of the Servant (Hebrew *ebed*) of Yahweh in Isaiah xl–lv; the passages central to the discussion are the Servant Songs in xlii 1–4; xlix, 1–6; 1, 4–9; lii, 13–liii. I. Engnell, in 'The Ebed Yahweh Songs and the Suffering Messiah in Deutero–Isaiah', *Bulletin of the John Rylands Library*, 31, 1948, pp. 54–93, introduced a new element into the discussion. He claimed that, while in these passages we are being presented with the figure of a Servant who is still to come, motifs from two overlapping circles of cultic ideas have been utilized in the description of the Servant: the ideology of divine kingship, particularly in its aspect of ritual humiliation and suffering present in Israelite tradition in certain of the Psalms, and the ideology of the dying-rising god cult, found in the Adonis–Tammuz myths in Babylon and in the Baal–Mot myths in Canaan.

It is possible to feel sceptical about the detail in certain of these studies. For example, it is not at all clear that we need to go to divine kingship or the dying-rising god cult for an explanation of the suffering, yet triumphant Servant. Victory through persecution and suffering is part of the experience of the Old Testament prophets, notably Jeremiah. What is not open to dispute is that all such studies are pointing us to a more synthetic view of the religion of Israel. Prophecy is only one strand, albeit a very important strand, in this religion.

WISDOM

Our discussion of the wisdom literature (cf. Chapter 2, pp. 98 ff.) has already hinted at some of the religious problems which this literature poses. Although wisdom may have its roots in early Hebrew family and tribal life, its place in the community of faith in Israel is not immediately obvious. Not only does it have a strongly international flavour, but it seems to lack many of the distinctive emphases in the religion of Israel. In particular, any reference to God's activity in history is conspicuously absent. The concept of 'Wisdom', however, came to be of ever increasing importance in the religious thinking of post-exilic Judaism. It became one of the means by which Judaism sought to communicate and relate her faith to the non-Jewish world. How did this happen?

In a superb poem now to be found in Job xxviii, although this is probably not its original setting, wisdom is described as being inaccessible to the seeking intelligence of men. The way to wisdom is known only to God. In Proverbs viii–ix, wisdom appears as a woman, calling men to learn prudence from her. Created by Yahweh, to be his delight, she existed at his side before the rest of creation. Happiness, fullness of life, and the favour of Yahweh are hers to give. She invites men to feast in her house. What is the purpose and origin of this figure of Lady Wisdom, drawn in sharp contrast to the 'strange woman' against whose deadly seductive wiles the opening section of Proverbs repeatedly warns (ii, 16–19; v, 1–6; vi, 24–32; vii, 6–27)? There is little doubt that in the context of Proverbs i–ix, generally regarded as the latest section in the whole book,[29] the figure of Lady Wisdom is one of the ways in which the wisdom tradition is being integrated into the distinctive religious heritage of Israel.[30] This interpretation would be all the more likely if, as has been frequently urged, the warnings against the strange, 'alien' woman are a plea not simply for marital fidelity, but for religious fidelity in face of the seductive attractiveness of pagan fertility cults. Another, less speculative, way of bringing the wisdom tradition within the orbit of Israel's religion is through the equation of wisdom with 'the fear of Yahweh' (Proverbs i, 7, 29 etc.).

But what kind of figure is this Lady Wisdom? Is she merely a poetic personification of some attribute of Yahweh, or is she an independent entity or divine agent distinguishable from Yahweh, i.e. a hypostasis? Out of extensive discussion of this issue there seems to be emerging a consensus of critical opinion that, as far as the Old Testament itself is concerned, we are dealing with no more than a poetic personification of an attribute of Yahweh. The development of this personification may have been helped by motifs taken from the mythology of the mother-goddess figure.[31] It has been argued that Wisdom began life as a hypostasis of an aspect of the Canaanite god 'El, and was already a Canaanite goddess before finding her place in Hebrew wisdom literature; but the evidence for this falls far short of proof.[32] When we move beyond the Old Testament into the field of later Jewish Apocryphal writings, the personification of Wisdom increases in intensity to the point where we must take seriously the concept of a hypostasis. Here influences have been sought, somewhat inconclusively, in many quarters: Iranian, Greek, Babylonian and Egyptian. A valuable survey of views will be found in W. Baumgartner's article 'The Wisdom Literature' in *The Old Testament and Modern Study*, pp. 210–35.

Wisdom plays several roles in Apocryphal literature. She is a convenient means of claiming universal significance for Jewish religion. In *The Wisdom of Jesus ben Sira* (*Ecclesiasticus*), early second century B.C., Wisdom is described (xxiv) as the word uttered by God before creation. This cosmic Wisdom, at God's command, finds her home in Israel. She is equated with *torah*, God's law or self-revelation contained in the five books of Moses. *Baruch*, first century B.C., draws upon the poem in Job xxviii to make this same identification of Wisdom with *torah* (iii, 9–iv, 4). *The Wisdom of Solomon*, a first-century B.C. Jewish Hellenistic document, probably emanating from Alexandria, ascribes to Wisdom many of the events in Hebrew history in which the Old Testament itself speaks of the Spirit of God at work. Thus cosmic Wisdom is given her place at the very centre of Israel's religious

traditions.[33] *The Wisdom of Solomon*, however, is not merely a
Jewish document. Consciously and unconsciously, it reflects the
outlook of the cosmopolitan Hellenistic world in which it was
born. In this it was no exception. Many Jewish writers, notably
Philo of Alexandria, first century A.D., sought to communicate
their faith in terms intelligible to the culture in which they lived.
The figure of Wisdom was a useful bridge builder since she was
easily identifiable with concepts such as *Sophia* and *Logos* which
were familiar in the thought world of the day.[34] Likewise Wisdom
provided Christianity with one of the categories through which it
developed its Christological thinking (e.g. 1 Corinthians i, 24).[35]
Many streams in both Israel's religious heritage and in the non-
Jewish religious world were to meet in the figure of Wisdom.

One of the important tasks for the future would seem to be a
continuing reassessment of the place of the Wisdom tradition as a
whole within the religion of Israel. Not least, we need a positive
evaluation, in the light of comparative Near Eastern material, of
that radical questioning of accepted religious presuppositions
which finds expression in Job and Ecclesiastes, and which has
links with other material outside the wisdom literature, for
example the Psalms of Lamentation and the Confessions of
Jeremiah.

We have touched briefly upon various aspects of the religion of
Israel. But it must never be forgotten that this religion, in spite of
its different traditions and inner tensions, was a living unity.
Jeremiah was persecuted to ensure that 'law shall not perish
from the priest, nor counsel from the wise, nor the word from the
prophet' (Jeremiah xviii, 18). The priests, the guardians of *torah*,
were responsible for the continuing education of the community in its traditional religious heritage. The wise men made
their shrewd comment on personal living, politics and the
ultimate enigmas of life. The prophets claimed to speak a word
from God of direct relevance to the situation of their day. They
are different, but not sharply antithetical, elements in the religion
of Israel. 'The picture which now presents itself to us of Israel's
religious development is not that of a successive elaboration of
the religious insights obtained by the great prophets of the eighth

and seventh centuries, but a series of traditions preceding and developing side by side. Law, psalmography, wisdom and prophecy all had their own distinctive place and maintained their particular traditions' (R. E. Clements, *Prophecy and Covenant*, 1965). No one of these traditions can be properly understood in isolation from the others.

Five

The Theology of
the Old Testament

The task confronting the historian of the religion of Israel has
been well described as follows: 'to offer a history of the religion of
Israel with respect not only to its historical development but to its
essence and inmost character as well' (Th. C. Vriezen, *The Religion of Ancient Israel*, p. 7). He seeks to describe as fully and as
fairly as he can a historical process. This is no easy task in the
light of the nature of the sources at his disposal. He can supplement his primary sources, the books of the Old Testament, with
data supplied to him by archaeology, comparative religion and
psychology. Increasingly, the tools of literary criticism, form
criticism and modern linguistic studies are at his disposal in
helping him to understand his primary sources. In the very act of
describing, however, he is evaluating, both in his selection of what
he considers to be relevant evidence, and also in the way he
handles that evidence. To this extent a personal equation can
never be entirely eliminated from his work although he will strive
for the kind of historical objectivity which allows the data at his
disposal to control his conclusions. In all this the historian of
Israel's religion is no different from his academic colleague who
seeks to elucidate Egyptian religion or Ancient Greek religion.

The results produced by the application of historical-critical
methods to the Old Testament in the nineteenth century were exciting. Instead of a book all on one level, and unquestionably
authoritative as the word of God, there emerged an intricate historical pattern with religious ideas ranging all the way from
primitive animism to ethical monotheism. This led many to look
upon such a historical study as the supreme goal of Old Testament scholarship. *Religionsgeschichte*, the descriptive, phenomenological account of the religion of Israel in terms of its historical

development, came into its own. This raised a serious problem for both Judaism and the Christian faith. How was this approach to be reconciled with the fact that historically the Old Testament had been handed down not merely as the literature of an ancient people, but as a Canon or part of a Canon of Sacred Scripture, regarded as authoritative and normative for belief and conduct? Is there not something inherently irreconcilable between the way in which modern critical scholarship will handle an Old Testament book or passage, making us perhaps only too painfully aware of its limited perspectives and primitive character, and the way in which appeal is made to the Old Testament in many of the classic documents of the Christian faith. *The Confession of Faith* of 1647, chapter 2, entitled 'Of God and the Holy Trinity', cites as proof texts for doctrine not only passages from the New Testament, but passages from Genesis, Exodus, Deuteronomy, Kings, Isaiah, Jeremiah, Ezekiel, Malachi, Psalms, Proverbs, Job, Nehemiah and Daniel, as if all were of equal validity in constructing Christian doctrine. Has the religious historian finally destroyed such an approach for all but the unthinking?

The conviction that, even on this side of the revolution in biblical studies, Jew and Christian cannot hand over the Old Testament solely to the antiquarian interest of the religious historian, has led to many attempts in recent years to write 'The Theology of the Old Testament' in addition to 'The Religion of Israel'; and to even more, indeed bewilderingly numerous, attempts to clarify the methodological problems involved in so doing. It is impossible to deal with all the many issues raised, but several may be said to have dominated much recent debate.

THE RELIGION OF ISRAEL AND THE THEOLOGY OF THE OLD TESTAMENT

Here we face the problem of the inherent tension between critical method and valid theological reconstruction. It is possible for two very different reasons to deny that there is any relationship between the approach of the historian and the theologian to the Old Testament. It may be done to undermine the academic integrity of the theology. R. H. Pfeiffer, in a posthumously published volume *Religion in the Old Testament*, 1961, declares

> The point of view and method of the historian are radically different from that of the theologian and the philosopher: he searches for actual historical reality, not for normative faith and doctrine valid for all times. With serene objectivity he will present impartially what is religiously obsolete and what is still alive, either a passing phase or an eternal truth, an ancient superstition or an intuition of an abiding article of faith. His own personal faith does not colour the presentation of his findings or at least it should not.

Per contra

> A statement of the religion of the Bible from the point of view of faith and dogma would inevitably reflect the faith of the researcher and the doctrines which he defends: a Jew, a Roman Catholic, a Lutheran, a Unitarian and a Moslem would differ widely in their presentation of the religion of the Bible from the point of view of their particular faith and doctrinal beliefs (op. cit., p. 9).

This view would seem to be unduly naïve both with respect to the methods of the historian *and* of the theologian.

On the other hand, it may be done to ensure the validity of the theological approach as a legitimate discipline in its own right with its own methods. O. Eissfeldt in an article published in 1926, 'Israëlitsch-judisch Religionsgeschichte und alttestamentliche Theologie', in *Zeitschrift für die alttestamentliche Wissenschaft*, xliv, pp. 1–12, which reflects, though not uncritically, the theological influence of Karl Barth, argues that the religious historian looks at things purely from the phenomenological point of view; the knowledge which he seeks depends upon proofs which compel assent and is always immanent and relative. The theologian's concern is with faith which lays hold on the ultimate, the transcendant, which is not accessible to the historian *qua* historian. Both approaches to the Old Testament are legitimate and necessary, but there must be no mixture of the two. They may be thought of rather as parallel lines of understanding.

It may be convenient for the theologian, particularly in an age of historical scepticism concerning some of the material in the documents he handles, to believe that his way of understanding in no way depends upon work being done in the historico-critical field; but it is doubtful whether this can ever be a satisfactory dichotomy in the study of the Old Testament. The very nature of the religious material within the Old Testament militates against it. Many of the credal statements in the Old Testament are in the form of recitals of the mighty acts of God, *Heilsgeschichte*, 'sacred history'. They contain not merely a philosophical statement about the general relationship between God and the historical process, but the affirmation that God spoke and acted in this and in that particular event. The Old Testament claim is that he acted, for example, in the Exodus from Egypt, and in the destruction of Jerusalem by the Babylonians; that he spoke to a particular community, Israel, or to this and that person within the community: Abraham, Moses, Samuel, the prophets . . .

Without accepting an absolute dichotomy between the approach of the historian and the theologian, G. von Rad has pointed the contrast by claiming that, while historical investigation searches for 'a critically assured minimum', the picture drawn by faith within the Old Testament 'tends to be a theological maximum' (*Old Testament Theology*, volume 1, p. 108). But what if the picture which emerges from this critically assured minimum seems to bear little or no relationship to the theological maximum? We can do one of three things. (1) We can absolutize the theological maximum which may exist in the Old Testament in the form of confessions of faith, and say that it does not matter, and indeed is of no theological significance, that we cannot probe behind it to what is historical and factual. If the historian says we can know nothing with certainty about the Exodus from Egypt, it is comforting to take refuge in the attitude which says, 'Never mind, at least it was an act of God!' (2) We can regard the theological maximum as so much pious wishful thinking. (3) We can, perhaps we must, query the assumptions of a historical method which leaves us with this critically assured minimum so much at variance with Old Testament traditions as we now have them.[1]

It has been suggested that the *Heilsgeschichte* of the Old Testament is related to the actual course of events in Israel's history 'somewhat as a portrait is related to a photograph'.[2] The analogy is helpful as far as we may take it. The media are different. The photograph is in a way much less controlled by the subjectivity of the photographer than the portrait is by that of the painter. Yet Karsh's famous photograph of Churchill is deliberately interpretative, just as much a work of art in its own way as what the sitter himself described as a 'remarkable example of modern art', Graham Sutherland's portrait. Both photograph and portrait, however are of the same man. If it were not so we could not pass any valid comparative judgement on either. Behind both the historical and the theological approach must be one and the same thing, 'Israel', and this must be demonstrable for both approaches. Unless the theologian of the Old Testament listens, even sometimes with irritation, to what the historian has to tell him about the religion of Israel in its historical development, essence and inmost character, he may be guilty of imposing upon the Old Testament material a totally alien theological system. Unless the historian is willing to listen to the theologian he may never be able to penetrate to that essence and inmost character since so many of Israel's historical traditions have come to us in theological form. There may always have to be tension here, but it ought to be a creative tension.

OLD TESTAMENT THEOLOGY –
THE PROBLEM OF METHODOLOGY

On the assumption that Old Testament theology is not the pursuit of a dogmatic will-of-the-wisp, how ought it to be handled? Instead of coming to us all on one level as the word of God, the Old Testament seen through the eyes of modern critical method is a diverse collection of documents, varied in authorship and date, varied in religious insight and emphasis. What kind of theology is it possible to find amid this diversity? Is it possible to say that 'in spite of differences and changes there is a distinctive pattern which is to be recognized almost everywhere, so that something of a family likeness can be detected as between different parts of the Old Testament and the different periods it records'?[3] To see how various people have attempted to locate and define this distinctive pattern and its theological significance may be more useful than any abstract discussion of this issue.

The first, and in the opinion of many still the greatest, and most comprehensive treatment of Old Testament theology in the modern period was that of W. Eichrodt, *Theologie des Alten Testaments*, Vol. I 1933, II 1935, III 1939. The whole is now available in English translation in two volumes, *Theology of the Old Testament*, Vol. I 1961, II 1967.[4] Eichrodt rejects on the one hand any attempt to imprison the Old Testament within categories derived from dogmatic theology or bloodless abstractions like 'ethical monotheism', and on the other any purely descriptive account of the religion of Israel in its historical development. He defines as his task 'the problem of how to understand the realm of Old Testament belief in its structural unity and how, by examining on the one hand its religious environment and on the other its essential coherence with the New Testament, to illuminate its profoundest meaning' (Volume 1, p. 31). The way to do this is to take a cross-section through the historical material in the Old Testament and thus seek to show how all its parts are related to one another. The three principal categories which he finds useful at this point – and here he admits his indebtedness to other scholars, particularly O. Procksch, whose *Theologie des Alten Testaments* appeared posthumously in 1950 – are *God and the People*, *God and the World* and *God and Man*. Throughout the first section *God and the People* all the material is grouped under the concept of the covenant. Thus we have 'The Covenant Relationship', 'The Covenant Statutes', 'The Name of the Covenant God', 'The Nature of the Covenant God', 'The Instruments of the Covenant', 'Covenant-Breaking and Judgement', 'Fulfilling the Covenant: The Consummation of God's Dominion'. In the second and third sections, however, *God and the World* and *God and Man*, the word covenant disappears.

Eichrodt has often been accused of forcing his material into a covenant straitjacket. The criticism is at once valid and irrelevant; valid, in so far as he has taken *one* – albeit a very important one – of the symbols found in the Old Testament to describe the relationship between God and Israel, and used it to classify his material; irrelevant, in so far as his use of covenant is merely a convenient symbol which corresponds to the fact 'that every expression of the Old Testament which is determinative for its faith rests on the explicit or implicit assumption that a free act of God, consummated in history, has raised Israel to the rank of the People of God, in whom the nature and the will of God are revealed' (Preface to fifth revised edition, p. 14). At this point, while there may be argument about the details of his presentation, and whether the mass of detail does not proliferate to the extent of making it difficult at times to see the wood for the trees, Eichrodt's general approach is surely sound. Any presentation of the faith of the Old Testament, any claim that this faith may have lasting significance in terms of revelation, depends upon a historically conditioned relationship between God and a particular, politically never very significant, nation. Anything that the Old Testament has to say concerning God and the World and God and Man comes as a by-product of this relationship.

But what of the 'essential coherence with the New Testament' to which Eichrodt referred in defining his task? Would it have made any difference to his presentation of the material if he had said instead 'essential coherence with Rabbinic Judaism'? Curiously, Eichrodt gives little place to the Old Testament – New Testament relationship except to say that while the old method of finding detailed New Testament fulfilment of specific Old Testament prophecies is wrong, all the hope of the Old Testament looks forward to the consummation of God's sovereignty, a consummation of a particular character linked to time and history, space and form. At the heart of it is an experience of real communion with God, a communion whose depth is realized through suffering . . . 'it is these basic features, inseparably connected with the essence of the Old Testament picture of God, and not any other individual details, which must decide whether the Gospel of the New Testament has a right to be understood as the real answer to the problem of the Old Testament prediction' (volume 1, p. 507).[5]

Eichrodt's methods are the methods appropriate to a religious historian: describing and classifying. His theological standpoint consists in his positing ultimate significance in terms of Christian faith for what he describes. The religion of the Old Testament, claims another Old Testament scholar, 'is the relationship between the Hebrew people and their God as they experienced it and as they described it. If this relationship has no spiritual significance for our faith then the book means nothing to us, however diligently we look for something as a substitute'.[6] Eichrodt's *Theology* excels in laying bare the inner meaning of this relationship. He has no doubts that once the inner meaning is grasped, it will be seen to have continuing spiritual significance.

Th. C. Vriezen's *Hoofdlijnen der Theologie van het Oude Testament*, 1949, second edition 1954, appeared in English translation in 1958 as *An Outline of Old Testament Theology*. The presentation is very different. Whereas Eichrodt plunged straight into a description of the covenant concept, Vriezen devotes an 'Introduction', which is approximately a third of the entire book, to the discussion of the problem of methodology, and in particular the place of the Old Testament in the Christian Church. He rejects Eichrodt's approach on the grounds that with respect to both its object and methods, Old Testament theology as a theological subject must differ from the history of Israel's religion (cf. p. 121). Its object, he claims, is not the religion of Israel but the Old Testament. The essential point of difference here is that the Old Testament 'is not merely a collection of ancient Israelite religious texts, but is the book of the religion of Israel as it was reformed in the period of exile under the influence of the prophets, whose critical insight was formed under the guidance of the Spirit of God in times of great distress' (pp. 14–15). That is to say, the Old Testament is the product of prophetic orthodoxy. As for its method 'it is a study of the Old Testament both in itself and in its relation to the New Testament' (p. 121). An Old Testament theology is therefore concerned with the element of revelation in the Old Testament message and with evaluating it on the ground of its Christian content.

This gives us a firm and unequivocal statement of presuppositions, but it inevitably means that a theology of the Old

Testament in Vriezen's terms can only be written by a Christian, and that in a far more pointed way than in the case of Eichrodt's theology, we are forced to ask how far such a theology both in its selection and handling of material must consciously or unconsciously read back Christian comment into the Old Testament. Vriezen himself is well aware of the problems and the dangers. The Old Testament theologian must be truly critical, endeavouring to abandon all *a priori* assumptions in his thinking. Yet there is a relationship between the Old and the New Testaments, and for Vriezen it exists in a twofold way; a historical relationship, the New Testament originating in the same historical milieu as the Old Testament yet exhibiting important differences from it, and an organic relationship which implies a very close spiritual affinity between the two.

When he turns in Part Two to describe the content of an Old Testament theology, Vriezen begins with a brief survey of the contents of the books of the Old Testament from a theological standpoint. This provides the essential data for outlining the basic ideas which run through the Old Testament. In describing these basic ideas, he begins, as Eichrodt does, with a relationship: what he describes as 'The nature of the knowledge of God in the Old Testament as an intimate relationship between the Holy God and Man'. He then proceeds to discuss in turn, 'God', 'Man', 'The Intercourse between God and Man', 'The Intercourse between Man and Man', 'God, Man and the World in the present and in the future'. Although not dissimilar in general outline to Eichrodt's classification of the material, his approach is much more consciously systematic. He draws material from all sections of the Old Testament and often makes little attempt to assess the historical relationship between the data he uses. Thus the chapter on 'Man' begins with a discussion of the narratives in Genesis i–xi. One must immediately say that this is not where Israel's understanding of man began, not even where prophetic understanding began. Genesis i–xi utilizes myth to provide reflective comment on factors in human life which forced themselves upon Israel first in the course of her historical experience. It would be truer to the Old Testament to begin with the historical experience of man in relationship both with God and his fellow man. It is true, of course, that Genesis i–xi is where the Old Testament, as opposed to the religion of Israel, begins, but if the Old Testament theologian begins here, it is difficult to see what relevance, if any, historical critical method has to the theologian's task. Part One is by far the most valuable section in Vriezen's book since it does pose the questions which haunt any Christian appeal to the Old Testament as the word of God.

E. Jacob's *Théologie de l'Ancien Testament*, 1955 (English translation *Theology of the Old Testament*, 1958) has been described as an invaluable student's tool because of its clear and systematic presentation of the material. Like Eichrodt, Jacob refuses to accept any radical parting of the ways between the history of the religion of Israel and Old Testament theology. 'Each has its proper function to fulfil, while remaining in each case an historical and descriptive subject; the first will show the variety of the history and its evolution, the second will emphasize its unity' (p. 29). The theology of the Old Testament may therefore be defined as 'the systematic account of the specific religious ideas which can be found throughout the Old Testament and which form its profound unity' (p. 11). Such a theology links up with the New Testament – Jacob indeed describes it as a Christology – not because we read the Old Testament in the light of the New, but because 'a perfectly objective study makes us discern already in the Old Testament the same message of the God who is present, of the God who saves, and of the God who comes which characterizes the Gospel' (p. 12). This statement either means much less than it seems to mean – a God who is present, who saves and who comes is as characteristic of Judaism as a living faith as it is of the Christian Gospel – or it assigns particular nuances to these activities of God, in which case we may well ask what 'perfectly objective' means in this context. Jacob narrows the scope of his 'theology' by insisting that it should concern itself solely with God and his relationship with man and the world. He thereby excludes from the subject matter of the Old Testament theology, piety, religious institutions and ethics. If we take seriously, however, the relationship between God and Israel, and Israel's self-understanding as the 'people of God' as being determinative for Old Testament theology, it is difficult to see how this limitation can do anything other than impoverish the treatment. To omit ethics, for example, is to miss seeing the theological significance of the fact that Israel's ethical outlook is represented in the Old Testament as the ethics of response of the people of God.

Two closely related themes, the presence and the activity of God, control Jacob's systematization of the material under the following headings: Part One, 'Characteristic Aspects of the God of the Old Testament'; Part Two, 'The Action of God according to the Old Testament'; Part Three, and much more briefly, 'Opposition to and Final Triumph of God's Work'. The tension between the broad systematic presentation which Jacob employs and the material within the Old Testament is well exemplified in Part Two. Although he is well aware that faith in God as creator is for the Old Testament theologically secondary to and derived from faith in the God who acts in history, nevertheless he treats God as Creator of the World before he turns to God, the Lord of History. Of course it is true philosophically and theologically that all Israel's experience of God in history could only take place within the framework of prior creation, but it is difficult to see how an adequate theology of the Old Testament can be built upon reversing the order in which knowledge of God came to Israel, particularly when it is emphasized that the theology of the Old Testament, like the history of the religion of Israel, must be basically historical and descriptive in its approach.

The most original, and in many ways the most exciting, Old Testament theology is that of G. von Rad, *Theologie des Alten Testaments*, volume 1 1957, 2 1960 (English translation *Old Testament Theology*, volume 1 1960, 2 1962). In Volume One, subtitled 'The Theology of Israel's Historical Traditions', von Rad, after a brief historical sketch of the different phases in Israel's faith and religious institutions, tackles the question of what the true subject matter of an Old Testament theology ought to be. It cannot be the spiritual or religious world of Israel, or the ideas which she held. At best, such things are only conclusions which we may draw from the documents at our disposal. It must be what Israel herself testified about her God Yahweh. The form-critical, traditio-historical analysis of the Hexateuch (cf. Chapter 2, pp. 72f.) reveals to us at the core of Israel's faith a series of credal statements or testimonies, e.g. Deuteronomy xxvi, 5–9; Joshua xxiv, 2–13. They all witness to certain mighty deeds of Yahweh in Israel's history. Israel's faith is therefore grounded in a theology of history. It points to certain events which come to us shaped and reshaped by faith. Its form is *Heilsgeschichte*. The most legitimate form of theological discourse in the Old Testament is therefore 're-telling', re-telling the mighty deeds of Yahweh in a context of worship, in such a way that they become for ever contemporaneous for faith.

As we have seen (cf. pp. 79ff.), the unified picture which the Old Testament gives us of God acting in Israel's early history, from the promises made to the patriarchs, through deliverance from Egypt and the Sinai covenant, down to the settlement in Canaan, the promised land, is regarded as the end product of a lengthy process of dovetailing and re-interpreting what were once the separate traditions of different tribes. In particular, the Sinai covenant event is notably absent in some of the earliest credal statements, for example, Deuteronomy xxvi, 5–9. If then at the roots of Old Testament tradition we have a series of different, and originally unrelated witnesses to God, must we not say that von Rad has solved one of the major problems in Old Testament theology by side-stepping it? Has he not simply given up the search for some unifying centre within the Old Testament and left us, not with a theology of the Old Testament, but with a series of theologies in the Old Testament? To this von Rad in one sense is prepared to plead guilty. 'The most urgent task today', he claims, 'is that of avoiding all conceptions of unity which are not fully authenticated by the material itself. This appears to me as the surest way to a better understanding of what was characteristic of ancient Israelite conceptions of God' (volume 2, p. 427). Nevertheless he has his own conviction concerning what unites Israel's divergent testimonies to God. Further work may be necessary on what may be described as the typical element in Yahwism, but if we examine Israel's historical traditions closely the essential subject of Old Testament theology is clearly seen to be 'the living word of Yahweh coming on and on to Israel for ever, and this was the message witnessed to by his mighty acts. It was a message so living and actual for each moment that it accompanied her on her journey through time, interpreting itself afresh to each generation and informing every generation what it had to do' (volume 1, p. 110).

It is probably wrong to accuse von Rad of taking refuge in Israel's credal testimonies as the only way of coping theologically with the historical scepticism concerning Israel's early traditions which is implied in recent form-critical work to which he himself has so ably contributed. He claims to be directing our attention to the nature of Israel's confessional statements as the only sound basis for a theology of the Old Testament. The theology of the living word of Yahweh which he finds therein would be consistent with either a negative or a positive attitude to the history which lies behind such testimonies.

Following the historical traditions within the Old Testament, von Rad sees Yahweh's saving acts unfolded in two great cycles of events, the one spanning the period from Abram to Joshua, the other centring on the advent of the monarchy and the Davidic royal family. It is not only these saving acts, however, which are of theological significance, but also Israel's answer to them. Not only did Israel testify to what God had done, but she responded in praise, in questioning and in complaint. This enables the Psalms and the Wisdom literature, Proverbs, Job and Ecclesiastes, to be given their place within the structure of Old Testament theology.

In volume 2, subtitled 'The Theology of Israel's Prophetic Traditions', von Rad, after a historical survey of prophecy in the Old Testament, analyses with great clarity precisely why prophecy occupies such a dominant role in his theology. The prophets mark a decisive watershed in the Old Testament. Although the old credal testimonies were normative for their faith, the prophets see that these credal traditions are no longer adequate for Israel. The guilt of the community had cancelled their effectiveness; the old pattern of faith no longer dominates the nation's life. Hence the prophets looked for a new act of God in the future. 'The prophetic message differs from all previous Israelite theology, which was based on the past saving history, in that the prophets looked for the decisive factor in Israel's whole existence – her life or her death – in some future event' (volume 2, p. 117). This future event might be described in categories drawn from Israel's past, a new Exodus, a new covenant, a new Davidic king, but it is eschatological in the sense that Israel has been ejected from the security of the past to find the basis of her salvation in a future act of God.

Volume 2 concludes with a discussion of the relationship between the Old Testament and the New. Central to the discussion is the character of the Old Testament itself as von Rad analysed it. In the Old Testament we find a continuous reshaping and re-interpretation of Israel's early traditions. In particular, in the prophets there is a radical break with the old traditions. They take such traditions with greater seriousness than many of their contemporaries yet give them a predictive character. The old here becomes a 'type' of the new, pointing towards it. What we find in the New Testament, and in the remarkable freedom with which New Testament writers treat the Old, is precisely the same kind of re-interpretation, the Old grasped anew in the light of Jesus Christ, the Old a 'type' of the New. This general principle von Rad proceeds to spell out in terms of the Old Testament understanding of the world and man, saving event and law.

No brief summary can do justice to the wealth of scholarship and insight which mark von Rad's theology. It is generally recognized to be one of the great books on Old Testament theology even by those who dissent most strongly from some of its presuppositions. More than any other comparable work, it shows the way in which there can be a marriage of true minds between radical critical scholarship and theological insight, a marriage which, far from leading to uneasy tension, produces new depths of insight. His Theology could not have been written except on the basis of a full acceptance of the picture of Israel's historical traditions which has emerged from recent form-critical studies. Yet it must be recognized that his approach raises serious questions. To take but two:

There is a deep ambiguity in the phrase 'theology of the Old Testament'. We may use it in the sense in which we speak of the 'theology of Aeschylus' or 'Babylonian theology', that is to say, a purely descriptive account of what was believed about God, without raising the question of the validity or otherwise of such beliefs. On the other hand we may use it in such a way that the question of truth and the ultimate validity of such beliefs is involved. It is in this latter sense that von Rad seems to use it since, as a Christian, he is concerned with the relationship between the Old and the New Testaments and the continuing relevance of the Old for Christian belief and practice. Let us grant that in terms of a purely descriptive approach, much of the Old Testament is historical narrative. To us it is very peculiar history; history described in terms of God's activity. The Exodus, for example, is not the escape of some Hebrew slaves out of Egypt; it is the mighty act of a God who delivers these slaves for his own purposes. Why should this description be in any sense normative for us today? What makes an event an 'act of God'? May not the Israelites themselves have been deceived when they used this kind of language? Indeed is there not an element of deception built into such description, if what is here recounted as the story of God's mighty acts for Israel bears little relationship to the factual content of Israel's early history?

The extent to which God's activity in history can be applied to the whole of the Old Testament is open to serious doubt. Many books in the Old Testament are not historical narratives; and in some of them, e.g. Proverbs, Job, Ecclesiastes, Song of Songs, there is no concern at all for history. Von Rad himself is aware of this and tries to make a theological virtue of it. He claims that this emphasis is often present implicitly where it is not explicit. This is true in many of the Psalms. Where it is absent its very absence produces serious theological dilemmas as in the case of Job and Ecclesiastes. But are we being given a theology of the Old Testament, or only a theology of parts of it, if we are driven, as von Rad is, to say concerning the Wisdom tradition preserved in Proverbs that it only passes over into theology when it contains some kind of pointer to the activity of God or to what pleases or displeases him? This effectively disenfranchises theologically most of Proverbs. May it not be that 'theology' in this case is being too narrowly defined in terms of *Heilsgeschichte*?[7] No one denies that witness to God's activity in history is an important element in Old Testament tradition, but how, for example, is this related to what we may call religious experience or personal encounter with God? Moses' encounter with God at the burning bush is prior to, and in some sense surely decisive for, the Exodus event in the Old Testament. An over-concentration on 'God who acts' may blind us to other equally important characteristics of God in the Old Testament. When the last critical word has been said, however, we may have to confess that it is much easier to criticize than to emulate von Rad's achievement.[8]

OLD TESTAMENT THEOLOGY AND LINGUISTICS

Any Old Testament theology must justify itself at the bar of the text of the Old Testament, by appealing to documents written in Hebrew. It also tends to focus attention on what it believes to be distinctive in the Hebrew outlook on life. Since it has often been argued, or assumed, that the distinctive outlook of a people finds expression in the structure of its language, appeal has been made to the peculiarities of Hebrew as a language to substantiate theological statements. In particular it has been claimed that Hebrew with its emphasis upon verbal rather than nominal forms, and its lack of abstract concepts, points to an attitude towards ultimate reality which is in sharp contrast to the world of Greek thought. This thesis was worked out most systematically by T. Boman, *Hebrew Thought compared with Greek*, 1960 (English translation of *Das Hebraïsche Denken im Vergleich mit dem Greichischen*, second edition 1954).[9] Further, single Hebrew words have often been made the subject of linguistic and lexical analysis and appeal made to their presumed etymology or root meaning as an indication of the meaning which they bear in particular contexts. A good example of this type of argument is to be found in E. Jacob's *Theology of the Old Testament*. After discussing in terms of their root meaning four Hebrew words for man, *'adam, 'ish, 'enosh* and *geber*, he concludes that from these words certain conclusions can be drawn concerning man and his vocation. 'If it is true that *'adam* insists on the human kind, *'enosh* on his feebleness, *'ish* on his power, *geber* on his strength, then we can say that added together they indicate that man according to the Old Testament is a perishable creature, who lives only as a member of a group, but that he is also a powerful being capable of choice and dominion. So the semantic inquiry confirms the general teaching of the Bible on the insignificance and greatness of man.' (op. cit., p. 157). The picture of Old Testament man here drawn may be true, but can it seriously be held that the fact that Hebrew has these four words for man proves it or even supports it? Does this mean that people who spoke a language that did not have four similar words could not have this kind of anthropology?

James Barr in *The Semantics of Biblical Language*, 1961[10] has utilized modern studies in the field of general linguistics to make a vigorous attack on this type of appeal to language to support theological conclusions. He is not concerned necessarily to deny the theological conclusions; he *is* concerned to show that they cannot legitimately derive from, or be strengthened by, the linguistic arguments used. Not only is the correlation between language structure and thought patterns highly dubious, but the Hebrew–Greek contrast is highly misleading since many of the linguistic features noted in the contrast are features which, on the one hand, Hebrew shares with many other Semitic languages, and on the other, Greek shares with many Indo-European languages. Moreover Barr has little difficulty in showing that, in the main, words are not concepts which bear an unchanging, sometimes complex meaning, which can be discovered by examining the ideas surrounding their root. Rather they are 'semantic markers' which depend to a large extent for their meaning on their context in a particular sentence. Anyone who has ever attempted translation work, whether it be from Hebrew into English, or German into French, or from any language into another, knows the truth of this. Many of the worst translation howlers are firmly grounded in an appeal to a dictionary which has indicated the basic meaning of the word. It is the sentence or larger literary unit which is the bearer of theological meaning, claims Barr, not one word or its particular form.

If it is true that words are 'semantic markers' which take their particular meaning from context, then the question of context becomes of vital importance, and may not be quite so simple as Barr sometimes seems to imply. In self-consciously theological documents, for example, the meaning conveyed by words often cannot be adequately grasped by reference to the sentence or even paragraph in which they occur. Their context may be much larger, not only the particular document in which they occur, but the theological tradition within which this writing must be placed. It is by no means impossible, or indeed unlikely that, within such a tradition, whether it be that of a theological school or of liturgical usage, a particular word or group of words may bear a fairly constant meaning which is at least consistent with its root meaning. Barr is heavily dependent on modern linguistic theories, and indeed on one out of several such theories, which may not have said the last word. On occasion he tends to push his argument to the extreme; but there is little doubt that he has issued a salutary warning. Sound Old Testament theology cannot be based on, nor does it need the support of, questionable linguistics.

THE OLD AND THE NEW

It is wrong to assume that the Old Testament only has theological significance when it is seen as part of a whole which includes the New Testament. Much rich contemporary Jewish scholarship – we may mention in particular the work of M. Buber and A. Heschel[11] – is the living disproof of the assumption. Indeed it may be that one of the clamant needs in the field of Old Testament theology at the present day is Jewish–Christian dialogue. All the theologies of the Old Testament, which we have reviewed, however, since they were written by Christians, have in one way or another posited a link between the Old and New Testament. The assumption of such a link becomes explicit in the title of G. A. F. Knight's *A Christian Theology of the Old Testament*, 1959, revised edition 1964. It is written out of the conviction that 'the Old Testament is nothing less than Christian scripture', p. 7. The distinctive thing in Knight's approach is his thesis that, just as there are significant moments in every human life, particularly birth, marriage and death, so in the life of Israel there were five such significant moments, birth at the Exodus, marriage in the covenant between Yahweh and Israel at Sinai, death in the destruction of Jerusalem in 587 B.C., resurrection in the restoration and renewal after the Babylonian exile, and a fifth and final moment to which the prophets witness in hope, the total reconciliation of all things as planned by God (cf. pp. 275 ff.). This makes the Old Testament, according to Knight 'in a most interesting way, the divinely given commentary upon the New Testament' (p. 244), since we find a similar five-moment pattern in the New Testament witness to Jesus. In the case of Jesus, birth and marriage are one moment when in the Baptism of John he has his call and identifies himself with Israel in the purposes of God. The third moment is his crucifixion and death, the fourth moment his resurrection and the fifth moment his second coming.

Knight's talk of the five moments of Israel's life raises difficulties. Is this a necessary or indeed an obvious interpretation of the Old Testament? Does he not rather impose upon the Old Testament a pattern which has either been derived from a particular interpretation of the New Testament, or has been chosen out of several options because it is the most capable of dovetailing into such an interpretation? This is the kind of question which is raised again and again by the detail of Knight's interpretation throughout. It is noteworthy that in neither Eichrodt's nor von Rad's theologies, which from their different standpoints are probably the most thorough analyses of the faith structure of the Old Testament we possess, do we find this five-moment pattern. Nor does New Testament scholarship seem to have worked with it. How far are we justified in such 'Christianizing' of the Old Testament? The process has been carried out with great exegetical ingenuity by W. Vischer in *Das Christuszeugnis des Alten Testaments* (volume 1, 1939, Vol. II 1942, an English translation of volume 1, *The Witness of the Old Testament to Christ*, appearing in 1949).

This is more than an academic issue. It concerns the way in which the Church may legitimately use the Old Testament in its worship, thinking and living. It was a particularly acute issue in the German Church under the Hitler régime when the standing of this Jewish book was seriously called into question. It is no new problem. In the second century, Marcion was calling for the rejection of the Old Testament by the Church on the grounds that the God of the Old Testament was not the God and Father of Jesus. It received classic expression in the light of modern critical interpretation from A. Harnack in a study of *Marcion: Das Evangelium vom fremden Gott* (second edition 1924). 'The rejection of the Old Testament in the second century was a mistake the Greek Church rightly refused to make; the retention of it in the sixteenth century was a fatal legacy which the Reformation could not avoid, but for Protestantism since the nineteenth century to continue to regard it as a canonical document is the result of a paralysis affecting religion and the Church' (op. cit., p. 217).

The problem of hermeneutics, that is to say, the inquiry into what constitutes valid principles of interpretation (in this case the interpretation of the Old Testament within the Church), has been very much to the fore in recent years. Some of the more significant contributions to the discussion, particularly in Germany, have been gathered together in two volumes in the S.C.M. Preacher's Library Series, *Essays in Old Testament Interpretation*, edited by C. Westermann, 1963 (hereafter *Essays*), and *The Old Testament and the Christian Faith*, edited by B. W. Anderson, 1964 (hereafter *O.T.C.F.*). The issues touched upon in these volumes are diverse, far-reaching and not altogether free from obscurity, particularly in the case of the English translation of certain essays which originally appeared in German. Nonetheless there is a certain unity. The *advocatus diaboli* in both cases is R. Bultmann (for his contribution to New Testament studies see pp. 257ff.). In the introductory essay in *O.T.C.F.*, 'The Significance of the Old Testament for the Christian Faith', an essay first published in 1938, Bultmann dismisses as theologically irrelevant any consideration of the Old Testament–New Testament religious relationship in historical terms. He looks at the Old Testament in terms of what he calls 'the basic possibility it represents for an understanding of human existence' (p. 13). The Gospel cannot really be grasped unless we first see the demand which God continually makes upon man. This unconditional divine demand, although it may come to man in other ways, comes with peculiar clarity in the Old Testament, particularly in the teaching of the prophets. Here Bultmann is following a strong Lutheran tradition, which has its roots in Pauline theology. It contrasts the Old and New in terms of 'Law' and 'Gospel', 'Law' being regarded as the necessary presupposition for life lived under the Gospel.

Bultmann is well aware that 'Law', in the sense of the demand God makes, is in the Old Testament found within a framework of grace. The Exodus, the deliverance of a people out of captivity, precedes the demands made upon them in terms of the covenant at Mt Sinai. There is thus Gospel in the Old Testament, as there is also hope and promise, but, claims Bultmann, it is often ambiguous. In particular it suffers from a nationalistic limitation and distortion, since it is directed towards the life of one nation, the Hebrews. The faith of the New Testament is different; it is a faith which has found fulfilment. It gathers up into itself all the elements of hope and promise in the Old Testament, but is free from all the ambiguities and limitations inherent in the Old. 'Jesus', he claims, 'is God's demonstration of grace in a manner which is fundamentally different from the demonstrations of divine grace attested in the Old Testament' (p. 29). Here we find God's eschatological deed of forgiveness, an immediate word to us, to everyman. For the Christian, therefore, the Old Testament can no longer be revelation in the same way as it was and still is for the Jew. We can indeed enter into historical dialogue with the Old Testament events, but they are merely events in the history of the Ancient Near East. We are no more entitled to describe the Exodus as our history than to say that the Spartans fell at Thermopylae for us, or that Socrates drank hemlock for us. The Old Testament is not God's word for the Church in any direct sense; but the Church may use it as such in an indirect way, in bringing us to the point where we can understand God's word to us in Christ. It can only be thus used provided that attention is paid to proper historico–critical methods of interpretation, and all resort to allegorical interpretation shunned.

In 'Prophecy and Fulfilment', (*Essays*, first published in 1949, pp. 50–70) he surveys the way in which New Testament writers appeal to Old Testament prophecy and rejects it as theologically irrelevant and critically untenable. His thesis of a radical discontinuity between the Old and New Testaments is illustrated by analysing three key Old Testament concepts, covenant, kingdom of God and people of God. In its equation of the people of God with a particular nation, in its bringing God's activity, both in terms of covenant and kingly rule into line with the empirical history of that nation, the Old Testament message can only be described as a miscarriage containing within it promise which finds its fulfilment in the eschatological teaching of the New Testament; 'faith requires the backward glance into the Old Testament as a history of failure and so of promise in order to know that the situation of the justified man arises only on the basis of this miscarriage' (*Essays*, p. 70).

Bultmann's arguments are important because they spring from two basic premises which no Christian would wish to dispute: the centrality of Jesus for Christian faith, however that centrality may be conceived, and the element of contrast and discontinuity between the Old and New Testaments. It may be doubted, however, whether he has correctly stated or defined these premises. In the first place we may ask whether Bultmann's essays tell us more about the Old Testament or about his own theological position in the light of which he interprets, and as some would say misinterprets, the New Testament. When Bultmann sets out to examine the Old Testament for the 'basic possibilities it presents for an understanding of human existence', he is using the language of modern existentialism. His whole approach to the New Testament is deeply influenced by this (see New Testament section pp. 333ff.). As J. L. McKenzie, a Roman Catholic scholar, puts it in *O.T.C.F.*, p. 105 f. 'The significance of the Old Testament for Christian faith is determined by what one's Christian faith is. The existentialist faith of Bultmann is not the faith of Roman Catholicism; and his own exposition of the significance of the Old Testament, consequently, is not the exposition which a Roman Catholic would present, even if the Roman Catholic were existentialist in his thinking' (cf. G. E. Wright, *O.T.C.F.*, p. 177). This is a frank plea for the recognition of the different presuppositions we bring to the handling of the Old Testament even within the Christian household of faith. Marcion, having decided that the God of the Old Testament was not the God of the New, had to operate with a very restricted New Testament, so much of it being contaminated with Old Testament ideas. Harnack was inevitably troubled with the Old Testament because, true to a certain type of liberal Protestantism, he had reduced the Gospel to the Fatherhood of God and the Brotherhood of man. Bultmann's particular difficulty with the Old Testament is closely related to his existentialist interpretation of the Christian faith.

In the second place we may ask whether, in his concentration on the discontinuity between the Old and the New Testament message, he has been blind to real elements of continuity. To take but two points:

The essential historical continuity between the Old and New Testaments is of far greater theological relevance than Bultmann admits. From the standpoint of the New Testament, Jesus appears as the climatic event in the history of Israel, the goal and meaning of that particular history and of no other. That history claims significance in its entirety precisely because from beginning to end it is the story of the unfolding of the activity and purposes of a God of a particular character. The theological problem, therefore, is whether in the light of this we can ever dispense with historical symbols in our witness to God, whether in fact it is the God of Abraham, Moses, the prophets, the God of Israel who is the God and Father of Jesus Christ (see F. Voegelin *O.T.C.F.*, pp. 64–89, G. E. Wright, *O.T.C.F.*, pp. 176 ff.). Similarly what we find in the Old Testament is not merely the 'imperative of the divine command', but commandments stamped with a particular character, and this character is closely related to what is believed about God in Israel. Thus Deuteronomy commands 'you shall love Yahweh your God with all your heart . . .' (vi, 5), because Deuteronomy sees the character of God in his relationship with Israel summed up in the word 'love' (cf. Deuteronomy vii, 6–11). The demand of Leviticus is for the people to be holy, 'because I, Yahweh your God, am holy' (Leviticus xix, 2; xx, 7; xxi, 8). The prophets demand national righteousness of a certain quality because Yahweh is a God characterized by this kind of righteousness. There is no understanding of the basic possibilities of existence in the Old Testament which is not directly related to the Old Testament witness to God. This is the pattern which we find likewise in the New Testament, whether in the Sermon on the Mount with its call to be 'perfect as your heavenly Father is perfect' (Matthew v, 48) or in the '*imitatio Christi*' for which Paul pleads in Philippians ii.

Bultmann concludes an essay entitled 'The Concept of Revelation in the New Testament'[12] with the words 'in response to the question what the New Testament understands by revelation, it (i.e. the New Testament) asks the counter question whether it itself is heard as revelation'. Repeatedly he insists that the New Testament message only becomes fully the Word of God, existentially real, when it is grasped in faith. It is strange that he does not see the same point made within the Old Testament. Whatever the Old Testament historical traditions may be, they do not come to us merely as events in Ancient Near Eastern history. They *are* that, but more. Not only particular events, for example the call of Abram, the Exodus, and the destruction of Jerusalem, but also the entire sweep of Israel's history, are interpreted in the light of faith and are of continuing significance only in so far as they are grasped by faith. Israel knew this. The covenant at Mt Sinai/Horeb is not merely a past event but an ever repeatable event. Deuteronomy v, 2 f. declares 'Yahweh our God made a covenant with us in Horeb. Not with our fathers did Yahweh make this covenant, but with us who are all of us here alive today.' Israel of every generation could be at Horeb and relive, reactualize the covenant experience, but only on the basis of a response of faith and obedience to the God who had there first made covenant with his people (see especially M. Noth in *Essays*, pp. 76–88).

We do not rightly understand the Old Testament – and this must be said over against the nationalistic limitation and distortion which Bultmann strongly emphasizes – until we realize that for the Old Testament, the nation of Israel and the people of God are not synonymous. The people of God was always that community of faith *within* Israel which responded to the God who came in the events of Israel's history. The contrast between the nation Israel, and Israel the people of God, could be sharply pointed. The prophet Jeremiah spoke and acted to ensure the downfall of the Judean state because he believed that only through the political destruction of the nation could the people be liberated to find again their destiny as the people of God (cf. Jeremiah xxxvii; xxxviii). It is of course possible to read the Old Testament in such a way that it is never anything other than ancient history, but it is equally possible so to read the New Testament. To rephrase Bultmann, we may say 'in response to the question what does the Old Testament understand by revelation, it asks the counter question whether it itself is heard as revelation!'

If we accept that the Old Testament and the New Testament witness to God are basically one, how do we express this in terms of our use and interpretation of the Old Testament? Does it mean that in the light of modern historico-critical methods 'every form of allegory is idle talk or nonsense' (Bultmann, *O.T.C.F.*, p. 33). If allegory is banned, what of its sister typology? It is important at this point to try to define terms carefully. The distinction between allegory and typology has usually been drawn in the following way. For allegory, history as such is of little importance, and the literal meaning of any text irrelevant. The records of the past, the documents being used are important because they provide us with illustrations or corroboration of truths which we already know from another source. Thus Abram's 318 retainers (Genesis xiv, 14) are important to the *Epistle of Barnabas* because 318, when converted into Greek letters, signified 'Christ crucified'; presumably 318 palm trees at

Jericho, or 318 gods and goddesses in some Ancient Near Eastern pantheon, would have served this argument equally well. Within Christian tradition, allegory became, notably in anti-Jewish controversy, a useful exegetical tool for proving that the Christian gospel lay hidden in the Old Testament.[13]

Typology does claim to take history seriously. Looking at events from some decisive viewpoint it sees previous events as an anticipation of what it holds to be the decisive event. Thus, if within the pattern of faith of the Old Testament the Exodus is the demonstration of God's saving initiative in Israel's history, it becomes in the teaching of Second Isaiah a 'type' of a new coming demonstration of that same initiative which he proclaims to a people once again in enslavement (Isaiah xl, 3–5; xli, 17–20; lii, 11–12). Later it becomes a type of that greater deliverance which the New Testament claims to see accomplished in and through Jesus.[14]

While few Old Testament scholars today are prepared to revive allegory as a way of interpreting the Old Testament, except in so far as certain passages within the Old Testament may be examples of allegory, there is considerable divergence of opinion over typology. There are those who argue that 'for the sake of scientific veracity, typological and Christological interpretation today is an anachronism which cannot be permitted' (F. Baumgartel, *Essays*, p. 150, cf. F. Hesse, *Essays*, pp. 283–313). G. von Rad, however, sees in typology 'the simple correspondence to the belief that the same God who revealed himself in Christ has left his footprints on the history of the covenant people' (*Essays*, p. 36, cf. H. W. Wolff, *Essays*, pp. 160–99, W. Vischer, *O.T.C.F.*, pp. 90–101 and much more cautiously W. Eichrodt, *Essays*, pp. 224–41).

Typology is being used by many today as a valid protest against a narrowly literal and historical approach to the Old Testament which seemed to rob it of everything but limited historical value. It has, however, its dangers. There is the danger of regarding an Old Testament event or character as important solely because of the way in which it is usable as a type, pointing forward to the New Testament. If this happens then we are in danger of no longer listening to what that event meant as revelation in its own particular context in the life of Israel. How then can we ever know whether it may still be heard as revelation today? Typology also carries with it the danger of limiting our vision, by leading us to concentrate too exclusively on the parts of the Old Testament in which we find easily recognizable correspondence to the New Testament. But the Old Testament is painted on a much broader historical and literary canvas than the New Testament. It explores, for example, the response of faith to social change, and realms of protest and doubt, witness Job and Jeremiah, which are not easily paralleled in the New Testament. We need first to listen to the faith of Israel in all its richness and complexity, its depth and its shallowness. This is a *sine qua non* of any sympathetic interpretation whether it be by Jew, Christian, Moslem or humanist. Then only will we be in a position to decide for or against the verdict of the author of the Letter to the Hebrews: 'In many and diverse ways God spoke of old to our fathers by the prophets, but in these last days he has spoken to us by a Son . . .' (Hebrews i, 1–2).

The problem of hermeneutics is very much one of the 'in' subjects of the contemporary theological scene. So much is discussed in terms of general principles that the debate as far as the Old Testament is concerned often seems confused and confusing. One prominent Old Testament scholar has been known seriously, though somewhat facetiously, to describe hermeneutics as 'the science of interpreting the Bible without having read it!' At the end of the day the proof of the pudding is in the eating. Can the general principles discussed be converted into guidelines for the interpretation of specific passages, particularly passages such as Psalm cxxxvii with its vindictive ending, and the story of Saul's slaughter of the Amalekites in 1 Samuel xv, which are immediately offensive to the Christian conscience? Two recent volumes, J. D. Smart, *The Old Testament in Dialogue with Modern Man*, Epworth, 1965 and J. Bright, *The Authority of the Old Testament*, S.C.M. Press, 1967, have attempted this marriage of responsible critical handling of text with a theological interpretation which, not shirking the difficulties, still believes that the Old Testament has something relevant to say for faith today. We need much more of this, both in specialized studies and in new commentaries. We need it because, as has been well said, 'a theology of the Old Testament, properly so called, is possible only through some kind of participation, so that we come to take the God of the Old Testament quite seriously as God'.[15] If it is no longer possible to believe this then we ought to cease talking about Old Testament theology.

The New Testament
by A. R. C. Leaney

Six

New Discoveries:
Archaeology and
History

Man's intense desire to understand himself has taken remarkable forms in the last thirty years; subjects like ancient history and philosophy, once assumed to be the preserve of scholars and un-coveted by practical men, are now popular in the lists of evening classes. Highly significant is the thirst for knowledge of the past, evidenced in the enormous interest taken in archaeology. It is as if we hoped to find something dug up from the past which will answer insistent questions about the present. A similar interest is shown in the New Testament: an uneasy feeling that it contains a clue to the riddle of the universe, if only because some persist in claiming that it contains *the* clue to that riddle, led many to buy the New English Bible version of the New Testament, often, it seems, with the wistful hope that because it was 'new' it would reveal the real facts contained in it and render them intelligible at last to 'modern man'. Any who bought the volume with such a hope must have been acutely disappointed: however ingeniously the translators had transformed what are virtually technical terms into modern-sounding phrases, often they found themselves defeated in their laudable attempt to make everything plain. Nothing could be a more eloquent example of the hopelessness of a translation adequate for such a task than the opening of the Gospel according to John, which still contains even in this modern translation the mysterious words, 'the Word became flesh'.

There will probably always be those 'simple Christians' to whom the gospel, in spite of its expression in terms no longer current, is clear and compelling (and some of these may be identical with those whose most familiar aspect is that of the learned scholar); but genuine intellectual puzzlement with unfamiliar language is widespread. It can be removed by explanation rather than by exhortation. Such explanations must always include relating the documents of the New Testament to the world in which they arose.

A great deal about the world of the New Testament has been always known to scholars: the great commentaries of such scholars as Wellhausen, Harnack, Lightfoot, Westcott[1] and many others throw abundant light upon the milieu in which the writings were produced. Reference to Josephus the Jewish historian,[2] to Philo the Jewish philosopher of Alexandria,[3] and to classical authors illuminated the world of thought in which these books were written. Less well-known to the general student was the fascinating information to be derived from comparison with contemporary Judaism, which afforded often far more relevant clues to the meaning of the concepts and phrases common in the New Testament but without parallel in secular writing. Since Jesus and his earliest followers were all Jews, whose political outlook was bounded by the tiny state of Judea and by the history of its almost always disastrous contacts with far greater powers, it is important to stress the contribution made by those scholars who have familiarized themselves with Jewish thought contemporary with the events which brought the New Testament into being. Further, those who by historical and archaeological research have brought to light new, or brought to life old, knowledge make in our time a contribution of enormous value to our understanding, if we will give a little time to assimilating their discoveries and to relating them to writings which are familiar but in modern days less and less understood.

In order to appreciate such work, we must present a summary of the events surrounding the birth of the New Testament. In the ancient world the time round the year 200 B.C. was important: Rome had broken the power of Carthage in 202, and turned her attention to the east, partly because the Carthaginian Hannibal, exiled for his failure in 195, took refuge with Antiochus the Great of Syria, descendant of Alexander the Great's general Seleucus and inheritor of his portion of Alexander's huge and swiftly won empire. When Antiochus was killed in 187 B.C. he had lost to

Rome a considerable part of his empire but that which he passed on to his sons was still vast and included Syria and Palestine. The eventual successor after some violent intrigues was Antiochus IV ('Epiphanes') whose attempts to unify the culture of his empire constituted for the Jews a cruel oppression against which the rise of the Maccabees was the most clear-cut and best known reaction. It is less well-known that an intrigue begun under the immediate successor of Antiochus the Great, Seleucus IV (the elder brother of 'Epiphanes'), involving the Temple treasure and the office of its priest, resulted in the murder in 171 B.C. of the legitimate high priest, Onias II, presumed to be a descendant of Zadok of the time of Solomon. This was the first specifically religious trauma inflicted on the Jews in the time of the Seleucids. The second was inflicted by order of Antiochus Epiphanes himself; this was the deliberate defilement of the Temple by offering a pagan sacrifice on the altar of burnt-offering in 168. The heroism and success of the early Maccabees in their revolt, for which this sacrilege was the flash-point, was succeeded by bloodthirsty tyranny in the later leaders of this house, who arrogated to themselves the title of high priest as a step to their eventual claim to kingship. Since they were not Zadokites, and their line was further debased by foreign blood, this was a great offence to strict Jews, and it is no wonder that some of them, weighing the defilement of the Temple as well as the cruelty and technical disqualifications of the secular ruler, concluded that Israel, the people of God, could survive as such only if recreated entirely.

The wilderness was the obvious place for such a recreation, in conscious imitation of Moses and the early life of Israel after their deliverance from Egypt, and it was apparently enjoined by the words of Isaiah xl, 3: 'In the wilderness make a way for the Lord'. Some were ready to undertake this exacting task and retired to an ascetic life in the wilderness at a place subsequently known as Qumran, in a barren spot on the north-west shore of the Dead Sea about five miles from Jericho. The place might have been suspected to possess historical importance, for it seems to have been known to Pliny the Elder[4] who refers to it accurately enough in his *Natural History* (5.15) and says it is the dwelling-place of the Essenes. He may have been right in this; even if he was wrong about the name of the sect whom he describes briefly and trenchantly, we now know that there was a sect living there from about 160 B.C. to A.D. 68. For it was in caves associated with the ruined buildings at Qumran (subsequently excavated and shown to have been occupied during this period by a considerable group of people) that the famous Dead Sea Scrolls were found, the first among them accidentally in 1947 by a Bedouin lad, and others since then both by Bedouin and by archaeologists in search of them.

These scrolls are the scriptures of just such a sect as has been described, a number of earnest and very strict Jews who were appalled by the lawless and unclean state into which Israel had sunk, and were convinced that all was soon to be set right, in favour of the few righteous, by divine intervention. They believed indeed that there would yet be great activity on the part of evil forces, pagan persecutors and renegade fellow-countrymen assisted by fallen spiritual powers; but the present period of history, when Belial wields power over the world, is part of a schematized sequence of events which God will shortly bring to an end. Two Messiahs, one priestly and the other secular, are to be expected in the end of the age, and their forerunner has already come in the person of the Teacher of Righteousness, a member of the sect who arose twenty years after its foundation and became a highly respected leader, and is now dead. All these beliefs, together with their Rule, or way of life, they derived from a profound searching and special interpretation of the scriptures.

Such an explanation of the people of the scrolls will perhaps suffice, for all its brevity, to show how natural it is that these writings should possess the character which they have revealed on being examined. Since they belonged to a Jewish sect, they naturally include books of the Bible, that is of what Christians call the Old Testament. Every book is represented except that of Esther, but some in very fragmentary form. One manuscript contains virtually the whole of the book of Isaiah and its text does not differ in any substantial degree from the standard text already known (see p. 105 in O.T. section). This fact is of great interest to biblical scholars, for they now have evidence of the state of the text of the Old Testament at a stage one thousand years before the oldest manuscripts known to exist before the discovery of the scrolls. Since the scriptures were their authority, but needed divinely guided interpretation, it is natural that one very intriguing class of scroll found at Qumran was the commentary. Modern theologians make commentaries on the Bible, and sometimes think that only their comments are right, now found out and published for the first time. Few commentators have been so downright and certain of their interpretations as the men of Qumran. One of the main works of this kind is a *Commentary on Habakkuk*; the commentator quotes a few verses of the prophet and then says very confidently, 'its meaning is . . .', and follows with a reference to recent history, events closely connected with the sect. This is a very important point about the scrolls: their authors thought that they were living at the divinely appointed end of the age, and that *they* had been divinely appointed as the 'sons of light' to assist in winding it up. When the end of the age came, the new Israel they had been trying to form would be established and all wickedness would be abolished. The word just translated 'meaning' in the phrase 'its meaning is' is the Hebrew word *pesher*, so scholars sometimes like to call these scrolls *pesher* scrolls. The *pesher* which the commentator gives is quite obviously not that which the prophet originally intended, as we can see easily enough for ourselves by reading the scrolls in such a book as *The Dead Sea Scrolls in English*.[5] This is important: the sectarians believed that secrets had been hidden in the scriptures by God and that they needed a specially gifted man to discern their true meaning, which, they believed, went 'beyond what the prophets have said'. Other commentaries which we possess are more fragmentary than that on Habakkuk; two of the most important are a *Commentary on Psalm 37* and a *Commentary on Nahum*. They provided some useful clues about the history of the sect, clues however about which there is much disagreement as to their significance.

Passing on to scrolls not quite so closely linked with the Bible as we usually think of it, we find there are some manuscripts of books of the Apocrypha represented at Qumran. The Apocrypha is rather a curious collection of works – in this sense, that no two great branches of the Church quite agree on which books ought to be in it, even after making clear that to put them in this category gives them only second-class status. A good illustration of the varying fortunes of such books is provided by the *Book of Enoch* (or *I Enoch*); this composite writing was once regarded as proper holy scripture, and it may be surprising to some to recall that we know this is so because it is quoted as though it were authoritative in our New Testament, in the Letter of Jude. Yet it wandered off to Abyssinia, was forgotten in its original Greek form for ages, and never entered the canon of the western Church. In other words, it is not even in the Apocrypha in our Bibles. There are a number of books of this kind which are very interesting because they show us the way in which religious people were thinking in the first two centuries before the Christian era. Some we have always known about and have been able to study in order to see the character of religious thought in what we call the intertestamental period. Two more such books may be mentioned as examples, the *Book of Jubilees* (a kind of rewritten Genesis) and the *Testaments of the Twelve Patriarchs*. The great scholar of this kind of literature in our country in the nineteenth and early twentieth centuries was R. H. Charles. With the help of other scholars he published two huge volumes, the first containing the Apocrypha, the second containing works of the kind under discussion, called in an omnibus way Pseudepigrapha[6] (which means writings which are attributed to writers who did not really write them). One of these works seemed mysterious: it seemed to be about a sect otherwise unknown and they seemed to be much taken up with the sons of Zadok as possessing authority as true priests, that is, true members of the family from which alone the high priest ought to be chosen. Charles called it *Fragments of a Zadokite Work*. He was absolutely right, although he worked long before the scrolls were discovered. It seems that this tract was written by the men of Qumran. It describes them, their history (though in a rather cryptic fashion) and their rules; for in the caves fragments have turned up which evidently belong to this writing. Certainly men of Qumran set great store by the Zadokite priesthood and sometimes called the whole sect 'Sons of Zadok'. Because this writing mentions a sojourn of 'the penitents of Israel' in the land of Damascus (perhaps meaning Damascus literally, perhaps referring to their going into the desert) it is usually called now the *Damascus Document*, or *Damascus Rule*, because it contains as part of its content rules for living in the community. This *Rule* envisages a way of life which could be lived in families and in different towns and villages. It might apply to the movement of Essenes in general. Another document which was totally unknown before, and which was one of those which came out of Cave 1, is often called the *Manual of Discipline*, but sometimes appropriately the *Community Rule* or the *Rule of Qumran*. Like the *Damascus Document* it is composite, but is composed of rules and liturgy, with at least one striking passage of doctrine about the two spirits which rule and guide mankind for their good or ill; it does not contain any history. Like all those mentioned so far, most of the scrolls are in Hebrew, but in Cave 1 one was in Aramaic, the language of the same family as Hebrew, more widely spread over the fertile crescent of the Middle East, and the usual language of everyday speech in Palestine in New Testament times, and therefore the mother tongue of Jesus and his disciples. This scroll, written in Aramaic, has been called the *Genesis Apocryphon*. It fills out imaginatively the story of Abraham, and contains some flattering descriptions of Sarah which caught the journalists' imagination when it was first published, and, apparently contained in a part which is all too fragmentary (and which is reminiscent of part of the *Book of Enoch*), a description of the appearance of Noah at his birth, whose wonderful aspect frightened his father Lamech into thinking that his wife had borne the child to a demon. Two points emerge here: the first is the doctrine about demons or fallen angels which is implied. The story in the beginning of Genesis vi about the fallen angels received some amplification in *I Enoch* and *Jubilees*, books which have already been mentioned; and this feature of the *Genesis Apocryphon* is one of several pieces

175

of evidence that the men of Qumran took seriously the role and significance of angels, both good and bad, in the universe. The second point is that we may have here further evidence of the one-time existence of a *Book of Noah*, part of which Charles felt sure was to be found in the *Book of Jubilees* as it has come down to us.

The passage about the two spirits in the *Rule* is very interesting; they are the spirits respectively of truth and of perversity, and mankind is divided according as they belong to one or the other. The details of this belief are not clear, but it is clear that the author believed that those who belonged to the spirit of truth were adversely affected by the spirit of perversity and caused to stumble by him. The doctrine is closely related to two strands of thought which are easily understood: the summons expressed in Deuteronomy xxx,15 ff. to choose good and to reject evil, and the related belief in a conflict in the spiritual world between the Spirit (or spirits) of God and the demonic beings, once 'Sons of God', who oppose them and him. It is therefore related to the 'Two Ways' of the *Didache* and the *Epistle of Barnabas* (early Christian works of the late first or early second century),[7] to the Jewish doctrine of the evil and good 'inclination', and to the concept of the struggle of light versus darkness. To these ideas we must add that of cleanness. All Jews of the time desired ceremonial cleanness; they had come to believe not only the rather primitive notion that some things, such as dead bodies, wounds and their discharge, excrement, and so on, rendered a man ceremonially unclean (the reason why the priest and Levite had to avoid going too near the wounded man in Jesus' story of the Good Samaritan). They had made a rather interesting advance in thinking that moral sins not only needed repentance and actions which showed repentance, but also defiled a man just as those other things, which we should call taboos, defiled a man. This is why John the Baptist practised baptism (ceremonial washing) *and* insisted on 'fruits worthy of repentance'. The men of Qumran emphasized very strongly this idea of cleanness, not distinguishing as we should the moral from the ceremonial cause of defilement. For them it would be as bad to eat meat with the blood in it as to steal something. It was probably their horror at the defilement of the Temple and of the high priesthood which led them to lay such an emphasis on this idea of cleanness. Thus they value highly a spirit of holiness, and we can see that this means something rather different from the Christian idea of the Holy Spirit, although the two ideas approach one another. For example, if a man has the Holy Spirit he will be pure from sin, and this is rather like, though not the same as, having a spirit of holiness. The final thought about cleanness or holiness is that at the end of the age God would purify for himself some of mankind by pouring upon them a spirit of holiness like purifying water.

Since the sect thought as it did about mankind and its divisions, and believed it was to be ready to fight for God in the final war of the age, it is not at all surprising that one of their scrolls should be about *The War of the Sons of Light against the Sons of Darkness*, in which the organization of the sect and the method of fighting to be employed are set out in elaborate detail. This document shows how the sect thought of itself as like the old Israel in the wilderness in the days of Moses, and also how seriously they took their duty to be prepared for the final war of all time.

Another important scroll which came out of Cave 1 is a collection of hymns or psalms, using often the language and phrases of the Old Testament Psalms. It is called the *Psalms of Thanksgiving*, since each one begins with 'I thank thee, O God . . .' From this collection of hymns we can learn a great deal about the sect: their sense of being specially chosen by God to represent his people at the end of the age; their sense that this was due to the grace of God and no merit of their own; their sense of the utter helplessness and worthlessness of man before God, so that only God is righteous; their apparent experience of persecution and of solidarity as an elect group; and things of this kind which reflect the basic doctrines of the Old Testament, especially those which can be distilled from the book of Isaiah and which we find also in a special form in the New Testament. There is even the same sense of being chosen by God which lends itself to interpretation as a consistent and watertight doctrine of predestination, though neither in the scrolls nor in the New Testament is this actually intended. Another and very important feature of the *Psalms of Thanksgiving* is that, contrary perhaps to the impression given so far, they are very personal; that is, they are the utterances of an individual. He speaks for his community but at times speaks poignantly for himself alone. He gives the impression of a leader whose position made him sometimes feel lonely, and who had powerful enemies to resist. We are therefore interested in his identification and we shall return to this matter.

In Cave 3 was found the Copper Scroll. This had been formed from three plates of copper, joined by rivets and then inscribed and rolled up as though it had been of parchment or some other usual writing material. When found it had broken at the second line of rivets and looked at first like two scrolls. Great care and much technical skill were needed to preserve this scroll, which had completely oxidized, but it was successfully preserved and cut into strips, the only way to 'unroll' it without destroying it. It was then found to be a list in Hebrew of buried treasures, with indications where they were to be found. The treasure was in gold, silver and perfumes. No one can be certain whether this is a work of the imagination or a real list of real treasures, perhaps those smuggled out of the Temple before its destruction.

Caves 4 to 10 are different from the other caves. 1 to 3 are apparently natural caves but these, 4 to 10, are man-made in the marl terrace at the foot of the cliffs which are really the sides of the Judaean hills. This terrace stretches out in three blunt prongs towards the Dead Sea, looking rather like the clumsy foot of some huge pachyderm. The caves made in this part of the terrain no doubt supplemented as living quarters or store-rooms the buildings which have been mentioned, but about which we have yet to say a little more. It is very sad that the local Bedouin tribesmen are totally unable to understand that such finds as fragmentary old manuscripts are priceless to scholars because of their historical value; they therefore suspect that there is some hidden wealth in them, get first to any cave they can, steal the contents and then sell them through an agent in Bethlehem. This arrangement has been accepted perforce by the archaeologists. The tribesmen do not know how to treat their finds so as to preserve them from damage; we have therefore to accept the fact that a great deal has been and will remain wholly lost to us. The way of working has been that the archaeologists get all they can and recover by purchase if necessary.

Cave 4 was the most fruitful of all the caves, but the haul was in an indescribable muddle. From time to time a scholar entrusted with the piecing together of a number of fragments finds that he has probably completed his task as far as this is possible and publishes the result in a learned journal. Here we shall indicate the kinds of scrolls found, mostly fragmentary, in the famous Cave 4. The Bible is well represented, and it is because of the finds in this cave that we can say with so much confidence that the sect read all the Old Testament with the possible exception of Esther, which has not been found. There are also commentaries on books of the Bible, and then many of these works which we have described as being so near to and yet not part of the 'official' Bible; there is the *Book of Tobit* (which is in our Apocrypha), the *Book of Jubilees*, the *Psalms of Joshua*, and other works written as though they were by a famous figure of the past, though without intent to deceive, pseudo-Jeremianic works, *I Enoch*, and most interestingly fragments of the *Testaments of Levi* and *Naphtali* in Aramaic. We possessed the *Testaments of the Twelve Patriarchs* before only in Greek and knew it to be a translation. Now we are free to wonder if this book was not built up gradually, various authors writing separate 'Testaments' in the name of this or that patriarch. This way of writing a religious tract is interesting because something like it may be seen in the New Testament. Both Jude and 2 Peter can be thought of as fictitious testaments of this kind.

Cave 4 contained also editions of the *Rule* and the *Damascus Document*, books of laws, numerous liturgical works, hymns, wisdom literature and calendrical works. The calendar was a matter of great importance to the sect. Other Jews regulated their calendar and therefore their festivals (an all-important part of their religion) by a lunar calendar. The men of Qumran used a solar calendar, and made an issue of it; in their view the moon was unreliable, and the sun had been set in the heavens to change the point of his rising and setting against the heavenly background by divine decree so that feast days could be observed, and (they thought) would thus fall regularly on the same day and date each year. As may well be guessed, they thought of the equinoxes and solstices as very important days of the year. The calendar by which they went is to be found in *I Enoch*. It is in a separable section and may have been composed by one of the leaders of the sect.

This discovery at Qumran of the already-known solar calendar has stimulated discussion of an important aspect of the narrative in the gospels about the Last Supper; how are the accounts in the synoptic gospels, Mark, Matthew and Luke, on the one hand, to be reconciled with that in the gospel of John on the other? The tradition is united that Jesus was crucified on a day of the week which we should call Friday (assuming 'Sunday' as the Jewish 'first day of the week' and 'Saturday' as the Sabbath). The last Supper therefore in either form of the tradition takes place on what we should call Thursday evening, but what for the Jew is the beginning of Friday, because his day begins with the evening of the Gentile's previous day. Differences, however, arise over the date. The Passover was always celebrated on Nisan 15 and according to the synoptic gospels the Last Supper was a Passover meal; the sequels followed so closely upon one another that Jesus was arrested, tried, died on the cross and was buried within twenty-four hours. The same sequence of events is narrated (though with differences as to detail) in John, but the Passover meal occurs after Jesus is dead and buried, on Friday evening, the beginning of Nisan 15 which was the Sabbath or what we call Saturday. In John, therefore, the Last Supper is not a Passover meal and Jesus' death is connected more directly with the Passover than by means of the Last Supper; for in John Jesus is dying on the cross at the time when the lambs are being slaughtered in preparation for the Passover, so that the evangelist may well be telling his readers that Jesus was *the* Passover Lamb of God. Many Christians would be content to derive some of the significance of the death of Jesus for themselves from its associa-

The Last Supper.

tion with the Passover, which in any case must be close. But interpretations of the Eucharist, the great central rite of Christendom, depend a great deal upon whether the event from which it arose, the Last Supper, or perhaps better, the Lord's Supper, was a Jewish Passover or not. A full account of the discussion on this matter cannot be given here, but two points may be made.

The first is that the discovery of a sect contemporary with the New Testament events which used a solar calendar has suggested a solution to the apparent conflict between the synoptic gospels and John as to whether the Last Supper was a Passover or not; if Jesus and his disciples followed this ancient calendar while the other Jews in Jerusalem followed the official lunar calendar, both versions of the timing may be correct. Such a theory would claim that the synoptic account gives a version of what actually happened according to the ancient calendar, and the Fourth Gospel an account of the events according to the official calendar.

The second point is closely connected with the first: the synoptics are held, according to the theory outlined, to have given us a version of the actual events, a version which is false only to the extent that it condenses too much the time taken by them. A clue to this possibility is supplied by the fact that Luke gives a slightly different version from Mark, though not different in the essential matter under discussion, the identification of the Last Supper with a Passover meal. The theory based on the hypothesis that Jesus adhered to the ancient solar calendar takes advantage of the fact that the solar calendar made all the festivals fall not only on the same date each year but on the same day of the week. Nisan 15, the Passover day, fell on Wednesday (starting on what we call Tuesday evening). Now if it is accepted that Jesus was crucified on the following Friday, it is possible to give more space to the events which led up to the death of Jesus, allotting to Tuesday evening the Last Supper as a Passover meal, and the arrest. On Wednesday Jesus is a prisoner of the high priest and under interrogation. On Thursday he is tried by the high priest and brought to Pilate who keeps him prisoner until the next day when he tries and condemns him to death. The crucifixion follows on the same day. This theory was put forward by Mlle A. Jaubert in 1957 in a book which has now been translated into English and entitled *The Date of the Last Supper*.[8]

Such a solution does not perhaps commend itself greatly to those who see no need to reconcile the accounts of the synoptic gospels with that of the Fourth Gospel on the ground that the latter is too heavily theologically orientated to claim defence as a historical document. The close condensation of the events of 'Holy Week' in the synoptics may rightly demand some relaxation, but many critics would doubt the relevance of an exercise which assumes that the pattern of the Passion Narrative is historical enough to profit by it: here too, they would say, theological considerations have been highly influential. Such questions must be mentioned again, but it will be clear already in what way the scrolls may bring new interest to the study of the New Testament.

Some students of the scrolls would say that the discovery of the material at Qumran has a further bearing upon the Christian Eucharist, since the sect practised a similar rite. This would be a most interesting conclusion; it would suggest that the ceremony which Jesus adapted as a memorial of his coming death was not the Passover but some other ceremony. There is no evidence to suggest that Jesus was a member of the sect, for his wholesale abandonment of the Jewish cleanness laws, so strictly kept by the sect, would outlaw him in their eyes; nor can it be argued fairly that he was nearer to them even in his revolt against so much in Judaism than to any other branch of religious practice, for he shows considerable signs of having understood the Pharisees best, and in some ways remained close to them. If therefore he did use a ceremony of the sect this question would be reopened. There seems little likelihood that this was the case. The words from two of the scrolls, the *Rule* and the *Two Columns* or *Rule of the Congregation*, merely give instructions that there is to be a priest to every ten men and 'when they shall prepare the table to eat or the grape-juice to drink, the priest shall be first to stretch forth his hand to bless at the beginning the bread or the grape-juice'. Such slight instruction, apparently enjoining the rules for 'saying grace', have been blown up into a ceremony like the Eucharist of the early church in the early excitement of discovery. No parallel exists beyond the eating of bread and the drinking of grape-juice (which may or may not be wine, i.e. fermented), and these two simple actions need an accompanying rubric to give them any special meaning. This is altogether lacking in the scrolls, where the point being made is that the priest (in the *Rule of the Congregation* the priestly Messiah) is to have pre-eminence at the board of the community.

The personality of Jesus has so intrigued and challenged men in every generation since he lived that it is to be expected that comparisons would be made between him and any other personalities of the same period who rose to prominence as religious leaders. It is worth remarking that he has not commonly been identified with any other known person, although the way in which the gospels have presented him, natural to their own time, has tended to afford material to those who have striven hard to make him disappear by arguing that such a person never existed. With the discovery of the scrolls such speculations were granted a new impulse: anyone who wished to make Jesus less important or to argue that he is falsely presented in the New Testament, could identify him with a personality among the men of Qumran, or at least compare Jesus unfavourably with him. The fact that we do not possess any really substantial knowledge about such personalities or their dates has done nothing to deter and something to encourage this activity.

We do not know the name of the founder of the sect or community which lived at Qumran. It was a part, perhaps the headquarters, of the Essene movement according to one reasonable theory. After they had been in existence twenty years their great man arose. They called him the Teacher of Righteousness, a title which they used sometimes for one who held a leader's position in the sect, but which was applied certainly in some cases to this one historical person. The men of the community thought of him, and he thought of himself (though in a very attractive and modest way), as directly gifted by God in the interpretation of the scriptures, especially the prophets.

We have seen that part of this interpretation consisted in seeing the 'true' meaning of secrets or mysteries of God hidden, as it were, in what the prophets had said. Another way in which he was held to possess great authority was in the adaptation and application of the laws of the Old Testament to the strict Jewish way of life which the sect wished to follow. If he wrote the *Psalms of Thanksgiving*, this would be completely in keeping with the way in which he is revered in references to him elsewhere. He is not mentioned in the *Rule* but appears in the *Damascus Document* and in the *Commentary on Habakkuk*. In the latter there is a strange passage which interprets a text of Habakkuk (which of course originally meant something quite different) as being a description of a scene when a character called the Wicked Priest confronted the Teacher of Righteousness on a day when the latter was celebrating the Day of Atonement. What this Wicked Priest did to the Teacher is not quite clear, but it is this passage which has been used to claim that he took him away to crucify him. Even those who originally made this claim agree now that the passage does not mean this, but it could mean that the Wicked Priest did destroy the Teacher. It seems more likely that he merely interrupted and confused him, making his keeping of the Day of Atonement invalid. In the *Damascus Document* a gentle and ordinary phrase is used about the death of the Teacher which is consistent with his having died a natural death.

We cannot identify the Wicked Priest; there are several people who might qualify, since those who usurped the title of high priest and ruled as bloodthirsty tyrants (for example, Alexander Jannaeus, 103–76) could very suitably be so described. But we may need someone who fits into history a little earlier (perhaps about 140) so we cannot be clear about this.

We have a corresponding difficulty with the Teacher of Righteousness, but there are one or two things we know about him. In addition to those already mentioned, about his being good at interpreting the law and the prophets, it seems clear that he was regarded eventually, if not during his lifetime, as the prophet promised by Moses in Deuteronomy, xviii, 15, and as such to be the forerunner of the Messiahs. Apart from this unexpected plural, which marks a difference between Qumran and the New

Testament, nowhere in the scrolls is there any reference to the Teacher as the Messiah, nor to his resurrection, nor to anything else which would make him look like Jesus before his time.

The two Messiahs deserve a little more explanation: when after the Exile devoted men were trying to re-establish the state of Judea, they formed the conception of two leaders of the people, one the anointed priest, the other the anointed secular ruler descended from David. These hopes were not realized but the idea did not die. It is found in the *Testaments of the Twelve Patriarchs* where it is agreed that Levi has the priesthood and Judah the kingship. Great reverence for the priesthood is shown in the fact that Judah is subordinate to Levi. Qumran is similar: they looked for the coming of the two Messiahs but the priestly one was to take precedence; and incidentally they show no sign whatever of either Messiah being claimed to be of divine nature as well as human, as is claimed by Christians for Jesus.

Although the men of Qumran made no claim for the Teacher like that made for Jesus by the Christian church, since the Teacher seemed to them to qualify as the forerunner of the Messiahs, we might compare him with John the Baptist. Such a comparison is fair so long as it is general: both were great religious leaders and desired a revival of the nation, and both lived very strict lives. But the Teacher is the leader of a community, whereas John is a solitary. The Teacher taught the necessity of many lustrations or ritual baths for the sake of ceremonial cleanness: John taught and practised a once-for-all baptism at what he thought was the end of the age, when the Lord himself would come in judgement very soon. The Teacher evidently thought it was necessary to remake the community of Israel. John hoped to bring Israel as it was to repentance. The fact that the Teacher of Righteousness existed and led a religious community in the days just before the life of Jesus has no relevance whatever for the claims made by the Christian Church that Jesus may be best described by calling him the Son of God. If the existence of such a leader is a threat to Christian faith, so is – and always was – the existence of John the Baptist, whose movement indeed rivalled that of the early church

185

for a long period, a fact we see reflected in the New Testament itself.

A natural and reasonable conclusion about the Dead Sea Scrolls is therefore that they are of the greatest importance in providing further material for the study of the history and thought of the Jewish people in the time between the Old and New Testaments. They do not throw a flood of light where all before was darkness, and the interpretation of the New Testament and its meaning and relevance for contemporary man are problems not fundamentally changed by their discovery, though it is very helpful to have them to consult when trying to reach a correct conclusion about some of the details of interpretation, just as other evidence of the period, which was already available, is also of the greatest importance.

Less has been heard in public about another discovery of ancient manuscripts, in 1945, two years earlier than that of the Dead Sea Scrolls. This was the accidental unearthing of a gnostic library of documents in Coptic at Nag Hammadi[9] in Upper Egypt.

There were many forms of Gnosticism, and their diversity is one of the factors which has led to controversy as to whether any existed in New Testament times, or whether it is better to accept the views of early Christian writers, such as Irenaeus (c. 130–200), bishop of Lyons, that Gnosticism arose as a Christian heresy. It seems certain that various streams of thought which contributed to it were in existence in the time when the events recorded and interpreted in the New Testament took place. These streams included religious and philosophical ideas borrowed from various sources; but what distinguishes the 'gnostic' is his attitude of mind. This is illustrated by his high valuation of *gnosis* (Greek for 'knowledge') by which he meant special knowledge revealed to him, possession of which secured serenity in this life and happiness in the next. He held, as it were, a pass, an identity card, into a state of being denied to those whose ignorance bound them to this world. The knowledge in question varied from system to system but always betrayed a preoccupation with the inferiority of the world of matter and the superiority of the world of spirit, special revelation from or a special relation with a redeemer from the world of spirit granting release from this world of mere sense by intellectual enlightenment.

It was inevitable that, given minds with such an outlook, 'Jesus' or 'Christ' should be represented in some quarters as such a redeemer; his work as a historical person gathering outcasts, healing spirit and body, challenging the false, embodying the true in conduct and teaching, finally giving his life in that challenge – all this is transformed into that of a redeemer entrusted with no more than a body of doctrine.

Although the sudden appearance of the Nag Hammadi library in 1945 did not immediately cause much excitement, part of the discovery eventually received considerable attention, for the *Gospel of Thomas* was published in full in newspapers, and headlines invited their readers to consider the possibility of the existence of 'another gospel'. Again, this document gains its true importance when seen in perspective. Many gospels of a kind or kinds fundamentally different from the four in the New Testament have always been known to exist; a standard work on the apocryphal books of early Christianity lists under 'Gospels', apart from fragments, three Jewish Christian books of this kind, an Egyptian gospel, a Gospel of Peter, 'gospels' of the infancy of Jesus, and many gnostic gospels, several of which bear the name of apostles (and one that of Mary), others being the 'gospels' of various leaders of gnostic sects. The find at Nag Hammadi contributed many to this list. Each of these works has its own characteristics, but they all share at least one – their lack of concern with history. The canonical gospels invite criticism by narrating miracles and apparently legendary material (such as the Infancy narratives), but their authors evidently wish to relate what to them are facts. The apocryphal writings almost show a contempt for facts. The few events they narrate are fantastic and their contents are for the most part teachings of a rather mysterious kind purporting to be a special revelation with divine authority and to be the true meaning of Christianity. The speaker is sometimes one who has received this revelation from the risen Jesus, sometimes it is the risen Jesus himself. In either case, it is to be observed that contact

187

with the historical Jesus is not so much lost as already abandoned before the book is composed. In general the teachings given are those of a supernatural teacher who, though he may be formally identified with the risen Jesus, may also show such independence of him as to be speaking at the same time as the earthly Jesus is being crucified.

Not all the apocryphal gospels are gnostic, but the library at Nag Hammadi certainly was, and the *Gospel of Thomas* is usually regarded as a gnostic gospel. The date of its composition lies in the fourth or fifth century. The primary importance of such writings is therefore as first-class evidence for the development of one strand of teaching within what may rightly be called Christendom, although often this teaching can hardly be recognized as Christian, so far does it stray from the path which would, if retraced, lead back to the New Testament. The *Gospel of Thomas* is nevertheless relevant to New Testament study; for while much of what is attributed to Jesus here is manifestly gnostic doctrine quite alien from him and his Jewish contemporaries, interest is quickened when a well-known saying of Jesus is recognized, even if it appears always in a different form from that in the canonical gospels. The question which arises for New Testament study is not therefore, 'Is this a collection of sayings of the historical Jesus hitherto unknown?' but 'Have we in this collection evidence for the original form of sayings of Jesus already known to us?'

An example will make this clear. Logion 100 reads: 'They showed Jesus a gold coin and said to him, "Those who belong to Caesar demand a tax from us." Jesus said to them: "Give Caesar the things which belong to Caesar, give God the things which belong to God, and give me what is mine." ' At first sight a reader might think that here is an alternative version of the famous passage in Mark xii, 13–17 and its parallels in Luke and Matthew. But a closer examination based on a comparison of the synoptic texts with the *Gospel of Thomas* shows that important steps in the original argument have dropped out; there is no mention of the image and inscription on the Roman coin, and the question 'Is it lawful . . .?' has been transformed into a statement which includes the description 'those who belong to Caesar', thus categorizing some class of people in a manner very typical of gnostics.

Gärtner in *The Theology of the Gospel of Thomas*[10] points out that Clement of Alexandria interprets 'Caesar' as 'the temporary Archon', one of the semi-divine figures of a gnostic system. Gärtner remarks that Heracleon (an early gnostic teacher, active c. 145–180) uses such a phrase for the Demiurge, that is the Creator considered as a lesser divinity than the absolute God in gnostic systems, in which Jesus himself often takes a place alongside other celestial beings. Since the *Gospel of Thomas* is clearly a collection of sayings purporting to come from Jesus and not at all a gospel in the sense of a narrative of his ministry, death and resurrection, we see that the most likely explanation of the changed form of the canonical gospel saying found in it is that it has been 'gnosticized'. The gnostic is to render due reverence and service to the three divinities, 'Caesar' (i.e. the Archon), God, and the divine being, Jesus. It seems always possible and sometimes essential to give such explanation of the sayings in the *Gospel of Thomas* which bear a striking resemblance to those familiar from the synoptics. While this does not by any means exclude the possibility that the author of this gnostic work had access to a collection of the sayings of Jesus which came to him independently of the canonical gospels, it shows the great difficulty of being sure of this. Moreover, it is now perhaps clear from the example given that it is unlikely in the extreme that the sayings in the form which they bear in the *Gospel of Thomas* represent in themselves a collection of sayings of Jesus which came from him unchanged and which rival in authenticity those used by the evangelists.

The Nag Hammadi collection then appears to illustrate the development of Christian thought, in a form deviating from the mainstream which endeavoured to adhere to the historical facts more conscientiously. It was a form of interpretation which was more interested in ideas than in history, it might even sometimes be said, than in the possibility of their corresponding to any reality. One further item of interest illustrating the materials and methods of scholars who try to build up a true picture of the development just mentioned is this: as long ago as 1897 and 1903, fragments of papyri were found at Oxyrhynchus in Egypt and published by B. P. Grenfell and A. S. Hunt which contained in Greek sayings or parts of 'sayings of Jesus'. It now appears that these sayings may have been parts of a *Gospel of Thomas* in Greek (probably earlier than the Coptic version found at Nag Hammadi) but differences of arrangement forbid us to say the Oxyrhynchus sayings are simply parts of a Greek writing from which the Coptic *Gospel of Thomas* was translated. Such evidence suggests the existence of a collection of sayings of Jesus, made at a date very difficult to determine, but late enough for it to be possible either that parts of it predated the canonical gospels or that it drew upon them. Many of the sayings in this collection would be gnostic but not all can be shown to be so. It was used by the author of the *Gospel of Thomas* as well as by other gnostic writers, some of whom are represented in the Nag Hammadi collection.

So far, under the general heading of archaeological discoveries only documents have been considered; but some of the most interesting have been archaeological discoveries in the form more usually associated with archaeology. Thus Israeli scholars have carried out an immense labour of excavation at many places, including Caesarea and Masada, while in the part of Jerusalem which is in Jordan important discoveries have been made in recent years.

Caesarea was originally 'Strato's Tower'[11] and was built by Herod the Great as a capital for the Roman province of Judea and named by him Caesarea Maritima in honour of Augustus Caesar. The theatre and aqueduct are striking features, but, from the point of view of New Testament study, perhaps the most interesting find is a stone which had evidently originally been part of a 'Tibereum', the first whole word on the stone and meaning a building dedicated to the Emperor Tiberius (A.D. 14–37). On the line below, TIUS PILATUS is quite clear, and on the line below that is ECTUS IUDAE, which should obviously be restored as 'praefectus Iudaeae'. The letters missing are permanently lost by the cutting away of the original surface at an angle, when the stone was used in a building of a later date; but the restoration 'Pontius Pilatus' is certain, and supported by his title *praefectus* which incidentally confirms that the governors of Judea were so entitled, the term *procurator* being introduced by the Emperor Claudius in 41.

The immensely thorough excavation of the fortress of Masada, on the west coast of the southern half of the Dead Sea, opposite the Tongue of Moab, was undertaken by Yigael Yadin in 1963-5, and the full story of the use of an army of volunteers from many different countries of the world, and of the resources and some of the personnel of the actual Israeli army, is told by him in a book of great interest and clarity, beautifully illustrated, entitled *Masada*.[12]

The discoveries made are not of direct importance for the New Testament, but are easy to link with its story. Herod the Great built – or rebuilt – the Temple at Jerusalem and according to Mark xiii, 1, Jesus was invited by his disciples to admire it. His response was to prophesy its destruction. The prophecy was fulfilled in 70 at the completion of the tragic and terrible siege which virtually ended the Jewish rebellion against Rome; but a number of zealots (fanatical patriots devoted to resistance against pagan overlordship on religious grounds) escaped and joined some of their number who earlier in the rebellion had gained possession from the Romans of another structure of Herod's. This was an extraordinary fortress-palace built in three stories on the precipitous northern face of the natural hill-fortress of Masada earlier in Herod's career. Here, thanks to the elaborate provision which Herod's architect and engineers had made for the conditions of a siege, zealots held out until 73 when, according to Josephus, almost all committed suicide rather than fall, as they saw to be otherwise inevitable, into the hands of the Romans. The discovery by Yadin of some documents of the same kind as those found at Qumran lent support to those who had argued that the men of Qumran were zealots; but if the evidence that they were some kind of Essenes seems too strong, a ready explanation would be that a remnant from Qumran, destroyed in 68, fled to join the zealots in Masada, willing to take part in fighting what their religious convictions assured them was to be the final war of the age. Pathetic evidence of the rough way in which the defenders lived among the deserted palace buildings was discovered and is clearly shown in Yadin's book.

Such discoveries whet the appetite for archaeological discoveries which would illustrate directly the story of Jesus. In fact, so much has changed over the centuries, which have treated Jerusalem and Judea very harshly, and brought about the virtual obliteration of the original Nazareth, that it can be confidently stated that all that remains for us to see of things seen by Jesus and his contemporaries are the tombs of the Hellenistic period in the valley of the Kidron in Jerusalem, structures which bear the entirely misleading titles of the Tomb of Absalom, the Tomb of St James, and the Tomb of Zechariah. The bare possibility remains of some stones having been re-used in the ruins of the synagogue at Capernaum, which goes back to the third century and probably stands on the site of that which Jesus attended. The countryside in Galilee, less populous now than in his day, distinguished by an unusual beauty of form and colour, remains the most rewarding scenery for those who wish to look at things which he saw, and is frequently the most appreciated part of a discerning traveller's tour when the appetite has been jaded and the intelligence insulted by a surfeit of phony sites elsewhere.

Sacred sites in Jerusalem have indeed their own interest; but from the historical point of view this is confined to that which they arouse through having been venerated from sometimes as early as the fourth century, from the time when such piety was encouraged under Constantine. It is difficult, for example, to be thrilled by the announcement that a certain shrine on the slope of the Mount of Olives marks the spot where Jesus wept over Jerusalem; but evidence that there was such a shrine here as early as the fourth century, marked by the remains of a mosaic floor, has its own historical interest, like the sixth-century basilica in Bethlehem which appears to stand on a site venerated since the fourth century as the site of the birth of Jesus and is in any case an excellent example of an early Christian basilica.

The Church of the Holy Sepulchre in Jerusalem is perhaps the most interesting of such sites associated with the account in the gospels of the life and death of Jesus. Eusebius and archaeological evidence make it certain that a truncated part of it stands on the site of the original building by Constantine, and incorporates remains of the original structure. It is therefore fortunate that some relevant account can be given of archaeological discoveries here during the last few years. It will be well to begin with an outline of the sad history of this building.

The original was built by the Emperor Constantine in 335 but this building was ruined in the Persian invasion of Chosroes in 614. It was restored by the Patriarch Modestus in 629 and when Jerusalem was taken by the Moslems in 637 the buildings were not injured; but in 1010 the church was utterly destroyed by order of Khalif Hakim. The Emperor Constantine Monomachus obtained permission to rebuild in 1040 and this was effected by the Patriarch Nicephorus about fifty years before the entry of the Crusaders in 1099. The latter added considerably to the buildings and there were no further changes until they were ejected in 1187. No more than mere patchwork repairs were carried out over the centuries before 1808 when the church suffered severe damage by fire and was restored on a 'first-aid' basis. Eusebius[13] (c. 260–340), in his *Life of Constantine*, and Sozomen (a church historian of the early fifth century) say that the sites of the crucifixion and resurrection were occupied by a Temple of Venus under Hadrian; and Eusebius says that Constantine ordered this to be demolished and the materials and earth forming its podium to be removed. Shafts sunk in 1961 show the church to have been built on blocks of stone and red earth and reveal no evidence of the remains of the Temple of Venus underneath, a fact which somewhat negatively supports Eusebius. These soundings were undertaken by C. Couasnon, the Dominican architect appointed by an agreement of the three churches most concerned and with the most prominent rights in the church, the Latin (as the Roman Catholic is called in Jerusalem and its environs), the Greek and the Armenian.

It appears that the site was, probably in pre-New Testament times, a quarry. The rock known as that of Golgotha was not quarried but left protruding from the surrounding area. This formation is invisible from the outside of the church and is shown to the visitor inside, the steps which take him to the top being now all within the structure. It was probably covered by the fill under the Venus temple and rediscovered by the builders under Constantine. A curious fact (as it seems to the visitor) is that what seems to have been indeed an ancient Jewish tomb but is sometimes called the Tomb of Joseph of Arimathaea and Nicodemus (John xix,38–42) was mutilated so that the circular wall of the Anastasis (the part of the church erected over the tomb of Christ) could pass through it. This western circular wall has lower courses which in the opinion of all writers date from the time of Constantine. The site of the tomb of Christ, as understood by the architects, must have been within the Anastasis; it is not known whether Constantine erected any structure over this site. If he did, the present structure (which is shown to visitors as the tomb) may or may not occupy the same position; and it is too early to say whether the present excavations will throw light on either of these questions.

It is unnecessary to describe the rest of this fascinatingly interesting building; for we must sternly remind ourselves that its interest lies in its formation about the fourth century and its beliefs, not about facts connected with the New Testament other than the fact that in the fourth century men believed they knew the site where Jesus had been crucified and buried. Whether the site was well-known to Christians is a question whose answer must depend not on archaeology but on what historical reconstruction we make of the gospel stories and how far we believe they report actual events. Did the disciples flee for fear of arrest (Mark xiv,50)? Was Peter's subsequent stealing back pretending not to be a disciple (Mark xiv,54 ff.) a return near enough to allow him to see all or even any substantial part of what happened? Did Joseph bury Jesus and two women followers named Mary actually see where he was buried (Mark xv,42–47; Nicodemus is mentioned only in the Fourth Gospel)?

Some may think that the synoptic gospels contain hard historical facts and that the account of the death and burial of Jesus consists of such facts; even then, excavation of the famous church at Jerusalem will show only where fourth-century men thought

194

these events took place; opinion may be divided as to whether they were right or not. Others may dismiss the story of the resurrection as legend and regard the account of the arrest, trial, crucifixion and burial as heavily encrusted with doctrinal deposit. In that case, the building will remain no more than evidence for the belief current in the period of Constantine. We shall not be greatly encouraged towards naïve acceptance of this belief when we reflect that at Bethlehem the place of the birth of Jesus is similarly marked by a basilica standing over a cave, and that no cave is mentioned in Luke ii or Matthew i. Indeed, the nearest we can get to one in the tradition is a cave said to be the place of the nativity by Justin (c. 100–165) who locates it 'between Jerusalem and Bethlehem'.

Far less open to any obvious sceptical criticism is the site of the Fortress Antonia, built by Herod the Great and called after his friend and patron Mark Antony as a garrison for Roman soldiers to use when on duty in Jerusalem at the northern end of the Temple area (cf. Acts xxi, 27 ff.). Destroyed in 68, it left behind an impressive pavement area covering large underground cisterns which the sisters of the Convent of the Dames de Sion now occupying the site will show the visitor with great courtesy and intelligence. On any showing, this site with the huge blocks of stone bearing marks of Herodian date, scratched with curious signs perhaps due to a game played by bored soldiers, and forming the pavement just mentioned (originally the courtyard of the fort) must rank as that in Jerusalem which brings the visitor closest to New Testament history.

It is hotly contested whether the fort was used as a praetorium, the residence of the prefect when he came up to Jerusalem from the Roman capital Caesarea. In 1955 Marie-Aline de Sion, now Mother Superior of the convent, reviewed in masterly fashion the differing views on this point and pleaded for recognition of it as the place where Jesus was brought before Pilate (John xix, 13).[14] The evidence of the experts which she reports is about equally divided, the rival place to be regarded as that used as a praetorium being the palace of Herod further west. If the Antonia is the place where Jesus was brought before Pilate, visitors can walk over and touch the actual stones on which he stepped as a prisoner; further, it is at least possible that the scratched stones mark the place where the soldiers used their prisoner in mockery as part of a game to pass the time between hearings of the case and between condemnation and execution of the accused. The connexion of this possibility with the gospel story is too obvious to need comment. It may however be remarked in passing that this topographical point arises from the Fourth Gospel and illustrates the uncharacteristic historical interest of that gospel in the Passion Narrative section of it.

In the next chapter we shall consider in outline the course of criticism of the New Testament as it has explored the Jewish background against which or within which the early Christian authors thought and wrote. Important advances have been made in this sphere, and these raise in the student's mind the question of the importance of the synagogue as the institution where the scriptures were taught and expounded, both within divine service on the sabbath and in its associated school on other days. While the institution is important and the buildings where it met less so, the discovery of remains of synagogues in Palestine and elsewhere in the Mediterranean world cannot but be of interest to students of the New Testament and the history of its times.

The origins of the synagogue as an institution are obscure. Though no doubt much earlier, it is not mentioned before the Christian era except in Greek inscriptions of Egyptian Jews, the earliest dating from the reign of Ptolemy III (227–221 B.C.). It may be that Psalm lxxiv, 8 – perhaps of Maccabaean date – refers to synagogues as the Authorised Version and Revised Version would have us believe. The word is a general one meaning an appointed time (thus used for a festival as the Greek version takes it here) or appointed place. *I Enoch* 46, 8 and 63, 6 may also refer to the synagogue, and also possibly Ecclesiasticus xxxix, 6, whose silence is otherwise odd. Modern criticism has nothing to offer which would clarify this matter, but in the realm of archaeology discoveries have been made which are of great interest though they are not sensational (in the sense of reversing what historians would expect).

The Schweich Lectures in Biblical Archaeology for 1930 were given by the Jewish archaeologist and scholar, E. L. Sukenik, and these were published in 1934 under the title of *Ancient Synagogues in Palestine and Greece*. The descriptions of the remains of these synagogues are fascinating, as indeed is the actual sight of them to the visitor to Palestine; but none of them go back to New Testament times and the problems associated with them and their unexpectedly ornate architecture must not detain us.

We saw in the previous chapter that the remains found at Capernaum may be presumed to stand on the site of a synagogue frequented by Jesus. No synagogue contemporary with Jesus was known until very recently; Qumran has not yielded the remains of any building which might have been a synagogue. But it fell to the lot of Yadin, son of Sukenik,[15] in his excavation of Masada, described in the book with that title referred to on pp. 191–2, to discover for the first time the remains of a synagogue in fact earlier than New Testament times. Pages 180 ff. describe and illustrate the remains of a building believed by very critical experts to be that of a synagogue dating from the building by Herod the Great and modified by the zealot defenders.

For the story of New Testament criticism such discoveries are interesting but not vital. Jesus, his disciples, Paul, and other personalities who are the subjects or authors of New Testament books were educated in their own homes and in the schools attached to the synagogue of their native place. It is not the buildings which are of the greatest importance but what was taught in them, and the spiritual and intellectual world inhabited by those who taught and learned in them. In knowledge of this sphere some advances, perhaps less of discovery than of insight and clarification, have been made in the last thirty or so years. It will be possible to give only a suggestion or two and an outline of this process, doing less than justice to the work of many scholars who must perforce remain unmentioned. To this task, however restricted, the next chapter is devoted.

Seven

New Horizons:
The Background
of Judaism

Although archaeological and historical evidence is important for
the study of the New Testament, an understanding of the thought
of Judaism in the time of Jesus and of the early church is even
more important. The Dead Sea Scrolls may seem to belong to
archaeology and history; but their value lies in their contribution
to our knowledge of that Judaism.

This is a sphere of study which is familiar to New Testament
scholars. It has always been recognized that Jesus and his immediate followers were sons of the synagogue and its associated
school in the places where they were brought up. It is often
thought that this means only that these men were familiar with
what Christians call the Old Testament and Jews call the Scriptures, or the Law, the Prophets and the Writings. Jesus and Paul
both quote the ancient scriptures and it is often imagined that this
alone was the clue to their thought, just as non-Jews in the
modern world often think that the guiding principles for Judaism
are to be found simply in the Old Testament. This is to leave out
a most important factor: throughout the history of the people of
Israel and Judah, of Judaea, and finally of the Jews in their homeland and in the dispersion, a great continuous and thorough work
of applying and adapting the Law to the contemporary scene was
carried out.

Thus there grew up an enormous body of Oral Law, at first not
written but preserved orally, but, beginning at a date or dates still
obscure, gradually and increasingly committed to writing. Thus
was created a formidable body of law or regulation for everyday
life; its Hebrew term is *halakah*, literally, 'way'. The 'way' of
the sect of Qumran was embodied in various documents, such as
the *Rule*, another term by which the Hebrew word could be

translated. There were several 'ways' which a pious Jew might follow; one was that of the Pharisees, another in due course arose as a result of believing that Jesus was the Messiah. In other words, Christianity was at first known as a 'way' within Judaism, as the book of Acts makes quite clear (for example, ix, 2 and xxiv, 22). It is not the Old Testament but the *halakah* which governs the life of the devout Jew and governed it at the time of Jesus and the early church. Moreover, there was another and closely associated scholarly discipline among the Jews, that of explaining and illustrating by story or legend or parable matters of belief about God and man and the relation between them. *Midrash* is the term for explanation of scripture carried out by certain acknowledged rules but often seeming to the modern scholar highly fanciful.

More fanciful still, but, like the parables of Jesus, often showing remarkable insight, are the stories and legends and parables which go to make up what is called *haggadah* (literally, 'story'). The Mishnah, the authoritative collection of *halakah* finally edited by Rabbi Judah ha-Nasi about 200 was mainly the product of scholars whose headquarters had been founded by Johanan ben Zakkai at Jamnia on the coast of Judea (the site is halfway between Tel-Aviv and Ashdod) after the fall of Jerusalem in 70, but its sources must sometimes reach back into the remote past.

The Mishnah is not a book which anyone would wish to read, but it must be studied and referred to from time to time by all New Testament scholars. It is an excellent sign of the way in which scholarship has developed in the last forty years that the standard translation into English trusted and used by Jewish and Christian scholars alike, was made by the English scholar, Herbert Danby, canon of St George's, Jerusalem.[1]

The Mishnah was itself a selection of material when it was first formed, so that much which has existed separately and often been given names suggesting that it is additional to the Mishnah is really as old or older than some of its parts. Further commentary upon it or upon its subjects continued to be made until the Talmud was formed, in Babylonia, in the sixth century. In addition to all this, the great world of *midrash*, that is, scriptural commentary and exegesis and explanation, continued to grow. The great collections of this material often leave little clue as to date, and Jewish scholars do not even yet show the enthusiasm for chronology which their Christian colleagues would like them to show. There is no edition of the Mishnah which treats the material by the standards of modern critical scholarship. For the Jewish scholar authority is lent to his material by that of the collection in which it is found, and by the fact that it belongs to his tradition. He does not find it necessary to try to determine its origin.

Two first rank Jewish scholars, C. G. Montefiore and H. Loewe, have made available a large quantity of the material not in the Mishnah or Talmud, as well as drawing also on those sources, in *A Rabbinic Anthology*,[2] and providing New Testament scholars with an indispensable tool. Characteristic are the words of the preface by Dr Montefiore, 'The book may be much criticized for one particular reason .... It makes no attempt at any chronological arrangement of the extracts upon any particular subject.' The point is of great importance to New Testament scholars, for it is raised again and again when parallels are adduced to show that Jesus or one of the authors of a New Testament work, often Paul, was merely reproducing the standard or at least well-known teaching of the Judaism of the period. This difficulty was recognized by the German Christian scholars Strack and Billerbeck when they produced their monumental commentary on the New Testament from Jewish parallels, *Kommentar zum Neuen Testament aus Talmud und Midrasch*;[3] they give when possible the date of the sage whose saying they are quoting. These volumes, published 1922-8, were the work of Protestant scholars, but in the sphere of learning the distinction between Protestant and Catholic often disappears. It is not through the necessity to correct denominational bias that J. Bonsirven, for example, published in Rome in 1955 *Textes rabbiniques des deux premiers siècles chrétiens pour servir à l'intelligence du Nouveau Testament*, but, as its title indicates, to provide a limited and more specific aid for such study. 1948, the year after the discovery of the scrolls, saw the publication of *Paul and Rabbinic Judaism* by W. D. Davies.[4] The theme of this influential book is well summarized in the author's own words: 'The Gospel for Paul was not the annulling of Judaism but its completion, and as such it took up into itself the essential genius of Judaism.'[5] Such a judgement may seem to disregard the obvious fact that for Paul not only his religion but his life 'was' Christ, and was therefore centred on a person. How then could a religion centred on Torah (the Law and its teaching) survive in such a faith and devotion? Davies tackles this very point: Paul applied to Jesus those concepts which Judaism applied to its greatest treasure, the Torah, 'so that we felt justified in describing the Pauline Christ as a New Torah'. It is not necessary to enter into the discussion whether this particular argument is finally justified, for the point is made that study of the New Testament works within these categories, and defines its central figure in relation to them.

The entrance of Jewish scholars upon New Testament criticism as partners in the enterprise of establishing the historical truth is another welcome phenomenon of this century which has made great advances during the last thirty years. Not only is the New Testament now studied scientifically at the Hebrew University in Jerusalem, but Jewish scholars in this country, in the United States and on the continent of Europe are beginning to study the New Testament using the techniques and approaches which have been evolved during the centuries, and which are described mostly in the chapters on the criticism of the gospels (10 and 11).

It had long been the custom for Jewish scholars to look at the gospels uncritically, ignoring the arguments which would make it hazardous to accept without careful consideration any saying ascribed to Jesus as his *ipsissima verba*. This made it natural to point to parallels with rabbinic teaching in that of Jesus, even sometimes to represent him as another of the leading rabbis of his time with a school propounding its own *halakah*. Criticism makes it clear that the most probable explanation of such parallels is often that the whole story of the ministry and of the teaching of Jesus has been 'judaized', as it manifestly has in the Gospel of Matthew.

The older approach is still used by some Jewish scholars, but more radical criticism gives others a sharper picture of the situation. It is therefore strange to the student who is accustomed to the techniques of gospel criticism to find that when a Jewish scholar publishes a book revealing a critical approach, the matter becomes a nine days' wonder in the popular press, the public thinking quite wrongly that this criticism is being promulgated for the first time. In reality, the criticism, in the sense of radical inquiry into the important and sometimes decisive influences which have gone to the making of a book, has been learnt from Christian scholarship; what is new is the application of such critical principles from the point of view of one who is used to a different atmosphere and a different sphere of knowledge.

An excellent example of significant and useful work of this kind has been provided in this country by David Daube, a Jewish scholar whose interests include studies in *halakah* and its origins. In a book called *The New Testament and Rabbinic Judaism*,[6] he uses his knowledge both of Judaism and of gospel criticism to make some valuable suggestions about not only the context and original meaning of sayings and teachings, but also the structure of the gospels. He ventures, for example, the notion that the famous series of questions and controversies in Mark xi, 27–xii, 44 are arranged upon a pattern suggested not only by the niceties of rabbinic discussion, but also in part by rabbinic elaboration of the custom, when a family is celebrating the Passover, by which questions are asked by the sons concerning the origin of the feast and its parts. This was to use form criticism (see pp. 246ff.) along with knowledge of Judaism, and meant that the author was expert in the work which Christian scholars had developed over the centuries.

The Jewish background has very largely determined the outlook of another book by W. D. Davies called *The Setting of the Sermon on the Mount*,[7] which patiently seeks to show the whole gamut of influences which have gone to compose this famous compendium of early Christian teaching, relating it both to what can be reasonably taken to have been the original teaching of Jesus and to the influences at work on the author of the gospel.

The book is therefore useful as a work of reference, even if many have doubted the truth of one of the author's theories, that the Sermon may be looked upon as a counterblast to the re-establishment of legalistic Judaism at Jamnia (p. 199).

In view of the obvious historical facts, it might seem that it is unnecessary to emphasize the Jewish character of the early church. The point has in fact been obscured by a number of factors, some of which do no credit to the church. One is the anti-semitism which has often prejudiced and still does prejudice the minds of so-called Christians who cannot bear to think of the Christ as a Jew, forgetting that the term Christ is but a Greek translation of an entirely Jewish concept. Other reasons are entirely outside the moral sphere and are due to the history of interpretation and criticism. The first illustration of this lies within the New Testament itself, in the Book of Acts, which (as will be briefly argued in Chapter 13) strives to be true history, but whose author not only lacked enough trustworthy information but was also unconsciously influenced by the desire to show Paul in a favourable light. He represented him as a loyal Jew, but loyal in the sense which included loyalty to the state, and excluded the murderous fanaticism of those who thought they were loyal Jews but showed their blindness by rejecting the Christ of God; thus a bias in this book in favour both of Rome and of the Gentile in general presents Paul as evangelizing the Gentiles in opposition to Judaism rather than in opposition to a narrow school within Judaism. It would be foolish to deny that Paul is rightly described as 'the great apostle to the Gentiles', but if this description is taken to imply that he rejected and condemned Judaism altogether, it produces a false picture of the apostle and of the relation of Judaism to the early church.

Although the picture is false one can understand how it was arrived at; it is easy to pass from the idea of Paul as insisting that salvation was intended also for other nations than Jews to the idea of Paul as condemning Judaism altogether. This step was made even easier by the way in which criticism was applied in comparatively modern times. In 1831 Baur began the great school of Tübingen New Testament criticism by applying

Hegelian doctrine to the interpretation of early Christian history, positing a Petrine (roughly speaking, Jewish Christian) and a Pauline (Gentile Christian) version of Christianity as the two foci of doctrinal development; the ultimate resolution of these two antithetic poles was Catholic Christianity, anticipated in the 'Christ' party at Corinth (1 Corinthians i,12). Although the philosophy of history upon which Baur had founded his views was later discredited, the conviction persisted that there had been a Jewish Christianity, the task being to show good evidence for it and to determine its character in the face of its virtual eclipse by a Christianity which rested on Pauline doctrine.

When reaction against Baur grew, the task had to be carried out under the cloud of disapproval which his philosophy had attracted. In 1933 Kirsopp Lake wrote in the fifth volume of *The Beginnings of Christianity*,[8] a large work oriented round the Acts of the Apostles, 'There are many problems with regard to the Jewish-Christian party which are likely to remain permanently obscure.' In 1949 Hans Joachim Schoeps wrote *Theologie und Geschichte des Juden Christentums*[9] to put forward a 'purified Tübingen point of view' based on much more comprehensive evidence than Baur had used. Schoeps pointed out that the evidence of Justin *Dial.* 47 showed that the phrase 'Jewish Christian' carried two meanings: one to designate those Jews who had become Christians and were members of the church which also contained Gentiles, and another to denote Jews who accepted Jesus as the Messiah but who would not associate with Gentile Christians who refused to obey the Law. Schoeps's investigation confined itself to this latter intransigent section of Jewish Christianity, but immensely widened the scope of inquiry into their beliefs and practices. His subject embraced the Ebionites (mentioned by Justin, Irenaeus and later Fathers), Nazarenes (Acts xxiv, 5; cf. Matthew ii,23) and other sects whose origin, meaning and exact delimitation will probably remain for ever obscure. Schoeps valiantly defends all Jewish Christianity against charges of gnosticism, but believes, as Cullmann had argued, that Essene influence might be present among Ebionites.

We are being drawn away from the sphere of criticism to that of interpretation and away from the New Testament; but the distance through which we have been removed may clarify the view. We can look back upon the New Testament through a clear glass such as that provided by the distinguished French scholar, Jean Daniélou, whose original work[10] has appeared as the first of a series of volumes on the history of early Christian doctrine in English and entitled *The Theology of Jewish Christianity*[11] now much enhanced by clearer arrangement. Daniélou devotes his second chapter to 'Heterodox Jewish Christianity' – the sphere of Schoeps, and one which we can leave on one side, pausing only to remark that Daniélou does not acquit this Jewish Christianity of gnosticism. The form which Daniélou describes is that which uses the vast architecture of thought-forms, images cosmic and historical, of late Judaism whose sources are to be discovered partly among books normally ranked among the Pseudepigrapha of the Old Testament, but some of which are more correctly dated to the Christian era. A second source, which is really indivisible from the first, is provided by the books of the New Testament Apocrypha. Books of both kinds have already been mentioned in connexion with the Dead Sea Scrolls and the Nag Hammadi documents; it will be enough to quote a sentence or two from Daniélou; there are certain Old Testament apocrypha

in which it is hardly possible not to notice Christian features . . . the *Ascension of Isaiah*, *II Enoch* and the *Testaments of the Twelve Patriarchs*. These works certainly have a Jewish background, and are typical of Later Judaism in their literary forms – visions, ascensions, testaments. Moreover, they have a literary relationship to known Jewish works: *II Enoch* is related to *I Enoch*, the *Testaments* to the *Book of Jubilees*, the *Ascension* to the accounts of the martyrdoms of the prophets.

In the main part of this book the sources used are the Jewish Christian writings classed as apocryphal, but at point after point passages of the New Testament are quoted or referred to, showing that the ideas clearly to be found in such apocryphal literature are clearly echoed and provide the way of thinking in the New Testament books themselves. In his Conclusion Daniélou writes,

At every point of the investigation three concepts have constantly recurred; cosmos, apocalypse, gnosis. The subject ... is essentially history, but not simply ... history constituted by the recorded affairs of nations, and acted out within ... sea and land. Its concern is with cosmic history, from the Beginning of things to the End of time, and from the great abyss, through Sheol, earth, firmament, planets, stars to the last infinite Heaven of God. The axis pinning together this immeasurable sphere of things and events in the Incarnation ... It is the Son of God who is the source *par excellence* of the great revelation, and the reception of this revelation affords *gnosis* to the men who receive it.

Except for this last clause, claiming that *gnosis* is part of the key to the revelation, all these assertions are relevant to the New Testament, which may be regarded as the centre of a spectrum whose outer fringes contain the material which afford the picture painted here. The New Testament books are controlled also by the conception of a historical Jesus, and this essential feature influences even the most 'theological' of them, since the point is that the person of theological significance has come in the flesh; yet the way in which his significance is set out is the way which was natural to a community born within the womb of a nation, whose thought-forms are historical rather than philosophical, and apocalyptic rather than inquiring.

The Jewishness of Christianity is concealed by the fact that the New Testament is written in Greek. This is due to the prevalence of the Greek language rather than to the acceptance of Greek ideas by Jews. The battle of the Issus in 331 B.C. gave Alexander the opportunity to turn southwards through Syria and Palestine to Egypt, and with him went a great flood of Greek-speaking peoples and their culture. Even before this Jews had spread into the cities of the Mediterranean world and learnt Greek, the *lingua franca* of that region. Many were strongly influenced by the new ideas with which they thus came into contact; but those who were most concerned to preserve their religious heritage resisted Greek 'pagan' influence even though they could speak Greek. This is obviously true of the Maccabees and of the Qumran sect. It is less obviously but no less firmly true of Paul (an Aramaic- and Greek-speaking bilingual), who to reach both

Jewish and pagan converts wrote in the Greek which they both normally spoke; for however orthodox and conservative a Jew might be, his everyday circumstances forced him to use Greek, a fact illustrated clearly by the widespread use of the Bible (i.e. the Old Testament) in Greek for two centuries or more before Christ. Paul indeed preached emancipation from the Law, but not from the moral law which it enshrined nor to a pagan manner of life. His language is Greek but his ways of thinking are derived from his Bible.

The gospels were written in Greek by authors familiar with the language, though none of them writes with perfect ease and in uniformly Greek idioms (even Luke has many passages whose style is modelled on the Greek Old Testament). Their language is Greek, but their subject is the Jewish Messiah and the story of his relations with his fellow-Jews. Still later, writers of the New Testament turn often to the ideas of their Jewish spiritual ancestors for guidance in everyday affairs, the ethics of marriage, money and manifold relations with one's neighbour, including the occupying political powers. Thus it is clear that they write Greek but think Jewish, not least in the Book of Revelation whose author's Greek would deserve expulsion for any pupil in a British public school who was capable of writing it.

The current of orthodox Judaism derived from the Old Testament was strong; but it could not fail to be influenced by some Greek ideas: the very course of history meant that by the time of Christ Judaism was Hellenistic, that is influenced by Hellenism or Greek culture. It is when we take this to mean that Jews took over Greek philosophy wholesale that the great mistake is made. Philo of Alexandria (c. 20 B.C. – c. A.D. 50) will illustrate the point excellently. He wrote for an educated public who knew something of Greek philosophy; he commended the Jewish scriptures by allegorizing them in such a way as to present the doctrines of philosophy. Moses becomes the teacher of Plato at a remove. There is little doubt that Paul borrowed some of Philo's notions; but he does not use or show any trace of the more extravagant ingenuities of the philosopher. Philo himself refused to doubt the importance of the literal meaning of scripture, even while he gave it a further 'spiritual' connotation. Paul's interpretations, equally assuming the literal meaning, do not go beyond the extravagances of the rabbis, and are cast in a rabbinic rather than a philosophical mould. As a Greek-speaking Jew he illustrates Hellenistic Judaism as clearly as Philo; as clearly he shows by comparison with Philo the vast spectrum covered by the term. These facts are clearly seen today: Greek ideas penetrated Judaism but did not change its fundamental ideas. Thus it is unnecessary for interpreters of the New Testament to argue for Hellenism or Judaism as the main influence in a particular passage; the Judaism behind the New Testament is Hellenistic, but it is Judaism unchanged in its essentials, using Greek language and sometimes Greek ideas to express itself in a mixed world.

It remains to indicate a few of the consequences of accepting Judaism as the background of the New Testament before going on to show how criticism has recently made use of knowledge of the character of this background, and of the particular interpretation given to it by that body within Judaism which became the nucleus of the Christian church. First, even the most uncompromisingly theological book of the New Testament, the Fourth Gospel, can be seen more and more clearly against the background of Judaism. This background may be exceedingly wide, embracing Hellenistic Judaism with its philosophical colour (see Chapter 11), but it is now seen very clearly to embrace Palestinian and Rabbinic Judaism.

Second, a work which shows obvious Jewish traits will not for that reason be early. This is a very important point when, for example, the date of the Gospel of Matthew or of the so-called Epistle of James is considered. For years some critics have argued that such phrases as 'treat him as you would a pagan or a tax-gatherer' (Matthew xviii, 17), or the use of the term 'synagogue' (James ii, 2), indicate an early date, and indeed reminiscences (not quotations) in James of the teaching of Jesus as found in Matthew tend to bind these works together as belonging to a period before the rise of Pauline Christianity or even of Paul as a missionary. The same critics were naturally puzzled by the manifest signs of lateness in both gospel and epistle (developed church discipline, rules and doctrine, verses like Matthew xxviii, 15 and James v, 15 and many other details) but they gave more weight to the signs, as they thought them, of an early date. In the case of the Gospel of Matthew we have the whole structure of synoptic criticism (Chapter 10) to enable us to see that this gospel is relatively late, and though the evidence in the somewhat baffling Epistle of James is nothing like so clear, the signs of Judaism are best explained (manifestly so in the case of the gospel) as rejudaization, an attempt to show that the gospel and the church which proclaims it are the true Judaism.

Third, we may urge that the very term 'Jewish Christianity' is misleading. New Testament criticism has been haunted by the ghost of Baur who has successfully prevented one from seeing the utter psychological impossibility that Paul, who describes himself as having been a 'Hebrew of the Hebrews' and a Pharisee (Philippians iii, 5), could have preached a gospel in non-Jewish terms. In fact, when we are discussing the early church, the church of the New Testament, instead of speaking of Jewish Christianity as though it were a body separate from that church, we should rather speak of the Jewishness of Christianity.

We may now turn to see the ways in which such a recognition of Jewish thought-forms assists understanding of the New Testament from a critical point of view. For example, no doubt the Sermon on the Mount is *halakah* with a difference (and this point is made very clearly by Matthew or perhaps by Jesus himself when the phrase recurs 'but I say . . .' in Matthew v), but the intention of hinting that this is a new Moses giving a new 'law', or, better, 'way' to the new Israel is unmistakable: the very idea of collecting the teaching of Jesus into this comprehensive sermon purporting to have been delivered at one session derives from the author's picture of Moses on Sinai. Traces of the use of the scriptures divided into their portions, a *seder* from the Law, a *haphtorah* from the prophets, may be more readily discernible in some parts of the New Testament than in others, and the theory is described in the chapter on the Fourth Gospel, but there is an attractive illustration of some influence of scripture in Matthew xxi,1–9. Comparison with the Marcan original (Mark xi,1–10) reveals the awkward way in which Matthew has introduced a second donkey, leaving it obscure to what extent it was – or could be! – a mount for Jesus along with its mother. The simplest theory seems to be that Matthew has allowed the passage Zechariah ix,9, which he quotes in verse 5, to be understood as demanding the presence of two donkeys.

This example will also illustrate another feature of the way in which the scriptures were used in contemporary Judaism; it is hardly possible to assume that Matthew was ignorant of the fact that Zechariah ix,9 did not mean 'an ass *and* the foal of an ass' but 'an ass, *that is*, a foal'. But if anyone wished to be over-ingenious, he might argue that there was a further hidden meaning in the scripture which did imply the presence of two animals, even when he and his hearers knew all the time that the plain meaning indicated one. This curious 'double-think' furnished rabbis with some of their most ingenious notions, as is made clear by the invaluable book, *Scripture and Tradition in Judaism*, by G. Vermès.[12] Since Matthew must have known all about these linguistic matters, he must have had a reason for his two donkeys and it may be that he had heard a story that there were two present.

Of the existence of *midrash*, in the sense of story or anecdote inspired by the need to find significance in scripture, there can be no doubt. While it has belonged to Christian belief for centuries to take the stories in the first chapters of Luke and Matthew as historical, it can hardly come naturally to contemporary generations to do so, and they will seek not so much reasons for believing them in spite of their incredibility as explanations for the rise of such stories. Once the nature of *midrash* has been grasped or even partly understood, these phenomena fall into their place. Stories grew up in Judaism round great personalities and illustrated their greatness without regard to their historicity. It is important for our general understanding of the New Testament to see that some stories would be quite historical, others founded on fact or invented. No student of these matters today would wish to deny for a moment that this is true of Moses, and many critics would readily admit that these remarks apply to stories inside the Bible as well as to the rich tradition outside it. It is altogether probable that the same is true of what is said about Jesus, and that the material in the early chapters of Luke and Matthew belongs to *midrash* in the sense of *haggadah* already explained. To give an example, remembering the scriptural origin of such stories as well as the free inventiveness which produced them, that of the Flight into Egypt and the return of Joseph, Mary and Jesus to their homeland in Judea is explicable on the basis of the need to find the Christian significance of Hosea xi, 1, 'I have called my son out of Egypt', once the word 'son' made students of the scriptures sure in their own minds that this had been written under divine guidance to refer to the Messiah. How far the famous passage in Isaiah vii, 14, whose Greek version uses the word 'virgin' to translate the Hebrew 'young woman', is responsible for the story of the birth of Jesus from a virgin must be a matter for speculation. It may well have played a major part in the formation of the story.

Midrash in the sense of *haggadah* is thus easily illustrated in the New Testament. Daniélou does not instance these as Christian *midrashim*, but discusses many which occur in and indeed form the bulk of such writings as the *Epistle of Barnabas*. However, he is inclined to regard Matthew xxvii, 52 – part of the strange story of the resurrection of 'saints' (i.e. Old Testament worthies) at the moment of the death of Jesus – as reflecting an ancient Christian *midrash* traceable also elsewhere. It can hardly be regarded as historical.

Eight

New Horizons:
The Literary Heritage
from Judaism

In the previous chapter something has been said about the ways of thinking and of expressing religious ideas which were current in New Testament times. The early church inherited these ways of thinking and these ideas, and it inherited also a number of books in which they were set down. It must be clear already that not all of these are in the Old Testament; the question therefore arises, 'What books did the early church regard as sacred scripture?'

Part of the answer has been supplied by Dodd in a small and influential book called *According to the Scriptures*;[1] in it he showed clearly that the thought of the early church upon the significance of Jesus and the events associated with him were formed by certain well-defined blocks of Old Testament scriptures, which themselves suggested a pattern for the way in which God dealt with his people, demanding obedience, punishing for disobedience, but refining by and restoring after suffering. The line pursued in this book was followed with great thoroughness and patience, as well as remarkable insight, by B. Lindars in his *New Testament Apologetic*.[2] Lindars was able to show the ways in which, once a scripture had received attention, it affected further writing based on it in a progressive way. Thus Judas' rather incidental money reward in Mark xiv,11 becomes the famous thirty pieces of silver in Matthew xxvi,15 through the influence of Zechariah xi,12 ff. which then gives rise to the story of the use to which this blood money was put, in Matthew xxvii,9 f.

The question about the sacred scriptures of the early church remains unanswered. So far we have seen only that there were most-favoured passages from the scriptures which we should have expected New Testament writers to regard as authoritative. The question was prompted by the evidence that the church regarded other books, not now part of the 'Old Testament', as equally authoritative, and the point at issue is to try to decide what list a Christian of the time of Paul would have given of books which he regarded as sacred. No doubt different people would have given different answers but if we consider the New Testament as a whole we can compile a list all of whose items would be acknowledged by at least someone in this sphere.

Technically speaking, we are therefore occupied with the question, 'What was the canon of the Old Testament acknowledged in New Testament times by the Christian church?' (the word 'canon' meaning 'list'; in this connexion, 'list of authoritative books'). This sphere of study has received a considerable amount of attention for the reason that the writings revered by a group of people must determine to an extent their outlook. To take only one, but important example; if the early Christians were great admirers of the Maccabees and regarded the books about their exploits as sacred scripture, we may find a tendency to represent Jesus and his followers as heroes or martyrs of the Jewish people. If there is on the other hand some evidence that the evangelists at least were dissatisfied with such an interpretation of Jesus, although themselves admirers of the Maccabees, it may be that they saw more in him than a hero or a martyr, and the question must at any rate be raised whether the otherwise scarcely credible picture of Jesus (judging from a naturalistic point of view) which they give may have been forced upon them by the historical facts. These arguments are introduced here not to plead a case, but to show the relevance of the present apparently remote subject to a question which it cannot indeed settle, but concerning which it can contribute interesting evidence.

Before we proceed to this discussion it is worthwhile to reflect on its importance for the vexed question of the authority of scripture for Christian believers. If the Bible is to be regarded as a closed record of revelation and as the Word of God, in the naïve sense that the words written in the Bible are the words of God spoken to man, it is important to know what books are included or ought to be included within its covers. If this is already decided, it is reasonable to ask whether those who decided it had the authority to do so. The matter can be represented as much simpler in regard to the scriptures inherited by the church than for its own writings; for a very simple view would be that those scriptures of the old covenant are authoritative which Jesus and the apostles regarded as such. On the other hand, there would still arise the difficult question as to which scriptures can be shown to have been so regarded by them. Perhaps then the only reasonable way to proceed would be to assume that, in the absence of any contrary indication, Jesus regarded those scriptures as authoritative which were so regarded by his contemporaries, since controversies which arose between him and his interlocutors turned not on which scripture it was cogent to quote but on what was its proper application. At this point it becomes appropriate to return to the discussion of the extent and character of the literary heritage of the early church.

The list of those scriptures regarded as authoritative seems indeed to have been larger than a list of the books of the Old Testament as printed on the contents page of a modern Bible. It is not merely a matter of comparing, as we did to a certain extent in the last chapter, the ways of forming and expressing thought in the New Testament with those of contemporary Judaism. A writer may be strongly influenced by other writings without 'officially' regarding them as authoritative, in the sense that if he appealed to them they could fairly be taken to settle an argument.

For many years the question of the canon of the Old Testament, essentially a matter for historical judgement, was a subject of Catholic–Protestant controversy. Early in the debate Protestants claimed that the canon of the Old Testament had been closed by Ezra and 'the men of the Great Synagogue'(best understood to mean the early scribes who completed Ezra's work in the period about 350 to 200 B.C.), so that only the books of the Hebrew canon had been used in the New Testament. If Catholics claimed (as they rightly did) that other works were cited in the New Testament in a manner clearly showing that they were cited as authorities, Protestants counterclaimed that the canon should in that case be even larger than that decreed by the Council of Trent (1545–63) which admitted books of the Apocrypha. The

Protestants were right on this point but had to concede that the Apocrypha had been accepted widely at least since the fourth century and several favoured some form of the theory that the New Testament church had inherited the canon of Jews living in Alexandria, which they took to have added the Apocrypha to the Hebrew canon.

The Ezra theory was foredoomed: several Old Testament books are later than his time and rabbinic evidence is clear for a much later date for the closing of the canon. In the passage of time the evidence from the rabbis has been used more objectively.

A more thorough and a more critical study of rabbinic sources, applying historical criticism to Mishnaic and Talmudic evidence, has led to the adoption of a reasonable theory regarding the canon of rabbinic Judaism – that the text of the Pentateuch was fixed and accepted about 400 B.C., the Prophets about 200 B.C., and the Writings about A.D. 90.

If the history of the Old Testament canon is clearer now in its main outlines than it once was, yet the canon accepted by the New Testament writers still poses its problems. So far the theory of an Alexandrian canon – the Hebrew canon plus the Apocrypha – was, and in many quarters still is, in possession of the field. There is an awkwardness about this theory which may be obvious to those who have read this book so far; increasing evidence shows the Palestinian provenance of much of the thought behind the New Testament previously ascribed, because of its character, to Hellenistic circles outside Palestine. The point need not be laboured here, but used to justify a further look at the problem of the canon. A. C. Sundberg has argued persuasively for a wider view of the canon accepted by the New Testament,[3] giving the evidence which a careful perusal of the New Testament by one familiar with the late Judaistic literature must reveal. It then becomes apparent that New Testament authors were familiar with the books of the Apocrypha, and in addition used the *Psalms of Solomon*, *I Enoch*, the *Assumption of Moses*, the *Assumption of Isaiah* and *IV Maccabees*. As illustrations of these facts (the whole of the evidence is too extensive to quote), Jude 14–16 quoting *I Enoch* i, 9 and the very probable allusion in Hebrews xi, 34 f. to *II Maccabees* vi, 18–vii, 42, and in Hebrews xi, 37 to a passage in the *Martyrdom of Isaiah*, will show the use not only of the Apocrypha but also of books outside that division.

In the face of these facts the evidence of Christian Fathers raises a problem: the earliest Christian list of Old Testament books is that of Melito, bishop of Sardis in c. 170. It is parallel to the Hebrew canon except for the lack of Esther and Lamentations. From this time onwards the lists of the Fathers tend to be based on the Hebrew canon but to add the Apocrypha. Other witnesses to the practice of the church on this question are the famous Alexandrine manuscripts, the oldest of which date as early as the fourth century; Vaticanus adds the Apocrypha to the Hebrew canon but lacks the books of Maccabees; Sinaiticus lists Tobit, Judith and I and II Maccabees; Alexandrinus adds *III–IV Maccabees*, the Wisdom of Solomon (not always regarded as part of the Apocrypha) and the *Psalms of Solomon* to the Apocrypha. It has been another advance in knowledge that it is now less than ever possible to believe that all the apocryphal books, which marked the so-called Alexandrian canon by being added to the Hebrew canon, were written in Greek. The preface to Ben Sira's Ecclesiasticus shows that it was originally written in Hebrew, and a considerable part of this Hebrew version has been found in the Cairo *geniza*, fragments also having appeared in Qumran and Masada. While Greek was the original language of some of the apocryphal books (including Wisdom and parts of II Maccabees), others were composed in either Hebrew or Aramaic even if they survive now only, or at least in any complete copy, in Greek. Besides Ecclesiasticus Judith was originally in Hebrew as well as minor works of the Apocrypha, and among those originally in Aramaic may be included Tobit and Susannah. Among the Pseudepigrapha only the *Letter of Aristeas*, the *Sibylline Oracles*, *III* and *IV Maccabees*, the Slavonic version of *Enoch* and the Greek *Baruch* were originally in Greek.

Since all the books of the New Testament were written in Greek but are inspired by events on Palestinian soil, the right interpretation of the fact of the presence of Greek in Palestine is all-important. Here again there has been a decided shift of opinion among scholars. The point of puns and other similar verbal devices in teaching ascribed to Jesus and often apparently likely to be authentic depends on their native Aramaic. The evidence is well set out in M. Black's *An Aramaic Approach to the Gospels and Acts*.[4] But there is no doubt that Greek was spoken by a large number of Jews, which may have included such a widely travelling person as Jesus, and some at least of his disciples who inhabited the towns on the shores of the Lake of Galilee, a centre of traffic, especially at its northern end at Capernaum. They would easily learn it by contact with the Greeks of such a district as the Decapolis. In any case there were many Greek-speaking Jews, not only in the dispersion (which will include Paul if he must count as of Tarsus more than of Jerusalem) but also in Palestine, those who had returned or whose ancestors had returned from the dispersion and brought back with them familiarity with Greek as an everyday tongue and as the language of their scriptures. Qumran has yielded a few Greek manuscripts; more important, it has yielded some Hebrew manuscripts of the Old Testament with readings showing affinity with the Septuagint.

It seems then that Hebrew versions of the Old Testament exist which have been influenced by the Greek version. Moreover, the Septuagint is the Greek version mainly used in the New Testament. There was evidently no difficulty for many Jews living in Palestine or in the dispersion to regard books written in Greek as sacred writings if their contents seemed to assign them to this rank. Sundberg argues that in Judaism itself before 90 there were closed collections of the Law and the Prophets 'and a third group of religious writings of undetermined proportions . . . throughout Judaism'. Again, 'it was before the decision closing the canon for Judaism that Christianity arose and became distinguished from Judaism'. This is why a large 'undefined group of writings constituted part of the Christian heritage of religious writings from Judaism'. This seems an unexceptionable judgement.

Greek scriptures as well as Aramaic and Hebrew writings could then be accepted as sacred and authoritative by New Testament authors. Once again, the Qumran sect may illuminate the situation, and Sundberg may be quoted: 'Here are two Jewish sects, the one probably coming to an end in Palestine about A.D. 68, the other arising in Palestine subsequent to about A.D. 30. Both used the apocryphal literature, the former in Hebrew and Aramaic, the latter in Greek. And we are now unable to distinguish their use of this literature from their use of the books of the Hebrew canon.' Emotion rather than historical judgement has sometimes led to the claim that the Christian church is directly dependent on Qumran. It is certainly wiser to say with Sundberg that 'A more probable explanation of the similarities between these two groups is that they represent parallel developments under similar circumstances . . .' These circumstances included the existence of a number of scriptures eventually excluded from the rabbinic canon in 90, though not all of them were then regarded as pernicious but rather as 'not defiling the hands' (that is without the aura of sacredness possessed by the Law and to a lesser extent by other scriptures). These excluded writings, along with some not formally considered in the rabbinic academy at Jamnia (p. 199), continued to circulate in Jewish circles and were therefore available to the New Testament authors. Some were written in Greek.

An interesting situation had in fact arisen: on the one hand a number of writings were venerated as the record of a fixed revelation given once for all by God himself to his chosen agents; but, on the other hand, new ideas and new events set up demands for explanation and for consolation, demands which could not be withstood. They could be met in part by reinterpretation of the old scriptures, both Law and Prophets; but reinterpretation was not enough: new pronouncements, warnings and encouragements were essential to meet new situations. New writings raised at once the question of their authority. They could claim divine authority only if they purported to come to the writer, perhaps in a vision or dream, through an ancient medium such as Moses, Jeremiah (or his secretary Baruch), Ezra (the last inspired author of strict Jewish tradition) or Enoch (suitable through his having been carried away to heaven without dying, although the reputed survival of his revelations caused trouble even in uncritical ages, since they implied a claim to be older than the Mosaic revelation). The divine voice, the controlling sage from the past represented as the real author, the existence of secret books other than those canonized – all these devices are illustrated in II (IV) Ezra xiv, 44 ff. This 'control' of the author is a vital factor and its importance has been neglected: the concept is found in a special form in the New Testament (e.g. in the enigmatic appeal by the Fourth Gospel's author to the spiritual being whose witness he is, in John xix, 35).

We can, therefore, explain the addition of some books to the long revered ancient scriptures: they were written to comfort and encourage, and claimed the authority of sages or heroes. Many of these writings were doomed to be quite soon discarded; for the earliest canons of the Old Testament in the church appear to consist of the Jewish canon plus the Apocrypha, relegating many to the third division, the Pseudepigrapha; this is in fact a title which many other books, both in the Old Testament and the Apocrypha, equally well deserve.

There seems little doubt that the Christian church decided for itself what books were authoritative for Christians. Both Melito and Origen seem to have shown commonsense in travelling to Palestine to discover what books Christ himself had accepted; but Origen undertook the task partly in order to see in what ways Jewish texts differed from those in his church, suspecting that the differences were to the discredit of the Jews. Melito needed a correct list in order to develop the arguments by which the whole mystery of Christ and the sacraments could be seen foreshadowed in the Jewish scriptures; he could then more effectively reproach Israel for rejecting their own Messiah. Justin also attacked the Jews for having altered the scriptures. In this he was mistaken, but he is the first to have observed that there were differences between Jewish and Christian versions of some Old Testament writings.

In time the conception of a true Hebrew canon crystallized: Athanasius (c. 296–373) undertakes to supply a correct list of the Old Testament; but no less than earlier Fathers, he quotes and refers to apocryphal works as though they were just as authoritative as writings in the canon. Some apocryphal works became added to the Hebrew canon under the umbrella of a name safely within it already. Thus the *Epistle of Jeremy* and *Baruch* came to be included, along with Lamentations, with the Hebrew Jeremiah.

Some doubtful books were then included in the official list; others, such as Ben Sira, though excluded, continued to be widely read. We need some explanation therefore of the rejection of other books, such as the *Apocalypse of Moses* and *I Enoch*, which had once been highly regarded.

One explanation seems to be that some books were disdained by Jews. Tertullian (c. 160–220) shows this to be true of *I Enoch*, for example. Such books could not be used effectively in controversy with Jews; and since such controversy occupied much of the energy of the early Fathers, this goes far to give us an explanation of their gradual decline. Their apocalyptic character may also go far to explain both their early popularity and their later eclipse.

The fortunes of the books of Maccabees provide a somewhat different story. They were rejected at Jamnia. I Maccabees at least seems to have been originally in Hebrew; there was therefore no language bar, and the explanation of the rejection probably lies in the hostility of Jamnia to violent political activity. That these books found a place in the affections – and some of them in the sacred canon – of the Christian church is probably due to the way in which the Maccabeans were later regarded by some as forerunners of Christian martyrs.

Further examples of waxing or waning popularity are unnecessary. The point is made that the Christian literary heritage from Judaism was not confined to books officially regarded as authoritative. It included those which were not part of the official Old Testament. The books we know as the New Testament were gradually added to this rather floating body of extras, so that the history of the canon of the Christian church is continuous and is the literary history of books concerned with the covenant of God with men.

Nine

New Knowledge:
Language, Text
and Canon

The kind of reconstruction touched upon in the last chapter can take place only when a great deal of preliminary study has been devoted to the material of the New Testament itself. Modern criticism of the gospels is of obvious importance in the attempt to find what the real facts are – a phrase whose meaning in this context, as we shall see, defies explanation; but before the serious student of the New Testament undertakes such a task he must clearly be able not only to read Greek but also to appreciate what sort of Greek was employed by the authors. Just as clearly, he must have some knowledge of the means of determining, or trying to determine, the original text of the books he is studying. Inevitably asscciated with these studies is the question of the canon, for it is part of his study to know not only what books the early church regarded as authoritative, but also (what is perhaps more important) what books were at first accepted and then rejected; if possible, also on what grounds they were accepted or rejected.

This last task cannot be set out in any detail for it amounts to a sizeable part of the study of church history; it must suffice to indicate the existence of this field and some of its principles. First we must look at language and text, in that order.

The picture of Paul in Acts xxi, 38 and xxii, 2 as surprising the Roman tribune by speaking to him in Greek, and the mob by speaking to them in Aramaic, is true to life. He could have written his letters in Aramaic but his determination to summon all men, not only Jews, to repentance in Christ's name gave him a sphere of activity demanding Greek. It is largely owing to Paul, unquestionably one of the greatest men of history (unless you count only those whose greatness consists in their ability to spread blood and misery over the face of the earth), the world of Christianity became that of the Mediterranean, whose *lingua franca* was Greek. Essentially the language of Homer, Sophocles and Plato (as modern Hebrew is essentially that of the Bible), in grammar, syntax and vocabulary New Testament Greek is sufficiently different to excite curiosity as to its origins. For years it was thought to be a special form peculiar to the New Testament, but a more scientific attitude began with the discovery in 1897 and 1903 of thousands of papyrus documents in Oxyrhynchus and elsewhere in Egypt, including collections of sayings of Jesus previously unknown, but for the most part secular documents (legal, financial, private, miscellaneous business) and dating themselves, stretching from 311 B.C. to the seventh century A.D. A German pastor, A. Deissmann, was the first to recognize that the language used in these documents had close affinities with that of the New Testament. An Englishman, J. H. Moulton, appreciated this insight and extended it to the grammar. They were dealing in the *koine*, that is, the common language of the Greek-speaking peoples of a wide area. The discoveries were too late to influence the Revised Version of the Bible, but lexicons became available to students. The best known in English is J. H. Moulton and G. Milligan's *The Vocabulary of the Greek New Testament* (completed in 1930)[1] and G. Abbot Smith's *A Manual Greek Lexicon of the New Testament* (1937),[2] the latter being distinguished by the compiler's alertness to the influence of the Septuagint.

The Septuagint needed more consideration than Moulton in his first enthusiasm thought to be necessary. Later he modified his views. The opening of Luke's Gospel will give a splendid example of this. Luke begins with a studied four verses to align his work with the histories of his time, in stylish Greek and with a sophisticated vocabulary. Having thus prefaced his book he adopts a no less studied solemn biblical style, almost certainly because he wished to give his readers the surprise of finding they were beginning volume two of a history whose first volume was the Old Testament ending (in the Hebrew canon) with the Books of Chronicles, which supply the clue to understanding the organization of the priesthood in the Temple and the status within it of Zechariah, the father of John the Baptist. It might seem that the use of *koine* Greek plus the conscious or unconscious use of Septuagintal Greek would be enough to explain the language of the New Testament writers. An obvious objection to this simple solution is that these writers differ immensely in their styles and vocabulary. Deissmann thought that the Septuagint was 'the mother of the Greek New Testament', but some New Testament authors do not use the Septuagint and may not have known it, although they employ a language reminiscent of it. Thus contemporary students of this aspect of our study entertain the possibility of a Jewish Greek, a language which had come into being through the contacts between the two cultures and which was that used alike by those who translated the Old Testament into Greek and by the authors of the New Testament.[3]

The study of 'semitisms' in the Greek of the New Testament is a branch of investigation in its own right.[4] Sometimes they are due to the Septuagint, clearly when they occur in an actual quotation, almost as clearly in a reminiscence. This last class shades off into many examples which may be reminiscence and may be unconscious use of a word in an Old Testament sense. Indeed, sometimes the modern investigator may mistakenly attach a 'semitic' meaning to a word in a way not intended by the author. Again, since Aramaic was the language spoken by some of the authors, and by Jesus himself, it is natural to ask whether some books now in the New Testament in Greek might have had an Aramaic origin, in the sense that they were originally written in Aramaic. This view has been put forward seriously by C. C. Torrey whose *Our Translated Gospels* was succeeded by *Four Gospels* in 1933,[5] and by C. F. Burney in *The Aramaic Origin of the Fourth Gospel* in 1922.[6] There is no evidence for the truth of such a wholesale theory – no manuscript survival even in fragments and no reference to the gospels in Aramaic in ancient authors, if we except the reference of Papias to the work of Matthew; the latter is probably better regarded as evidence for a gospel circulating among Jewish Christians, not really by Matthew (either the disciple, or the author of the Greek gospel bearing that name) and perhaps best identified with *The Gospel according to the*

223

Hebrews of whose existence several church Fathers were well aware.

The method of M. Black[7] in his *An Aramaic Approach to the Gospels and Acts* (already mentioned in the previous chapter) is better, showing how sayings originally in Aramaic have sometimes lost their immediate thrust, though not their whole meaning, by translation and incorporation into a Greek writing; but it is unnecessary to regard the whole gospel as originally written in Aramaic.

When there is good reason for thinking that a word owes its force to the way in which it is used in the Old Testament, the Hebrew term or terms which it most often represents in the Old Testament can be discovered by consulting *A Concordance of the Septuagint and the other Greek Versions of the Old Testament*.[8] Thus it now becomes clear how necessary it is for the serious New Testament student to be familiar with the Old Testament and with its language as well as with the Greek of the New Testament itself.

No study of the ancient world which involves literature is so richly furnished with texts as that of the New Testament. Classical scholars must envy both the number and the antiquity of manuscripts which its students can consult. About 5,000 Greek manuscripts contain all or part of the New Testament. They are usually divided into the categories of Papyri, Uncials (manuscripts written in 'capital' letters separate from one another) and Minuscules (written in a flowing or cursive hand with the letters joined to one another). B. M. Metzger has produced a useful summary of this science in his *The Text of the New Testament*[9] and much of the following is taken from that book.

Papyri are the earliest witnesses to the text; they are grouped for the most part in two important collections, those of Sir Chester Beatty in Dublin and M. Martin Bodmer in Geneva. These give invaluable witness to the text of much of the gospels (not of all, though P75, a Bodmer papyrus, gives Luke and John completely), to Acts and to the epistles, and fragmentarily to Revelation.

Even the most important Greek uncials are too numerous for all to be mentioned here. Some English readers will remember subscribing to buy from Moscow in 1933 the Codex Sinaiticus (usually denoted by the Hebrew letter *aleph*), whose original home was the monastery of St Catherine on Mount Sinai, where the monks had no idea of the value of this or of their other similar treasures, when it was rescued by the patience and care of von Tischendorf in 1844 and 1859. This, the only uncial manuscript with the New Testament complete (it once contained the whole Greek Bible) is often on open exhibition in the British Museum. Visitors to the Vatican might be shown the Codex Vaticanus, denoted B, like the Sinaiticus dating from the fourth century. A (Alexandrinus) and C (Ephraemi) date from the fifth century. D is used to signify the remarkable manuscript presented by Beza, the French scholar who succeeded Calvin as leader of the Genevan Church, to the University of Cambridge in 1581. Of the fifth or possibly sixth century, Codex Bezae has most of the Gospels and Acts and a small piece of 3 John; especially in Acts it presents a series of unique and unexpected readings which have stimulated a whole literature of their own. It is noteworthy also for being in two languages, in Greek on the left hand page and in Latin on the right. Largely for its glamour we mention only one of the other important uncials, N, or Purpureus Petropolitanus, written in the sixth century in silver or purple vellum, except for the gold used for the contracted names of God and Jesus. Various leaves are now in different places all over the world.

Minuscules are of great importance when they represent a tradition of text older than themselves and bear witness to it stoutly by agreeing with one another in their variations from other traditions. Some few have accordingly been grouped in families named after their 'founder' members. Well-known are those of 'fam. 1', of 'fam. 13' and of 'fam. 1424'.

Two other groups of witnesses to the text must be mentioned – the ancient versions, that is, translations into other languages undertaken so early that they are often evidence for a reading as early as that found in the most venerable Greek manuscripts; and lastly, quotations from the Fathers. The most important versions are the Syriac, Latin, Coptic, Gothic, Armenian, Georgian and Ethiopic; but the Old Slavonic is also significant. The existence of these versions reflects the often heroic history of missions of the church in early centuries.[10]

To save space, our survey of the study of the text of the New Testament cannot begin at its true beginning but at a chosen point. We choose the printing of the standard text in England, that of the Parisian printer Estienne's (or Stephanus') third edition of 1550. It is this 'Textus Receptus' which is the centre for scholars who study this branch of learning in English, and it still enjoys great respect. But a new era began in 1881, which saw the publication of the text of Westcott and Hort (upon which was largely based the Revised Version translation of the English Bible of 1885). Basing their work on the past scholars Griesbach and Lachmann, they issued a new view of the transmission of the text by dividing the manuscripts and other witnesses into types: the Syrian, Western Alexandrian and Neutral, of which the latest was the Syrian (not to be confused with the Syriac version). Although there were many important scholars who contributed to the science, it will be effective if we follow here the main line of research and mention next B. H. Streeter, who devoted the first half of his monumental *The Four Gospels*[11] (discussed further in chapter 10) to a study of the manuscript tradition. The outstanding feature of his grouping was the isolation of forms of text current at the great centres of Christianity, attempting to show also that these 'standard' texts were used at times to 'correct' the variant readings of manuscripts acquired from other lines of transmission from travelling Christians who visited some great centre. The question-begging 'Neutral' text of Westcott and Hort was abandoned, and Streeter thought that the originals (now lost) had given rise to the Alexandrian (which absorbed most of the so-called 'Neutral'), the Eastern (which sub-divided into Caesarean – a discovery of Streeter – and Antiochene) and Western. The last boasts for its most interesting representative the famous D, supported by some versions, especially by the old Latin; but it is also supported by manuscripts of eastern provenance, and so, especially after Streeter, the term 'Western' is often enclosed in quotation marks. Streeter was content to sub-divide Western into Italy–Gaul and Africa.

Progress in this sphere has been marked by a refusal to be over-impressed by famous ancient manuscripts, and a tendency to judge readings on their individual merits, apart from the venerability of the manuscript which has supplied them; but other principles are invoked, such as the style of the author or linguistic considerations, better knowledge of the language sometimes rendering quite explicable a reading long regarded as certainly wrong. Part of the science consists in being aware of the mistakes which a scribe is bound to make from time to time, such as those caused by his eye falling on a similar ending of a word a little further on from that which he is copying, so that the intervening words are accidentally omitted. It is concerned also with alterations made deliberately, for doctrinal reasons.

The manuscript D will illustrate this last point. In 1933 A. C. Clark, a classical scholar of Oxford, issued a controversial edition of the Book of Acts based on the ingeniously argued theory that D provided the nearest to the original text from which the others had diverged. The idea was startling and did not settle the debate; we may bring it rather arbitrarily up to date by mentioning a monograph by E. J. Epp called *The Theological Tendency of Codex Bezae Cantabrigiensis in Acts* (1966),[12] which argues rather more persuasively that the variants provided by D can be best explained as due to a hand or hands whose owners were concerned to increase disrespect for the Jews in the story of the early church, and to enhance the reputation of the apostles; this explanation is quite opposite to that of Clark, and is likely to gain more support from the majority of scholars than Clark's over-ingenious arguments. Thus it is the scribe of D rather than all the rest who is convicted of deviation.

D is not the only manuscript to be affected by doctrinal considerations; its story should be taken as a clear example of phenomena which appear in less obvious forms in others. The result is that textual criticism is now ceasing to look for the impossible, although it was originally the avowed aim of the science; that is, the establishment of the original text. Such an operation would be regarded by many scholars today as both too complicated and too controversial. The study has become in fact a part of historical study, revealing evidence by which the preoccupations and prejudices of the times represented by the scribes can be seen and evaluated against evidence from other sources.

It remains to correct an impression which may have been given inadvertently. The variations within the text are never of sufficient size or importance to call in question the contents in any degree which vitally affects the meaning, and they are for by far the greater part quite minor. Rare exceptions to this rule, such as the ending of Mark's Gospel or the *Pericope Adulterae* (printed in the received text as John vii, 53–viii,11) are clearly indicated in all editions of the Bible likely to be used by students.[13]

The problem of the canon may well mean for a modern churchman the problem of deciding what ought to be the canon of a reunited church, having regard to the religious or historical value (the latter now better known through critical study) of various books which have at some time been venerated by Christians. For our more limited purpose, a review of the ways in which the New Testament is studied, the question is reducible to the form, 'What is the New Testament?'; that is, 'What books constitute it?' By the New Testament is meant a collection of books which the church came gradually to regard as sacred and authoritative, and worthy to be added to the writings now called the Old Testament which were already so regarded. To answer the question 'What is the New Testament?' is thus quite easy, but only if we are allowed to give a different answer for different people at different times and different places.

Ignatius, Papias and Justin represent a generation more concerned with what we should call the canon of the Old Testament than with that of the New. This is because they were able to appeal to living Christian tradition in oral form. In a passage beset with obscurity as to its precise meaning Ignatius at least bears unconscious witness to the fact that for him the supreme authority for his faith is Jesus Christ. In his letter to the Philadelphians, 8, his situation appears to be that there are men who will not believe anything which they do not find 'in the charters', that is, probably the Old Testament. Ignatius roundly proclaims with this as text, that 'to me the charters are Jesus Christ, the inviolable charter is his cross, and death, and resurrection, and the faith which is through him' (Loeb edition translation). Papias, in a passage preserved by Eusebius and important for what he says in connexion with the origin of the Gospels, explains that he would ask information of various authorities who had access to what the apostles had said and what others were saying, because he expected more profit from the living voice than from writings. In Justin we meet the end of this period, when the written gospels, which he calls 'memoirs of the apostles', are beginning to enjoy some authority.

In fact we have to do here with the concept discussed earlier which we have called the 'control'. For all these early Fathers Jesus is the control as he is for Paul, both in the sense that they all believe they have access to his words as he uttered them while on earth, and in the sense that he is the unseen spiritual authority for what the apostles, and others taught by them, continue to teach. Indeed, K. Aland, in a brief monograph entitled *The Problem of the Canon*,[14] divides the development of the canon into seven stages, the first of which is that in which the words of Jesus gain an authority equal with that of the Old Testament. He believes that they circulated orally but were also written down in collections from which quotations were taken. It should be noted that this is the judgement of a New Testament scholar, not of a church historian, and that the question of the canon here overlaps with that of the origin of the gospels. The second stage is that of writings believed to be by apostles, again attaining an authority like that of the Old Testament. In about 150, as has already been implied by the remarks on Justin above, the period of the canon, from the point of view of a church historian, begins. At this point the Fathers begin to discuss books by their titles and authors without going necessarily into the question of their contents when they are claiming or repudiating authority for them. In the fourth stage (by 200) the canon of the gospels is well recognized and a group of apostolic writings stands beside it. In the fifth 1 Peter and 1 John have gained recognition but that accorded to 2 Peter, 2 and 3 John, James and Jude is only partial. And at this stage the eastern church recognizes Hebrews and rejects Revelation whereas the western church does the opposite, at first sight an odd set of circumstances because Hebrews was probably written in the west where it was slow to gain acceptance and the book called Revelation in the east where it was for a long time rejected. All these facts have a powerful influence on the judgement of scholars when assessing the question of actual authorship, as distinct from, though not necessarily different from, the traditional authorship. In the sixth stage official decisions are made at councils and in the seventh dissident churches come slowly into line. On such a basis of stages, which corresponds well to what most scholars would accept, the seventh stage may be regarded as still operative. Our concern is almost wholly with the first five.

The heretic Marcion, who disliked the God of the Old Testament, taught in the years round 160 on the basis of a canon of his own according to which he recognized only the Gospel of Luke, in a form purified by himself, and his own editions of Galatians, 1 and 2 Corinthians, Romans, 1 and 2 Thessalonians, 'Laodiceans' (possibly Ephesians), Colossians, Philemon and Philippians. Such individual action provoked response from Irenaeus who makes much of the fact that there are four apostolic gospels standing, as it were, four-square in their witness. We know that he accepted Revelation as well as 1 John and 1 Peter. More interesting, he accepted also the *Shepherd* of Hermas and the Wisdom of Solomon. It is noticeable how the distinction between what belongs to the old and what to the new dispensation is blurred. The next evidence to list is a curious fragmentary document written in very bad Latin, found in Milan by L. A. Muratori who published it in 1740. It probably represents the canon of Rome about 200, and it gives some interesting information, much of which has been badly misinterpreted in the past by emending the admittedly bad Latin unnecessarily. Thus the point was missed that in speaking of Luke this document calls him 'a kind of legal expert' on the staff, as it were, of Paul. B. F. Westcott (for example) in his standard work, *A General Survey of the History of the Canon of the New Testament*,[15] emended the Latin so as to mean that Luke was Paul's journey companion, thus failing to see that the point made by the document was that Luke was in a sense defending

Paul by his writings, an insight first reached by A. A. T. Ehrhardt in 1953 who, on the basis of historical knowledge of Roman law, showed that phrases not before understood and therefore emended were metaphors from Roman legal and constitutional spheres.[16] This is an excellent example of discovery by cross-fertilization from one field of learning to another.

The Muratorian Fragment of the Canon rejects the *Shepherd*, telling us that the book is recent, written by the brother of a Roman bishop Pius I (140–155). Missing from the list as we might expect to find it appear to be 1 and 2 Peter (remarkable in a Roman document), Hebrews, James (both known in Rome a century earlier), and 3 John. The great uncial manuscripts may be used to show the situation in the fourth century: Sinaiticus contained, of apocryphal books, the Wisdom of Solomon, Ecclesiasticus, Judith, Tobit and I and IV Maccabees; and also the *Epistle of Barnabas* and the *Shepherd*. Vaticanus originally contained both the Old and New Testaments with the Apocrypha *except* the books of Maccabees. It is interesting to find the two great fourth-century uncials thus reflecting the ambivalent attitude of the church towards the Maccabees.

The question, 'What is the New Testament?', in the sense of 'What books *are* included in it?', can therefore be answered by setting out the facts, for these are not in dispute. The question, 'What books *ought* to be in the New Testament?', is a matter for ecumenical debate and not a matter only for New Testament scholars, who may be blamed for attempting to inflict on others what may seem to be no more than their opinions as to the authority of certain books, based on judgements as to their date and authorship. But it is worth remarking that the Muratorian Canon both insists that the authors of canonical scriptures must be apostles, yet knows that neither Mark nor Luke were apostles. Again, it does not appear to doubt the apostolic authorship of the *Apocalypse of Peter* but is reserved as to the title to be accepted. This need not surprise us: the human mind can (rightly) point out that the wall of Damascus as far as it dates from New Testament times exists only in low-standing fragmentary remains, if at all, and in the next breath point with triumph to the wall of a medieval fortress as that down which Paul was let in a basket. It can therefore certainly believe that an epistle has the authority of a particular apostle while knowing that he cannot have written it. Nor is it a matter of surprise that the period of decision, the sixth stage in Aland's convenient summary of the history of the canon, was that very much influenced by Athanasius who, as we have already seen, commended a particular list as canonical and yet shows clear evidence of holding in equal regard a number of other writings. It may be not far from the truth to say that the authority of the church may be claimed with all sincerity by some minds as at least one of their 'controls', in the sense in which this term has been used already in this book, but that unconsciously they use some other or some others, such as their own judgement, or it may be the guidance of the Holy Spirit.

Modern New Testament scholars would like to think that these two guides may not be incompatible; for the situation among them is such that they frequently quote evidence both from within and without the New Testament canon in order to show the practice and thought of the church at the time under discussion. Thus neither Catholic nor Protestant would hesitate to cite the evidence of the *Didache*, an early manual of church procedure and discipline of uncertain date, not indeed as pronouncing authoritatively upon doctrine but as a witness to the facts of the past. Again, no one would complain if the *Letters* of Ignatius or the works of Athanasius were recommended as illuminating reading for the inquirer into the genius of Christianity. Some might say they were of more value on any ground than the Pastoral Epistles or those of Jude and 2 Peter. Our real canon is less rigid than that of the official decisions of the church.

Ten

New Methods:
The Synoptic Gospels

LITERARY CRITICISM

To appreciate the issues involved in the critical study of the New Testament, we need some historical introduction, however brief. To find a starting-point we must go back to the early eighteenth century when J. D. Michaelis (1717–91), professor of oriental languages in the university of Göttingen from 1746, began scientific study of the New Testament, inquiring critically how it came into existence. He put on one side the dogmatic assumption of the inerrancy of scripture which was fashionable in his day, and insisted on reading the Old Testament historically and the New Testament without doctrinal assumptions. His work was made known to English readers by the translation by Herbert Marsh (1757–1839), professor of divinity at Cambridge 1807–16, but the stir which it made was slight compared to that created by the writings of Thomas Arnold (1795–1842) and Connop Thirlwall (1797–1875); these two English scholars did not follow Michaelis so much as B. G. Niebuhr (1776–1831), a German critical historian who demonstrated the importance of source criticism in his studies of the history of Rome.

D. F. Strauss (1808–74) began the really significant era of criticism of the New Testament with his two-volume work, *The Life of Jesus* (1835).[1] He pointed to the 'mythical' character of such passages as the Transfiguration. Moreover, it was useless to turn from the synoptics to the Fourth Gospel for more reliable historical facts, even though it appeared to be written by an eye-witness who ardently insisted that his witness was true. To quote a sentence of Schweitzer's which sums up Strauss's thesis, 'The Gospel of John is inferior to the Synoptics as a historical source just in proportion as it is more strongly dominated than they by theological and apologetic interests.' After Strauss it seemed that

233

little remained that was historical. The very title of his work, *The Life of Jesus*, is misleading; since it was published it has been impossible in the judgement of many scholars to write such a *Life*, although this judgement does not deter novelists, playwrights or film producers. According to Strauss not only the order but the events themselves are unhistorical. The events are doctrinally conditioned and the order is in each case imposed by the evangelist.

Meanwhile in the sphere of literary criticism conclusions were emerging which would modify this view, for they led to the belief that criticism could establish the historical reliability of Mark in contrast to the doctrinal presentations of the other gospels. Later we shall see that this view was destined to be called very seriously in question and to produce once more a radical historical scepticism. Strauss had used neither textual nor literary criticism, being content to contrast the synoptics with the Fourth Gospel. He did not consider the historical and doctrinal causes which might have explained the differences between them, and have left a core of material for reasonable historical reconstruction.

F. C. Baur (1792–1860), professor at Tübingen from 1826 to his death in 1860, worked over the material more critically: he recognized that the naïve picture in the minds of so many believers that the New Testament presents the plain history, and that subsequent thinkers within the church worked out its significance, is false. The authors of the books of the New Testament are themselves interpreters, as Strauss saw clearly with regard to the gospels. Baur studied the whole New Testament thoroughly but unfortunately he applied to this study the Hegelian theory of history, namely that a statement which can be regarded as thesis is succeeded by antithesis, and the two then reconciled in a synthesis. Baur went to work with the enthusiasm of a fundamentalist and explained the New Testament books on the basis of Judaic Christianity (thesis), Pauline Christianity (antithesis) and Catholic Christianity (synthesis). He was right indeed to begin with Paul, for his letters are the earliest documents in the New Testament. Baur's conclusion that Romans, 1 and 2 Corinthians and Galatians are alone authentic is a starting-point for all subsequent Pauline studies, although it has been necessary to discard some of his absurdities, such as the judgements that certain other letters (even including Philemon) are post-Pauline. However sadly Baur was misled by *a priori* assumptions derived from his philosophical convictions, he saw clearly the falsity of the assumption current in his day, before Strauss, that the Fourth Gospel was the right starting-point for reconstructing the history of Jesus. He was rightly convinced that the synoptics bring us nearer to the facts. This is the point which we shall take up in the next section, and which leads to a considerable discussion involving not only the relation of the gospels to one another but also the whole question of their historicity.

For the moment this must be postponed to allow for the entrance upon the stage of New Testament studies one who exemplified the Anglo-Saxon scholarly virtues at their best – enormous patience, sound judgement and persevering research. This was J. B. Lightfoot (1828–89) whose books on the New Testament, notably on the writings of Paul, and on related subjects, are still of such enormous value that they represent the clearest examples in English of that very rare type of literature, the theological volume whose appreciation in monetary value is due not to its character as a curiosity but to its continued relevance for modern study. Lightfoot's work established the genuineness of the *Epistle of Clement* and of seven letters of Ignatius (c. 35–107) which make clear references to certain people and books of the New Testament, and thus provide a basis for a reasonable chronology of the books of the New Testament. The details of this chronology still supply a host of unsolved problems, but it is unnecessary any longer to subscribe to Baur's extravagances, such as that the Gospel of Mark, now regarded almost universally as the earliest gospel and to be dated round A.D. 70, was a late book dating from not earlier than the middle of the second century.

Baur died in 1860, the year which saw the publication in England of *Essays and Reviews*,[2] a book which today would not arouse any strong feelings, but which led to considerable disturbance at the time, because it showed that scholars were departing from the fundamentalism which the layman, even today, often assumes to be the orthodox basis for study. Lightfoot, Westcott and Hort all contributed to it, though it was the essay by Jowett which caused the disturbance. For our purposes it is enough to notice the date coinciding with the death of Baur. Before we pass on we must also note the important position which the Gospel of Mark was gradually and ever more surely taking up in the sphere of gospel study and criticism, and we must pause to observe very briefly the rise of the particular branch of criticism which is concerned with the relations of the gospels to one another, and in particular of the synoptics to one another.

THE SYNOPTIC PROBLEM

Critical study of the gospels demands not only recognition of the different character of the Fourth Gospel from the synoptics, but also of the distinctive characteristics of the synoptics themselves. Harmonization of all four into one consistent account is fairly easily and quickly seen to be impossible, and a further great step forward is made when we recognize that the attempt to create a historical account by an amalgam of the synoptics is bound to fail; for they are not three independent accounts of the same story, but stand in some dependent relation one to another. The story of the emergence of the standard statement of this relation has recently been retold in a critical review of the process by which it was reached, in a book called *The Synoptic Problem*, by W. R. Farmer.[3] J. J. Griesbach (1745–1812) was the first to set out the synoptic gospels in three parallel columns for the sake of study and comparison, including this first 'Synopsis' (in this technical sense) in the first edition of his Greek New Testament in 1774. In 1783 Griesbach published his statement of the relations between the synoptics, claiming that Mark was dependent on both Matthew and Luke. In 1794 J. G. Eichhorn (1752–1827) published another solution of the synoptic problem, arguing for a number of sources behind the four gospels; his most important idea was that Matthew and Luke, but not Mark, used an early revised edition of the 'original gospel'; he thereby offered an explanation of passages where Matthew and Luke agree with one

236

another but differ from Mark. More radical views soon appeared: in 1835 K. Lachmann (1793–1851) took up a study by Schleiermacher of the evidence derived from Papias (c. 60–130), bishop of Hierapolis, which is preserved in Eusebius. Papias says that Mark wrote a gospel which was the result of his listening to the sermons of Peter, and that Matthew composed the *logia* (sayings) of the Lord in 'the Hebrew dialect' (usually taken to mean Aramaic). Papias adds that everyone interpreted Matthew's *logia* 'as he was able'. Lachmann followed Schleiermacher in taking Papias to have referred to *an original gospel* written by Mark, not our Gospel of Mark. The idea of an original or Urgospel had been introduced by Lessing (1729–81) in 1778, in a work which was published after his death. He believed that Matthew's gospel was a combination of the Ur-gospel and the 'sayings' of Papias.

Two alternative methods of study of the synoptic gospels and of their relations to one another thus appeared early. One was that associated with Griesbach; he believed Mark wrote a concise gospel by abbreviating Matthew and Luke, no matter what stages lay behind them. This is the way of study which Professor Farmer has sought to reopen by showing weaknesses in the other method; but this other method has captured the loyalty of almost all New Testament scholars. Farmer's book is thorough and distinguished but he is not likely to reverse the long trend of following the method set forward by Lachmann and crystallized by C. H. Weisse in 1838; this is based on the view that both Matthew and Luke were the result of combining the narrative of the Ur-gospel with the sayings source. We have not yet quite reached the form of the solution to the synoptic problem which was to be the triumph of the Oxford scholars of the early twentieth century. The reason is that the scholars whom we have so far summarized were haunted by a ghost – the Ur-gospel, a ghost which was to be laid by materializing him into Mark himself.

It is unnecessary to go into the details of the study which followed, but it will be useful to notice the solid work of H. J. Holtzmann (1832–1910) for his painstaking factual verification of the views of Lachmann and Weisse, and because of the great in-

237

fluence which his work exercised on subsequent scholars.[4] For him Mark was the original *apostolic* document (the ghost was not yet laid, Holtzmann still believing in the existence of a document now lost which stood behind Mark); moreover, Mark was historically reliable. Even further, and of great consequence, the non-Marcan document used by Matthew and Luke contained authentic words of Jesus. Such convictions were nearer the facts than the extravagant *a priori* views and errant chronology of the Tübingen school. They led to the belief, still alive in many quarters, that a historical life of Jesus could be reconstructed.

The denial of this possibility is a most important element in the present situation and will occupy us fully later, but we are not yet quite in the position to appreciate the factors involved in the argument: work of immense significance remains to be described, and this will take us well into the period with which our book is chiefly concerned. Indeed it will take us into the present situation, and it may be useful to observe that the position now foreshadowed, that Mark is the earliest gospel, and therefore deserves the most devoted study by those occupied with questions of historicity, is the basis of such important discussions at the present time. In the next section the relation of Matthew and Luke to Mark will come out more clearly.

THE FUNDAMENTAL SOLUTION

Holtzmann's definitive statement of the synoptic problem, made in 1863, was essentially a two-document hypothesis: Matthew and Luke used a sayings source not known to Mark and also independently copied an Ur-gospel which Holtzmann called Ur-Marcus.

The scene shifts from Germany to Oxford where William Sanday (1843–1920), a professor in Oxford from 1882, undertook a programme of the gospels and their relation to one another inspired and actuated by the work of the German scholars; a hesitant man, he did not accept the two-document hypothesis at once but inaugurated a seminar for the study of the material in 1894. His own book, in conjunction with other scholars, *Oxford*

Studies in the Synoptic Problem,[5] and Sir John Hawkin's *Horae Synopticae*[6] were fruits of this seminar's work and are still used for the material collected in them; but the main results have been enshrined for all time in the definitive book by B. H. Streeter, *The Four Gospels, a Study in Origins*, first published in 1924.[7] The fundamental solution of the synoptic problem, as Streeter calls it in this book, includes as a major fact, that both Matthew and Luke independently used Mark. The ghost had in fact already been laid, a fact shown by another English scholar, F. C. Burkitt (1864–1935) of Cambridge,[8] reflecting the opinion of J. Wellhausen in Germany. Matthew and Luke also used the sayings source (now universally known as Q – the reason for which is unknown, the explanation that it stands for *Quelle*, the German for 'source', being an English-speaking aetiological myth). Matthew and Luke also each had access to a further source peculiar to his own gospel. The material peculiar to Matthew Streeter called M, and that peculiar to Luke he called L. This four-document hypothesis remains to this day the basis of synoptic literary criticism, though some of M and some of L may well be the creation of the evangelist in question.

Two further points about the theory thus crystallized by Streeter deserve mention. One is the relation of Mark to Q, and the other the Proto-Luke theory. To begin with the first: if there once was a collection of sayings whose origin either was, or was believed to be, Jesus himself, and which was old enough to be earlier than the Gospel of Mark, it becomes relevant to ask whether Mark may have known this document. It is all the more relevant when we look carefully at the three synoptic gospels side by side in a synopsis and note how often a saying exists in two forms, the Q form and the Marcan form. Indeed it is often possible to argue with plausibility that Luke, for example, has not only reported a saying of Jesus twice, once when following Mark and once when using Q, but also that he has allowed the form of the saying in one place to be influenced by its form in the other. An example will make this clear. Mark iv, 21 has the famous saying about the absurdity of hiding a lamp under a 'bushel', i.e. a meal-tub or something of that sort. Here Luke (viii, 16) follows him, though

239

not using his exact words. When we come to Luke xi, 33 we find a very similar saying but one sufficiently different for us to look for the possibility of another source. Matthew v, 15 gives us Matthew's version of this saying; and it seems nearer to Luke than Mark. It seems that the version at Matthew v, 15 and Luke xi, 33 is the Q version while Luke viii, 16 is that which Luke has derived from Mark. If he was using two sources, Mark and Q, we have a natural explanation why he should include in his gospel two versions of what is substantially the same saying, and this explanation seems all the more likely when we know that this is but one example of a saying apparently existing in the two forms, the Marcan and the Q form. The necessity for a disciple to take up his cross (Mark viii, 34; Matthew xvi, 24; Luke ix, 23; cf. the apparent Q version Matthew x, 38; Luke xiv, 27), the reward of those who have left behind earthly ties (Mark x, 23; Matthew xix, 23; Luke xviii, 24; cf. the apparent Q saying Matthew x, 37; Luke xiv, 26), the denunciation of separation and remarriage as adultery (Mark x, 3 f., 11 f.; Matthew xix, 7, 9; cf. the Q version Matthew v, 32; Luke xvi, 18) may be mentioned as examples of this double appearance of sayings of Jesus in the synoptic record.

We noticed just now that Luke viii, 16 seems to be derived from Mark iv, 21 since this seems to be a point at which Luke is following Mark; but we also noticed that Luke did not use the exact words in Mark. If his version at xi, 33 (which seems to be a Q saying) is compared to Mark iv, 21 and Luke viii, 16, the facts are clearly consistent with the theory that Luke has allowed his version at viii, 16 to be influenced by Q, which he followed at xi, 33. An interesting small point, small but of some importance arises here. If the explanation which we have given of Luke's double reporting about the lamp not to be hidden is correct, he altered the Marcan version *before* he came to the place in his gospel which was to include the Q form. This implies that he was very familiar with Q and that perhaps it influenced him without his realizing it. This fact, if it be a fact, lends some force to the Proto-Luke theory which we must now explain.

Streeter observed Luke's preference for the Q version of sayings, but he observed something far more important still: leaving aside the non-Marcan (but certainly not Q-derived) first two chapters of Luke's gospel, which are unique in their substance and style, he saw that at iii,1, which reads like an opening or a re-opening of a book, Luke was still not using Mark, and that he did not obviously depend on him until Luke iv, 31. Even after that there came a passage, vi,1–11, about the call of Peter to disciple-ship, which is unique in the gospels, although it is reminiscent of John xxi,1–11. Streeter, who thought the Lucan Passion Narra-tive to contain enough elements different from Mark or peculiar to Luke to be ranked as non-Marcan, believed that 'the editor of the Gospel found Q . . . embodied in a much larger document (Q + L), which was in fact a complete gospel, somewhat longer than Mark . . . though Luke valued Mark highly, he regarded the document Q + L as his primary authority; when this and Mark contained alternative versions of the same incident or saying, he usually preferred that of Q + L. This document Q + L may be styled "Proto-Luke".'[9] Streeter therefore looked on Luke's other material as the framework into which he had fitted Marcan material.

The importance of such a theory, if it could be shown to be probably true, is obvious; in an age when Mark was held to represent an unsophisticated gospel deriving from the unstudied reminiscences of Peter, the discovery of another of similar anti-quity suggested close contact with the historical Jesus along not one but two lines of tradition. Vincent Taylor developed the theory[10] to an extent which most scholars regard as unwarranted, finding in passages which are closely parallel to Mark reason for assigning them to the special source with which Luke now came to be credited.

The failure to produce a copy of Q or even to agree about its exact delimitation makes it possible to doubt whether it ever existed. It could be regarded as a body of tradition in Aramaic known by heart by members of the Christian church in Palestine and represented as appearing in Greek form only when written down by Matthew and Luke; such a notion may be attractive through its consistency with the habit of learning by heart in that time and place. Yet such a view suffers from a very serious weakness: the main argument for the existence of Q is the great similarity in the actual wording of at least a considerable part of it as found in both Matthew and Luke. Since all this was written in Greek, the main argument for Q's existence is valid only for a Greek Q; it would be strange and remarkable if both Matthew and Luke, writing in different places and each translating an Aramaic document, hit so often upon exactly the same Greek versions. Use of the hypothetical Q is a 'common source' theory, that is, the similar characteristics of two or more documents are explained as due to their sharing common sources rather than one depending upon another. Such a hypothesis is useful and may well be right when other characteristics are present which suggest the improbability of either author having had access to the other's work. In the case of Matthew and Luke this improbability is usually held to be great and the position can be described in Streeter's words:

> If ... Luke derived this material from Matthew, he must have gone through both Matthew and Mark so as to discriminate with meticulous precision between Marcan and non-Marcan material; he must then have proceeded with the utmost care to tear every little piece of non-Marcan material he desired to use from the context of Mark in which it appeared in Matthew – in spite of the fact that contexts in Matthew are always exceedingly appropriate – in order to re-insert it into a different context of Mark having no special appropriateness. A theory which would make an author capable of such a proceeding would only be tenable if, on other grounds, we had reason to believe he was a crank.[11]

Most scholars would still accept this account of the matter as substantially stating their own position, and it may seem strange that anyone could suppose that Luke, if he copied Matthew for any of his material, should have done what Streeter shows he must have done: but A. M. Farrer, in an essay entitled 'On Dispensing with Q',[12] was unabashed, and argued that this is exactly what Luke did. The theory argued by Farrer has great interest, for it proceeded from a lively mind capable of a most enjoyable style, and one which dared – or rather rejoiced – to make a way against the stream. More important, it drew attention both to the fact that it was possible to swim against the stream, and to what struggles this must involve. Reflection upon Farrer's arguments will convince us that in this matter of synoptic criticism, we must look not for proof but for the most reasonable hypothesis; and that of Farrer does not seem the most reasonable when we consider not only the argument taken from Streeter, but also the facts that according to Farrer himself Luke did sometimes prefer not only Mark's order but even Mark's version to that of Matthew. There is no room to argue this in detail. It is interesting to see the revival of the outlook which believes that one of the synoptics had access to *two* of the others, an outlook which we can place in the Griesbach tradition, but we must observe that Farrer does not think for a moment that the position of Mark as the earliest gospel is at all upset. He combines elements of both the Griesbach and Lachmann traditions.

THE GOSPEL OF MARK AND ITS RELATION TO OTHER SOURCES

We have seen that the ghost of Ur-Marcus was laid by identifying the ghost with Mark himself; and we have mentioned the evidence from Papias that this gospel depended upon Peter. We have also raised the question of Mark's possible knowledge of Q, which led us aside to consider the Proto-Luke theory. The matter of Mark's relation to Q must now be briefly reviewed more directly.

In an essay contributed to *Oxford Studies in the Synoptic Problem*, Streeter thought that the overlap between Mark and Q was due to Mark having drawn upon Q. The passages where comparison can be made include the Temptation (Mark i,12 f.; Matthew iv,1–11; Luke iv,1–13) and the Beelzebub Controversy (Mark iii,22–27; Matthew xii, 22–30; Luke xi,14–23), and will serve to illustrate the subject. In the first instance Mark provides what at first sight looks like a summary of the account in Matthew and Luke (i.e. a Q account). A closer look shows that while the bare fact of temptation by Satan is common to all three gospels, this conceals a rather important point. Mark calls him Satan in his brief statement in verse 13; for the story in Matthew and Luke he is 'the devil', except that at Matthew iv, 10 Jesus addresses the tempter as Satan. The way in which he addresses him (the famous 'Get thee hence, Satan!' reminds us of the more famous 'Get thee behind me, Satan!' at Matthew xvi, 23) is most probably a Matthean touch, for Jesus speaks in this way only in these two places in the gospels, the phrase 'Get thee behind me, Satan!' in Luke iv, 8 being certainly an interpolation into Luke's text and accordingly found in the Authorized Version but omitted in the Revised Version and all carefully edited texts. Again, Mark's intriguing 'and he was with the wild beasts' is entirely without parallel in Matthew or Luke. Finally, the appearance of the ministering angels in Matthew (iv,11) after the temptations are over has accustomed us to think of them appearing at the same point in Mark, but if we read Mark as though for the first time, we find that he is telling us that while Jesus was in the wilderness forty days being tempted by Satan, angels were ministering to him. This point is made by Streeter in his *The Four Gospels* where he gives his reasons for now thinking that the evidence for Mark knowing Q is weaker than he had thought. He emphasizes the difficulty of supposing that Q lay before Mark in a *written* form, and the phrase, written in 1924, is a useful reminder of the necessity of regarding Q as a fluid concept, not insisting on its having existed as a written document, or if there were such a thing, that some of what we call for convenience Q material was orally preserved when Matthew and Luke used it.

The detail into which we have entered over the Temptation narratives may serve to excuse a similar exercise in the case of the Beelzebub Controversy where parallel though not precisely similar arguments lead to the same sort of conclusion, and whose study would give a similar glimpse into the meticulous care over small pieces of evidence which is vital in criticism of the gospels. Further, it may be claimed that we have arrived at a position where it is natural to contemplate the existence of a body of tradition which has been used by the synoptics in their different ways, each imprinting upon their material a certain theological stamp. While this theologizing of the material was from early times re-

garded as a characteristic of Matthew and Luke, the establishment
of Mark as the original gospel which both used led to the natural
conclusion, accepted no doubt without conscious examination,
that Mark was a primitive gospel. It was thus not only in the
technical sense that it was the 'foundation' gospel but in the
sense that it exhibited primitive ideas uninfluenced by theology.
Thus Burkitt in 1906 could write with great confidence:

> In St Mark we are, I believe, appreciably nearer to the actual scenes
> of our Lord's life, to the course of events, than in any other document
> which tells us of Him, and therefore if we want to begin at the beginning
> and reconstruct the Portrait of Christ for ourselves we must start from
> the Gospel of Mark. The other Gospels, even the Gospels according to
> Matthew and Luke, give us an interpretation of Jesus Christ's life. An
> interpretation may be helpful, illuminating, even inspired, but it
> remains an interpretation. The thing that actually occurred was the
> life which Jesus Christ lived, and our chief authority for the facts of
> that life is the Gospel according to Mark.[13]

Such views were by no means universal. Two famous German
scholars may be quoted in opposition, namely Wilhelm Wrede
(1859–1906), professor of the New Testament at Breslau, and Julius
Wellhausen (1844–1918), the famous biblical scholar and orient-
alist of Halle, Marburg and Göttingen. Both published studies of
Mark (Wrede in 1901, Wellhausen in 1903) arguing that Mark
was a highly theological document. While the belief that Mark's
material was derived from Peter still lingers on in Great Britain in
some quarters, even here there have been many who have seen
clearly the impossibility of thinking of Mark as primitive and
merely historical reminiscence. In this respect the commentary
published in 1925 by A. E. J. Rawlinson (an Oxford scholar who
became bishop of Derby in 1936) may be quoted. While there are
aspects which contrast with Matthew and Luke and suggest a
more obviously human Jesus, and certainly more obviously fal-
lible disciples, stories in Mark like the Baptism (i, 9–11), the Walking on the Water (vi, 45–52), and the Transfiguration (ix, 2–8)
make it impossible to deny the theological nature of his writing.

One may hazard the guess that such a judgement about Mark
could not have arisen if gospel criticism had not adopted its own

particular method – that of comparing one gospel with another and deducing the apparent use of Mark as a source by the other two synoptics, partly by observing more of the supernatural in them. If it had judged all the gospels from that critical point of view which does not hesitate to pronounce as mythical all that 'modern man' would so pronounce, such as voices from heaven, the appearance of beings long dead, and the like, Mark could not have been thought of as an authority for what actually happened in contrast to interpretations of what happened. The long road which led to the clear and true vision of Mark as the earliest gospel afforded another vision which was false, that of Mark as a mainly historical account of what really happened. True, Luke and Matthew used Mark and added interpretations. But Mark had himself already given them – and us – an interpreted history.

We are therefore led to ask, what was the nature and origin of the material used by Mark, by the compiler of Q (if there was only one such person), and by Matthew and Luke in those portions of their gospels where they commanded other material (M and L)? This brings us directly to the next section.

FORM CRITICISM

Examination of Mark by itself shows that the gospel is a sometimes quite rough joining together of a number of incidents and sayings which can very easily be isolated. This is even clearer in a synopsis where Matthew and Luke are arranged side by side with Mark, for it is then obvious that the same unit of the material often appears in different contexts. A most fruitful procedure of criticism arises from this fact of the easy distinguishability of one section from another. They can be isolated and then put into categories according to their form or content. In fact categorization according to form was the method used, and this kind of investigation is called form criticism.

The section of this book devoted to the Old Testament explains how this method has been profitably used in its study. Its story in connexion with the New Testament goes back to the work of Dibelius and K. L. Schmidt in 1919 and the most famous work of

Bultmann in 1921. The standard work of the first appeared in English in 1934 (M. Dibelius, *From Tradition to Gospel*),[14] and that of Bultmann not until 1963 when it was published under the title of *The History of the Synoptic Tradition*.[15] This delay reflects the slowness of British scholars at first to accept the new method; their tradition was that represented by the Oxford school brought to consummation with the work of Streeter, the publication of whose book was met with the reproach from German scholars that it entirely ignored all the form-critical work which had been going on for a number of years on the Continent. Indeed, while Streeter was working at his *Four Gospels* he must have been aware of the form critics, who had a right to be a little surprised that he ignored them, for they showed no opposition to the literary criticism, perhaps better called source criticism, carried out mainly by the Oxford school. Literary criticism is a necessary preliminary to form criticism. Now that the importance of each step is understood, criticism of the text, followed by source criticism and then, as a natural sequel, by form criticism with its inquiry into the material used by the writers or their sources, seems to be an inevitable procedure.

Opposition to form criticism has arisen less because of the alleged unsoundness of the method than because of the sceptical attitude which tends to result. It starts from the assumption that all the gospels are the product of the early church and reflect its beliefs and needs; they are held to be its presentation of Jesus as identical with the risen and exalted Lord, and not the product of eye-witnesses concerned to tell the writers what actually happened. Curiosity about the events was far from the hearts of the members of the early church. They needed stories to tell them what the absent Lord required them to do or to believe, or to enable them to represent him before a world used to 'gods many and lords many' as one just as capable of performing great miracles as his pagan rivals.

Accordingly, some of the units from which the synoptic gospels are composed are pronouncement-stories, accounts of conversations of Jesus with contemporaries, often opponents, on a controversial theme. Each one ends with Jesus' own authoritative pronouncement. Others are miracle-stories the point of which is not to exhibit a decision or piece of decisive teaching assigned to Jesus but to show him as the wielder of divine power. Each kind has its own form, the pronouncement-story clearly enough consisting of the introduction of the controversial matter, almost always by someone who either is or may be hostile, but sometimes by a short dialogue or else an unanswered question put by Jesus, and finally his own pronouncement on the matter. In *form* the pronouncement-story is not unlike many funny stories of all ages: dialogue leads to the 'punch-line' or 'point'. Thus the famous scene in the Temple when Jesus is asked about tax to Caesar (Mark xii,13–17) ends with what might be called a 'punch line'. The audience is not of course brought to laughter, but to something which may be recognized as the appropriate equivalent when they are struck with great seriousness: 'they marvelled at him'.

Miracle-stories also show consistency of form – the sufferer is brought or comes, the disease is described, healing may be requested, Jesus heals, the crowd marvels. It is true that the order could hardly be otherwise, but the form does not consist only in the order but in the elements corresponding in so many of such stories. They are, so the form critics would urge, to a large degree, and with only few exceptions, stereotyped as to form.

An important part of the theory is to ask and to answer the question, from what situation in real life do these stories arise? What situation produced them? If we ask the question in the latter form we are aware of an ambiguity: do we mean produced the *event* or produced the *story*? The form critics have good reasons for meaning the *story*: in the case of miracles they point to the likeness to stories circulating in both the Jewish and the Hellenistic world of the time when the gospels were being written, and to the presuppositions of such stories; these were very often that the illnesses were caused by demons, so that the effectiveness of the story and therefore its truth depends upon belief that Jesus exorcized the demons and so worked his cures. Since we now know that demons are not the causes of diseases we cannot believe the stories; but we can assign a reason for their having been told of Jesus – the desire to enhance his reputation. This desire lay in the minds of members of the early church.

This introduces us to another aspect of form criticism. Every passage in the gospels has a life-situation which produced it. The uncritical reader believes this life-situation to be that given in each case by the gospel. For example, according to Mark xii,13–17 Pharisees and Herodians ask Jesus a question about taxes and he gives them the famous answer, 'Render unto Caesar the things which are Caesar's, and unto God the things which are God's.' The situation is a point in the life of Jesus when he is teaching in the Temple at Jerusalem and his opponents are trying to trick him into a damaging statement. On form-critical lines it is possible to suggest another origin for the story: members of the early church needed guidance on the question whether in view of their loyalty to God alone and their belief in an imminent judgement on this world, they ought to pay taxes to the Roman Empire. It was safer to do so, but was it consistent with Christian principle? To answer these doubts, a story was invented which invested a prudent practice with the Lord's authority. On this view, the life-situation which produced the story is that of the early church. Form critics use this notion a great deal; they look for a plausible situation-in-life, in German Sitz im Leben, where a story or a saying might have arisen to meet a particular need.

In the example chosen, it is possible to believe that Mark gives the true situation, and that the dialogue between Jesus and his opponents occurred just as he describes. In that case, the form critic would rejoin, at any rate the reason for the preservation of this incident lies in the situation of the early church. In this story they found an answer to their own problem, and they therefore remembered and repeated it. The story about the coin in the fish's mouth, Matthew xvii, 24–27, is far less credible; in this instance the form critic commands more attention when he suggests that it is quite unhistorical, and that the Sitz im Leben can be dated after the destruction of the temple in A.D. 70 when the tax was still being collected – but for the Roman government.

The form critics' theory about the pronouncement-stories is the same. They arise from the need to quote the Lord for teaching purposes. Here again the reason for scepticism is that such stories often imply interests and preoccupations which were not those of Judaism in the time of the ministry of Jesus, but of the early expanding church in its missionary situation, often in the Hellenistic world, wider than Palestine. As we have seen in connexion with 'Render unto Caesar . . .', sometimes a saying of Jesus may be authentic yet significant for the situation of the early church. In such a case one may detect the re-use rather than the invention of a saying. There has been a *Sitz im Leben* in the ministry of Jesus itself, but the significance of the passage was then different. Thus, for example, the well-known reference to the lost sheep appears in different contexts in Luke xv, 1–7 and in Matthew xviii, 10–14. In Luke, if we read from the beginning of the chapter, we see clearly that the saying is a defence by Jesus of his own practice of associating with unclean persons to the scandal of devout Jews. He appeals to the latter by in effect saying that his conduct is natural and like that of any shepherd faced with a parallel situation. In Matthew, if the whole passage is read in order to see the context, it is clear that this evangelist has used it to emphasize the importance of not one sheep being lost. Matthew is thinking of a situation – his own – where the church deprecates the loss of even one member. In this instance there is no difficulty about imagining the *Sitz im Leben* being originally in the ministry of Jesus and correctly preserved by Luke, because Jesus' association with unclean persons is not likely to have been invented. Whether the discussion took place at the point in Jesus' ministry represented by Luke's account of the matter is an entirely different question. Our judgement of what was the original situation which produced the saying and of what was the situation in which Matthew used it is based on our conception of the historical probabilities.

Less likely to have had any original situation in the life of Jesus himself are passages reflecting the concerns of a later age. Thus for example it seems that the early church, regarding itself as a branch of Judaism and having no thought of being other than orthodox, observed all the customs of Judaism. Only by degrees did they abandon the normal fasts and the observance of the Sabbath. Thus Mark ii, 18–28 contains units, easily separable, which may well seem to have been assigned to Jesus to say in order to give the necessary authority for these changes, which gave offence to Jews unconverted to belief in Jesus as the Messiah. It remains possible that Jesus taught these things substantially as they are reported, but in that case we have to explain why the early church, as we know it from evidence in the epistles and even in Acts, did not apparently follow his teaching.

It will be clear that the *Sitz im Leben* allotted to any particular unit of tradition is of the utmost importance: if this can reasonably be seen as belonging to the life of Jesus, the unit concerned may be authentic; if it appears to have owed its origin to the community, it seems that it must be at least in some respect unhistorical. In some instances the *Sitz im Leben* is likely to be the Palestinian church since the point at issue would not constitute a problem for the church in the Hellenistic world. When it is necessary to find dominical authority for abandonment of the Sabbath, stories such as that found in Mark ii, 23–28 arise. It is regarded as noteworthy that Jesus is not compelled to defend himself but his disciples, that is the church. Again, arguments settled by appeal to scripture clearly argue at least a Jewish milieu, while the performance of miracles enhances the reputation or commends consideration of Jesus to non-Jewish audiences accustomed to stories about the exploits of demi-gods and heroes. Bultmann admits that some of the miracle-stories (such as exorcisms) are more at home on Palestinian soil, but claims that the overwhelming majority must originate within the Hellenistic environment.

A clear and interesting example of the influence upon a saying of the evangelist's situation lies in the addition of forbidding a woman to divorce her husband (Mark x, 12), meaningless within Judaism but significant in Rome where Mark probably wrote. There are no doubt many such additions to sayings explicable by the *Sitz im Leben* in which they are used; Matthew xxii, 7, a reference to the destruction of Jerusalem in A.D. 70 and an incongruous element in the story being related, is intelligible as an example of the aggressive apologetic of a Jewish Christian church claiming in opposition to the local synagogue to be the true Judaism. Such illustrations cannot prove that nearly all the material arises from the community rather than from Jesus; but the needs of the community sometimes suggest the most probable explanation of an incident. Thus Matthew xvii, 24–27 is hard to accept as historical but gives a good argument for Christians paying the Temple Tax (still levied by the Romans after the Temple's destruction). In this passage the argument is represented as spoken by Jesus himself and clinched by an accompanying miracle.

FORM CRITICISM AND THE HISTORICAL JESUS

Form criticism could therefore lead to the discovery as far as possible of which sayings of Jesus are authentic, at the same time setting them in some credible milieu of his ministry. Such a use of this method would also be able to show clearly, at least in a number of instances, how such material was re-used by the writers of the early church (the evangelists) who used the material by putting it in such contexts and altering it, perhaps only slightly, to give the impression that this was the original milieu. They put it in a situation in the life of Jesus, but this situation is made to parallel that in which they themselves lived. Thus Jesus is made to argue with the Pharisees: this is really the early church arguing with the Jews of their own time. Such a theory of re-use can be regarded with equanimity by even conservative Christians.

Less welcome to them is the other direction in which this method may influence scholars who use it; this is the direction which leads to an extreme historical scepticism founded perhaps on grounds easily understood by those with any knowledge of human nature, but not on altogether logical grounds. The psychological grounds which may be so sympathetically understood are capable of being summarized simply as follows. The origin of certain material can be attractively and ingeniously explained in such a way that almost none of it *need* be ascribed to the Jesus of history – therefore none of it *can* be rightly ascribed to him. Indeed, among the criticisms which have been brought forward against form criticism, that which will have occurred to many readers is perhaps the most interesting and fruitful: this method severs the material from Jesus apparently absolutely; but is not the object of such investigation to show how such material is *connected* with Jesus, for all critics agree that ultimately he is in some important sense the cause and origin of all the material? It would not have come into existence but for him; is it not therefore an extreme and unlikely point of view to deny that *anything* which has survived comes from him?

Can the impasse be broken down? There are several ways in which this might be done and it is now necessary to explain some of these. First, we can begin by modestly taking this position: granted for the time being that the evangelists and even their sources so surrounded Jesus with interpretation that we cannot see a clear picture of him or of his teaching, we can take up the story where it will be agreed that history is firmly based. This point will be the activity of the earliest Christians as represented by their own writings (the clearest example is Paul) and by the earliest narrative sources about their activity. If we take these narrative sources first, we are faced with the book of the Acts of the Apostles, a book whose origins are very difficult to determine. What actually happened in those earliest days in Jerusalem represented by the first eight, or even twelve, chapters of Acts, is quite lost to us. No doubt Luke did his best, and he was careful and thorough, but he did not dispose of the material which would give us a certain account. This may well be true, but perhaps by paying careful attention to what he has given us we can find, not the sequence of events, but at any rate what the apostles preached. For even though Luke was compelled to make up their speeches, we may find traces of very ancient material in them, a kind of ground base or recurring theme upon which these speeches are constructed. If this can be distilled out of the early chapters of Acts we could then check to see whether it is reflected in Paul, whose writings are very early. This was the very procedure which was followed by C. H. Dodd, who in 1935 delivered at King's College, London, three lectures, published in 1936 in a short book entitled *The Apostolic Preaching and its Developments*.[16] In the sphere of New Testament study this is the book *par excellence* which may be referred to in the cliché, 'whose importance is out of all proportion to its size', without any fear that the truth of the cliché can be denied.

The essence of Dodd's work in this book is this: a concise and highly significant formula expressing the conviction and the matter preached by the earliest preachers can be recovered and reconstructed from speeches in Acts and from Paul. It would be better to say that the earliest protagonists proclaimed rather than preached; they acted rather like heralds who proclaim aloud something important for all to hear. The Greek for herald is *kerux* and that which is proclaimed is *kerugma*, usually anglicized into *kerygma* in connexion with our subject. The early *kerygma* can be seen clearly in the words of the New Testament as it occurs in different places in Acts and Paul by turning to the excellent chart at the end of Dodd's book, and may be fairly summarized in these words: 'As prophesied, Jesus, marked out by God as his Son by the mighty works which he did, was delivered up to be crucified. He died, but God raised him from the dead. We are witnesses of these things. Believe, repent, be baptized!'

Subsequent criticism of Dodd's thesis has cast doubt on whether there ever was such an explicit formula, and this is perhaps quite an important historical point, to decide whether or not the apostles or other missionaries of the early church consciously crystallized their message into a formula of this kind and so handed it out to converts who wished to take their place as missionaries. It is clear for example that Paul did receive something from the church which he began by persecuting and went on to serve, but it is not clear that he would have reduced it to exactly these terms. Nevertheless, the *kerygma* thus reconstructed cannot by any stretch of the imagination be held to falsify what the early church actually preached. It may never have been in any of the forms, so like one another, which Dodd discovered; but any one of them may well represent in essence what the church did preach. For example, after reading all that is extant of Paul, we could not say that such a summary was an unfair summary of the basis of his gospel. It must be admitted that no form of the *kerygma* derivable from Paul would contain an explicit reference to miracles performed by Jesus and this may be an important weakness in the chain of descent from the historical Jesus which we should like to establish; for the *kerygma* as derived from Acts derives from a source or sources of unknown date. The attribution of miracles to the historical Jesus will remain suspect for the modern investigator. The other elements are clearly derivable from Paul and it is striking that they include the physical resurrection of Jesus.

It may be that the results of this line of inquiry are meagre in quantity. If this is meant to provide some link with the historical Jesus, we must admit that it gives us little. We may well claim that any reconstruction of the historical Jesus must be consistent with it, but such a condition will easily be met by the very fact that it leaves all too much to be supplied. This is true and is in itself an important point, but it must not blind us to the quality of the result. The early *kerygma* was not about the Jesus of history to which some critics have reduced him, the easily credible teacher of a moral ideal called in the quaint language of his own day 'the kingdom of God'. It was about a person of more than human spiritual stature, who rose from the dead. It was about a person in relation to whom a man's own final destiny is determined. Any reconstruction therefore must be true to a figure who could cause his contemporaries to write about him as they did.

The description of the course of criticism which has been given so far has led into the sphere of interpretation, into the sphere of the quest for the historical Jesus which, strictly speaking, lies outside that of this book; but it is impossible to avoid the necessity of giving some brief indications of the results for that inquiry which arise from the development of criticism. The kind of source criticism which appeared in the classical statement by Streeter was in its infancy when Albert Schweitzer (1875–1965) wrote *The Mystery of the Kingdom of God*.[17] In this Schweitzer interpreted the life of Jesus on the basis of the eschatological expectations which Jesus seems in the synoptics to entertain, and which had been in an increasing measure regarded as unauthentic and attributed to the evangelists and their contemporaries by the prevailing 'liberal' school of theologians, some of whom were Schweitzer's theological tutors at Strasbourg.

In 1906 he wrote a great theological classic, one of the most brilliant and interesting books of the century. The original German *Von Reimarus zu Wrede* was translated in 1910 into English with the appropriate title, *The Quest of the Historical Jesus*,[18] giving an account of some of the most important attempts at reconstruction of the life of Jesus from the eighteenth century until his own day, and culminating in a restatement of his own solution. This dramatic (and it has been said even Wagnerian) picture of Jesus convinced of the imminence of the kingdom of God on this earth and, during his ministry, of the necessity for him to sacrifice his own life deliberately in order to save his people from the period of woes believed to presage the kingdom, and so to usher it in – this picture has exercised a fascination over many readers. Its construction involved a theory of dislocation of order in the Marcan story and the use of a passage in Matthew as pivotal which most scholars would regard as historically unacceptable; indeed the latter method disregarded the result of criticism which thought of Matthew as dependent on Mark at this point. Schweitzer, long regarded as the deliverer of the *coup de grâce* to liberal theology, seems in greater historical retrospect the last and most giant-like of the old liberals. Such a reconstruction rendered a view of Jesus which saw him at his end a deeply disillusioned man, uttering a cry of despair from the cross as he died. Logically Schweitzer provided a Jesus who, in the judgement of intelligent lay thought unfamiliar with the gospel criticism which has been outlined above, was completely credible historically and quite incapable of being erected into a figure who may be the object of worship. It is no part of our task to pursue an apologetic course at this point, but the story is incomplete without the observation that the Jesus thus reduced to human dimensions nevertheless exercised upon Schweitzer the same sovereign claim which more orthodox Christians have ever felt and which the earliest *kerygma* expressed. Schweitzer never ceased to be a follower of the Jesus who, according to his interpretation had died bequeathing to his followers no kingdom, and no hope of one, but only dis-illusion and despair.

These facts have their relevance. They suggest an unease with the solution and invite others. In fact the long course of critic-ism's development was to issue not in a despairing unbelief but in extreme historical scepticism. In 1935, for example, appeared R. H. Lightfoot's *History and Interpretation in the Gospels*, [19] in which the priority of Mark and the form critical atomization of Mark were used, along with the insight that Mark was a highly theological document, to produce a radical scepticism as to the historicity of the material contained in all the gospels. If Schweit-zer could say at the close of his book that Jesus 'comes to us as One unknown', [20] he could at least thereby suggest a nearness (though in what sense is not clear) of the unknown person of Jesus to his followers; Lightfoot, a more orthodox Christian, in a clos-ing passage almost as famous, has to confess 'that the form of the earthly no less than of the heavenly Christ is for the most part hidden from us. For all the inestimable value of the gospels, they yield us little more than a whisper of his voice; we trace in them but the outskirts of his ways'. [21]

This impasse, this extreme scepticism, has been largely due to the work and influence of Bultmann. In him historical scepticism is allied to a particular concept of history derived from existential philosophy. On this view the real historical event is not an event or a series of events in the past, but the coming of Christ to the potential believer (who must make an existential decision at this confrontation) in the Word preached by the church. The form of Christianity thus commended is a demythologized *kerygma* re-presented in the terms of existentialism. What therefore matters to Bultmann is the bare historical fact of Jesus, that there was a Jesus of Nazareth, plus the church's *kerygma* concerning him. Faith must not and cannot depend upon conviction about the historic-ity of certain events confined to the past. The resurrection does not consist in the rise of Jesus from the dead as a physical fact, but in the *kerygma* and its impact.

Bultmann's position is hard to overturn, but it is small wonder that it leaves a discontented feeling that the importance of the historical events must be greater than this, that Christian conviction must rest at least in part on the assurance that the Jesus presented by the gospels is continuous with and consistent in character with the Jesus proclaimed by the church. This conviction has led to the latest development along this line, the New Quest for the Historical Jesus. Description of it will take us a little out of the way of the story of biblical criticism, since here we are very much involved with historical judgement and interpretation; but a brief account is necessary, in order to show what the present position is.

It is fundamental that it is no longer assumed that the historical Jesus is the centre of Christian faith. This place is taken rather by the *kerygma*. Already, before Schweitzer, M. Kähler (1835–1912) had published a book[22] in 1892 showing that the gospels could not be sources for the life of Jesus and that their Christ, and not the 'historical Jesus', was the concern of Christian faith. Bultmann extended this position to the point where what is claimed about this Christ is the centre of faith. Historical study must not try to reconstruct the Jesus of history because such an attempt is both illegitimate and impossible. It is the former because it implies the use of analogy with our own consciousness, and we cannot say that Jesus' understanding of himself would offer any analogy with our understanding of ourselves. It is in any case impossible because of the nature of the sources.

The New Quest starts from this position but seeks to modify it; it makes this attempt under the conviction that there must be a continuity between the historical Jesus and the Christ of the *kerygma*. This point is taken up explicitly by Käsemann who – significantly enough – believes that we have some knowledge of the historical Jesus obtained from the application of criticism of the kinds we have been describing, including form criticism. We can assert for example that the messianic claims of Jesus are explicit in the *kerygma* but already implicit in his own teaching. The development of this continuity has led to the new hermeneutic or interpretation of which Fuchs (born in 1903, and since 1961 Bultmann's successor at Marburg) and Ebeling (born in 1902, and since 1962 director of the Institute for Hermeneutics at

Tübingen where he is also a professor) are two main exponents among continental scholars.

Fuchs establishes the Pauline gospel and then looks for its reflection in the account of Jesus which he wins from criticism of the synoptic outline. The Pauline gospel and what Jesus said both about his own and about our relation to God are fundamentally the same. Paul had a vision of the risen Christ and accepted him as Lord (1 Corinthians ix, 1). Henceforth, in place of the anxiety before judgement which separates man from God, Paul has the joy which unites an individual to God, because Christ sits on the throne with God. The judge has become gracious. To find the essence of what Jesus taught about his own and our relation to God, Fuchs interprets the Parable of the Prodigal Son. In this story Jesus is defending his own conduct in rejecting no sinner, and implies that he bases his conduct on the will of God. The Father in the story is Jesus acting for God. 'Jesus therefore implies that God, despite his severity, mercifully receives the returning sinner, as he himself does.' This attitude, Fuchs claims, is essentially the same as that of Paul; but the claim of Jesus is that his own conduct reflects the will of God. Jesus' enemies 'could not tolerate his claim to assert through his own conduct that God's will was a gracious will'. This was the main reason for their bringing about his death. During his ministry Jesus demanded of his hearers a decision, the same decision as that which he had made; it concerned the time of the rule of God. Jesus, more radical even than John the Baptist, attempts 'to make the time of the rule of God his own'.

Although Fuchs gives careful reasoning to account for these results, it is necessary only to state his viewpoint to see that it is highly individual, and perhaps reminds us of a characteristic of the old liberal approach; the scholars of that period had shown a great confidence that they could reconstruct what Jesus *really* thought about himself. Fuchs – and he is not alone in this – seems to claim to know what Jesus *really* taught about the rule of God and even implies some insight into Jesus' mind. This introduces a second point in Fuchs's interpretation; Jesus revealed that his decision was 'to make the time of the rule of God his own' not only by his teaching but also by what he *did*. He gathered 'together the unorganized group of the eschatological community in the midst of a perverse generation' (cf. Matthew xi, 16 f.). This action gave the outward appearance of a challenge both to Rome and to the authorities of his own nation, but the reality was quite different: it was 'to be interpreted in a purely religious sense', and it concerned his relationship with God.

D. E. Nineham has complained about another book in this sphere, that of G. Bornkamm, *Jesus of Nazareth*,[23] that it is based too optimistically on 'assumed' or 'generally agreed' results; in the case of Fuchs this complaint, well justified, might be reinforced by another against the extremely individual interpretation of what might be called the character and outlook of the historical Jesus. Bornkamm represents Jesus as 'of unmistakable otherness,'[24] a prophet of the coming kingdom of God whose authority resides in his fulfilling the present will of God and who therefore exhibits a unique sovereignty. He proclaimed both by his teaching and his life (which included his faithfulness to death) 'the light of the coming God'.

The Teutonic genius for making an issue clear by ruthless investigation and for making subsequent reconstruction of startling novelty is exemplified no less in the new quest than in the old. If German scholars work so hard that their lives must seem a perpetual study of books akin to a life sentence, for the readers of their results there is never a dull moment. American scholars have been much occupied in keeping pace with German speculation, in surveying it, and in evaluating it. Thus many English-speaking readers made their first acquaintance with the new quest through *A New Quest of the Historical Jesus*, by J. M. Robinson,[25] although the author put forward a position of his own as well as reviewing both the old and new quests as far as that time. In this book he makes a great deal of the modern view of history which, in the words of N. Perrin, 'seeks to mediate an encounter with the past at the level of self-understanding, and approached the historical Jesus and his message in this way'.[26] Robinson thought that this 'modern historiography' (the language is distinctly American) 'mediates an existential encounter with Jesus' just as the *kerygma* does. To quote Robinson himself, 'we have, for example, in the parables, in the beatitudes and woes, and in the sayings on the kingdom, exorcism, John the Baptist and the law, sufficient insight into Jesus' intention to encounter his historical action, and enough insight into the understanding of existence presupposed in his intention to encounter his selfhood'.[27] Put differently, the encounter of the historian and the encounter with the *kerygma* make the same existential demand, that of recognizing in this message clothed in its Jewish form, eschatology and all, 'the eternal word of God'.

Subsequently Robinson has dropped his emphasis on the encounter with the historical Jesus through the historical approach, and now lays emphasis rather on the parallel between the message of Jesus and the *kerygma* of the early church. Some phrases have already been quoted from the book called *Rediscovering the Teaching of Jesus* by Norman Perrin,[28] which exhibits the same American ability to survey a very wide field and to summarize it, and then to suggest another possible approach to the problem. The title indicates the book's main subject, but phrases so far quoted come from a final chapter on 'Knowledge of the historical Jesus'. The teaching of Jesus is a distinguishable subject but intimately connected with that of the search for the historical Jesus since his recorded teaching is always given in relation to events actual or imminent in the historical sphere. The uninformed asumption that the teaching of Jesus can be represented properly as a series of unconnected maxims (in form at least parallel to the thoughts of Chairman Mao) cannot survive an attentive reading of any one gospel. However, since there is imperfect agreement among scholars on some vital points connected with what Jesus thought about history and current or imminent events, any attempt to decide what Jesus actually said must be attended with great risk of error.

Perrin's book can hardly therefore be the end of the debate, but will serve very well to indicate its present impasse. The author proposes as criteria for his quest those of dissimilarity, coherence, and (with safeguards carefully explained) multiple attestation. It is obvious that a saying, to be authentic, must cohere with what Jesus stood for or taught as a whole, and we have seen that there is some broad agreement about what these things were; it is equally obvious that if a saying is attested by a number of different sources in different circumstances, and it does not appear that the circumstances have dictated the saying, then this saying has a claim to be considered authentic. The criterion of dissimilarity from the church or contemporary Judaism is remarkable, for it shows less clearly a way of gaining specimens for a collection of historically trustworthy sayings than a way of excluding doubtful members from such a collection. It will tend to exclude rather than to include, for some actual sayings of Jesus may well either serve the need of the early church or reflect contemporary Judaism, or both; and these are the two means suggested for testing in this way. Perrin sees this clearly but regrets that 'the brutal fact of the matter is that we have no choice'. It would not be unfair to sum up the situation in Perrin's words: the 'early Christian equation' of Jesus with the risen Lord 'justifies us in using that historical knowledge [gained by modern criticism] to test the validity of claims made in the name of *Jesus* Christ and the authenticity of a *kerygma* claiming to present Jesus *Christ*: to be valid and authentic these must be consistent with such knowledge as we have of the historical Jesus'.[29]

'Such knowledge as we have' suggests that it is meagre, and that in the amassing of such knowledge we have not advanced beyond the old liberals; and, alas, that the men of the new quest may be as subject to the accusation of subjectivity as they were. But there is a vital difference. The old liberals were puzzled by the apparently unbridgeable gap between the simple teaching of Jesus and the theological structure of Paul. With the insight that the gospels are theological documents and that from them we cannot extract an unembroidered picture of the 'historical' Jesus has come the more positive insight that they present a theology consistent with that of Paul. The way in which a Fuchs or a Bornkamm presents the outlook of either may be highly individual, but they and many others have shown there is a real correlation between them. For both, all depends on the resurrection. Paul proclaims the risen Lord; he emphasizes that Christ is risen and that his earthly days are now of no importance. The gospels claim that his earthly days had the same significance: they showed that this was the son of God, destined to die and rise again *because* he was, is, the son of God.

It is impossible to prophesy how this debate will continue; it must seem to all who contemplate it to have reached a profoundly unsatisfactory stage. Dissatisfaction with form criticism itself has also been voiced by many critics, but on the whole all serious critics of the New Testament have allowed it some validity. The most significant statement of its limitations has come from Sweden, not because scholars there have entered upon a detailed study of those limitations, but because they have sought to find an alternative road of advance in gospel criticism, largely under the conviction that Jesus himself must have had far more influence in the creation of the tradition about him than the form critics have often been willing to allow.

The two scholars mainly concerned have been Harald Riesenfeld and Birger Gerhardsson. The former delivered something of a manifesto at the opening of a Congress on 'The Four Gospels in 1957' held in that year at Oxford. In his lecture, entitled *The Gospel Tradition and its Beginnings*,[30] he drew attention to the references to the *paradosis* or tradition in the New Testament itself. Excellent examples of passages which betray the existence of such a tradition are 1 Corinthians xi, 23 and xv, 3, where Paul refers to his having received and passed on a tradition evidently entrusted to him by the church when he was converted. The receiving and passing on, Riesenfeld argued, were technical terms known also in Judaism, where such a process had its own history and technique. The facts about the latter were set out in B. Gerhardsson's *Memory and Manuscript*,[31] but neither scholar has been very successful in persuading his colleagues anywhere that there was, as these two claim, a body of 'holy word' from and about Jesus, which was preserved and communicated orally like so much of Jewish law and story.

It may well be that this line of approach has yet much to give. A positive gain, besides drawing attention to the possibility that the tradition in the New Testament may have included a body of material used subsequently and perhaps after some changes by the evangelists, is to have brought into consideration the picture of Jesus himself in some way controlling the formation of the tradition about himself. It is not necessary to believe that Jesus actually said he would do this by means of the Holy Spirit whom he would send; but we must acknowledge the manifest importance of this belief in the early church as it produced the New Testament, and many other books, some written later, which the church was unable to regard finally as authoritative. Indeed there were some which it had to repudiate from the beginning.

It may be well to observe what the church seems to have held quite clearly, as it is expressed in the Fourth Gospel: there Jesus is represented as saying to his disciples as he prepares to leave them, two things about the divine guidance which they will receive from the Holy Spirit who will act in his stead. The first is that the Holy Spirit will bring to their remembrance all the things he has said to them (xiv, 26); this seems to guarantee the reliability of what authorized reporters tell the church and the world about the teaching of the historical Jesus. The other point made about the divine guidance which the disciples will enjoy, a point credited to the utterance of Jesus himself, is that the Holy Spirit will lead them into further truth which will rest upon the authority of the Father and upon his own authority. If we read with attention John xvi, 12–15 we see that this is the meaning.

Further reflection will show that belief that the teachers within the church were thus guided was bound to blur the distinction between the words spoken by the historical Jesus and those which the apostles felt able to represent as his. Paul in 1 Corinthians vii, 10, 12, 25 very clearly makes a distinction between what he says 'on his own authority' and what he says on that of the Lord; but it later appears that 'his own authority' is really that of the Lord, for in verse 40 at the end of the chapter he claims to have the Spirit. It may be, as most scholars hold, that in 1 Corinthians xi, 23 what Paul received 'from the Lord' he really received from his fellow-apostles, though perhaps not directly from them. At any rate the account he gives here of the institution of the eucharist differs from that given in the synoptic gospels. However careful Paul may have been, at least in 1 Corinthians vii, to distinguish what Jesus had said and what Jesus was now saying through the Spirit, this care was not always taken, for there was no need for it in the minds of those who were convinced that the authority was no different for the one kind of teaching than it was for the other.

It becomes clear that those in the early church who wrote what Jesus had said and done were sometimes influenced by their conception of the historical Jesus, and sometimes by that of the risen Lord. It may be that Q comes fairly near to a document (if it existed) which a memory confined to the historical Jesus might produce.

At the other end of the spectrum there are many documents which were composed under the influence of a conception of the risen Lord in the mind of the writer, sometimes in the form of a curious mixture, that of a heavenly being of mysterious nature who was yet one who could talk to his disciples on the earth. Such ruling conceptions would, at this end of the spectrum, produce the extraordinary 'teachings' of the gnostics who were vexed by no scruples at all as to what they might say was the true gospel, what Jesus had really taught. In their case the invention is quite clear. If we shift this controlling conception back into the time of the historical Jesus and imagine that it played a part even in the minds of those who set out to give the actual facts (Luke i, 4), we are not surprised at finding stories like that of the Transfiguration.

We need not be surprised either if we find one gospel which combines a highly theological picture of Jesus with a representation of him as active in Judea and Galilee; nor to learn that this gospel was not immediately accepted, and that it made its way into the canon, the list of accepted books, only by degrees. This is the Gospel according to John which, in order to emphasize both its different nature from that of the synoptics and the doubt that it was written by any John of whom we know from the pages of the New Testament, is often called the Fourth Gospel. We must now give some account of criticism as it has affected this gospel.

Eleven

New Insights:
The Fourth Gospel

THE FOURTH GOSPEL

The history of the criticism of this gospel is very important for understanding influences at work in two different directions. One set of influences tends to move people to regard some New Testament book as authoritative; another urges them to discover the factual situation with regard to its authorship. The two sometimes sharply conflict. The traditional view of the authorship has seemed – and still seems even to many well-informed critics – to be tenable, and even to be the most plausible; but if certain basic ideas are accepted it is a view which becomes quite impossible.

The first basic idea is that the Jesus of the synoptic gospels, although he is represented there to some extent 'theologically', is nevertheless in part a credible historical figure. He is a workman, he forms a group of disciples, he goes forward in faith and does not claim to be more than the expected Messiah or deliverer; though probably he did not claim even that. He repudiates even the idea that he may be called good, he is baptized by John, and so forth. If this picture is anywhere near that of the historical Jesus, the figure of the Fourth Gospel is fictional.

The second basic idea is more radical: the figure in this gospel is not *a priori* credible. Conscious of his divinity, he argues for it, claims to be 'one with' God, calls himself the resurrection and the life, condemns his contemporaries not because they are blind to the call of God's kingdom but because they are blind to who he is. These and similar claims may even repel the modern reader ('I am the bread of life', 'I am the Light of the world'). There is no Gethsemane agony, soldiers sent to arrest him fall to the ground; even when crucified his words are not indicative of distress, but 'to fulfil the scriptures'.

No doubt on any presupposition, whether of belief or active anti-Christian unbelief, Jesus must be held to have been a remarkable and compelling person, remarkable enough for the most painstaking historical criticism to find it so far impossible to reach a convincing reconstruction of what he was 'really' like. The figure in the Fourth Gospel is remarkable, but hardly compelling. He repels as much as he attracts, he does not often appear to be a credible figure at all, and his chief characteristic is that of being out of contact with his fellow-men and absorbed in what or who he is. If this is how he appears to a modern reader uninfluenced by the conventional Christian's uneasy conviction that he must love the person of whom he is about to read, it becomes necessary to show how it was possible for this gospel to be regarded for many years as historically the most reliable of the four.

There can be no doubt that the main reason was the tradition which can be traced back at least to Irenaeus (c. 130–200) that 'John, the disciple of the Lord who leaned upon his breast, himself too set forth the gospel while dwelling in Ephesus the city of Asia'. Two figures from the gospel story are identified here. One is John the son of Zebedee, more prominent by this designation in the synoptics and the early chapters of Acts than in the Fourth Gospel itself. The other is 'the beloved disciple' who appears so prominently in the Passion Narrative, beginning with the Last Supper in chapter xiii and ending with the famous post-resurrection story in chapter xxi where he is explicitly identified with the witness of the crucifixion appearing in chapter xix. The name of this very mysterious figure is not revealed; in fact the author carefully and even laboriously avoids it. The identification in the tradition, therefore, has seemed to many to be so fantastic as itself to demand rather than to afford an explanation. John son of Zebedee was a fisherman of Galilee, not illiterate but in the tradition clearly not a scholar (Acts iv, 13); one as far removed from the world of philosophy and rabbinic expertise as the author is steeped in it. It is possible that Papias unwittingly provides a clue to the explanation of this unexpected identification of John son of Zebedee with a quite different person, by mentioning both

John the disciple and another John, an 'elder', still alive evidently in Papias' own day, who lived in Ephesus. Many have thought that perhaps this second John was the author and that the son of Zebedee was his eye-witness informant. This means identifying the Elder with the Beloved Disciple and a difficulty at once arises: according to the gospel this disciple is he who claims to be the eye-witness *and* author. It is small wonder that the authorship problem is regarded by many as insoluble.

The tradition that the author was the disciple, John son of Zebedee, was established at the time of Irenaeus – it may well be, *by* Irenaeus in his battle with the heretics; but it has unfortunately blinded some critics to the fact that this conviction was not shared by everyone in the church at that time. Irenaeus himself knew of people who repudiated it; the Roman presbyter Caius, writing at the beginning of the third century, ascribed it to the gnostic Cerinthus. In so doing he demonstrated two points of view which, for almost any modern student, it seems impossible that anyone could have held simultaneously. Caius saw that the gospel diverged from the synoptics and used this as an argument for the heretical provenance of the book; but he ascribed to the same author the gospel and the book of Revelation, which is written in an entirely different Greek and from a radically different outlook. Hippolytus of Rome also gives evidence for the gospel's failure to find acceptance at Rome, for he defended it. We have seen that even in this early period those who believed that it had been written by John the apostle might be conscious of difficulties. This is further illustrated by the words of Clement of Alexandria (c. 150–215) who said that 'the tradition of the elders from the first is that John at last, having observed that the bodily things had been set forth in the gospels, on the exhortation of his friends, inspired by the Spirit, produced a spiritual gospel'. This 'traditional' view did not include the deduction (inevitable to a modern critic) that the gospel had been written by someone who was not an eyewitness, nor that it was a gospel in which the incarnate Logos speaks rather than the man Jesus; for this would have been impossible in the mental climate of most of the centuries between the birth of Jesus and the twentieth century.

It is unnecessary to go back far to begin the modern story of criticism of this gospel; it had provided for many scholars the framework of a reconstruction of the ministry of Jesus because of the manifest attractiveness of an account of that ministry which took three years or more, in contrast with the swift and condensed story of Mark which made it inevitable to see the public ministry of Jesus as lasting only one year. This, supported by the apparent eye-witness claim, made the Fourth Gospel for many years the gospel most to be trusted as history.

It was D. F. Strauss in his *Leben Jesu* (1835-6) who pointed ruthlessly to the 'mythical' character of the gospel, more prominent here than in the synoptics; and to the consequent fact that the gospel could not be admitted as a source for historical reconstruction. Baur in 1847 argued that the gospel did not contain any historical traditions but was intended to convey an idea, a notion which we have seen to go back to Clement of Alexandria. Other views ranged from the conservative view, going back to Irenaeus, to partition theories, claiming either that the gospel as we have it is the result of chapters or pages having been misplaced accidentally or that it is the product of a number of sources and editors. This view of the gospel as being less than a unity is based in part on doctrinal difficulties, such as the apparent contradiction between 'My flesh is real food; my blood is real drink' (vi, 55) and 'The spirit alone gives life; the flesh is of no avail' (vi, 63); and also upon historical difficulties such as the apparent necessity to change the positions of chapters v and vi if the sequence of events, the movement of Jesus from Galilee to Jerusalem, is to be made natural. As the chapters stand, Jesus is suddenly in Jerusalem at the beginning of chapter v, though at the end of chapter iv he is in Galilee, as he is at the beginning of chapter vi. Such partition theories may have something to commend them if they are concerned only to remove manifest contradictions in narrative which no author can have intended. They are not so probable when they depend upon supposed doctrinal contradictions, since it may be possible to explain how these would not appear contradictions at the time of composition.

For sympathetic understanding of the gospel, the commentary by Hoskyns[1] can probably hardly be bettered; it does not concern itself much with critical questions but implies that the author of the gospel knew the synoptics and that he was theologizing upon a known tradition. The meaning of the writing is beautifully brought out without sides being taken upon critical matters. For the history of criticism the commentary by Bultmann[2] is of greater importance. He thought there were three classes of material in the gospel, a 'Book of Signs', 'revelation discourses' and a tradition of the Passion Narrative peculiar to this gospel; the last might be a continuation of the Book of Signs and in any case the evangelist has edited his material in the interests of his theology, though he has not removed all the contradictions between his sources. Some comments ought to be made at this point for the sake of clarity: first, the Book of Signs is in some sense a reality. This can be seen by looking at the gospel itself, for at ii, 11 the author draws attention to the fact that the incident at Cana which he has just narrated is the 'beginning of signs', and xii, 37–50 is an eloquent peroration to this 'book' which verse 37 clearly shows has now been completed. Owing to the rejection of Jesus and his signs, the Passion begins (xiii, 1).

The 'revelation discourses', which are mingled with the 'Book of Signs', came into the gospel from gnostic sources, according to Bultmann. Such a view depends on the general historical judgement that there was already before New Testament times a developed system of gnosticism on which it was possible for New Testament authors to draw, as a medium in which to express their ideas. Many scholars would hold rather that the seeds of such a system were indeed present at that time but that the developed system awaited the coming of Christianity; thus Irenaeus and Hippolytus were largely justified in regarding gnosticism as a Christian heresy, or rather series of heresies. It is true that the author's emphasis upon the reality of the humanity of Jesus may seem to draw attention unconsciously to his own uncertainty on this point, an uncertainty with which he himself is grappling; nevertheless, he is clearly anti-gnostic, if there was a gnosticism to combat.

The greatest objection to Bultmann's general view of the gospel is provoked by his implication that the author was so much of an editor and compiler, for the thought is highly original; and we must find somewhere an author of great talent, some would say genius, to account for the book. If, as Bultmann thinks, the author took over the gnostic elements, he was more than a mere compiler to have used them so skilfully, and the theory seems to demand a talented thinker, talented enough to be responsible for all the material.

When Dodd brought out in 1953 a work which had occupied him for many years, *The Interpretation of the Fourth Gospel*,[3] he used the conception of a Book of Signs, and saw in the material which preceded it a Prologue (using the term Proem for the famous passage usually called by this name, i, 1–18) and in the material at the end, of course, the Passion Narrative, which itself contains a number of important farewell discourses. Allowing the book to fall naturally into these divisions evidently intended by the author, Dodd did not base any theory of sources upon them but was content to show as clearly as possible the media in which the author had expressed his ideas. The evangelist was familiar with Judaism, but like Philo, though in Dodd's view independently of him, he wrote to commend his theology to the 'higher paganism' of the Hellenistic world. Philo did this for Judaism; the author of the Fourth Gospel did it for the Christian *kerygma* but in the form of an account of the ministry of the historical Jesus. There is no doubt that Dodd in this work made a great deal clear, but he may have erred in not using what was then known of the Qumran documents, whose main interest for New Testament scholars may turn out to be the demonstration that certain key concepts which look so Hellenistic owe their presence in this gospel to their being the counters of Palestinian Jewish theology. This is probably true of such important themes as life, light, and truth, which are among those which Dodd explains in masterly fashion.

Dodd's book is not a commentary, but a work which is very like it in outlook was published as a commentary by C. K. Barrett, once a pupil of Dodd, in 1955, although the manuscript was finished in 1951 and therefore was not actually dependent upon Dodd's book.[4] Barrett represents the earlier opinion of Dodd on the question of the Fourth Gospel's relation to the synoptics, which was that the author knew them and used them, sometimes as it were commenting upon them, or taking for granted that the reader knew the gospel of Matthew or perhaps of Mark. To take but one example of such apparent use by the fourth evangelist of the synoptic record, it must be the impression of many that after perusing John i, 29–34 they have just read a description of the baptism of Jesus by John (the Baptist, though not called by the title in this gospel). Such an impression is due to the fact that they are familiar (perhaps in a vague way) with the story in the synoptics, according to which the occasion on which John sees the spirit descend like a dove upon Jesus is that of the baptism. In fact, the baptism of Jesus is not narrated in this gospel. It may be a significant parallel that the institution of the eucharist is also absent; yet in chapter vi there is a long discourse on eucharistic doctrine, usually regarded as beginning at verse 51, though some would say at verse 32.

A new note is struck by a controversial book called *The Fourth Gospel and Jewish Worship*, by Aileen Guilding,[5] which puts forward a theory of the construction of the gospel based on a little known line of research. This is the line of following the clue provided by the fact that there appears to have been in New Testament times, as also later (when it is undisputed), a lectionary of the Jewish scriptures allotting passages for reading in synagogues on feast days and sabbaths, and designed to complete the reading of the Law in three years. The passage from the Law appointed to be read was called the *seder* and associated with it was a 'second lesson' taken from the Prophets (from either the 'former' or 'latter' prophets, i.e. from the historical books or from those we should call prophets). This passage from the prophets was known as the *haphtorah* or *haphtarah*. It is the essence of the theory that there are passages in the New Testament which betray their origin as expositions of a *seder* and its associated *haphtorah*. The process and the appropriate scene is well illustrated by Acts xiii, 13–41, where the *seder* may be Deuteronomy i, 1–ii, 1 and the *haphtorah* the passage beginning with Jeremiah xxx, 4. Dr Guilding remarks, 'Certainly Paul's whole discourse turns on the double sense of "raise up" in verse 9 of the haphtarah, and his allusion to the judges, unique in the New Testament, echoes the theme of Deuteronomy i, 16–18.'[6]

The application of this theory to the Fourth Gospel produces material which provokes gasps of surprise, of the kind which do not indicate even to the one gasping whether they are of admiration or incredulity. Dr Guilding's studies of the scriptures associated with the feasts of the Jewish liturgical year often bring to light passages which it is very reasonable to suppose were in the mind of the author relating the discourses spoken by Jesus at those feasts; they carry less conviction when an attempt is made to identify the sabbath lections which may have inspired material in the gospel not associated directly with a feast. An example or two will make this clear. The first is taken from chapter 9 of Dr Guilding's book: John x, 22 dates the events being described to the Feast of the Dedication, the feast which Jews still celebrate as Chanukkah. 2 Maccabees x, 1 ff. shows the importance of light and lighted lamps to this festival, which required *sedarim* for seven of eight days; it had become customary in later times (it is by no means certain from any independent evidence that this was as early as the New Testament) to allot passages beginning with Numbers vii for those days. Legends which gathered round this feast included a miraculous fall of fire from heaven, as is clear from 2 Maccabees i, 18–36. It is therefore natural that 1 Kings xviii, 38 should be found as a *haphtorah* for it. Such evidence enhances the insight, not in itself controversial and available from even a fairly superficial reading of the gospel, that it is founded on a chronology not historical but liturgical, fitting the ministry of Jesus to the round of feasts and making it extend in this manner to three and a half liturgical years.

For our second example we may take the Raising of Lazarus (John xi, 1–44) discussed in chapter 10. Now the theory is applied to sabbaths and attempts to fill out the scheme to show that the whole gospel is rightly understood against a lectionary background. It is pointed out that the lections for the period between Chanukkah (x, 22) and the next Passover (xi, 55, xii, 1) 'are full of mournful associations'. In them are written the accounts of the deaths of Jacob, Joseph, Moses, Joshua and Eleazar, and there are many references to sickness, not least in the psalms which were probably also allotted to particular sabbaths. The details given in the book are not needed here to show the appropriateness of these lections to the story of Lazarus, which falls in this period according to the theory being explained.

It is perhaps not altogether surprising that Dodd, when he published another large book on the Fourth Gospel called *Historical Tradition in the Fourth Gospel*,[7] confined his comments on this type of work to the single sentence in a footnote, 'That the "festival" framework may reflect in one way or another liturgical usage is a theory, advanced in various quarters, for which there is much to be said.'[8] Dodd did not venture to say it, but subjected the gospel to a very thorough examination on conservatively critical lines, concluding that the author may have had at his disposal an independent tradition which gave fuller information than the synoptics have preserved for us about John the Baptist, a credible account of a ministry of Jesus in southern Palestine, some material about Jesus as healer, something about the Galilean ministry and about the Passion, some sayings, and topographical information not paralleled at all in the synoptics. It is this last item which, without doubt, shows that the author had access to accurate information about Palestine, including Jerusalem, before the Fall in 70. Whether any of the other material (which alone can provide history as distinct from geography) is really independent of the synoptics (when it is, as Dodd frankly admits it often is, 'closely related to the Synoptic tradition'), or whether it owes its origin to history rather than to doctrine when it manifestly is quite independent of the synoptics – these questions cannot easily be decided.

For one example of the last category we can take the turning of the water into wine at Cana of Galilee (ii, 1–11). Like the famous stone jars in the story, the passage – the 'beginning of signs' (ii, 11) – is brimful of symbolism: the new wine of Jesus' teaching replaces sterile Judaism, the redemption by blood replaces merely ceremonial purification, the baptismal eucharist replaces cleans-

Cana in Galilee.

ing by lustration. It is possible to imagine that some event took place on which such passages are founded; but when the characters of such events are suggested they usually remove all point from the story as it has come down to us in the gospel. If indeed the master of ceremonies made a joke about water as being 'the best wine', the story would have been worth preserving as an example of tact on the part of that amiable man, but not a candidate for inclusion in a gospel about the incarnate Logos, the Lord of Life. We are forced to the conclusion that it is the unhistorical element which has led to the inclusion of the story.

The conclusion of F. W. Beare in a review[9] will do very well to summarize the verdict of most scholars of weight on this book:

After all has been said, and every last particle of primitive gold-dust extracted, the Fourth Gospel is in its total character a much less reliable source of historical (especially biographical) information than Mark, even though it may in some instances preserve a more accurate recollection of what occurred. The 'new look' on the Fourth Gospel has already, in my opinion, set a number of my colleagues dancing down a false path; and I would beg that due weight should still be given to the patently unhistorical aspects of the Johannine picture of Jesus, as well as to the presence within the composition of elements of good primitive tradition.

Roman Catholic attitudes are less radical. The Roman Church's view of Christ makes it easier for its adherents to accept as historical miracles of a type which others will find best explained as making a doctrinal point in the form of a story. Thus R. E. Brown[10] is able to regard a Johannine tradition, parallel to the synoptic tradition, as the basis for a series of developments arising from the pressure of philosophical and religious ideas upon disciples of the original author, himself an eye-witness, at various stages; and to minimize the extent to which the synoptic tradition has been used. The source of the Johannine tradition is probably John son of Zebedee and his disciples may have included John the elder, mentioned by Papias. It is remarkable that a work so hospitable to criticism has received the Imprimatur, but the liberal temper and erudition of such a commentary has become typical of much Roman scholarship during the last decade or two. From the point of view of cool judgement which this survey attempts to adopt (with full awareness that this itself implies a particular point of view), the work of R. E. Brown illustrates a very ingenious and honest attempt to combine the long tradition with thorough criticism. It has been implied in this chapter that the success of such a venture is really impossible, and that the tradition is not founded upon the original facts but came to birth in the mind of Irenaeus after a period when this enigmatic gospel had been perhaps a hundred years in existence but without gaining anything like universal acceptance.

Twelve

New Groupings:
Paul and His Letters

Study of the great missionary Paul raises these questions: how far can we make a historical reconstruction of his life? Which letters are genuinely Pauline?[1] Lastly, how can his genuine writings best be understood?

If we take these in turn, we may be surprised to find that Paul, so often known as 'Paul of Tarsus' because according to Acts he was born there (xxi, 39 and xxii, 3), never mentions the town in his own writings; and in Acts xxii, 3 goes on to say, 'I was brought up in this city, and as a pupil of Gamaliel[2] I was thoroughly trained in every point of our ancestral law', thus implying that he was by early training a Jerusalem Jew. It is consistent with this that he calls himself a 'Hebrew of the Hebrews' (Philippians iii, 5) and his instruction by Gamaliel must mean that he was familiar with rabbinic ways of thinking, as he demonstrates in Galatians iv, 21–31. Yet he uses the Septuagint and often shows the attitude of a 'Hellenist' Jew. We find this problem reflected when we take up the question: how can his genuine writings best be understood? For it is obviously relevant to ask: did Paul think like a Jew or like a Greek? Or is this a false question because he thought partly as a Jew, and partly as a Greek? Or perhaps he thought within the framework of a Judaism profoundly influenced for some time (since the days of Alexander the Great) by Hellenism? All these questions will now be illustrated, but no attempt will be made to give them final answers. They all belong to the criticism of Paul but no 'assured results' can be registered.

First, we can illustrate the difficulties met when we try to build a working reconstruction of Paul's life from his conversion onwards. The task is indeed by no means easy: his letters may be trusted to give reliable information for the very reason that they are not for the most part concerned to establish fact (although the first two chapters of Galatians may be a very important exception to this rule) and so artlessly yield information undistorted by argument. But, for a reconstruction of the life of Paul, the letters do not give us enough to work on. The conventional method is to retell the story of Paul in Acts with embellishments from his letters. This is unsatisfactory, because Acts does not dispose of sufficient trustworthy information for the task; in addition, many would say that Acts is hopelessly unhistorical and written from a biased point of view. The interdependence with Acts of the problem of the history of Paul is paralleled by its interdependence with the gospels, though in a different way. On this point there is fortunately now much agreement; Paul's letters can be considered by themselves and his teaching evaluated, and then an approach made to the gospels to see whether they reflect his outlook, in whole or in part. It is important for understanding the gospels, as we have already seen, to bear in mind the possibility that they have been influenced by Pauline conceptions; if Paul complicated the 'simple message of the gospel', it must have been the simple message of the gospel of Jesus; but we must now recognize, as the last chapters have shown, that it is the burning question of gospel criticism to try to find what that message was, and that there is very little agreement except about the difficulty of the problem. It is therefore even more difficult to judge whether Paul complicated it.

If we accept the moderate view of Chapter 13 that the author of Acts did his best with the sometimes sparse material which he had at his disposal, and was an honest historian, we must nevertheless admit that while he seems to have been quite well informed about the movements of Paul, he describes these less fully than we might have expected. To put an example very briefly: in the story of Acts Paul makes two visits to Corinth, but Paul implies at least three by his language in 2 Corinthians xii, 14 and xiii, 1, and although some critics would explain away these two references as if they meant only that Paul intended to make his third visit but never carried it out, and so earned the contempt of opponents at Corinth for changing his mind (2 Corinthians i, 17), they usually think that he did eventually make three visits. Again in 2 Corinthians xi, 23 Paul speaks about having been in prisons, in the plural. According to Acts, by this time he ought to have been in prison only once, in Philippi (Acts xvi, 23 ff).

Hapless students of theology struggling with 'A' levels or in their first year at a university know also the almost impossible problem set by the discrepancy between the information in Galatians i and ii and that in Acts. Among the problems set by the study of this matter is the question: is Galatians written to the North or South Galatians? If to the North Galatians we must find a time in Paul's life for the writing of the epistle after he had been in that remote district, a visit which does not appear to be narrated in Acts, although some critics would argue that Acts xvi, 6 or xviii, 23, or both, constitute sufficient evidence. Others argue that these verses refer only to passing through the northern part of southern Galatia, whose evangelization is narrated with much detail in Acts xiii and xiv.

Galatians — written to whom? [margin note]

In the first two chapters of Galatians Paul is arguing about his own authority which he says he obtained from the Lord, and in the course of this shows that he had not in the past deferred to the church at Jerusalem. For this claim to be justified, Paul must be sure to make no error, and his confident claim that he had visited Jerusalem only twice as far as the date at which he is now writing must be absolutely reliable. He is writing to the Galatians to counteract the teaching of those who say that his converts there must be circumcised, and who indeed go further and say that Paul himself usually preaches such a doctrine. He clearly had already evangelized *some* Galatians; indeed the letter is full of reflections of his visit. The earliest time in the Acts story would be after chapters xiii and xiv. It is therefore an immediately attractive theory that when Paul in Galatians ii, 1 ff. describes his second visit to Jerusalem, he is reflecting the same story as that of the 'council' described in Acts xv. Alas, for the unlucky student! For in that case, according to Acts this ought to be Paul's third, not second visit to Jerusalem since his conversion. Did then Paul write Galatians hastily from Antioch during the time vaguely expressed in Acts xiv, 28? This may be right, but then we

council of Jerusalem [margin note]

279

have to crowd a number of events, including the visit of Peter to Antioch (Galatians ii,11), not narrated in Acts at all, into a short time. Moreover, many would say that Galatians is full of advanced doctrine and well-developed Pauline ideas, such as can be paralleled in the Corinthian correspondence and above all in Romans; and it must therefore have been written at a much later date, perhaps from Ephesus during Paul's long stay there. But why then does Paul not mention the decision of the council of Acts xv, which he could have quoted so tellingly in his argument?

It is far from the purpose of this book to chronicle the different views, even the main views, upon these points. They are given to show the sort of problems with which the critic is faced. It is easy to add others which may well occur to the most casual reader. For example, what is the explanation of the fact that the story of Acts 'ends' without 'an ending'? The techniques of T.V. drama were unknown in those days, and there was no intention of leaving the reader 'up in the air'. Why then do we not read what happened to Paul? What is the relation of his own references to his impending death to the way in which Acts closes?

Before we go further, it will be well to make clear the relevance of such questions to the understanding of Paul as a thinker, and here again it is possible to give only a number of indications. If the Galatians ii visit is identical with the 'council' of Acts xv, and the latter account is trustworthy, this is the great debate of early church history, which marked a divide between the time when Judaism embraced unwillingly a mere deviationist sect which later came to be known as the Christian church, and the time when the Christian church, now well-established, stood out against what they regarded as an outdated and discredited Judaism. Paul's opponents in Galatia may well have been in league with those who provoked the council, that is, converted Pharisees (Acts xv, 5). The issue was circumcision. If Acts xv falls under suspicion of being unhistorical, we are at liberty to emphasize the fact that the letter purporting to have been sent from the council does not mention circumcision, but rather those minimal ritual rules for Gentile converts in Syria–Cilicia whose keeping would enable

280

Jews within the same church to associate with them (Acts xv, 20, 29). More important, and indeed fundamental, the council of Acts xv ceases to be the great watershed dividing early church history. There was no single classical debate about circumcision; it was an issue which must have arisen in different times and places and continued to do so for a long time. The Galatians complain that Paul had deceived them by not preaching the full gospel, which they now learn involves circumcision. This was no doubt the view of Jewish Christians, in the second sense mentioned in chapter 7.[3] Paul himself clearly thought that *for a Jew* circumcision and the whole Law were obligatory. He circumcised Timothy and accepted James's appeal to show he kept the Law, even according to Acts (xvi, 3 and xxi, 15–26). All this profoundly affects our view of Paul, who cannot be denied the title of the great apostle to the Gentiles, but can no longer be represented as the great opponent of Judaism.

No attempt has been made to give a list of scholars who hold different points of view with regard to the best way of reconciling the conflicting evidence about Paul's life. These are so many and differ so widely that it has seemed best to illustrate the problems rather than to try to give any of the answers.

The chronology of Paul is also teasing. The following references in Acts appear at first to promise links with secular history of a kind which will enable the reader to date the events. While they succeed in linking the story of Acts with that history, they just fail to give an assured chronology for the life of Paul. Just fail, because in each case the promise is not quite fulfilled when the matter is examined. There is indeed one reference which is definite enough to be a reasonably fixed point, but others are too imprecise and in any case hard to reconcile with this one fixed point. Here are the references in the order in which they occur in Acts: xii, 1 ff., Herod Agrippa I persecutes the apostles, perhaps A.D. 44; xiii, 7 ff., Sergius Paulus, known from a Roman inscription but not precisely datable from it for the Acts reference; xviii, 2, Anti-Jewish edict of Claudius, perhaps A.D. 41 but more probably A.D. 49; xviii, 12, the proconsul Gallio, the most nearly exact reference, dating to A.D. 51–52 or 52–53; chapters xxiii ff. (cf. Jos. *Ant.* xx, 168 ff.; Tac. *Ann.* xii, 54), the procurators Felix and Festus, about whose dates, particularly when Festus took over from Felix, controversy is sharp.

The way in which the date of Gallio can be determined may serve as an example of the careful argument which must be employed in this work. Fragments of a votive inscription found at Delphi refer to Gallio as proconsul, but it is not clear whether this is a title *emeritus* or that he was in office at the time when the inscription was made. The name of the emperor is given as Claudius who is given the 'date' of 'Imperator xxvi'; Roman historians often use the years of tribunician *potestas* and consulship assumed by emperors, given on inscriptions, to fix a date, but in this case these items are lost. However, another inscription gives Claudius as 'Imperator xxvii' at a date known to be 1 August 52, and he must have enjoyed acclamation as 'Imperator xxv and xxvi' some time between the beginning of 51 and mid 52, so that it is reasonable to suppose that acclamation xxvi fell in the first half of 52. If we are to understand from the Delphi inscription that Gallio was in office at that moment, part of the twelve months of his office fell in the same half-year 51–52. 52–53 is also possible, having regard to the fact that proconsuls left Rome for their provinces in the spring. If Gallio is referred to as a past proconsul, 51–52 is the latest possible date. This is the date usually thought the most likely.

The difficulty over Felix and Festus is somewhat complicated and turns upon the question when Felix can at the latest have been in Jerusalem for Paul to be his prisoner. As late a date as possible is required in order to find room for all Paul's activity between his clash with Gallio and his arrest in Jerusalem. Felix was recalled to Rome to answer charges of misgovernment and peculation; he escaped justice through the intervention of his brother Pallas, a freedman favourite of Nero, but it appears (though the evidence is not absolutely certain) that Pallas fell from favour in the summer of 55. Acts xxiv, 27 seems to imply that Paul was the prisoner of Felix for two years, but we may interpret this as meaning that Felix was procurator for two years and then succeeded by Festus. This would give 53–55 for the procuratorship of Felix and is a very awkwardly early date for the chronology of Paul; indeed, the date of Paul's arrest is usually put at 57, Felix being succeeded by Festus in 59, or some dates very near to these.

Once more we have merely given examples to show the kind of calculation and weighing of evidence necessary in the historical criticism of the New Testament. It is worth noting that if it is accepted that Acts is incomplete rather than false, and artlessly shows correct knowledge of the times about which it tells rather than betrays the time when it was written, then we may conclude that the sources of that book for the career of Paul are excellent in themselves, but too few or too short to give the full account which would enable us to reconstruct the whole of Paul's career and to give dates for each event. There is a strong tradition, not mentioned in the New Testament, that both Peter and Paul perished in the mad persecution of Christians instigated by Nero in 64, a tradition to which *I Clement* may well refer.[4] We cannot reconstruct the life of Paul so as to include this final martyrdom, but what we gather from the New Testament leads us towards this climax, and perhaps left the readers of those days when it was first published to reflect on the injustice of the execution about which they knew all too well.

Before any indication can be given of the way in which fashions in interpreting Paul have changed or developed it is logical to raise the question: which are the genuine letters of Paul? The canon lists fourteen as his. Hebrews, probably written in Rome or Italy, was first regarded as Pauline in Alexandria, then generally in the east, and since the fourth century in the west also. No scholar now thinks that it was written by Paul. Of the thirteen left, the so-called Pastorals can be subtracted in order to be discussed separately, for even the diehards who think Paul wrote them will agree to putting them in a sub-class by themselves. Ephesians also is regarded by many as pauline.[5] This leaves 1 and 2 Thessalonians, 1 and 2 Corinthians, Galatians and Romans as occasional letters.[6] This means that they were written when circumstances demanded, to correct error or to answer questions. Philippians, Colossians and Philemon then rank as 'captivity' or

283

'prison' epistles (written during Paul's imprisonment in Rome at the end of the Acts story), with the addition of Ephesians if it is Pauline.

At this stage a word may be said about the use of a computer. It will suffice to make two points. The first is that its usefulness in deciding authorship will depend on whether it is true that, as those who trust it argue, a writer may vary his style, but not his habits beyond a traceable amount. Thus an author, it is suggested, may indeed be influenced as to vocabulary by the subject he is pursuing; but the number of times he uses 'and' or 'but' and such small words, and the length of his sentences, with other small but vitally revealing, because unconscious, practices – all these betray him or, if absent, betray the imitator. It is debatable whether sufficient samples have been examined to establish this principle, although it may be true.

The second point is that in the case of Paul, the computer discovered nothing which had not long been suspected on other grounds. When the computer controversy, summed up in the *Observer*, was raging in the autumn of 1963, many theological students must have been writing essays for their tutors debating the authorship of (for example) Ephesians. On this matter a good many (being students and therefore somewhat conservative) will have decided, rightly or wrongly, that the epistle was actually written by Paul and found themselves at variance with the computer. More will have accepted the view that the Pastorals cannot have been written by him, and thus agreed with the computer. None will have found anything new in its verdicts. All will have or ought to have, asked themselves what the computer meant by 'Paul'. The answer is 'the author of Galatians'; the machine (like all idols humiliatingly dependent on its worshippers) had to be told what was typical of Paul by mere theologians.

It is worth while to note in passing, therefore, that New Testament scholars neither oppose the use of a computer nor feel outraged by its findings. In the realm of authorship, date, authenticity and related matters, it has told them nothing which they did not already know or suspect. Indeed, the proper use of computers is bound to increase in the sphere of literary criticism and historical inquiry, and scholars are becoming aware of its potentialities as an immense time-saver. For example, when the development of an idea or doctrine is being investigated, much depends on the use of key technical words by different authors. If steps are taken now to feed data into computers, much laborious consultation of indexes, concordances and lexicons can be avoided for future students. An informed computer will answer in a matter of seconds; but imparting knowledge to it in the first instance will take years. An international committee of New Testament scholars is concerning itself with this and similar matters. In the meantime it is well to understand that a computer is not in itself an infallible judge; it is rather a wonderful storehouse and – under informed direction – sorter of information.

In fact, since the beginning of the nineteenth century the Pauline authorship of a number of the letters bearing his name in the canon has been questioned. Baur, anticipating the computer by nearly a hundred years, regarded the 'pillar' epistles, Galatians, 1 and 2 Corinthians and Romans alone as genuinely Pauline. (In fact the computer's user, A. Q. Morton, is more conservative and adds Philemon.) This was due to Baur's certainty on doctrinaire grounds that Paul must in every case have been occupied with the struggle with Judaizers. Only letters which bore traces of this, therefore, could be genuine. This example of *a priori* reasoning may be repudiated now in favour of examination of the facts, but Baur still influences critics unconsciously – and unduly – by his Hegelian conception of the history of the church; moreover, books on Paul are still written in which the Jewish controversy is used as a dating device: on this view a writing must show awareness of the controversy if it is to be assigned an early date; and if it shows no such awareness it must be very early indeed, or very late.

In the meantime, much more objective work has been carried out upon Paul's letters, by study of vocabulary, style, word usage and his use of the Old Testament. By such means it has been possible to be a little less drastic than Baur. In 1924 a survey of New Testament study and criticism by Maurice Jones[7] could add to Baur's list 1 Thessalonians, Philippians and Philemon, as letters which most scholars would then regard as Pauline, with Colossians and Ephesians as debatable. Jones noted that most scholars would doubt the Pauline authorship of the rest; in 1929 Schweitzer, writing his great book on *The Mysticism of Paul the Apostle*,[8] refers to his previous conclusions in *Paul and his Interpreters*:[9] he is confident indeed about those regarded as genuine by Jones, but regards as non-Pauline not only the Pastorals but also 2 Thessalonians. Today among British scholars there is a strange tendency in some quarters to argue for the Pauline authorship of the Pastorals and not to regard these nor 2 Thessalonians, Colossians and Ephesians as worse than doubtful; Roman Catholic scholars on the Continent are just as conservative but the bulk of German scholars would class the Pastorals, Colossians and Ephesians as pauline, indeed, but not written by Paul himself.

The letters in the Pauline canon which are doubtful will be considered briefly in a separate section, in order to explain the grounds on which they are thought not to be by Paul and also to attempt to show how criticism succeeds in finding a significant place for them in the history of the church after Paul.

Happy in the august company of the 'foundation members' of the Pauline group, Galatians, 1 and 2 Corinthians and Romans (omitting the others as lighter in bulk and unnecessary for the establishment of Paul's thought) we pass on to ask: how can Paul best be understood? Before a survey, however brief, is given of the way in which this subject has fared at the hands of critics, it will be well to observe that the question is capable of being understood and answered in two different main ways; we can say firmly that Paul was a child of his time, that (for example) all his thinking was governed by his conviction that the returning Messiah would shortly bring to an end the age whose last events had been signalled by his resurrection. In this case, the task will be to understand what were the terms in which Paul thought and expressed his doctrine. On the other hand, we may be convinced either that Paul did not always think eschatologically, but accommodated his teaching widely to his hearers so that he only appears to think exclusively in that way; or that, although he did think within this apparently restricting framework, the whole message of his writings can be transposed into another key and understood on an existential basis. We reach again in fact the field of discrediting myths. Here we are in the sphere of interpretation, and we must defer until chapter 15 fuller discussion of the relation between criticism and interpretation.

One of the most decisive facts for the abandonment of Baur's account of early Christian history is that Irenaeus in c. 180 shows clear knowledge of all the New Testament books except Philemon. Again, Clement of Rome refers to the gospels, the epistles of Paul, that of James, and very often to Hebrews. If he is rightly dated to 96, Baur's chronology must be abandoned. A similar starting-point for investigation was to be found in the *Letters* of Ignatius, the genuineness of which was established by the work of J. B. Lightfoot and others. Lightfoot saw as clearly as Baur that the letters of Paul were the key to understanding the New Testament, and by his more correct dating of Clement, Ignatius and the other Apologists demonstrated that the true picture of the church in the first two centuries was not as Baur had painted it, and could be seen clearly as one which had developed from that in the New Testament. Throwing off the shackles of Baur's theory, Lightfoot expounded the letters of Paul in such a masterly fashion that his commentaries are still valuable standard works.[10] Lightfoot and scholars of the same approach have enabled generations who followed to understand the material against its own historical background, instead of within the framework of an artificial philosophy of history. Lightfoot expounded Paul on the basis of what Paul wrote, and showed thereby an understanding born of classical scholarship, knowledge of the ancient world, and the lucidity of a mind which knows perfectly what it means.

The Hellenistic influences which Baur regarded as a corruption of Paul's thought were seen as a main clue to his meaning by a large number of theologians in the early years of the twentieth century. It is true that Christianity appeared at much the same time as the oriental mystery cults (mainly those of Cybele and Attis from Phrygia, Serapis and Isis from Egypt, and Mithras from Persia) were being taken into the Hellenistic world to accompany its own Eleusinian mysteries and Orphism. It was inevitable that Christianity should be seen by many as one more of these eastern mystery cults; it was perhaps just as inevitable that the same point of view should be taken many years later by German scholars and their followers in England. In 1903 Heit-müller, for example, saw in Paul's words on baptism (e.g. in Romans vi, 1–11) and the Lord's Supper (1 Corinthians xi, 23–24) concepts from the mystery religions, and wrote *Taufe und Abendmahl bei Paulus* from this standpoint. Destined to have a lasting significance and influence were the writings of Reitzenstein (*Poimandres*, 1904 and *Die Hellenisten' Mysterien-Religionen*, 1910) and of Cumont whose *Oriental Religions in Roman Paganism* achieved paperback status in 1956.[11] These views, summarized for English readers notably by Kirsopp Lake [12] and by H. A. A. Kennedy,[13] were surveyed with typical mastery by Schweitzer in the book already mentioned, *Paul and his Interpreters*, and categorically rejected in favour of a view of his own to be described below.

There can be no doubt that early Christian thinkers knew about the mysteries and gnosticism. Clement of Alexandria uses their terminology and regards the Christian as 'the true gnostic'. In Paul we meet some of this terminology in such words as wisdom, knowledge, seal, 'psychic' (meaning natural as opposed to supernatural or spiritual) and 'pneumatic' (or spiritual). Reitzenstein was convinced that already formed gnostic systems existed in the time of Jesus and Paul, and was therefore able to say of Paul that he was 'not indeed ... the first but ... the greatest of all the Gnostics'.

The main and fundamental opposition to this judgement rests on the demonstration that such interpretations tend to make Paul the revealer of a religion which he himself has evolved, even if based on what he has heard and been taught, and to devalue the supernatural element. This turns what was for Paul essentially a revelation from Christ himself and ultimately from God, who was on his own initiative working the redemption of man through the life, death and resurrection of Christ, into a 'religion' whose myth and *kerygma* are the children of Paul's own brain. Such interpretations, which bring Paul and his teaching into the realm of anthropology, do no justice to the conviction of Paul that he had received his revelation partly from the Lord himself, and partly from the tradition of the church which his conversion made him join.

W. Bousset (1865–1920), like the rest of the *religionsgeschicht-liche* ('history of religions') school which we have been discussing, saw the rise of Christianity as part of a wider histor-ical phenomenon, but included in his explanation of its birth the Jewish background. He recognized the eschatological element and argued that this gave way in a worshipping community (which it was his merit to see was the most correct description of the church) to the concept of the *Kyrios* (Lord) present in the act of worship. This was the main theme of his book *Kyrios–Christos* (1913).[14] A. Schweitzer denied altogether 'the influence of the mysteries on Pauline thought. He regards the teaching of St Paul as eschatological through and through. All its peculiar features, its contradictions, and its problems are to be explained by the special circumstances of the period in which he found himself, the brief interval between the Death and Resurrection of Christ and His Parousia. In St Paul sacraments are in the nature of "sealings" which guarantee the ultimate salvation of the participant in the Parousia.' This is the just summary by Maurice Jones[15] of what Schweitzer wrote on this matter in *Paul and his Interpreters*, and which he developed to the full in *The Mysticism of Paul the Apostle*.

Most of the points of view which may be regarded in this field as classical still find adherents or partial adherents today. Klausner, Eisler and the contemporary Brandon have been strongly influenced by Baur and believe that Paul was the bitter opponent of the Jerusalem apostles. Indeed, on this bold identifi-cation of the opponents of Paul, Schweitzer is also of this school. It is in fact a fault of continental scholars and those who follow them that they are unable to see a middle way between extremes. Until recently a German or a Frenchman was unable to find a middle way between Romanism and Protestantism and suspected deliberate mystification in an Anglican who claimed to be both

Catholic and Reformed; similarly, it is not in the Teutonic or Gallic temperament as a rule to imagine that a man, a Paul, may have opposed his friends and either simply remained friends with them, being united on the main issue, or else made it up afterwards. J. Munck (a Dane) rejected altogether the idea of any sharp controversy between Paul and the other apostles,[16] but was a successor of Schweitzer in seeing that the Jewish eschatological element was of paramount importance in understanding not only what Paul taught, but also what he did, with such urgency; Munck however does not subscribe to the notion that 'mystic' union between Christ and the believer was a key to Paul's thought. Reitzenstein's introduction of *gnosis* as a – or even the – key to Paul is carried on by Bultmann and others, including Schmithals, who, largely on the basis of a questionable belief in the existence of a pre-Christian gnostic system, holds that Paul wrestled with *gnosis* in Corinthians and used its terminology.[17]

It would be foolish to try to dismiss the gnostic question out of hand, but it is certainly reasonable to protest against *gnosis* being regarded as the main, let alone the only, key to Paul's thought. If this were the case, then the church must have gone gnostic in a big way, and the comment of S. Neill[18] on an essay of Bultmann in 1960 is apt and thoroughly justified. Bultmann had argued that 'Paul changed overnight from an understanding of the *Ekklesia* which was based on the Jewish tradition of the Old Testament to a Hellenistic concept based on the gnostic understanding of the Body of Christ, and that neither he nor his followers at the time noted the inconsistency'. Neill's comment is that 'the essay bears the wrong date; it should be 1925, not 1955'.[19] We cannot now be persuaded that a man of Paul's intellect would make such changes without noticing that he had done so. Nor, as Neill argues elsewhere in the same book,[20] can we find any evidence for a congregation of the church which reflects such an outlook. In fact, the identification of the Body of Christ with both the crucified body of Jesus and with the 'body' of the believers who by baptism are united with him (Romans vi, 1–11) is Pauline, and it is Jewish, not gnostic. The way in which this can be understood and clearly seen is set out in a small book, *The Body* by J. A. T. Robinson,[21] who thus demonstrated his grasp of Pauline theology better than he demonstrated philosophical theology in the more famous and less valuable *Honest to God*.[22] This perceptive and interesting New Testament scholar has developed his theme in useful articles doomed to be left on one side in the prevailing search for more sensational material.

Among other influences thought by past scholars to be present in Paul is that of Stoicism; this theme too is sustained, if with less zeal and by fewer followers. In 1920 E. V. Arnold writing in the *Encyclopaedia of Religion and Ethics* could claim not only that some of Paul's ethics were very like what we know of those of Seneca and Epictetus but also that while at his conversion 'he parted alike from Hebraism and Stoicism', for him the true 'wise man' was Christ; and that his use of the term 'body' was Stoic. Such sweeping views must today be modified, though there is no need to deny the influence of Stoicism on any writer in the New Testament, so long as the manifest importance of the hard historical fact that they all arose from Judaism is given its true weight. In such circumstances studies like that of J. N. Sevenster's *Paul and Seneca* (1961)[23] become valuable.

If this were a book about the development of theology rather than of biblical criticism it would be necessary to do more than mention in connexion with Pauline questions the immeasurable importance of Paul's Romans; but Romans is accepted as in every sense Pauline, and has not detained us. It is nevertheless useful to remark that it has a decisive influence on all modern Christian theology through the experience of Karl Barth who after the First World War sought in it the foundation of a theology of the Word of God as opposed to the 'liberalism' of man-made 'religions'. If Barth is not now rightly represented by the commentary on Romans which he wrote in 1918,[24] yet it remains a magnificent example, for all its original confusion and violence, of what happens when a man listens not to the commentators but to Paul himself.

It is in fact not difficult to listen to Paul himself. There is no doubt that we can read the words which he wrote and can trust the text which we have before us, once we have satisfied ourselves which are the genuine works of Paul; and we have seen that there is almost universal agreement about the most important of these. Two further points in the sphere of criticism may be made, however; one is a minor point with nevertheless interesting consequences for our understanding of Paul and his activity. The other is a matter of detailed and expert study, and is speculative.

The first and relatively minor point concerns the famous letter to the Romans: without going into great detail it is easy to see that the last chapter (xvi) has a remarkable form, consisting largely of greetings. It is the extent of the greetings rather than their inclusion which is remarkable. Such personal messages are well-known in ancient letters, including those of Paul; but here is a long list – and we find that some of the people in it seem to be in Ephesus, not Rome. Reconstruction from clear evidence elsewhere in Paul shows this to be true of Aquila and Priscilla (Romans xvi, 3), and Epaenetus is described as 'the firstfruit [i.e. of Paul's missionary work] of Asia' (verse 5). Since Paul spent a great deal of time at Ephesus, it is altogether natural that he should have many friends there to whom he would wish to send greetings; but not in a letter to Rome, where indeed he presumably had few if any acquaintances, since at this point in his life he had never been there. A natural conclusion springs to mind: chapter xvi belongs to a recension of the letter which he wrote to the Romans (as i, 7 and 15 show quite clearly) but now wishes to send to the Ephesians. This is a very natural wish because he must have been aware that, whatever the exact circumstances which occasioned this letter, now that he had wrestled with the problems with which it deals, a definitive statement of his faith had emerged. This conclusion, that there were two recensions of Romans, is supported by a number of minor considerations connected with textual criticism; one of the facts is that some ancient Latin manuscripts give a series of chapter lists (not the same chapters as are now used to divide the letter) which imply without any doubt whatever that according to them the letter consisted of i, 1–xiv, 23 followed by xvi, 25–27. There is a host of other facts concerning this last chapter, but this is perhaps the clearest indication that the bulk of chapter xvi might well have been present originally only in the form of the letter sent to Ephesus.[25]

It we add to this conclusion the more obvious fact that Paul wrote his most famous and most comprehensive statement of his faith to a church with which he had no direct contact, it is necessary to find an explanation of this action, not too inconsistent with the boast of a man who did 'not want to build on another man's foundation' (Romans xv, 20). It is not really hard to find this explanation: Paul probably means that he wished to be the first preacher of the gospel as far as possible wherever he could go personally: it was his 'ambition to bring the gospel to places where the very name of Christ has not been heard' (the previous words in the same verse). When someone else had in fact preached the gospel in any place, this did not mean that he took no interest in it; in fact he then showed what was strictly speaking some inconsistency in his concern for Christians there.

This concern was not entirely centred upon them: both temperament and experience made him anxious that such converts had understood the gospel rightly as he saw it, that they knew the doctrine on which he insisted, that Christ had ended the period during which the Law was the dominant divinely given authority for men. He knew that he was the only teacher (except perhaps later on a close personal disciple such as Timothy) who could be trusted to ensure such an understanding in the minds of recent adherents to the church. He had won a position endorsing his right to act on this conviction some time before he wrote Romans. This is shown clearly in Galatians ii, 7 where he affirms that the apostles in Jerusalem had acknowledged his claim that he 'had been entrusted with the Gospel for Gentiles as surely as Peter had been entrusted with the Gospel for Jews'. If Paul then in the first place wrote such an authoritative statement of his own gospel to a church which he had not yet visited, and then thought it worthwhile to send forms of it to other churches (or at least to one other church), he gives us here the clearest picture we can find of the great 'apostle of the Gentiles' claiming and implementing precisely that position.

293

The other point in the sphere of criticism is too difficult to explain in a short compass, and difficult to explain at all without trespassing once more in the field of interpretation. It springs from the manifest fact that Paul tried to be 'all things to all men'. In passing we must say a brief word about the usual interpretation of this phrase, which takes it to describe the argumentative weathercock who may know his own mind but hypocritically conceals it, and agrees with each of his contemporaries in turn, however inconsistent this makes him. This interpretation cannot be applied to Paul. The words come from 1 Corinthians ix, 22 and their true meaning can easily be gathered by anyone who will take the trouble to read the passage in which they occur. This may be limited (lest we ask too much of Paul's critics) to the section which begins with verse 19, in which he writes, 'I am a free man and own no master; but I have made myself every man's servant, to win over as many as possible'.

Studies based on a right understanding of this passage have yielded some interesting results, if speculative theories can be so described. In a very thoughtful article H. Chadwick[26] (for example) showed the probability of the idea that Paul often took up a position side by side with the man whose opinion he wished to modify, perhaps quoted something which he had said, and then proceeded to bring his interlocutor (or correspondent) to another point of view by showing how the latter's view must be qualified. A good example is afforded by the way in which Paul apparently agrees with the slogan 'I am free to do anything', which he quotes in 1 Corinthians vi, 12, but immediately goes on to show how this is not by itself an adequate criterion for conduct. It may be interesting to note that the New English Bible has at this point adopted the theory we are now explaining by opening the verse with ' "I am free to do anything", you say', whereas the Greek strictly warrants only 'I am free to do anything' as though these were Paul's words and not quoted by him from someone else.

J. C. Hurd, in an exhaustive study of 1 Corinthians,[27] has employed all the possible clues of this kind which might lead to at least an outline reconstruction of the correspondence which passed between Paul and the Corinthians; although the results must be regarded as provisional, they illuminate the letter and the whole situation from which it arose.

Such studies disclose how Paul conducted, or may have conducted, an argument with those who were either opponents or puzzled inquirers asserting at least temporarily a view with which Paul could not agree. Another branch of this study is concerned with what Paul himself contributed to Christian doctrine and what he accepted from others. His history makes it natural to suppose that he received a great deal from his predecessors among the ranks of the apostles;[28] it has been very reasonably claimed that when he went up to Jerusalem to talk with Cephas (i.e. Peter) as he tells us in Galatians i, 18, it was presumably in order to talk not about the weather, but about the gospel, and that Peter, as spokesman of those apostles who had known Jesus from the first, must have had much that he could tell him both about what had happened and about what the original followers of Jesus believed as a consequence of their experience.

Whether first taught by Paul or not, the doctrine of justification by faith must be closely associated with him and with no one else in the New Testament to the same degree, even if it may seem legitimate to argue that other writers taught the equivalent of this doctrine. It may be that another characteristic feature of his own teaching was that the Christian received this 'justification' (being put right in the eyes of God by God himself) by being baptized, which meant dying to his old self and rising again to a new life in which he was closely united with Christ. All or part of this may belong to Paul's predecessors as much as it does to Paul; it becomes important when the question is asked: is this the way in which the Christian, according to Paul, may be assured of the forgiveness of his past sins so that he can enter with confidence upon his new life? Is it solely by this faith-union with Christ in his death and resurrection? If we return a positive answer to this question, we imply a judgement about any passage of Paul in which he seems to assert a further theory of the atonement, according to which Christ in some way by his death obtained for us such forgiveness. Such passages must then have a secondary importance for him and perhaps such theories were accepted only reluctantly by Paul.

This kind of criticism is illustrated by its attitude to a famous passage, Romans iii,21–26, in which Paul uses a vocabulary including important words not found elsewhere in his writings; one such word, and the most important, may be an adjective or a noun. If this is settled, there may still be controversy as to whether it is to be translated as referring to 'expiation' or 'propitiation' (the New English Bible translated rather freely here and used the phrase, 'means of expiating sin'); but in the minds of the scholars[29] whose work is now being considered a much more interesting problem arises. This goes beyond the matter of the exact meaning of this word, and raises the question whether Paul was really in sympathy with the statement that God provided in Christ an expiation or a propitiation. It looks, they argue, as if he quoted this and other parts of the passage as a concession to his readers, and inserted into the quotation his favourite words 'through faith'.

Such investigations must proceed by methods as scientific as possible: if the vocabulary is anywhere apparently un-Pauline one must weigh this against the fact that he might have introduced some rare word here, perhaps only here, because this was the best way to make an important point. Against such an argument might be urged that he makes the same or a very similar point elsewhere in different words. Obviously the convictions of individual scholars are found to exert a great influence in such research; but however inconclusive it is, it serves to focus attention in a new way upon passages which the uncritical reader may have passed over without particular notice and which now shine forth as possessing a great importance by themselves. This is true of Philippians ii,6–11, where Paul has long been thought by many to have introduced a Christian hymn praising Christ to reinforce his plea for humility, a theme which in itself does not warrant so full a statement of Christology.[30]

To decide what was Paul's original thought and what he took over, perhaps reluctantly, from his predecessors, might seem to be a game for scholars. A little reflection will show that it is of some importance: it is hard to restate in modern terms a theory which includes a doctrine of the atonement based on some cultic model no longer significant for contemporary man, but if the idea of a faith-relation with God is the essence of Paul's outlook, it is possible that it may be demythologized and restated in existential terms. It may even be the case that in contending with these arguments, we come to recognize that Paul was attempting to reconcile something which once was but 'is now no splendour at all' (to use words from 2 Corinthians iii, 10) with a revelation of which he claims 'I did not take it over from any man; no man taught it me' (Galatians i, 12), and that he was sometimes baffled as to how to express the events in which he was caught up. And in this situation we may see something very like our own; for we, no less than he, in attempting to present convictions in a manner true for our time, fall back on descriptive techniques which the very novelty of the situation seems to forbid.

Thirteen

New Interpretations:
Luke–Acts,
a Theological History

Glance at the opening of the Gospel according to Luke and at that of the book of the Acts of the Apostles; you immediately become aware that they were meant to be two parts of one work, so that a mental effort is demanded by which the gospel, so like Mark and Matthew in many respects, may be considered apart from them and in conjunction with its companion second volume. Since this second volume is manifestly not intended to be of the same character as the gospels, in the sense of being a proclamation of the *kerygma* about Jesus, but to be about those who made this proclamation; since therefore, unlike any other book in the New Testament, it is mainly concerned with narrative, it makes Luke–Acts a distinguishable subject for New Testament criticism. A book such as *The Making of Luke–Acts*, written by H. J. Cadbury in 1927,[1] exemplifies this fact, but examination of it shows that for the gospel the author must be closely occupied with the questions which also concern the other gospels, especially the synoptics. Indeed, the special character given to this enterprise in writing is seen most clearly by attending to Acts, although any conclusions at which criticism arrives must account for the character of the gospel as well. In this chapter, therefore, attention is given largely to Acts.

A long tradition ascribes Luke–Acts to Luke, the companion of Paul (Colossians iv,14; 2 Timothy iv,11; Philemon 24), a companion who used his own diary or notes in the famous 'we-passages' (xvi,9–17; xx,5–16; xxi,1–18; xxvii,1–xxviii,16). This tradition is as old as the Muratorian fragment of the canon and the Prologue to the Gospel of Luke (extant in only one manuscript) whose original dates from about 160. The obvious gaps in the author's knowledge, already noticed in the chapter on Paul, show that either he wrote with a non-historical motive or he did not know enough about his subject. Critics, beginning with J. D. Michaelis (1777), have taken one of these viewpoints; the non-historical motives suggested have included defence against Judaizing, defence of Paul against his accusers, desire to establish the divine origin of the church (by emphasizing the miraculous), or to extol the apostles, to insist on the centrality of Jerusalem in the growth of the church, to illustrate Pauline theology, to meet the special needs of Theophilus.

In 1836 Schrader and Baur gave a new turn to the story by emphasizing the discrepancies with the Pauline epistles, Paul's dependence on the older apostles, the evident desires to make Peter's and Paul's miracles parallel in fact and impressiveness, and to refer to Roman officials as friendly. Paul's death was excluded because it would nullify the effect of the book and show the emperor to be not a pillar of enlightened Roman justice, but the flouter alike of justice and humanity. In Baur's 'Tübingen' scheme Acts takes its place among the irenic writings concerned to reconcile Jewish Christians and Paulinists, and in this sphere of criticism as in others, the Tübingen school has exercised lasting, often undetected, and sometimes mischievous influence.

It might seem possible to maintain that Acts reveals apologetic motives but that the author has not departed from history in any misleading way. So believed Schneckenburger in 1841, but he provoked a long series of destructive criticisms from the Tübingen school. Unfortunately the sensible view of Schneckenburger was lost in a controversy in which the traditional view was held too rigidly by conservative scholars, while others produced even more extreme views such as those of Bruno Bauer (1850), who held that the author of Acts had no knowledge or understanding of the controversy between Judaizers and Paul because Acts belongs to a period long after this dispute raged. Catholicism already exists but is not a compromise; it is due to the development of Jewish legalism within the church. Other critics, such as Pfleiderer,[2] were more favourable to Acts, regarding it as an attempt on the part of the author to interpret the apostolic age in the light of his own, which was marked by a *rapprochement* between the saner elements in the two parties.

The year 1897 saw the publication of J. Weiss's work on Acts, putting forward a view which must contain much of the truth and can in any case never be neglected. He saw Acts 'as an apology for the Christian religion addressed to the heathen and directed against the accusations of the Jew, which shows how it happened that Judaism had been supplanted in its world-mission by Christianity'.

The outline so far given illustrates the obvious fact that the line dividing criticism from interpretation constantly tends to vanish; indeed, interpretation seems to be indistinguishable from criticism. It is hardly surprising, therefore, that under the waves of controversy about the trustworthiness of Acts the figure of Luke, feebly protesting his claims to be the author, seemed doomed to sink without trace.

In 1908, when he was about to go under for much more than the third time, no less a person than Harnack threw him a lifeline. It was a curious one: its strands were partly those of home-spun commonsense, but they included one which led back to Colossians iv, 14 ('Luke the beloved physician'). The situation was very unusual: Harnack,[3] the expert and widely read German scholar, had been persuaded by an uncritical enthusiastic doctor from Dublin named W. K. Hobart (1882),[4] whose examination of the Lucan vocabulary had convinced him that the author must have been a physician. This evidence, whose weakness was exposed finally by Cadbury in 1926, is now used more often in pulpits than in lecture-rooms. Harnack's interest in it makes no difference at all to his importance as a scholar of immense ability and deserved reputation; he re-established the possibility of believing that Luke wrote the works ascribed to him but nevertheless is as a historian open to severe criticism. Luke 'must be recognized . . . as a literary artist, but when it comes to content he proceeds where he was not himself an eye-witness in a most negligent fashion, chapter after chapter, and often confuses things completely. This is true both of the Gospel and Acts.' It was for later scholarship to suggest that what appeared to be negligence (one seems to overhear the German professor rebuking a junior member of his staff) might be design, and what appeared to be confusion an attempt to do justice to all his sources at once.

During the development of criticism many different views about the sources of Acts have been put forward. It is unnecessary to detail them all, for the reader can be asked to cooperate in a straightforward investigation, starting from a point (still widely considered valid) made by Harnack. This is that a natural break seems to occur at xv, 35 or perhaps xvi, 5. Leaving Harnack for a moment, let us work backwards and find him again at the beginning. The last part of Acts will now appear reasonably (though not wholly) homogeneous, largely about Paul, continuous and intelligible; though it may contain here and there miraculous elements which are hard to credit (less because they are about the miraculous than because they do not harmonize with the rest of the story), these can be dropped out and the continuous narrative is unimpaired. Thus the earthquake at Philippi (xvi, 26) appears to have affected no part of the town except the prison, especially its doors and the prisoners' shackles. Yet Paul and Silas no doubt really did run into trouble in Philippi (1 Thessalonians ii, 2 refers to it) and managed to get away. In passing it may be useful to draw attention to the possibilities of distinguishing the strata (one a plain itinerary, one a highly coloured tale) in this chapter, and to reflect that some such criticism is inevitable when one observes that the apparently victorious and vindicated apostles do nevertheless leave the town. Nevertheless, this latter part of Acts raises few problems.

As we persist in our backward progress, let us leave on one side xv, 1–35, and observe that xiii and xiv seem to belong to the Pauline cycle occupying the last part of the book. Acts xv, 1–35, thus isolated, is the account of the 'Council' in Jerusalem, which the chapter on Paul's epistles showed to constitute a problem when considered together with Galatians i and ii. It may be due to Luke's writing up an account which he possessed, though it did not originally belong to this stage in the church's history, but which he thought *must* come in here (or otherwise he could not understand how church history had developed as it had).

Backwards again; we arrive at some material concerned with Peter. This is ix, 32–xi, 18 and xii, although Luke may have added what he knew about the death of Herod Agrippa I, which he describes in xii, 19–23 in such a way as to make it seem that Herod was punished by God for his cruelty to the apostles. Acts xi, 19–30 is difficult to characterize. Perhaps Luke wrote it to link up other material; this looks like the truth about verse ix, 31, but can we say that ix, 1–30, all about Paul and his conversion, belongs to a Pauline cycle of tradition? If so, is it the same as the rest which we singled out and which begins at chapter xiii?

No doubt these are enough questions to ask and to leave unanswered, but something must be said about the remainder, i, 1–viii, 40. This is the region in which Harnack thought that sources could be discerned, and indeed that there were doublets among the sources; that is, Luke sometimes had before him two reports of the same thing and, thinking them to refer to distinct though similar events, recorded them twice. One main source Harnack ascribed to Antioch and another to Jerusalem. He was inclined to regard them as continuations of sources which Luke used in his gospel, and to value them somewhat arbitrarily in the opinion of a modern historian. It will be sufficient for us to observe that it is in this period of the earliest church that Luke seems to have lacked any certain evidence or sources, and may well have written up traditions about which he had heard, or which he combined, or which he selected from written sources. The story of Pentecost in chapter ii is clearly of the kind we should call 'mythical', but Luke would not and could not criticize it in this way, regarding some such event as necessary to explain how the church arose, how the apostles, naturally discouraged and afraid after the crucifixion, received power for the work which it is a fact of history that they did carry out. Modern critics may well say that they were impelled by some inner conviction which was very real to them, and that this is externalized and presented as an event by an historian without modern critical attitudes. This is fair, but if we convict Luke of being uncritical, we must observe that he is so from a modern point of view. He would regard the story of Pentecost as just what must have happened to explain subsequent events.

That Luke was not the muddler which Harnack accused him of being is now increasingly recognized: it may be said that the way was in part cleared by the form-critic Dibelius, whose *Studies in the Acts of the Apostles*[5] certainly looked at the work from an analytical point of view: Luke had access to the diary and to an itinerary, and composed a great deal himself; there was also at his disposal a mixture of sources, from a modern historian's point of view of no value, which may be called legends; but Dibelius thought the author was a companion of Paul. The result of such insights, summarizing and clarifying the work of critics and adding much of value from the same point of view, was to emphasize the theological character of Luke's writing, suggesting that he wrote to convey a picture of the early church which inevitably reflected the state of affairs when he was writing in about A.D. 90. The work of other critics in the same line of advance, notably Conzelmann and Haenchen, has done much to bring out the theological character of Acts, largely conveyed in the speeches given to such authoritative figures as Peter and Paul which are generally regarded as Lucan compositions. Haenchen found it difficult to believe that a companion of Paul had really written Acts, rightly drawing attention to the apologetic character of the book.

When we are satisfied that the problems raised by critics have been given due weight, it becomes possible to answer all the more clearly questions about Luke's knowledge of the times about which he was writing, using our knowledge of the times when he wrote. When we reflect upon this we recognize immediately that in a highly theological book which claims to be history we owe it to the author to examine minutely his knowledge of the earlier times (which he did not know at firsthand), not only through the spectacles provided by his own times, but side by side with what we know from quite different sources about them.

To give an example of such inquiry, Luke wanted to show that Paul, when accused of disturbing the good order of the Roman Empire, was not condemned by Roman officials. It will suit his purpose then to relate that in Corinth Gallio refused to regard Paul as deserving arrest. That is why Luke relates the incident in chapter xviii; it is a good instance to prove his case – but not if it did not happen. Luke then must have thought it did happen. If there were no such person as Gallio or if, though real, he was in Corinth only at such times as meant that he could never have clashed with Paul, Luke is unreliable on this point and may be unreliable on others. We shall then conclude that the explanation, 'Luke wrote this incident to show how things were and had no real knowledge of how they had been', is the right one and we shall cease to examine Acts with any hope of establishing through its material even glimpses of the early church. In fact, we have seen that Gallio may well have clashed with Paul in Corinth and that our difficulties over the exact date are not enough to make us abandon the historicity of an incident hard to think of as invented (it is hardly a victory for Paul).

Did Luke then perhaps know some history after all? Granted that he coloured it, was it there to colour? It is this last question which has slipped out of the bag on to the floor while the form-critics have monopolized the quiz game. Some scholars, not at first invited into the circle, have now with an apologetic cough picked up the card on which this question is written, and dared to give it some very positive answers. The arguments used by these scholars (among them the Roman historians, A. H. M. Jones and A. N. Sherwin-White)[6] include the observation that the attitude of the Roman government represented by the officials in Luke's story was not that of later governors known to Luke in his day; more important, the legal niceties which adorn the background of Paul's appeal to Caesar were as represented by Luke when Paul made the appeal, but they changed quite soon afterwards. In fact, it is the burden of Sherwin-White's studies that Luke reveals wonderful accuracy on several points in the period about which he was writing, accuracy which it would have been very easy for him to miss if he had merely assumed that the earlier days were like those in which he lived. Such evidence is conveniently reviewed in the New Clarendon Bible *Acts* by R. P. C. Hanson,[7] who shows among other items the 'very remarkable synchronization' which gives accurate information about the lives and offices of Ananias the high priest (xxiii, 2), Felix, Festus, Agrippa II, Berenice and Drusilla (xxiii, 24–xxvi, 32). The lives and relations of these persons changed a good deal in a relatively short time, but they were as Luke described them at this moment, as we know from Roman history and Josephus.

There is no need to abandon the insights acquired by radical criticism, but such criticism demands that Luke be credited with sources which are remarkably accurate as well as with others which a modern historian would not regard as historical sources at all. While we must not only admit but affirm that Luke wrote history theologically, we are bound to concede that he suffered rather less than the average from the occupational hyper-function of historians who as a class (in the words of Dean Inge) 'certainly do not share the disability attributed to the Deity of not being able to alter the past'.

Fourteen

New Judgements:
Later Books

The books of the New Testament which have so far received no more than mention need shorter treatment than that afforded to the gospels and to Paul; they illustrate for the most part the same principles and techniques which the rest of the New Testament demands for its understanding. They do however illustrate an important change of outlook in criticism; many very competent scholars adhere to what others regard as unduly conservative views, such as that 1 Peter can be shown to have been written by Peter the apostle or even that the Epistle of James was written by James the brother of Jesus. The other way of regarding these writings allows them to fall into a highly satisfactory and illuminating chronological scheme, but it involves giving up the cherished belief that in some of these writings we hear the words of the apostles themselves.

This latter way of regarding these works sets them in the line of historical and theological development where they reflect the later history of the church. One of the main features of such books is often the attempt to fill the gap between conviction about what has happened and what is going to happen, and life as it continues every day. To await the coming of Jesus Christ from heaven, strange as it may sound to our ears, was for some time the chief mental preoccupation of Christians, even if their manual preoccupations were necessarily indistinguishable from those of their unbelieving fellow-men.

Thus Paul in his lifetime left abundant evidence to show it was often in the intervals of his work as a tent-maker that he engaged in the preaching of the gospel, though when he could do so he concentrated his energies upon it. These writings reflect not only disappointment at delay in the coming of Christ to vindicate his followers, but also the church's anxiety as to what ethic was appropriate during this unexpected period. Neglect of this fact has led countless interpreters astray; for example, 1 Corinthians vii tackles the situation in its early stages, and answers questions put by the Corinthians on marriage in this context. Paul's words here are not a condemnation of marriage (a view possible only for those who have not read the chapter with attention) but advice about marriage during a time held by both himself and his addressees to be short. This is clear from verse 29, and his acceptance of marriage is really clear throughout the chapter. Verses 3 and 4 could hardly have been written by someone who condemned marriage as unholy.

Quite as pressing as time developed were the questions about wealth; while it would be easy to see that according to the Christian ethic there can be no countenancing riches gained wrongly or by making others poor, the question whether it is right to engage in profit-making enterprises at all, simple if you expect the world to enter shortly upon an age where such things will be entirely irrelevant, becomes complicated if that age does not appear, and if the present age persists and brings further trouble through persecution or other causes.

Many of the books of the New Testament awaiting notice reflect these problems and situations. They reflect also some sort of church life which shows the church becoming to a certain extent an institution. Such characteristics, especially if accompanied by others, such as style, may be used as evidence by which these writings can be assigned their natural place in the story of the early church.

It is natural to begin with those epistles, or letters, which have, or have seemed to have, a claim to be Pauline. Ephesians is the most obvious letter to take; it can boast of a long tradition of being regarded as written by Paul, but criticism has made the following points: there is no eschatology in the letter, the style is sluggish and ponderous, and therefore unlike the volatile Paul, it shows great affinity with Colossians but betrays its unPauline character by using key technical words found in that letter in markedly different senses, and it ends without any of the usual Pauline greetings.

Perhaps its most famous characteristic from a critical point of view is to be found at the beginning rather than the end, though it can be considered along with the lack of greetings at the end. In the opening sentence the writer appears in customary translations to address Christians 'in Ephesus' but these last two words are omitted in a formidable number of manuscripts and other witnesses. The theory has therefore arisen that the work was a cyclical letter, containing an epitome of Paul's doctrine and intended to be sent round to a number of churches; or, as some have argued, composed as an introduction to Pauline theology to be placed at the beginning of the corpus of his writings when these were, at the end of the first century, being copied and sent round the faithful because they had by now gained among some the status of sacred writing and were being commended by them for reading in other churches. The theory is attractive and could explain the undoubted absence of Paul's style combined with the presence of a large measure of his thought; that is, thought compatible with that known of Paul from the accepted authentic letters. Its weakness lies in the position of the letter now in the Pauline canon, and the theories by which this has been explained require rather too much ingenuity to remain altogether plausible.

While there is a good explanation for the lack of eschatology (since it can easily be shown that the writer had it in the back of his mind, as e.g. in i,13 f.), the differences in vocabulary and style are as important as the considerations already advanced. Of other points which might be added two may be selected. One is teaching about the relation of Christ to the gifts of the Spirit. The sophisticated use of scripture in iv,8, by which this doctrine is expressed, could certainly be ascribed to Paul, but the doctrine of ascension implied here, and its association with a doctrine of the gift of the Spirit through Christ expressed differently from Paul elsewhere, are considerations which make the reader familiar with Paul's accepted letters fairly certain (especially when he thinks of the other arguments) that Ephesians was not written by Paul. Doctrine in the letter is not strongly developed in any direction which would suggest a very late date, and it remains possible that the letter was composed by a follower of Paul, whether in his lifetime or not.

Here an interesting question emerges: it is obvious that if the letter is to be regarded as unPauline, it becomes possible to regard it as not a letter in the strict sense at all. The name Paul at the beginning, if we must regard it as an instance within the Christian church of the pseudepigraphy with which our outline of the matter of the canon has made us familiar, suggests at once that the work may be merely cast in the form of a letter, and never have been sent as one. In this connexion we remember the doubt about the intended recipients and the lack of greetings at the end (strange indeed if it had really been written by Paul to Ephesus where he must have made very many friends, a supposition well supported by the importance given to Paul's work there in Acts, and by the subsequent importance and reputation of the church at Ephesus).

Ephesians therefore may be an early example of someone using the apostolic epistle as a model to convey his teaching. His use of the name Paul is not intended to deceive but to say that this is what Paul would say in the present situation. The use of the epistle as a literary form rather than as an actual letter, destined to become a widespread practice outside the canon of the New Testament, is thus regarded as having begun within it also. The so-called Epistle to the Hebrews is really a tract, though it obeys the form of a letter at the end by introducing personal elements. Again, the Epistle of James is avowedly addressed to a very wide audience, and the author of the book of Revelation uses the epistle form in his 'letter to the seven churches', i, 4–iii, 22, at least in his opening utterances, but is really conveying to them 'what the Spirit says to the churches'. The incorporation of the 'letter' or 'letters', if they can be envisaged as seven separate messages, into an 'apocalypse' reveals that this is no more than a literary device to make the members of the several churches feel that the solemn words are addressed to *them*. In every case it is what the Spirit says which is conveyed and the Spirit says solemnly 'Write . . .'

It has even been urged by some that Paul's seven letters

(Romans, Corinthians counting as one only, Galatians, Ephesians, Philippians, Colossians, Thessalonians counting as one only) as they were originally issued as a corpus at the end of the first century, gave the author of Revelation the idea of writing the warning part of his message in this form. This receives perhaps some support from the odd claim in the Muratorian fragment of the canon that Paul followed John in writing this mystically significant number of *seven* letters, in the order Corinthians, Ephesians, Philippians, Colossians, Galatians, Thessalonians, the fragment quaintly admitting that writing to the Corinthians and to the Thessalonians had to be repeated 'on account of corruption'. He is anxious to be able to say that Paul wrote seven, even though he has to add that he also wrote to Philemon, Timothy and Titus 'on account of love and affection'. It is impossible to accept this relative chronology of the book of Revelation and Paul's letters, but it shows that some people in the relatively early days of the church thought in these – to us – odd and unacceptable ways, so that if the author of Revelation knew of Paul's letters, he may have used this form and even the number seven for his 'letters' section because he too thought that Paul had written seven main ones, or at least letters to seven churches. The fact that the Muratorian fragment reverses the order of the composition of John, author of Revelation, and Paul, is another indication of the uncritical attitude of much of the tradition within the church about its early literature.

Much of the teaching and many of the ways in which it is expressed are shared by Ephesians, 1 Peter, James and Hebrews. The considerable differences which they nevertheless reveal, side by side with some common subject-matter, are phenomena probably to be explained by a common fund of doctrine in the church, held also by many who committed nothing to writing. We can return to this fact and to a further discussion of these writings after we have reviewed in brief the somewhat complicated problem of the so-called Pastoral Epistles of Paul, 1 and 2 Timothy, and Titus.

P. N. Harrison's *The Problem of the Pastoral Epistles* was, in his own words, 'an attempt to show how the language of the

Pastoral Epistles can be used as a key to unlock the old secret of their origin'. The way in which Harrison used arguments from vocabulary was extremely painstaking and careful but has been subjected to much criticism, especially since the principles required to be observed by those who use statistics have been better understood. It is a great pity that glee in discovering that Harrison may be vulnerable on this score has misled some critics to give insufficient weight to the facts which enabled Harrison to announce from the outset that he was attempting 'to unlock the old secret of their origin'. However his efforts are to be judged he must not be accused of inventing the problem. Many who have criticized his method have been candid enough to admit that other reasons than word usage, namely style, doctrine and the impossibility of finding a place in Paul's life for these letters if they are genuine, all remain. Indeed, no satisfactory place can be found unless we accept the theory that Paul was released from Rome, made a journey again in the east, was rearrested, and finally put to death in Rome, writing 1 Timothy and Titus while he was temporarily free and 2 Timothy during his second imprisonment (along with Colossians, Philemon and Philippians) or some variant upon this. One difficulty is the extreme weakness of the evidence for such a release and rearrest; there is some slight evidence of a tradition of a journey to Spain, but this probably stems from Romans xv, 24, written before Paul knew he would be arrested but devoutly regarded as an apostolic prophecy which must have been fulfilled. There is no evidence at all for the further journey in the east which is required in order to find a place for the epistles in Paul's lifetime.

Harrison's solution was to identify three (in his original book five but in a later article reduced to three)[2] genuine fragmentary letters of Paul, two to Timothy, one to Titus, round which a devout Paulinist in Rome had built three 'epistles' addressed to the Timothies and Tituses (i.e. sub-apostolic supervisors of the churches) of his day, in order to meet in the name of the now dead apostle a situation in which the offices in the churches were held by unworthy men, and in which wrong, often morally harmful, teaching was being permitted by both slackness and ignorance. Whatever be thought about the genuinely Pauline fragments, the character of these brief epistles exactly fits this situation; there have been drunken and corrupt ministers in the church and gnostic, or proto-gnostic, teaching has been accepted. This situation is to be met by appointing worthy members of the church to the ministry and by guarding the 'sound doctrine'. It is remarkable how this conception fits the sort of time to which it has been suggested that these writings belong. It is not typical of Paul to urge retention of sound teaching, not because he would have countenanced what he thought was false, but because he would have argued each point dynamically and given his urgently expressed reasons for holding fast to the doctrine which he commended. Moreover, this doctrine would consist less of formally correct statements than of glowing accounts of what God had done for man in Christ. What Paul had hammered out on the anvil of his own experience, and that of the church which he had joined, has in the Pastorals crystallized out into a number of 'true sayings'. The situation is incidentally that to which Luke makes Paul refer in his speech at Miletus in Acts xx, 17–35 (see especially verses 29–30).

The Pastorals are interesting also for the stage in the development of the ministry which they reflect; in the rest of the New Testament it is very difficult to determine the exact status of 'presbyters', and whether, in a particular instance where the word is used, a specifically Christian or old Jewish-style official is meant. The word is not mentioned in the certainly genuine letters of Paul. In the technical sense of an officer of the church the word deacon is used by him only once, in Philippians i, 1, beside his sole mention of the word bishop. This last occurs twice in the Pastorals and the duties of presbyters and deacons are thoroughly discussed there.

The Pastorals may now be left, with the warning that many scholars still defend (by hook and episcopal crook) the possibility of Pauline authorship, on the grounds that at the end of his life he had perforce to turn to the defence rather than the creation of doctrine, and that he legislated for the continuance of his work in this manner before his death.

Hebrews is a puzzling work. On the one hand it appears to have existed for a time without a title, for that which it now bears does not appear in the text as a description of the recipients or as a word at all, and there is no hint accompanying this title (which is found in the early manuscripts) as to who the author might have been. On the other hand it is a very plausible guess that it was addressed to Hebrews who are being encouraged to see that Christianity is the fulfilment of Judaism, or possibly to Jewish Christians of the kind who regarded Jesus as a prophet indeed but had not acceded to the claim that he was far more than this, greater even than the angels in ontological status. Possibly, in view of the very stern warnings against apostasy, it is addressed to Christians, once Jews, in danger of falling away from their allegiance. Tertullian (c. 160–220) refers to it as though there were no doubt about its being a letter written by Barnabas, the companion of Paul in the letter's early journeys. The traditional view from the fifth to the nineteenth century was that Paul wrote it, but this is impossible on a number of grounds, involving both style and subject-matter. Quite often Luther's suggestion that Apollos (Acts xviii, 24 ff.; 1 Corinthians i, 12; iii, 4 ff. etc.) was the author is revived. It is possible, but no more than this can be shown. Apart from the references which suggest persecution and apostasy, the document is remarkable from the historical point of view for the list of 'martyrs' in xi, 32–40, which seems to include a reference to recent Jewish martyrs whose importance has already received some comment (p. 220).

The Christology of Hebrews is interesting both in itself and for the light which it throws upon the origin of the work. Christ is called the Son of God, and the author defines the meaning of this title very clearly, arguing Christ's superiority to angels in the order of being by a number of citations from the scriptures. Other arguments establish the reality of his humanity and his solidarity with his fellow-men. In this part of the argument there appears an interesting reflection of the same tradition as the narratives of the garden of Gethsemane (Hebrews v, 7; Matthew xxvi, 36–46; Mark xiv, 32–42; cf. Luke xxii, 39–46; John xii, 27), but the manner of Jesus' death is used to lend colour and emphasis to a remarkable interpretation of its significance as a sacrifice by and of the universal and sinless High Priest, once for all time, an interpretation based on the representative action of the Jewish high priest on the annual Day of Atonement.

This characterization of Jesus as the one only sinless High Priest sets out to distinguish him essentially from the hereditary Jewish high priest; but the Dead Sea Scrolls have revealed the one-time existence of a sect who ardently expected the coming of a messianic high priest, and have set several scholars re-examining the evidence for the influence of this concept upon New Testament Christology,[3] especially on Hebrews.

Hebrews v, 5 ff. associates closely the titles Christ (anointed one), Son and Priest, partly by means of a quotation from Psalm cx, 4 which introduces the enigmatic figure of Melchizedek, who enters the story of Abraham rather mysteriously in Genesis xiv. Hebrews vii elaborates the theme of this venerable figure in close connexion with that of the priesthood, clearly here meaning the high priesthood. It has therefore always been the task of commentators to discover if possible to what milieu these ideas could belong. The three themes, Son of God, High Priest and Melchizedek all occur in Philo, but the first two are not identified until Hebrews, where the mysterious origin of Melchizedek ('without father, without mother', vii, 3) is used to emphasize the uniqueness of the Son who is an 'eternal priest according to the order of Melchizedek' (this phrase from Psalm cx, 4 is repeated often in Hebrews; see v, 6, 10; vi, 20; vii, 11 ff.).

The general character of Hebrews does nothing to prevent the judgement that the Alexandrian Judaism represented by Philo may be the milieu from which the tract arose; but fresh examination of the question is demanded by the publication of a fragment from Qumran,[4] according to which it seems that Melchizedek is assigned largely eschatological functions such as belong to the Son of Man in the gospels.

The background of Hebrews is not clear; but it may be unnecessary to regard the evidence of Philo and the Scrolls as completely contradictory, since we now know that the Judaism of Alexandria was not always so different from that of Palestine.

Further difficulty arises from the evidence, both internal and external, that Hebrews was written in Rome or Italy. Hebrews xiii, 24 implies this,[5] and the great familiarity with the work displayed by Clement of Rome supports it. However, an author familiar with Alexandrian and Palestinian thought need not be confined to Alexandria or Palestine and might have been living at Rome when he wrote this remarkable treatise.

In the group of Jude and 1 and 2 Peter, 1 Peter is the longest and the most interesting, not to say the most attractive. On any showing it is also the oldest, since 2 Peter seems to imply the existence of 1 Peter, as we should expect, and Jude is clearly very close to 2 Peter in time.

Discussion about 1 Peter yields matters of great interest. It certainly appears to be a sermon or letter to Christians about the main characteristics of the Christian life in a situation where persecution is in progress, or is threatening. This would be universally agreed. A great deal of assent would be afforded to the contention that the author connects his sermon with baptism and its significance. He manifestly does this at some points, but some would say that the connexion is so close that a baptism service inspired the address which is here set down in writing. Perhaps it is even more than a baptism homily; perhaps it is, as has been urged by some, a baptism liturgy, that is, we may discern going on as it were in the background the Paschal Liturgy, the Eucharist on an Easter Day when, in the early church, catechumens reached the climax of their instruction by being baptized within the context of this solemn and joyful memorial of the Passover, on which the first Christian Eucharist (the Last Supper) was founded.

In such speculative theory we have once more inevitably strayed into the sphere of interpretation. To return to more strictly critical and historical matters, one obvious question which must be asked is: what are the arguments for and against Peter himself having written the letter, as it clearly claims for itself? A very closely connected question is: what persecution is in progress, or what persecution is actually affecting the recipients? If Peter did write it, the answer seems to be quite clear; it must be the persecution in which he was shortly to die, that set on foot by Nero in Rome in A.D. 64. Tacitus in his *Annals* (xv, 44) tells about this insane act of Nero, and the strong tradition in the church is that both Peter and Paul perished through it. This would be a persecution in progress but not affecting the recipients.

From among the many arguments which would illustrate the work of criticism on this writing we may select one which may be called an argument in the sphere of historical and we may add psychological possibility. The letter is addressed to Christians in various provinces in Asia Minor, as its opening shows; now we have no firm evidence of a church in Pontus–Bithynia at so early a date, but Pliny the Younger was governor of this Roman province in 112–13 and has achieved immortality partly through his letter to the Emperor Trajan asking for a ruling on how he is to deal with Christians. He implies that there were Christians there as long ago as twenty years before, but this does not bring us back anywhere far enough to imagine a church there founded by Peter, to whom he might now be writing. Nor have we any knowledge whatever of Peter which would enable us to say that he ever travelled in that region – nor, it must be admitted, is there any reason to suppose that he did not, for he certainly travelled over a wide area. (The matter raises points of criticism of Acts, for it would be most natural to suppose that Peter's travels began with his escape from Jerusalem (Acts xii,1–17) and that his appearance in the council of Acts xv is just one more reason for believing that the chronological position of that meeting, at least, is unhistorical.)

We may add to this historical argument what we have called a psychological argument: is it credible that even an apostle, caught up in a persecution which persuaded him that the eschatological act of judgement was 'beginning with God's own household' (1 Peter iv, 17) – that is, the church – would settle down to write not a brief farewell letter, but a longish, earnest and rationally argued treatise in which the main weapon against threat of persecution is recommended as the good life, which will put a stop to the slanders being circulated about Christians? He might well do this if he saw that the persecution was world-wide, but hardly at such length as here. Moreover, the writer expresses what in such circumstances is not only a naïve but an impossible optimism, with the words, 'Who is going to do you wrong if you are devoted to what is good?' (iii, 13). On the usual theory of authorship, the author could answer this question himself with the one word, 'Nero'.

Although the above arguments would be widely accepted as serious and important, they cannot prove that Peter did not write the letter. Paul too, after being flogged at the orders of Roman magistrates at Philippi and after witnessing the beating-up of his fellow-worker Sosthenes under the uncaring eye of Gallio, could write, 'government, a terror to crime, has no terrors for good behaviour' (Romans xiii, 3, thought by some, partly on these very grounds, to be unPauline, but probably wrongly, for the argument, *pace* these critics, is all of a piece here). It is perhaps to be expected that the New Testament, notoriously proclaiming very different values from the world's, should provide puzzles not only for the conservative but also for the critical.

More telling are other arguments, such as that the inexpert (though not illiterate) Peter could hardly have written such excellent and indeed sophisticated Greek. For this reason attention is drawn to the mention of Silvanus, perhaps to be identified with Paul's companion Silas (see the opening of 1 and 2 Thessalonians for his alternative name Silvanus) as having been more than the scribe, perhaps the part-author, or even more of an author than Peter. The trouble with this argument is manifest: the more you defend the Petrine authorship by saying that Silvanus wrote the work, the more difficulty you have in maintaining that Peter wrote it. One of the most thorough advocates of the conservative authorship position, E. G. Selwyn, has analysed the material used in 1 Peter, showing how it owes something to set instruction given to catechumens, something to *Haustafeln* or domestic ethical codes such as are known to have been popular in the more educated areas of Hellenistic civilization; this is done very largely by comparing the writing with epistles of Paul and other books of the New Testament. The odd thing is the failure to conclude on this very evidence that the letter is probably late, reflecting a situation in which the church has settled down, albeit uneasily, side by side with non-Christians in society, and earned a bad reputation partly by not joining in the life of the community, under the influence of its eschatological expectations; a church which the author urges to play its due part and to be ready always with a reason for holding their Christian faith (iii,15). Such considerations have moved many modern editors to see the letter as best understood against the very situation which Pliny reveals. The place is obviously right for this interpretation, and the time is too, if we will agree that in 1 Peter we have yet another example of a pseudonymous writing.

In this instance the author's writing in the name of the apostle from Rome seems reasonably natural but does not give a full explanation of the apparently very personal greetings at the end of the letter. A reference to 'Mark, my son' is natural if it is Peter who is writing, for we know of a close association between Peter and Mark through Papias, but for someone usurping the name of Peter the apostle, *any* personal reference without explanation is odd. This difficulty is eased by some critics who suppose that the original sermon consisted of i,3–iv,11 (where indeed it seems to 'wind up') and that i,1 f. and iv,12 to the end were added when it was enclosed in a letter on the occasion of an actual persecution. The personal reference would then be that of the otherwise unknown Silvanus of v,12 who in fact is the real sender, though not necessarily the author, of the whole of the letter.

1 Peter illustrates once more the historical and critical matters with which investigators of the New Testament must be occupied, and so deserved a little more space (though not a full account) than we can devote to the remaining books.

Jude seems to be understood most naturally as the basis of 2 Peter, with which it stands certainly in some kind of close relation. Jude is mentioned in the Muratorian fragment and by Tertullian, Clement of Alexandria and Origen, but Eusebius ranks it among the disputed books. With this licence criticism can afford to leave on one side any ultra-conservative claim that the tract was written by Jude, a brother of Jesus, for the writer, in giving his name at the outset, claims only to be a brother of James, calling himself a servant of Jesus Christ. Only if the James mentioned is the brother of Jesus with that name can Jude also be the brother; but he makes no such claim, and as we shall see James also makes no such claim and is probably not the brother of Jesus either.

The so-called Epistle of Jude is a tract seeking to combat the growth of false teaching within a church being divided by it. The tone and arguments are manifestly those of a man who writes for a church revering scriptures not now familiar to the average Christian, but which have received some notice in this book, namely the intertestamental writings such as *1 Enoch*. Balaam, prominent in the Old Testament story as one who in spite of temptation to the contrary did only what God commanded, is placed in Jude 11 among the enemies of the faith, bearing the character which he held in later Judaism as one of the manifestations of the arch-enemy of God's people. Careless hints reveal that the writer belongs to a generation subsequent to that of the apostles. The church is an institution to which many belong who must be exhorted into remaining members of it. The language is alien to one used to the forthright arguments of Paul or even the appeals of 1 Peter.

2 Peter seems to be an expansion of Jude. If it is not, Jude must almost certainly be an abbreviation of it. It is even possible that the writer of Jude means that he was busy writing 2 Peter when news convinced him of the necessity to write immediately the shorter tract. 2 Peter is concerned with the same troubles as the writer of Jude, but also contends with some members of the church who are asking naturally enough the question, 'When will the Lord come?' with some impatience, and indeed affirming at the same time their belief that the world order has continued since the creation and will continue thus for ever. Both Jude and 2 Peter refer to acts of judgement by God in the past history of his people, and 2 Peter clearly uses this recital to enable him to argue that God will inaugurate a final judgement of great severity in the manner which the prophets foretold. Both regard the apostles as authoritative for the conduct of the church in the meantime and

319

do not appeal to the authority of Jesus directly; he has become in fact a somewhat remote figure taking on the lineaments of the stern judge of the Old Testament LORD. 2 Peter uses the specious argument that 'with the Lord one day is like a thousand years' (iii, 8) to attempt to comfort those who had been led to believe that the vindication of the Lord for them would come soon. Since comfort could be derived from this doctrine only if the 'soon' were understood on the human time-scale, the argument reveals a preoccupation less with comforting the faithful (as Paul so earnestly tried to do in for example 1 Thessalonians iv, 13–18) than with saving the face of a discredited expectation. Such considerations make fairly clear and perhaps obvious that these writings are relatively late, and other characteristics already mentioned show that the milieu to which they belong is that of Jewish Christianity. They may therefore be classed with the genre of fictitious testaments of which *The Testaments of the Twelve Patriarchs* is so magnificent an example in the inter-testamental period.[6]

It is necessary only to glance at Jude and 2 Peter to see that they are cast only roughly into the letter-form and make no pretence to being letters addressed to particular recipients. They are therefore not letters at all, unless we are prepared to give them the title of 'Open Letters', which is perhaps something like what is meant by calling them, along with James and the three Johannine epistles, 'Catholic Epistles', i.e. universal letters, letters addressed to all Christians. Such is avowedly the character of the 'Letter' of James which addresses the twelve tribes in the Dispersion, most naturally taken to mean the Jewish nation outside Palestine. In the context of a writing addressed to Christians it may mean Jewish Christians, or possibly the author is addressing the world-wide Christian church in this manner in order to make clear that he regards the latter as the true Israel. This last interpretation is more likely when the critic is convinced that Christians are being addressed, a point on which some doubt has been raised by the scarcity of references which would make this certain; thus Christ himself is mentioned only at i, 1 and ii, 1 and the writer refers to the people assembled for worship not as a church but a synagogue; again, he chooses for example to follow, or from whom to take heart, heroes of the Old Testament, and thinks of Job as a good example of patience under adversity when one might have expected him to refer to Jesus himself. Suspicion that the work is or was originally a Jewish writing is allayed when we reflect that the undoubtedly Christian letter *1 Clement* also betrays the early church's habit of appropriating the ancient scriptures and using them as naturally as its predecessor the synagogue had done to illustrate and to enforce doctrine or exhortation. It is further allayed when it is seen that a Christian background is necessary to explain the argument at certain points, especially where the author seems to be arguing against the Pauline doctrine of grace rather than the works of the Law, as the way to salvation (ii, 14 ff.).

Other indications of a Christian milieu include reminiscences of the teaching of Jesus as recorded in the synoptic gospels. The modern trend of criticism is well illustrated here: in 1897 Mayor could use this feature as an argument for authorship by James the brother of Jesus, on the assumption that it would be natural for a brother to recall teaching which he had himself heard Jesus deliver in Galilee.[7] This is not only uncritical, but may even be called sentimental since the tradition about the attitude of the brothers of Jesus to him suggests that James is not likely to have listened to much of his teaching (there are several passages to support this contention but it is remarkable to find the tradition clearly preserved in John vii, 5).

But we are concerned with arguments arising out of the practice of criticism. The teaching of Jesus reflected in James is most often in a form near to that found in Matthew. That gospel, as we have seen, bears marks of being somewhat late, revealing the fact by artless phrases such as 'to this day', by the intrusion of a bitter reference to the destruction of Jerusalem where it is quite out of place in the original story (xxii, 7) and by a large number of traits betraying the outlook of a later age than that of Mark's gospel which he uses as an authority. The reminiscence of Jesus' teaching, therefore, at first sight an argument for the early composition of James, is really an argument for its relative lateness. The attitude to the Christian synagogue or church as a well-established institution supports such a conclusion.

It thus becomes open to the critic to look for the characteristics he might expect to find in a work of this date (about A.D. 100); these will include as one important characteristic some ethical instruction for Christians in everyday life, unrelated to the end of the age or any belief connected with it. 'James' is interesting in this respect since he chooses at least three themes about which the reader receives the impression that he has his own strong convictions, and perhaps thinks that they are neglected. These are: the danger of the uncontrolled tongue; showing favour to the rich; and the uselessness of a faith which does not issue in deeds. Some methods of New Testament criticism are illustrated in connexion with them.

First, the well-known diatribe against the tongue (iii, 1–12; cf. i, 26) is rightly called a diatribe, for while it shows (like other parts of this writing) affinity with Jewish Wisdom literature, it is an example of the diatribe of Greek orators – a form of speech or writing which concentrates on one subject, uses irony or sarcasm, and answers, sometimes with ridicule, imaginary opponents. Thus James shows his knowledge of Hellenistic culture, as also when he uses such phrases as 'the wheel of becoming' in iii, 6 or the technical astronomical terms of i, 17. Whether he had a profound knowledge of the thinking which used these counters, or was merely trying to show himself as 'in the know', it is a reasonable conclusion that the author was a Hellenistic Jew at least acquainted enough with Greek culture to admire it.

His warning about showing favour to the rich (ii, 1–21; cf. v, 1–6) is revealing in another way altogether. Favouring the rich is one danger against which the author warns, and then he is led to inveigh against the rich as being themselves in danger of unfavourable judgement before God. The author is thus speaking in a context in which the church has developed in such a way that there is a temptation to flatter the rich members; but he has a hatred of them as a class because they are representatives of those who encompassed the death of Jesus (v, 6) – and incidentally of the historical James himself who both in his lifetime and after his murder in A.D. 62 was generally known as 'James the Just' or 'Righteous' (the Greek word is that used in v, 6). Such a situation and such preoccupations would not accord so well with the earliest days of the church as with about A.D. 100. These passages are therefore support for a later date.

On mature consideration the same conclusion is reached when the famous protest against 'faith alone' (ii, 14 ff.) is studied. The initial thought that here Paul's doctrine of redemption by the grace of God and not by works of the Law is being opposed has to give way to the understanding that two elements have entered the debate since Paul, of which account must be taken. One is that 'faith' is taken to mean belief in one God. It is a little misleading to call this purely intellectual conviction, for such a belief carried with it moral implications; but James is thinking as a Jew (though no doubt a Christian Jew) and for him 'faith' does mean this commitment to ethical monotheism. The other element which has entered is that whereas Paul himself stressed the necessity of deeds which issue from faith (Galatians v, 6 is almost certainly to be understood in this way and cf. Romans ii, 6, etc.), opposing the notion that man could save himself by a strict obedience *to the Law* and by doing the works which it prescribed, it has been forgotten that he encouraged obedience to the moral law (e.g. Romans xiii, 8 f.) and would have scouted as strongly as James the notion that mere belief in God without consistent deeds, even if in the true God, was enough. In a word, James is correcting not Paul but a debased paulinism. Once again we find criticism being served by interpretation, pointing to both a date and a situation for this work much later than would be consistent with its having been written by James the brother of the Lord.

The chapter on the Fourth Gospel showed the difficulty of deciding who wrote it. The Johannine epistles share the mystery for it seems they must have come from the same pen or the same school. As early as the early part of the third century Dionysius of Alexandria (who died c. 264) wrote with intelligence and critical acumen on the extreme probability of the author of the gospel and first epistle being identical and different from the author of Revelation. This piece of criticism is unique in the ancient world in its clarity and incisiveness. While Dionysius suffered from the tradition, already very strong in his day, that John the son of Zebedee had written the gospel, what he says as a result of examining the actual writings is impeccable.

The First Epistle has seemed to a number of modern scholars to belong to a different kind from that of the gospel because of alleged differences in doctrine. Others see no such incompatibility, and the majority would agree cordially with the judgement of Dionysius; but the epistle does reveal some interesting facts about the situation in which it was written; some who had been members of the church had left it, apparently led astray by some gnostics who taught that 'Jesus had not come in the flesh'. This was not a general denial of the incarnation but reflected a positive doctrine that Jesus had come, but that his flesh, or body, was a human body in appearance only. They thereby exhibited a very common and by no means extinct tendency to reject the idea of the Son of God having been subjected not only to the actual suffering of crucifixion but to the humiliation of a human body. These were the Docetic Gnostics,[8] and it appears that they arose within the church and then left it (1 John ii, 18 f.). Once again the date required by this evidence is the end of the first or beginning of the second century.

The Second and Third Epistles appear at first glance to be unimportant. Although they seem to have been written by the same author, the evidence that he was also the author of the First Epistle, although quite strong (especially on internal grounds) is not uniform. Irenaeus quotes only 2 John and the Muratorian canon speaks of only two epistles by John which were accepted in the church. Again, Origen and Eusebius both know that the authority of both fails to be universally recognized in their days. It is possible that the explanation for this is quite simple: the gospel was thought to be by an apostle, and so any writing purporting to be from the same hand must not contradict this assumption. The First Epistle, for all its anonymity, does not, but the other two are from 'the elder' or 'presbyter' and this may well have rendered them suspect.

Käsemann[9] has suggested an approach from a direction opposite to that taken by most critics: let us begin with the short Third Epistle and interpret it without prejudice. The preconceived notion that an apostle is speaking with unquestioned authority then falls away; the author is no apostle – he makes no such claim. Rather it is someone who is being excluded from a congregation ruled over by one Diotrephes who 'likes being the leader'. He writes to a friend named Caius who is apparently a member of the congregation to which 'the elder' wants access. All the evidence falls into place, Käsemann urges, if we conclude that Diotrephes is the leader (perhaps the equivalent of a bishop in the early church) of a local orthodox congregation (for the elder does not accuse him of heresy, complaining rather that Diotrephes will have nothing to do with him). The elder is then the leader of a group which seeks to have representatives within each congregation, a group characterized by the teaching conveyed in the Fourth Gospel and First Epistle and alluded to as 'the truth' in the other epistles. Such teaching lies midway between orthodoxy (in the sense of doctrine founded upon belief in fulfilment of the Old Testament in Jesus) and the heretical gnosticism which the elder has clearly resisted. Jesus *has* come in the flesh, but his coming has been a manifestation of the transcendent God; and this manifestation is not to be understood primarily as the fulfilment of hopes based on the scriptures, which is the main way of interpretation used by all other New Testament writers.

Whether or not this theory is correct, it is a splendid example of that type of criticism which enables the student to see his material in a new light, even if he does not finally accept the critic's theory. The author clearly has indeed his own theology, and it is characterized by many of the traits which Käsemann lists, including those which have been mentioned here. Whether it must be regarded as so sharply contrasted with previous orthodoxy is less certain; but that it was developed largely as a reaction to gnosticism by someone who nevertheless shared something of the gnostics' conception of salvation would be hard to deny.

The so-far-neglected Second Epistle may illustrate the 'midway' character of this writer's doctrine: as in the First Epistle he protests, 'Do not think I am giving a new command' (his insistence on love as the key to Christian life shows that he is not really departing from orthodoxy); but he says, 'Anyone who runs ahead too far . . . is without God', and then goes on to recommend the exclusion of such gnostic heretics.

Further, if we consider this body of writings as a whole, it becomes clear that the author's highly individual teaching does in a sense advance from the orthodoxy of Paul or Luke. He takes much of what they teach for granted, and composes variations upon it. He gives less weight to the writers of scripture and more to the authority of God himself as shown in the life and work of his Son.

No book justifies better our former insistence on the influence of Jewish prototypes and Jewish ways of thinking than the Book of Revelation. Its use of the Old Testament, especially Ezekiel, but also Daniel, Isaiah and Zechariah (though even with the addition of these the list is far from complete), is so thorough and yet of such a transforming kind that A. M. Farrer's brilliant (though not perhaps always correct) interpretation is very justifiably called *A Rebirth of Images*.[10] Again, the extraordinary Greek, shattering so many rules of elementary grammar and syntax, is manifestly that of a writer who thought in a Semitic language. Moreover, strange though his grammar is, he keeps his own rules, and gives the impression of a new artist using his own novel idiom. We have seen that Dionysius of Alexandria could clearly distinguish this John from the author of the gospel and epistles, whom he thought to be John son of Zebedee. Some coincidences of thought are not enough to make plausible any contrary theory: the author is an otherwise unknown 'John' who held a high position in the church in Asia Minor, and probably also in society. Otherwise he would have been sentenced not to banishment on Patmos but to the salt-mines of Sicily. His punishment is clearly because he is a Christian, and he writes with a sense of urgency and terror against a background of persecution.

Ancient evidence, and that gained by a study of the text itself, makes clear that this author uses the legend of *Nero redivivus* in his chronological scheme. A popular and reasonable (though not universally held) interpretation of xvii, 1–11 is that the author writes *as though* in the time of the sixth emperor, Vespasian (counting Augustus as the first and the three ephemeral and unsuccessful pretenders Galba, Otho and Vitellius not at all). The seventh, destined for only a short reign (verse 10), is Titus, son of Vespasian (79–81), and 'the eighth who is also one of the seven' (verse 11) is Domitian (81–96), who is also Nero returned to life, as popular superstition feared that he would.

Domitian did not conduct a persecution of Christians as a set policy, but he liked to give himself the title 'Lord and god'. To exact such acknowledgement, in the context of pagan worship with which his 'genius' was associated in Asia Minor, meant refusal and consequent martyrdom for Christians and probably also for some Jews. The cruel and unrestrained character of such local persecution was enough to make John think this was the final series of woes which were to precede the return of the Messiah.

The evidence, thus interpreted, illustrates more than the historical background: it also illustrates the apocalyptic writer's habit of pretending to write at a somewhat earlier time than is the case in order to appear to prophesy some events which have in fact taken place, as well as some which he genuinely predicts. These and other characteristics are typical of apocalyptic literature such as the Old Testament book of Daniel which the author of Revelation uses so wisely. The latter writes under the terror of a comparatively local persecution about 96, the end of Domitian's reign, but pretends to write in the time of Vespasian (69–79). The revelation divinely given him to set down was transmitted through Jesus Christ himself (i, 1 f.), whose initial appearance in order to make the revelation (i, 12–18) makes him a much more gloriously heavenly figure than any other vision of him (such as the Transfiguration or the appearance to Paul in Acts) in the New Testament.

Study of these and related matters illustrates the clarifying effect of New Testament criticism; when the probable historical background can be indicated, the circumstances of writing understood and the imagery identified, then the apparent exaggeration of terror and hatred of the persecuting power – and much more – become perfectly intelligible. Fantastic theories which seek to equate some of the images with persons in contemporary history (a mania which has afflicted some readers in every age) are recognized as the absurdities which they are. Like the book of Daniel, Revelation is a tract for the times, a message of encouragement and hope expressed in a full parade of imagery culled from a Bible of which the author has a thorough knowledge.

Fifteen

Conclusion:
The Consequences
for Theology

Our survey has revealed important changes in the aims of New
Testament criticism. Thus, the object of studying the canon and
its history was once to determine what should be the true and
definite list of sacred books with the full authority of the church.
With changes in both knowledge and outlook, it has become a
study of the history of the canon itself, its changes and the uncertainties connected with it. Again, study of the text of the New
Testament was once the attempt to decide what was the true text
of the New Testament, that is, to recover the form of each book
as it was originally written. It has become the study of the changes
and variations in manuscripts and versions, and the historical
and doctrinal reasons for them. Certainty about either canon or
text now seems impossible.

We can go further. Criticism of the gospels was once undertaken in the hope of deciding 'what actually happened'; and
criticism of Paul to decide when he wrote this or that letter, and
to show how what he says or implies agrees with the account of
him in Acts. It has become a study of differing opinions at
different times on all these matters. This is especially true of
gospel criticism. But here the differing opinions include those of
the evangelists themselves. We recognize now that they, no less
than modern critics, had their own way of understanding the
tradition and of presenting it. No doubt their material had a
history even before they incorporated it into their writings; but it
had further adventures when they began to use it for writing
gospels. Form criticism looks for the *Sitz im Leben* of the different
units within this material, and has often come to the conclusion
that there were two 'situations in life' – one in the life of Jesus
himself, and one in that of the early church, a situation which

caused the church to adapt the unit to fit its own contemporary purposes. All this has been explained in Chapter 10.

Recently, critics have turned their attention more and more to the way in which the evangelists themselves have used their material and to the milieux in which they wrote; thus they have become concerned with a third *Sitz im Leben*, that of the author himself. This third aspect of criticism is called 'redaction criticism'. The term was first used by W. Marxsen (born in 1919, since 1961 professor at Münster) and we may prefer the term of E. Haenchen (born 1894, professor at Münster 1939–46), namely, 'composition criticism'. Some of the followers of Bultmann, as we saw in Chapter 10 (pp. 258 ff.), have thought of the possibility of a New Quest for the Historical Jesus, a quest which will take account of the critical and philosophical difficulties inherent in reconstructing history; Marxsen, on the contrary, making a study of the way in which Mark uses his material, rejects the notion that Mark's redactional principle can be turned into a biographical principle. The course of Jesus' life cannot now be reconstructed. Indeed, we cannot be surprised that he reaches this conclusion when we reflect on the several stages through which the material about Jesus has passed.

The great quest, the overall concern of critics, has thus joined those pursuits which began with a definite goal in mind; it has become a journey offering glimpses of almost everything but its end. We can give an excellent account of the way in which an evangelist envisaged both Jesus and his career, and we can learn to sympathize with and in a measure understand the story he tells, the picture he paints, the vocabulary he uses. We cannot say, 'This is what actually happened.'

For many, this may be an acute disappointment; but there are advantages. The Jesus who seems to have entered upon a career of self-advertisement, proclaiming in effect, 'I am the son of God; therefore anyone who questions my authority will be lost!' is now seen to be a fantasy. Always a caricature, it is now no longer even plausible; it was defensible when the Fourth Gospel could be regarded as historically reliable in the plain modern sense of 'historical', but criticism has enabled us to see that the figure in that gospel expresses what the author thought about him, not historical reality. Unfortunately we cannot substitute a reconstruction which expresses that reality, for it now appears a hard fact that all the gospels have their own theological orientations. Redaction criticism shows more and more of the preoccupations of the particular writer or of the people who formed his background, even if form criticism left some possibility of referring some of the material to a *Sitz im Leben* in the life of Jesus himself.

Thus it seems at first as if the *kerygma* must be substituted for Jesus as the subject about which missionaries must preach and theologians must speculate; but Bultmann and his followers have insisted that it is the Word of God which meets and challenges the person who hears the *kerygma*; it calls forth response from a person at present living an 'unauthentic existence', so that he decides for the Jesus whom he hears preached. This implies that Jesus is the Word of God and the believer who hears accepts him and identifies with him. This event of preaching and accepting is in fact the resurrection of Christ. If we identify this latter event with that narrated in the New Testament, our faith is dependent on a contingent historical fact and will disappear if we become convinced that the event did not occur. Indeed, it is not and never was faith, for faith is not of that order: it is a response, not a historical judgement.

The movement known as the New Quest for the Historical Jesus, with its adherents of many different outlooks, has this in common – a discontent with the complete relegation of the historical Jesus to the realm of the unknown and unknowable. Something can be known through criticism and through meeting him in his position in history as that history is studied; and this something is (and must be) consistent with the *kerygma* and its claims. If it is not, the *kerygma* is falsified. Although these scholars are rebelling against Bultmann, they acknowledge their debt to him and cordially agree with him that the old quest has been for ever rendered impossible. It is only those with insufficient understanding of the grave critical problems involved, or with sufficient hardihood to ignore them, who will continue to produce lives of Jesus. Such bold spirits receive some acknowledgement below.

The consequences for what theologians call Christology (the discipline which seeks to express in appropriate terms the person of Christ) are enormous and perhaps incalculable. The simple believer in the historicity of the myth of the virginal conception clearly attaches a straightforward meaning to the claim that Jesus is the son of God. No doubt he is often quite unaware of the consequences of this belief for the account he should then give of God and of Jesus. He is unaware because he is unconcerned to give any such account; yet investigation will often show that a simple believer of this kind harbours an unreal and fantastic notion of Christ; he thinks of someone with a body different from that of ordinary men, constituted only apparently like theirs; the great difference being that he was as it were constitutionally incapable of sinning, and even of feeling pain. The Jesus thus imagined is usually credited with omniscience, his predictions of his death being cited as evidence that he 'knew everything which was going to happen, so it was easy for him – he knew he would soon be in heaven'. Criticism has removed this figure, still seen every day in stained-glass windows, from the realms of historical possibility. We come rather to the conclusion that Jesus may be properly regarded not as a phantasm who came down from heaven to earth and went back again, but as a man of such quality that for those who wrote of him, only those terms were adequate which expressed his uniquely close relation to God and God's purposes for the world.

These considerations raise a host of others. For example, if the *kerygma* is all, did Jesus really rise from the dead? If not, is there any meaning in the resurrection story and the resurrection idea? We have seen one answer to this, and many others might be given; but here we must be content to have pointed out some of the consequences of criticism and some of the tasks which it sets theology.

Other considerations concern Paul: is there any meaning still to be given to his words when he says of Christ Jesus that 'God designed him to be the means of expiating sin by his sacrificial death, effective through faith' (Romans iii, 25)? Or, again, if criticism shows that Jesus did not found a church but sought to reform a community which he already regarded as the people of God, what authority – indeed, what point – is there in the church of today? Less dramatic in appearance but probably most fundamental of all, can we attach any meaning to the doctrine of the grace of God? Closely connected with this, is there a reality corresponding to the concept in the New Testament expressed in the words, 'the Holy Spirit'?

It is at this point that Bultmann becomes important for theology. As a critic of the New Testament he is, as we have seen in Chapter 10, assured of a place in history, but he may be judged more important still as an interpreter of the main teaching of the New Testament; for he has given a radical reinterpretation of the gospel according to Paul by re-presenting it in terms entirely different from those of Paul, although carefully examining Paul's terms. Thus, as a *critic* of Paul he may be seen as no more than one of the *Religionsgeschichte* school, since he holds that we can attribute Paul's soteriology (or doctrine of salvation) and Christology to Hellenistic sources; but when Bultmann turns to Paul's doctrine of man, or his anthropology, he makes history in the world of New Testament interpretation. In his view of the origins of this anthropology he is quite conservative: it is to be understood on a Semitic background; but at this point Bultmann brings into the discussion all-important philosophical considerations.

Bultmann's philosophical basis is the phenomenology of Heidegger. The latter is not a Christian, but the Christian Bultmann can follow him, because Heidegger is concerned with those foundations on which any account of man may be built. Thus it may be proper in view of the Christian revelation to go further than Heidegger and to form a doctrine of man which is specifically Christian; but in laying the lowest foundations the phenomenology of Heidegger, which is existentialist, affords for Bultmann an indispensable starting-point.

Bultmann's approach to Paul is therefore that of an existentialist. It is impossible to give a full account of his theology here, but it will be useful to indicate an outline by which his interpretation of Paul may be understood. As already briefly mentioned above in connexion with the *kerygma*'s displacement of Jesus, he borrows the concept of authentic and unauthentic existence. Truly to exist (to 'stand out') a man must realize by decisive choice his own possibility. If he makes no such existential choice or decision his existence is unauthentic, determined by factors within the grip of which he is in a spiritual sense dead. We must not imagine that each man is faced once for all in his life with such a choice: this would falsify the point which Bultmann makes. Man is faced continuously with this existential decision and should be always open to the possibility of his own existence.

It may be already clear that Bultmann interprets Paul as though the latter had delivered a doctrine of man rather than of God. This is in fact a criticism often made of him; but Bultmann uses here a point which is difficult both to understand and to refute: we cannot properly set forth a doctrine of God since anything we say of him makes him an object of knowledge like any other object, and this at once contradicts the very idea of God, who is always subject and never object. Indeed it is part of Bultmann's purpose in his fully developed theology to overcome the duality of subject–object thought. To explain this would take us beyond our boundaries, and we must return to the question of why, if it is improper to speak directly of God, it is proper to speak of man in relation to him. Bultmann claims that for the Bible God is not 'the mythological designation for an ontological state of affairs but the personal God, man's Creator who demands obedience of him'.[1] Thus God as creator 'concerns man's existence'.

Armed with these concepts of authentic and unauthentic existence Bultmann approaches the doctrines of Paul and divides what he has to say mainly under two headings, 'Man Prior to the Revelation of Faith' (chapter 4 of his *Theology of the New Testament*) and 'Man under Faith' (chapter 5). In Bultmann's view, death is the real enemy of man rather than sin, and to live according to 'flesh' (Paul's expression) is to live with a perverse intent, whereas true Life arises out of surrendering the self to God. The way to righteousness is seen by Paul first as eschatological and then as a present reality, 'revealed' by the occurring of salvation in Christ. Grace is bestowed in a salvation-event which emphasizes the death and resurrection of Jesus.

Two puzzles arise in the reader's mind: one is, how can the salvation-event be understood as an event which reaches man and happens to him? The other is, how far is Bultmann justified in reinterpreting the realistic eschatology of the New Testament as if it were entirely metaphorical? The answers are closely connected. The salvation-event reaches man in the Word as it is preached, as we saw already in Chapter 10. Further, Bultmann believes that the New Testament, especially Paul and John, uses the language of eschatology to express an existential truth. When the hearer hears the gospel preached it compels him to decide for or against it, and this is the true eschatological event. Paul may well have believed in a literal return of the Lord to this earth, but his basic teaching can be re-expressed in these existentialist terms. John knows the gospel in eschatological terms but is the first demythologizer, and seeks to reinterpret the primitive eschatology in the direction of a perpetually present Christ.

The importance of Bultmann lies now not so much in the contribution which he has made to criticism as in that which he has made to restatement on the basis of that thoroughgoing criticism which replaced the historical Jesus by the *kerygma* as the centre of New Testament theology. Briefly, the older liberals sought to re-establish Christianity on the basis of a reconstructed historical Jesus; their efforts in the end succeeded in showing the impossibility of this task. With the approach of Bultmann and those who follow him, Christianity as a gospel to be proclaimed is not the historical Jesus but the proclaimed Christ, as he appears in Revelation i, 17–18, 'the first and the last, the living one who became dead and is alive for ever . . .'

Bultmann is the acknowledged prince of demythologizers. Another category of theologian sees the problem of interpretation just as acutely as he does, but can offer no immediate solution. This category contains many different types of response to the situation. It is fair to say, however, that they are united by one attitude in common: they are loath to abandon the concepts in the

New Testament, because they do not believe that any equivalents, modern or otherwise, can be found for them. These concepts imply sometimes, but not always, a world-outlook which is no longer feasible. Thus we no longer live in a three-storied universe, but we are still guilty of sin. The 'predicament of mankind' (a modern phrase) is a situation which seems to many to have 'not a redeeming feature'. Does this imply that modern man is not after all unlike the jailor of Philippi who betrayed his 'predicament' by his curiously old-fashioned sounding sixty-four-thousand-dollar question, 'What must I do to be saved?' (Acts xvi, 30)? And why, such theologians ask, do we now speak of 'charisma' as though it were a word from modern slang, unaware that it is a technical term in New Testament theology? (It is the word which, usually in the plural, is rendered 'gift' in English versions of 1 Corinthians xii, 4, 9, 31, and many other passages.) If mankind is in a 'predicament', theologians are no exception; this is clearly illustrated by the dilemma which faced the translators who produced the *New English Bible*. When Paul used one of his favourite expressions, 'according to the flesh', they naturally looked for something more intelligible for a modern public. Sensibly enough, they did not always use the same phrase, but Romans i, 3 provides a good example of their solutions to the problem: they translate the expression there by 'on the human level'. This is reasonable, but what could they do when John i, 14 says 'the Word became flesh' except retain this old translation, however laudably they were seeking to be modern and up-to-date?

Many students of the gospels and of the story of their criticism, however much they were puzzled by the problems of interpretation, would regard as certain the proposition that Schweitzer dealt the death-blow to the older liberalism; but when he is viewed, as suggested on p. 256, as the last of the old liberals rather than the first of a new series of scholars, the way is apparently open for yet more and more modern attempts to discover the historical Jesus. Clearly those who persist in this attempt are not intimidated by the difficulty (which in the eyes of some amounts to an impossibility) of penetrating behind the theological presentations of Jesus in all the gospels, but believe that a historical reconstruction can be made. Such scholars are few, but sometimes catch the public eye. They therefore deserve some notice.

One type of reconstruction uses as a basis the theme of Jewish national martyrdom: thus Jesus is one of a number of martyrs who suffered for their nation's freedom at the hands of the Romans, inspired by the examples of the Maccabees in the days of Seleucid persecution. It is indeed true that New Testament writers seem to be constantly aware of the continuous tradition enshrined already in the Maccabean literature which was excluded at Jamnia and absent from Melito's canon of the Old Testament. This tradition reappears in Origen and there seems therefore to be a period when New Testament writers used such literature while it was out of favour with official Judaism. Yet it is doubtful if it can be said to have affected the evangelists' presentation of the main act of the 'martyrdom' of Jesus. According to them Jesus' agony is suffered before his crucifixion in Gethsemane in a private struggle and is inflicted by the situation in which the redeemer of the world faces the giving of his life; the heroes of Judaism and of Christianity suffer directly at the hands of their persecutors. There is a parallel with this in Jesus' own endurance of mocking, scourging and crucifixion, but there is at those points no description of his agony as there is in the garden.

Such a view would be contested by a tradition of writers who see Jesus clearly as one in a line of martyrs stretching from an indefinite point in the Jewish past through to the end of the Second Jewish War, and who reconstruct the story of Jesus on this basis. Such were J. Klausner with his book *Jesus of Nazareth* (1929),[2] and with a slightly different point of view R. Eisler, *The Messiah Jesus and John the Baptist* (the title of the abbreviated English version, 1931).[3] This kind of reconstruction depends upon an overdue recognition which such writers rightly afford to the importance of the Zealots, the party within Israel who resisted the Roman overlordship by force of arms, from the time of the census in A.D. 6 when, on the deposition of Archelaus, Judea came under direct Roman rule, until their terrible defeat at Masada in 73. They acted usually as guerilla fighters but on the rare occasions when it was possible in open conflict. The attitude of Eisler is represented in contemporary scholarship by S. G. F. Brandon, who has attempted a comprehensive reconstruction of the history of the early church on a naturalistic basis.[4] Work on the Zealots has meant a critical study of Josephus, whose unpatriotic pro-Roman views led him to represent the Zealots as no better than murderous brigands. M. Hengel has carried out such a study, providing a volume of evidence and justifiably stressing the extremely religious character of the Zealot resistance, and its easily recognizable prehistory in the Jewish tradition.[5] In 1967 Brandon published a representative work of the school which seeks not only to understand the background better as a result of such studies but puts Jesus firmly in this background, arguing that the Marcan story of Jesus is an apologia with more doctrine than history, that the actual historical Jesus was arrested and put to death by Romans, and that the consequences of this reconstruction must be fully faced.[6] Whereas W. H. C. Frend in a comprehensive book on martyrdom[7] regards Jesus as a martyr *against* his nation, not for it, Brandon thinks that for the original Jewish Christians (whom both in his earlier book and in this he regards as bitterly opposed to Paul and his gospel) Jesus was a martyr *for* Israel; but Mark and the other evangelists have for apologetic reasons represented him as martyred *by* Israel.

The weakness of this type of reconstruction is manifest. It has to suppose a stage in the tradition for which there is no evidence, that in which Jesus is a martyr for Israel and is honoured as such by those early Jewish Christians of whose outlook we know nothing except what seems to contradict the theory. It may be true that the evangelists present a theological view of Jesus, but this is not a warrant for reconstructing a view of him which is the direct contrary of that which they present. It is worth while giving an example of the sort of evidence and argument by which such theories are supported. It is pointed out, for example, that there was among the twelve disciples of Jesus one known as

Simon the Zealot. If this is taken as evidence of a contact between Jesus and the Zealots, it is impossible to complain; but if it is used to suggest that Jesus *was* a Zealot, an absurdity immediately becomes apparent. On such a theory all the disciples should be Zealots; hence to single out one is odd. If on the other hand, we follow the evangelists in seeing Jesus as distinct from all parties in the Jewish state, to label *one* of his disciples as a Zealot begins to have point. In view of the outlook of Jesus, it seems probable that this disciple is so called because he is not like the others. A further step in the argument is scarcely less reasonable: perhaps the evangelist meant to imply that Jesus called him when he *was* a Zealot, and not *to be* a Zealot, any more than he called the sons of Zebedee *to be* fishermen.

Such reconstructions may be abandoned without regret. It is less agreeable to have to admit the impossibility of envisaging Jesus as a historical person; or that some at least of the events recorded about him are mythical. It may be easy for theologians to regard the resurrection as a story expressing a 'spiritual reality'; others will want to know how they can believe in the Christian claims if the resurrection did not happen; and it must be admitted that at present no one has succeeded in pointing a way out of this dilemma. To be blunt, Bultmann's way, with its philosophical basis, is a way for intellectuals, and is far more difficult to understand than the New Testament.

This book was not the place in which to attempt a restatement of New Testament doctrines, nor to do more than indicate some of the ways in which criticism affects theology. Enough has perhaps been explained to show that while criticism presents problems to the theologian, it also shows the beginning of the way to solve them. It does not guide the theologian to the end of his path but it does set him in an open field. He may be puzzled to know in what direction he should go, but he can certainly breathe fresh air. Moreover, his puzzlement may seem to him to be preferable to ignorance, to nihilism or to wanton destruction. Men of the past believed passionately in the object of his studies. To debate whether they were justified or not is well worth his trouble.

Notes

INTRODUCTION TO THE OLD TESTAMENT

1. Grant, E., ed., *The Haverford Symposium on Archaeology and the Bible*, New Haven, Connecticut, 1938, pp. 47–74.
2. op. cit., p. 44.

Useful surveys of trends in modern Old Testament scholarship are to be found in Rowley, H. H., ed., *The Old Testament and Modern Scholarship* (*O.T.M.S.*), Oxford University Press, 1951; Hahn, H. F., *The Old Testament in Modern Research*, S.C.M. Press, 1956; Wright, G. E., *The Bible and the Ancient Near East*, Routledge & Kegan Paul, 1960; Black, M. and Rowley, H. H., ed., *Peake's Commentary on the Bible*, Nelson, 1962; Hyatt, J. P., ed., *The Bible in Modern Scholarship*, Abingdon, Nashville, 1965.

CHAPTER ONE

Much of the detailed information on current archaeological work appears in periodicals. Among the most important of these are: *Revue Biblique* (*R.B.*), *Palestine Exploration Fund Quarterly* (*P.E.Q.*), the *Bulletin* and *Annual of the American School for Oriental Research* (*B.A.S.O.R.* and *A.A.S.O.R.*), and the *Israel Exploration Fund Journal* (*I.E.J.*). Popular accounts of recent work appear in the *Biblical Archaeologist* (*B.A.*), some of the most important articles in which are gathered together in the volumes of the *Biblical Archaeological Reader* (*B.A.R.*). The Jubilee volume of the British Society for Old Testament Study, Thomas, D. W., ed., *Archaeology and the Old Testament*, Oxford University Press, 1968, gives an up-to-date report on the significance of the major site excavations.

The following are among the most useful of the many general surveys of archaeology in relationship to Old Testament studies:

Wright, G. E., *Biblical Archaeology*, Duckworth, revised edition 1962.
Gray, J., *Archaeology and the Old Testament World*, Nelson, 1962.
Kenyon, K. M., *Archaeology in the Holy Land*, Ernest Benn, 1960.
Pritchard, J. B., *Archaeology and the Old Testament*, Princeton University Press, 1958.

Notes

Comparative documentary evidence is available in Pritchard, J. B., ed., *Ancient Near Eastern Texts Relating to the Old Testament*, Princeton University Press, 1955 (*A.N.E.T.*), and Thomas, D. W. ed., *Old Testament Times*, Nelson, 1958 (*D.O.T.T.*).

Pritchard, J. B., ed., *The Ancient Near East in Pictures*, Princeton University Press, Second edition with supplement 1969, gathers together the graphic evidence from monuments, buildings and artefacts. A handy abbreviation and combination of the two Pritchard volumes is *The Ancient Near East, An Anthology of Texts and Pictures*, Princeton University Press, 1959.

1. Miss Kenyon has written a popular account of the expedition's work, *Digging up Jericho*, Ernest Benn, 1960.
2. See Kirkbride, D., 'Five Seasons at the Pre-Pottery Neolothic Village of Beidha in Jordan', *P.E.Q* 98, 1966, pp, 8–72.
3. See Malamat, A., 'Prophetic Revelation in Mari and Bible', *Supplement to Vetus Testament um* (*S.V.T.*), 5, pp. 207–27. Further reference to the importance of the Mari material is made in Chapter 2, p. 95.
4. Wiseman, D. J., *The Alalakh Tablets*, Occasional Publications of the British Institute of Archaeology at Ankara, no. 2, 1953.
5. Garstang, J., *Joshua–Judges*, Constable, 1931, p. 145.
6. *Yahweh* is probably as near as we can get to representing in English the four Hebrew consonants of the divine name in the Old Testament. The Authorised Version renders 'Jehovah'; most modern translations 'the LORD'.
7. Driver, G. R., *Canaanite Myths and Legends*, Clark, 1956; Gordon, C. H. *Ugaritic Literature*, Pontificium Instituteum Biblicum, Rome, 1949.
   A useful introduction to the significance of the Ugaritic material is Kapelrud, A. S., *The Ras Shamra Discoveries and the Old Testament*, Blackwell, 1965; English translation by Anderson, G. W.
8. *S.V.T.* 3, 1955, pp. 9–10, and Scott, R. B. Y., *Proverbs Ecclesiastes*, Doubleday, New York, Anchor Bible, 1965, pp. 57, 59.
9. See *P.E.Q.* from 1962 onwards.
10. *B.A.*, May 1967.
11. *A.N.E.T.*, pp. 287 ff.
12. Glueck, N., *The Other Side of Jordan*, American School of Oriental Research, New Haven, 1940; *Rivers in the Desert*, Weidenfeld & Nicolson, 1959.
13. Glueck, N., *Rivers in the Desert*, pp. 158, 165, and Bright, J., *History of Israel*, S.C.M. Press, 1960, p. 195.
14. *P.E.Q.*, 1962, pp. 5–71, and *God's Wilderness*, Thames & Hudson, 1961. Glueck has accepted many of Rothenberg's suggestions in *B.A.*, vol. 28, no. 3, pp. 70–87.
15. Wright, G. E., *Shechem*, Duckworth, 1965. See also *B.A.R.*, no. 2, 1964.
16. *P.E.Q.*, 1956, pp. 125–40.
17. De Vaux, R., op. cit. p. 133.

18. Reisner, G. A. R., Fisher, C. S., Lyon, D. G., *Harvard Excavations at Samaria*, Harvard University Press, Cambridge, Massachusetts, 1924. The results of later excavations directed by J. W. Crowfoot are contained in three volumes of reports

Samaria-Sebaste I, *The Buildings*, 1942

II, *Early Ivories*, 1938

III, *The Objects*, 1957

published by the Palestine Exploration Fund. An excellent popular survey is Parrot, A., *Samaria*, S.C.M. Biblical Archaeology Series, no. 7, 1956. A more recent discussion of some of the problems raised by the archaeological data at Samaria is to be found in Wright, G. E., *B.A.S.O.R.*, no. 155, October 1959, pp. 13–29, and *B.A.*, 22, no. 3, September 1959, reprinted in *B.A.R.*, no. 2.

19. Birnbaum, S., *Samaria-Sebaste*, III, p. 32.
20. Diringer, D., *D.O.T.T.*, pp. 218 ff.
21. Pritchard, J. B., *Gibeon where the Sun Stood Still*, Princeton University Press, 1962.
22. Avigad, W., *I.E.J.*, vol. 16, no. 1, 1966, pp. 50–53.
23. Translations by Thomas, D. W. in *D.O.T.T.*, p. 214.
24. Thomas, D. W., *The Prophet in the Lachish Ostraca*, Tyndale Press, 1946.
25. op. cit. p. 216.
26. Aharoni, Y., *I.E.J.*, vol. 16, no. 1, 1966, pp. 1–7.
27. Yeivin, S., *I.E.J.*, vol. 16, no. 3, 1966, pp. 153–9.
28. See McHardy, W. D., *D.O.T.T.*, p. 251, and the discussion by Bright, J., in *B.A.R.*, no. 1, pp. 98 ff.
29. Selections from the Chronicles are to be found in *D.O.T.T.*, pp. 75–83, *A.N.E.T.*, pp. 202–5, and *B.A.R.*, no. 1, pp. 113–27.
30. Yaron, R., *The Law of the Aramaic Papyri*, Oxford University Press, 1961.
31. See Cross, F. M., *B.A.*, 26, December 1963, no. 4, pp. 110–21.
32. Pritchard, J. B., op cit.
33. The Israelis are currently excavating in the Sinai peninsula and in parts of old Jerusalem previously in Arab control.

CHAPTER TWO

1. See the English translation of his article in *The Problem of the Hexateuch and Other Essays*, Oliver & Boyd, 1966, p. 1.
2. See Welch, A. C., *The Code of Deuteronomy*, Oxford University Press, 1924, and *Deuteronomy, the Framework to the Code*, Oxford University Press, 1932; Robertson, E., *The Old Testament Problem*, Manchester University Press, 1950.

Notes

3. Kennett, R. H., *Deuteronomy and the Decalogue*, Cambridge University Press, 1920; Holscher, G., 'Komposition und Ursprung des Deuteronomiums', *Zeitschrift für die alttestamentliche Wissenschaft (Z.A.W.)*, vol. xl, 1922, pp. 161–255. For a recent evaluation of the critical problem see Nicolson, E. W., *Deuteronomy and Tradition*, Blackwell, 1967.

4. *Hexateuch Synopse*, J. C. Heinrichs, Leipzig, 1922. Excellent surveys of the problem of Pentateuchal source criticism are to be found in Eissfeldt, O., *The Old Testament, an Introduction (O.T.I.)*, Blackwell, 1965 (English translation by Ackroyd, P. R.), Anderson, G. W., *A Critical Introduction to the Old Testament*, Duckworth, 1959, and North, C. R., 'Pentateuchal Criticism', *O.T.M.S.*, pp. 48–83.

5. Volz, P., and Rudolph, W., 'Der Elohist als Erzahler; Ein Irrweg der Pentateuchkritik', *Beihefte der Zeitschrift für die alttestamentliche Wissenschaft (B.Z.A.W.)*, vol. 63, 1933; compare *B.Z.A.W.*, vol. 68, 1938.

6. An excellent introduction to form criticism is now available in Koch K., *The Growth of the Biblical Tradition: the form critical method*, London, 1969 (English translations of second edition of *Was ist Formgeschichte*, Neukirchen, 1964).

7. See Baltzer, K., *Das Bundesformular, Wissenschaftliche Monographien zum Alten und Neuen Testament (W.M.A.N.T.)*, No. 4, 1960; Muilenburg, J., 'The Form and Structure of the Covenantal Formulations', *V.T.*, vol. 9, 1959, pp. 347–65.

8. See for example McCarthy, D. J., *Treaty and Covenant*, Pontificium Institutum Biblicum, Rome, 1963.

9. See Beyerlin, W., *Origins and History of the Earliest Sinaitic Traditions*, Blackwell, 1965; Gerstenberg, E., 'Covenant and Commandment', *Journal of Biblical Literature (J.B.L.)*, vol. 84, 1965, pp. 38–51; Kapelrud, A. S., 'Some Recent Points of View on the Times and Origin of the Decalogue', *Studia Theologica*, vol. 18, 1964, pp. 81–90; McCarthy, D. J., 'Covenant in the Old Testament: the Present State of Inquiry', *Catholic Biblical Quarterly (C.B.Q.)*, vol. 27, 1965, pp. 217–40; Newman, M. L., *The People of the Covenant*, Abingdon, Nashville, 1962; Stamm, J. J., and Andrew, M. E., *The Ten Commandments in Recent Research*, S.C.M. Press, 1967; Nielsen, E., *The Ten Commandments in New Perspective*, S.C.M. Press, 1968.

10. Noth, M., *The History of Israel*, A. & C. Black, second edition 1958, p. 136.

11. See Anderson, G. W., 'Some Aspects of the Uppsala School of Old Testament Study', *Harvard Theological Review (H.T.R.)*, vol. 43, 1950, pp. 239–59. For a statement of the formative place of oral tradition in Israel see Nielsen, E., *Oral Tradition*, S.C.M. Press, 1954. A critical assessment is to be found in Ploeg, J. van der, 'La Rôle de la tradition orale dans la transmission du texte de l'Ancien Testament', *R.B.*, vol. 54, 1947, pp. 8 ff.

12. In this linking of Deuteronomy with the historical books from Judges to

Kings, Engnell follows Noth, M., op. cit., though he dissents from Noth's literary critical analysis of the material.

13. See *S.V.T.*, 3, 1955, p. 109.

14. Traditio-historical method is applied to the narratives concerning David in 2 Samuel in Carlson, R. A., *David the Chosen King*, Almqvist & Wiksell, Uppsala, 1964. Tradition history is well used to supplement literary criticism in Clements, R. E., *Abraham and David*, S.C.M. Press, 1967. A lucid review and defence of the documentary hypothesis is to be found in the introduction of Speiser, E. A., *Genesis*, Anchor Bible, 1964. An alternative approach in the light of Jewish tradition is outlined by Weingreen, J., 'Oral Torah and Written Torah', in *Holy Book and Holy Tradition*, pp. 86ff., ed. Bruce, F. F., and Rupp, G., Manchester University Press, 1968.

15. See *The Psalms in Israel's Worship*, Blackwell, 1962, vol. 1, p. 199; vol. 2, note 28, p. 250 f. (English translation by Ap–Thomas, D. R.).

16. Schmidt, H., *B.Z.A.W.*, 49, 1928.

17. Birkeland, H., *The Evildoers in the Book of Psalms*, Oslo, 1955. A useful discussion of the various theories is to be found in Anderson, G. W., 'Enemies and Evildoers in the Book of Psalms', *Bulletin of the John Rylands Library*, vol. 48, no. 1, 1965, pp. 18–29.

18. Among those supporting Mowinckel's basic thesis are Schmidt, H., *Die Thronfahrt Jahves am Fest der Jahresende im Alten Israel*, J. C. B. Mohr, Tübingen, 1927; Leslie, E. A., *The Psalms*, Abingdon, Nashville, 1949; and in a modified and attractive form Johnson, A. R., *Sacral Kingship in Ancient Israel*, University of Wales Press, second revised edition 1967. For criticism of the thesis see Snaith, N. H., *The Jewish New Year Festival*, S.P.C.K., 1947; De Vaux, R., *Ancient Israel*, Darton, Longman & Todd, 1961, pp. 502 ff. (English translation by McHugh, J.).

19. A radical criticism of Kraus's thesis is to be found in Mowinckel, S. *The Psalms in Israel's Worship*, vol. 2, note 9, p. 230 f.

20. *Der Messias II*, Vandenhoeck und Ruprecht, Göttingen, 1929.

21 Westermann's book contains a valuable survey of trends in the study of prophetic literature over the past fifty years.

22. Lindblom, J., *Die literarische Gattung der prophetischen Literatur*, Uppsala Universitets Årsskrift (*U.U.A.*), 1924; Kohler, L., 'Deutero-jesaja stilkritisch Untersucht', *B.Z.A.W.*, vol. 37, 1923, the argument of which was further advanced in 'Der Botenspruch', *Kleine Lichter*, Zurich, 1945. Compare Ross, J., 'The Prophet as Yahweh's Messenger' in Anderson, B. W., and Harrelson, W., ed., *Israel's Prophetic Heritage*, S.C.M. Press, 1962, pp. 98–107.

23. An excellent statement of this approach to prophetic literature is Mowinckel, S., *Prophecy and Tradition*, J. Dybwad, Oslo, 1946. See also Jones, D. R., 'The tradition of the Oracles of Isaiah of Jerusalem' *Z.A.W.*, vol. 67, 1955, pp. 226–46; Eaton, J. H., 'The Origin of the Book of Isaiah', *V.T.*, vol. 9, 1959, pp. 138–57.

Notes

24. Nyberg, H. S., *Studien zum Hoseabuch*, *U.U.A.*, 1935; Birkeland, H., *Zum hebraïschen Traditionswesen: die Komposition der prophetischen Bücher des Alten Testaments*, Grondahl, Oslo, 1938; Engnell, I., *The Call of Isaiah*.

25. Mowinckel, S., op. cit.; Widengren, G., *Literary and Psychological Aspects of the Hebrew Prophets*, *U.U.A.*, 1948; Anderson, G. W., *H.T.R.*, op. cit.

26. See Mowinckel, S., op. cit.

27. Rankin, O. S., *Israel's Wisdom Literature*, Clark, 1936.

28. 'Eine ägyptische Quelle der "Sprüche Salomos"', *Sitzungsberichte der Preussischen Akademie der Wissenschaften*, 1924, pp. 86–93.

29. Whybray, R. N., *Wisdom in Proverbs*, S.C.M. Press, 1965.

30. Gordon, E. I., *Sumerian Proverbs*, Monographs of the University Museum, Philadelphia, 1960; Kramer, S. N. 'Man and his God – a Sumerian Variation on the Job Motif', *S.V.T.*, 3, 1955, pp. 170–82; Lambert, W. G., *Babylonian Wisdom Literature*, Oxford University Press, 1960.

31. See for example Albright, W. F., 'Some Canaanite–Phoenician Sources of Hebrew Wisdom', *S.V.T.*, 3, pp. 1–15; Dahood, M., *Proverbs and North West Semitic Philology*, Pontificium Institutum Biblicum, Rome, 1963.

32. For the political activity of the sages and the prophetic criticism which it provoked, see McKane, W., *Prophets and Wise Men*, S.C.M. Press, 1965.

33. See *S.V.T.*, 3, 1955, pp. 262–79; *Proverbs Ecclesiastes*, Anchor Bible, Doubleday, New York, 1966; McKane, W., *Proverbs*, S.C.M. Press, 1970.

34. *Wesen und Herkunft des "apodiktischen Rechts,"* *W.M.A.N.T.*, no. 22, 1966.

35. *Studien zum Alten und Neuen Testament*, vol. 15, 1966.

36. Von Rad, G., *The Problem of the Hexateuch and Other Essays*, Oliver & Boyd, 1966, pp. 292–301.

37. For the Psalms see Mowinckel, S., 'Psalms and Wisdom', *S.V.T.*, 3, 1955, pp. 205–24; for prophetic literature see Lindblom, J., 'Wisdom in the Old Testament Prophets', op. cit., pp. 192–204; Wolff, H. W., *Amos geistige Heimat*, *W.M.A.N.T.*, no. 18, 1964; Terrien, S., 'Amos and Wisdom', *Israel's Prophetic Heritage*, pp. 108 ff.

CHAPTER THREE

1. Wurthwein, E., *The Text of the Old Testament: An Introduction to Kittel-Kahle's Biblia Hebraica*, Blackwell, 1957, English translation by Ackroyd, P. R.

2. Cross, F. M., *I.E.J.*, vol. 16, no. 3, 1966, pp. 81–95; *H.T.R.*, vol. 51, 1964, pp. 281–99; Skehan, P., *B.A.*, vol. 28, September 1965.

3. See the criticism by Goshen-Gottstein, M. H., *The Book of Isaiah*, Hebrew University Bible Project, Jerusalem, 1965, introduction.

4. Goshen-Gottstein, op. cit., p. 17.

5. Driver, G. R., *S.V.T.*, 4, 1957, p. 5; Orlinski, H. M., *The Study of the Bible Today and Tomorrow*, University of Chicago Press, p. 151, says concerning the *apparatus criticus* of *B.H.* 'nearly every line ... swarms with errors of commission and omission as regards both the primary and secondary versions'; compare his article 'The Textual Criticism of the Old Testament', *The Bible and the Ancient Near East*, Routledge & Kegan Paul, 1960; Katz, P., 'Septuagint Studies in Mid Century'; Davies, W. D., and Daube, D., ed., *The Background to the New Testament and its Eschatology*, Cambridge University Press, 1956, pp. 176–208.

6. See Orlinski and Katz, op. cit.

7. See, for example, Gehmann, H. S., 'The Hebraic Character of Septuagint Greek', *V.T.*, 1, 1951, pp. 81–90; 'Hebraisms in the Old Greek Version of Genesis', *V.T.*, 3, 1953, pp. 141–8.

CHAPTER FOUR

1. See for example Hooke, S. H., 'Myth and Ritual, Past and Present', the introductory essay to *Myth, Ritual and Kingship*, Oxford University Press, 1958; and Vriezen, T. C., *The Religion of Ancient Israel*, Lutterworth, 1967, pp. 7–31.

2. Compare Albright, W. F., *From the Stone Age to Christianity*, Doubleday, New York, second edition 1957; Kaufmann, Y., *The Religion of Israel*, University of Chicago Press, 1960, English translation by Greenberg, M.; and the survey article by Anderson, G. W., 'Hebrew Religion', *O.T.M.S.*, pp. 283–310.

3. Rowley, H. H., 'Ritual and the Hebrew Prophets', *Myth, Ritual and Kingship*, pp. 236–60. Whitley, C. F., *The Prophetic Achievement*, Brill, Leiden, 1963, still argues that the prophets owe very little to Israel's early religious traditions. The best treatment of prophecy is Lindblom, J., *Prophecy in Ancient Israel*, Blackwell, 1962.

4. See De Vaux, R., *Studies in Old Testament Sacrifice*, University of Wales Press, 1964; Thompson, R. J., *Penitence and Sacrifice in Early Israel outside the Levitical Law*, Brill, Leiden, 1963.

5. *He That Cometh*, Blackwell, 1956, English translation by Anderson, G. W.

6. See also Hooke, S. H., *The Origins of Early Semitic Ritual*, Oxford University Press, 1938; *Middle Eastern Mythology*, Penguin Books, 1963; James, E. O., *Myth and Ritual in the Ancient Near East*, Thames & Hudson, 1958.

7. Hooke, S. H., *Middle Eastern Mythology*, p. 12.

8. Humbert, P., *Revue de l'Histoire et des Philosophies Religieuses* (*R.H.Ph. R.*), vol. 15, 1935, pp. 1 ff.

Notes

9. For example Meek, T. J., *Interpreter's Bible*, vol. 5, Abingdon, Nashville, pp. 91 ff.

10. Robinson, T. H., 'Hebrew Myths', *Myth and Ritual*, pp. 272–96.

11. Wildengren, G., *Myth, Ritual and Kingship*, p. 156.

12. De Langhe, R., *Myth, Ritual and Kingship*, pp. 122–48. For a general criticism of the myth-ritual pattern see Brandon, S. G, F., 'The Myth and Ritual Pattern Critically Considered', *Myth, Ritual and Kingship*, pp. 261–91; and Frankfort, H., *The Problem of Similarity in the Religions of the Ancient Near East*, Oxford University Press, 1951.

13. Hooke, S. H., *Myth and Ritual*, p. 8.

14. Engnell, I., *Studies in Divine Kingship in the Ancient Near East*, Blackwell, second edition 1967. Frankfort, H., *Kingship and the Gods*, University of Chicago Press, 1948, is critical of Engnell's generalizations. See Gurney, O., *Myth, Ritual and Kingship*, pp. 105–21, for a criticism of Engnell's handling of Hittite evidence.

15. A good discussion of these historical traditions is to be found in Noth, M., 'God, King and People in the Old Testament', *The Laws of the Pentateuch and Other Essays*, Oliver & Boyd, 1966, pp. 145–78. See also North, C. R., 'The Religious Aspects of Hebrew Kingship', *Z.A.W.*, vol. 9, 1932, pp. 27 ff.

16. See also his essays 'The Role of the King in the Jerusalem Cultus', *The Labyrinth*, pp. 71–114; 'Hebrew Conceptions of Kingship', *Myth, Ritual and Kingship*, pp. 204–35; 'Divine Kingship and the Old Testament', *Expository Times (E.T.)*, vol. 62, 1950–51, pp. 36–42.

17. For example Engnell, I., op. cit.; Bentzen, A., *King and Messiah*, Lutterworth, 1955, English translation of *Messias-Moses redivivus-Menschensohn*, Zwingli Verlag, Zurich, 1948; Wildengren, G., *The King and the Tree of Life in Ancient Near Eastern Religions*, *U.U.A.*, 1951; Haldar, A., *Studies in the Book of Nahum*, *U.U.A.*, 1946. An excellent treatment of Hebrew kingship ideology is to be found in Mowinckel, S., *The Psalms in Israel's Worship*, vol. 1, pp. 50 ff.

18. Compare Ringgren, H., *The Messiah in the Old Testament*, S.C.M. Press, 1956.

19. *Psalmenstudien II*, pp. 228 ff., and in a modified form *The Psalms in Israel's Worship*, vol. 1, p. 116, 184 ff.

20. For example Morgenstern, J., *Amos Studies*, Hebrew Union College, Cincinnati, 1941; Watts, J. W. D., *Vision and Prophecy in Amos*, Brill, Leiden, 1958. For a general discussion of the concept of 'the day of the LORD' see Cerny, L., *The Day of Yahweh and Revelant Problems*, Filosoficka Fakulta University Karlovy, Prague, 1948.

21. See 'The Origin and Concept of the Day of Yahweh', *Journal of Semitic Studies*, vol. 4, 1959, pp. 92 ff. and *Old Testament Theology*, vol. 2, p. 123 ff.

22. Notably Haldar, A., *Associations of Cult Prophets among the Ancient Semites*, Almqvist & Wiksell, Uppsala, 1945.

23. A balanced survey of the issues involved will be found in Rowley, H. H., 'Ritual and the Hebrew Prophets', *Myth, Ritual and Kingship*, pp. 236–60.

24. Rowley, H. H., op. cit., p. 242.

25. In addition to the bibliography in Chapter Two, compare Clements, R. E., *Prophecy and Covenant*, S. C. M. Press, 1965, and Porteous, N.W., 'The Prophets and the Problem of Continuity', *Living the Mystery*, Blackwell, 1967, pp. 113–26.

26. Compare Albright, W. F., 'The Psalm of Habakkuk', *Studies in Old Testament Prophecy*, ed. Rowley, H. H., Clark, 1950, pp. 1–18. Eaton, J. H., 'The Origin and Meaning of Habakkuk iii', *Z.A.W.*, vol. 76 1964, pp. 144–71.

27. Humbert, P., 'Le Problème du livre de Nahoum', *R.H.Ph.R.*, vol. 12, 1932, pp. 1–15; Lods, A., *R.H.Ph.R.*, vol. 11, 1931, pp. 211–19.

28. Johnson, A. R., 'Jonah II 3–10: a study in cultic phantasy', *Studies in Old Testament Prophecy*, pp. 82–102.

29. An early Solomonic date, however, has recently been defended by Kayatz, C., *Studien zu Proverbien 1–9*, *W.M.A.N.T.*, no. 22, 1966.

30. See Whybray, R. N., *Proverbs and Wisdom*, S.C.M. Press, 1966.

31. Whybray, R. N., op cit.; Ringgren, H., *Word and Wisdom*, Lundequistska Bokhandeln, Uppsala, 1947; Rylaardsdam, J. C., *Revelation in Jewish Wisdom Literature*, University of Chicago Press, 1946.

32. See Albright, W. F., *From the Stone Age to Christianity*, pp. 370–72; and *S.V.T.*, 3, 1955, pp. 7 ff. For a criticism see Whybray, op. cit., pp. 83–7.

33. A convenient brief introduction to such Apocryphal books is to be found in Eissfeldt, O., *O.T.L.*, pp. 571 ff. For the issues raised by the development of the figure of Wisdom see Rylaardsdam, op. cit., and Porteous, N.W., 'Royal Wisdom', *Living the Mystery*, pp. 77–92.

34. For Philo see Wolfson, H. A., *Philo*, Harvard University Press, 1947–62.

35. See Davies, W. D., *Paul and Rabbinic Judaism*, S.P.C.K., second edition 1962, chapter 7.

CHAPTER FIVE

1. Eichrodt, W., in an Excursus to the sixth revised English edition of his *Theology of the Old Testament*, S.C.M. Press, vol. 1, 1961, pp. 512–20, takes issue with von Rad, G., on this question. See also the articles by Wright, G. E. and von Rad, G., 'History and the Patriarchs', *E.T.*, vol. 71, 1959–60, and vol. 72, 1960–61.

2. Porteous, N. W., *Living the Mystery*, Blackwell, 1967, p. 18.

3. Black, M., and Rowley, H. H., ed., *Peake's Commentary on the Bible*, Nelson, 1962, p. 152a.

4. Eichrodt had laid down the guidelines for his approach in an article in *Z.A.W.*, vol., 47, 1929, pp. 83 ff., in reply to Eissfeldt's article of 1926.

Notes

5. A fuller statement is to be found in his essay 'Is Typological Exegesis an Appropriate Method', *Essays in Old Testament Interpretation*, S.C.M. Press, 1963, pp. 224–45.

6. McKenzie, J. L., *The Two-Edged Sword*, Bruce, Milwaukee, 1956, p. 20.

7. For a radical criticism of the over-concentration on *Heilsgeschichte* as the basis of Israel's faith see Barr, J., *Old and New in Interpretation*, S.C.M. Press, 1966, pp. 65–104.

8. In addition to the 'theologies' discussed, reference may be made to Davidson, A. B., *Theology of the Old Testament*, Clark, published post-umously in 1904; Robinson, H. W., *Inspiration and Revelation in the Old Testament*, Oxford University Press, 1946; Knight, G. A. F., *A Christian Theology of the Old Testament*, S.C.M. Press, second edition 1964. On a less ambitious scale, Burrows, M., *An Outline of Biblical Theology*, Westminster Press, Philadelphia, 1944; Baab, O., *The Theology of the Old Testament*, Abingdon–Cokesbury, New York, 1949; Dentan, R. C. *Preface to Old Testament Theology*, Yale Studies in Religion, New Haven, 1960. Many books have been published on topics within the general field of Old Testament theology, for example; Snaith, N. H., *The Distinctive Ideas of the Old Testament*, Epworth, 1944; Rowley, H. H., *The Biblical Doctrine of Election*, Lutterworth, 1950; Wright, G. E., *God who Acts*, S.C.M. Press, 1952; *E.T.*, vols. 73 and 74 have a useful series of review articles of the major Old Testament theologies.

9. Compare Snaith, N. H., op. cit.

10. See further his *Biblical Words for Time*, S.C.M. Press, 1962, and *Old and New in Interpretation*.

11. For example Buber, M., *The Prophetic Faith*, Macmillan, New York, 1949; Heschel, A., *The Prophets*, Harper & Row, New York, 1962.

12. *Existence and Faith*, S.C.M. Press, 1961, pp. 58–91.

13. It is doubtful whether allegory must be unhistorical; see Hanson, R.P.C., *Allegory and Event*, S.C.M. Press, 1959, and Barr, J., *Old and New in Interpretation*, chapter 4.

14. For a good discussion of the distinction between allegory and typology along the lines indicated, see Anderson, B. W., 'Exodus Typology in Second Isaiah', *Israel's Prophetic Heritage*, pp. 177–95. In general see Barr, Hanson, op. cit.; Daniélou, J., *From Shadows to Reality*, Burns & Oates, 1960; Lampe, G. W. H., and Woollcombe, K. J., *Essays in Typology*, S.C.M. Press, 1959; Smart, J. D., *The Interpretation of Scripture*, S.C.M. Press, 1961.

15. Porteous, N. W., *Living the Mystery*, Blackwell, 1967, p. 44.

CHAPTER SIX

1. For accounts of these scholars see *The Oxford Dictionary of the Christian Church*, and in this book for Wellhausen see p. 245; Harnack p. 300; Lightfoot p. 235; Westcott, pp. 230–31.

2. Josephus can be read in the old translation by Whiston, in the Loeb edition, and for *The Jewish War* in the Penguin translation by G. A. Williamson.

3. Philo can be read in the Loeb edition.

4. Pliny the Elder (A.D. 23–79) uncle of the younger Pliny (p. 316), served Rome in many capacities and was occupied in amplifying the veritable encyclopaedia known as his *Natural History* at the time of his death through the eruption of Vesuvius in 79.

5. G. Vermès, Pelican, 1962.

6. *Arocrypha and Pseudepigrapha of the Old Testament*, Oxford University Press, 1913.

7. These are available in the Loeb edition of *The Apostolic Fathers* (Greek and English) and in English translation in the S.C.M. Press Library of Christian Classics, Vol. 1, *Early Christian Fathers* (ed. C. C. Richardson), 1953.

8. Alba House, New York, 1965.

9. The find appears to have been actually at the village of Chenoboskion on the opposite (eastern) bank of the Nile, but the name of the town Nag Hammadi is usually employed in referring to the documents.

10. B. Gärtner, *The Theology of the Gospel of Thomas*, Collins, 1961.

11. Josephus tells us this many times but never explains the original name.

12. Weidenfeld & Nicolson, 1966.

13. The writings of Eusebius can be read in the Loeb edition. His *Ecclesiastical History*, translated by G. A. Williamson, is published as a Penguin Classic, L 138.

14. *La Fortresse Antonia à Jérusalem et la question du Prétoire*, Franciscalium, Jerusalem, 1956.

15. Like many in modern Israel, the family changed its original for a Hebrew name.

CHAPTER SEVEN

1. *The Mishnah*, Oxford University Press, 1933.

2. Macmillan, 1938.

3. Four volumes (strictly five, since the fourth is divided into two separate volumes) were published by C. H. Beck in Munich, 1922–8. Billerbeck, just before his death in 1932, committed to Professor Joachim Jeremias the task of completing a fifth volume, *Verzeichnis der Schriftgelehrten*, an index of the Rabbis quoted in the first four. Jeremias obtained the assistance of K. Adolph and published this volume in 1956. These two scholars then prepared a *Geographisches Register* published as a sixth volume in 1961. The fifth and sixth volumes were combined in a single volume when a second edition of them appeared in 1963. The work has not been translated.

Notes

4. S.P.C.K., second edition 1955.
5. The present author draws special attention to this judgement because he believes it to be correct and that it is incumbent upon all Christian scholars similarly convinced to draw attention to it.
6. D. Daube, *The New Testament and Rabbinic Judaism*, Athlone Press, 1956.
7. Cambridge University Press, 1964.
8. Foakes Jackson and Kirsopp Lake, Macmillan, five volumes, 1920–33.
9. H. J. Schoeps, *Theologie und Geschichte des Juden-Christentums*, Mohr, Tübingen, 1949.
10. J. Daniélou, *Théologie du Judéo-Chrstianisme*, Desclée, Tourai, 1958.
11. It is volume I of the series, The Development of Christian Doctrine before the Council of Nicaea. Translated and ed. by J. A. Baker, Darton, Longman & Todd, 1964.
12. Brill, Leiden, 1961.

CHAPTER EIGHT

1. It carries the revealing sub-title, *The Substructure of New Testament Theology*, Nisbet, 1952.
2. S.C.M. Press, 1961.
3. In *The Old Testament of the Early Church*, Harvard Theological Studies XX, Harvard University Press, 1964.
4. Clarendon Press, Oxford, first edition 1946, second edition 1954, third edition (with an appendix on *The Son of Man* by Geza Vermès), 1967.

CHAPTER NINE

1. Hodder & Stoughton, 1914–29.
2. Clark, Edinburgh, 1921, second edition 1923, third edition 1937.
3. Such is the plea of N. Turner in the third volume, devoted to syntax, of Moulton's *A Grammar of New Testament Greek*. (Volume I, *Prolegomena*, appeared in 1906 and Moulton had written almost all of volume II when he lost his life through submarine action in the Mediterranean in 1917. W. F. Howard issued it in three parts, in 1919, 1920 and 1929; volume III, by N. Turner, completed the series in 1963.).
4. A recent book illustrating this fact is Max Wilcox's *The Semitisms of Acts*, Clarendon Press, 1965.
5. Hodder & Stoughton; *Four Gospels*, Hodder & Stoughton, 1933.
6. Clarendon Press.
7. See chapter 8, p. 217, note 4.
8. By E. Hatch and H. A. Redpath, Clarendon Press, 1897 (two volumes).
9. Clarendon Press, 1964.

10. The Cyrillic alphabet itself may owe its origin to the ninth-century apostles to the Slavs, Cyril and Methodius; but it is more certain that Cyril invented the Glagolithic alphabet and not that called Cyrillic, although the latter came into being at the same period.
11. Macmillan, 1924.
12. Society for New Testament Studies Monograph Series, 3, Cambridge University Press, 1966.
13. See for example the Revised Version which shows clearly that these passages were not part of the original text.
14. Mowbray, 1962.
15. Macmillan, first edition 1885, seventh edition 1896.
16. In *Ostkirchliche Studien*, 2, 2.

CHAPTER TEN

1. D. F. Strauss published his *Das Leben Jesu* in two volumes, 1835 and 1836. The second edition was unaltered. The third edition, 1838–9, contained alterations but the fourth edition in 1840 agreed with the first. The English translation was made by the novelist George Eliot who completed her task in 1846. For an account of the effect of Strauss's work see for example S. Neill's *The Interpretation of the New Testament 1861–1961*, pp. 15 ff.
2. Ed. J. Parker, Longmans.
3. In *The Synoptic Problem: A Critical Analysis,* Macmillan Company, New York, and Collier-Macmillan, London, 1964. The book is a critical review of the process by which the standard statement has been reached.
4. H. J. Holtzmann published *Die Synoptischen Evangelien: Ihr Ursprung und ihr geschichtliche Charakter*, Leipzig, 1863, when only 31 years of age. He was to be the tutor of A. Schweitzer who dedicated his first book on the gospels to him.
5. Clarendon Press, 1911.
6. Clarendon Press, 1898, second edition, revised and supplemented, 1909.
7. Macmillan.
8. In *The Gospel History and its Transmission*, Clark, Edinburgh, 1906.
9. This summary is taken from Streeter's own précis at the head of his chapter 8 of *The Four Gospels*.
10. *Behind the Third Gospel: A Study of the Proto-Luke Hypothesis*, Clarendon Press, Oxford, 1926.
11. *The Four Gospels*, p. 183.
12. *Studies in the Gospels*, ed. Nineham, D. E. Blackwell, Oxford, 1955.
13. *The Gospel History and its Transmission*, pp. 102 f.
14. M. Dibelius, *From Tradition to Gospel*. Translated by Bertram Lee Woolf from the second edition of *Die Formgeschichte des Evangeliums*, Nicholson, 1934.

Notes

15. This English translation is by J. Marsh and published by Blackwell, Oxford, in 1963. The German editions are dated 1921, 1931, 1957, published by Vandenhoeck und Ruprecht, Göttingen.
16. Hodder & Stoughton.
17. This is the title of the English translation by W. Lowrie of 1925, published by A. & C. Black. The German original, *Das Messianitäts - und Leidensgeheimnis: Eine Skizze des Lebens Jesu*, was published in Tübingen and Leipzig in 1901, and dedicated to his tutor, H. J. Holtzmann.
18. The translator was W. Montgomery and the publishers A. & C. Black. A second edition appeared in 1911.
19. The book, published by Hodder & Stoughton, comprised the Bampton Lectures of 1934.
20. *The Quest of the Historical Jesus*, p. 401.
21. op. cit., p. 225.
22. *Der sogenannte historiche Jesus und der geschichtliche, biblische Christus*. was first published in 1892 in Leipzig, and reprinted several times. New edition by Ernst Wolf, Munich, 1953. It was translated into English, edited and given an Introduction by Carl E. Braaten, Fortress Press, Philadelphia, 1964.
23. *Jesus von Nazareth* was first published in 1956, second edition 1957, third edition 1959. English translation by Irene and Fraser McLuskey with James M. Robinson, *Jesus of Nazareth*, published by Hodder & Stoughton, 1960.
24. *Jesus of Nazareth*, p. 56.
25. S.C.M. Press, Studies in Biblical Theology, no. 25, 1959.
26. In *Rediscovering the Teaching of Jesus*, S.C.M. Press, New Testament Library, 1967, p. 230.
27. op. cit., p. 230.
28. See note 26.
29. Perrin, op. cit., p. 245.
30. Listeners to his lecture at the conference were gratified on returning to Christ Church to discover already on sale a booklet with this title, in which the lecture was printed, published by A. R. Mowbray, 1957.
31. The book carries the sub-title, *Oral Tradition and Written Transmission in Rabbinic Judaism and Early Christianity*, Gleerup, Lund & Munksgaard, Copenhagen, 1961.

CHAPTER ELEVEN

1. E. C. Hoskyns, *The Fourth Gospel*, ed. F. N. Davey, vols. 1 and 2, Faber & Faber, London, 1940.
2. R. Bultmann, *Das Evangelium des Johannes*, Vandenhock und Ruprecht, Göttingen, 1941, second edition 1950.
3. Cambridge University Press.

4. C. K. Barrett, *The Gospel according to St. John*, S.P.C.K., 1955.
5. Oxford University Press, 1960.
6. op. cit., p. 78.
7. Cambridge University Press, 1963.
8. op. cit., p. 10, n. 1.
9. In *New Testament Studies*, 10, 4, pp. 517 ff.
10. In *The Gospel according to John I-XII*, The Anchor Bible, vol. 29, Doubleday, New York, 1966.

CHAPTER TWELVE

1. It is a useful convention to use the word Pauline with a capital 'P' when we mean 'written by the apostle Paul himself' and pauline with a small 'p' when we mean 'according to his teaching but written by someone else who was influenced by him'. The term 'deutero-pauline' is sometimes used by theologians for this latter purpose, and is stretched by some to include almost anything affected by Pauline ideas.
2. Probably a son and certainly a disciple of Hillel, and president of the Sanhedrin early in the first century A.D.
3. The distinction is made by Schoeps on the basis of Justin Dial. 47. See p. 204.
4. *I Clem.*, 5.
5. Note, with a small 'p', meaning that it is in accordance with his doctrine, and of his 'school', but not Pauline, actually written by Paul.
6. This is true even of Romans which appears to be something of a continuous treatise; for it appears that Paul had to meet the objections of those Christians who felt that Christianity was the crown rather than the replacement of Judaism, and that Paul's doctrine as known already in Galatians implied that God had abandoned his original plan of world redemption through his own chosen people.
7. In *The New Testament in the Twentieth Century*, Macmillan, 1924.
8. The first German edition appeared in 1929. The English translation is by W. Montgomery, A. & C. Black, 1931.
9. The original German was published in 1911. The English translation is by W. Montgomery, A. & C. Black, 1912.
10. Published by Macmillan as follows: Galatians 1865, Philippians 1868, Colossians and Philemon 1875. Galatians contains an able exposition of the 'North Galatia' theory, Philippians incorporates a masterly essay on the Ministry in the New Testament from the point of view of liberal Anglicanism in the nineteenth century, Colossians and Philemon includes an essay on the Essenes still worth careful study.
11. Dover Publications, New York, 1911. The English translation was made in 1911 from the original French of 1907.
12. In *The Earlier Epistles of St. Paul*, Rivingtons, 1911.

Notes

13. In *St. Paul and the Mystery Religions*, Hodder & Stoughton, 1913. Kennedy is critical of this type of explanation.

14. W. Bousset, *Kyrios Christos: Geschichte des Christensglaubens von den Anfangen des Christentums bis Irenaeus*, Göttingen, 1913.

15. op. cit., p. 135.

16. In *Paulus und die Heilsgeschichte*, Universitetsforlaget, Aarhus & Munksgaard, Copenhagen, 1954. English translation by Frank Clarke, *Paul and the Salvation of Mankind*, S.C.M. Press, 1959.

17. W. Schmithals, *Die Gnosis in Korinth*, Vandenhoeck und Ruprecht, Göttingen, 1956, second edition 1965.

18. In *The Interpretation of the New Testament 1851–1961*, The Firth Lectures, 1962, Oxford University Press, 1964.

19. op. cit., p. 222.

20. ibid,. p. 182.

21. S.C.M. Press, Studies in Biblical Theology, no. 5, 1952.

22. S.C.M. Paperback, 1963.

23. Brill, Leiden.

24. K. Barth, *Der Römerbrief*, Kaiser, München, 1918. Several editions since published. English translation from the sixth edition by E. C. Hoskyns, *The Epistle of the Romans*, Oxford University Press, 1933.

25. The other facts to which allusion is made here include the varying position in the different manuscripts of the final doxology, xvi, 25–27, the strong suspicion on grounds of vocabulary that it is not from Paul, and the poor attestation for the alternative doxology, xvi, 24, which is omitted from standard Greek texts. It is puzzling that the favourite alternative position for xvi, 25–27 is at the end of chapter xiv; for no one wishes to argue that one recension of Romans ended there. Other interesting facts are the testimony in the margin of two manuscripts that some copy used by Origen lacked the words 'in Rome' at i, 7 and the omission in one manuscript of this phrase at both i, 7 and i, 15.

26. ' "All Things to All Men" (I Corinthians ix, 22)' in *New Testament Studies* 1, 4, May 1955, p. 261.

27. John C. Hurd, Jr., *The Origin of 1 Corinthians*, S.P.C.K., London, 1965.

28. See for example A. M. Hunter, *Paul and his Predecessors*, Nicholson & Watson, 1940.

29. E. G. Bultmann, Käsemann, Hunter.

30. R. P. Martin, *Carmen Christi: Philippians ii, 5–11*, Cambridge University Press, 1967.

CHAPTER THIRTEEN

1. The first edition was published by the Macmillan Company, New York, in 1927. It was reprinted unchanged in 1958 by S.P.C.K.

2. Pfleiderer's *Paulinismus* was published in 1873 and in English translation in two volumes in 1877.

3. A. Harnack, *Lukas der Arzt*, Leipzig, 1906. English translation by J. R. Wilkinson, *Luke the Physician*, Williams & Norgate, 1903 and 1907; *Die Apostelgeschichte*, Leipzig, 1908, English translation by J. R. Wilkinson, Williams & Norgate, 1909.

4. In *The Medical Language of St Luke*, London, 1882.

5. *Aufsätze zur Apostelgeschichte*, Greeven, Göttingen, 1951. The English translation, made by M. Ling and P. Schubert, was published by S.C.M. Press, in 1956.

6. A. H. M. Jones, *Studies in Roman Government and Law*, Blackwell, 1960; A. N. Sherwin-White, *Roman Society and Roman Law in the New Testament*, Clarendon Press, 1963.

7. R. P. C. Hanson, *The Acts in the Revised Standard Version*, New Clarendon Bible, Oxford, 1967.

CHAPTER FOURTEEN

1. Oxford University Press, 1921. The book should be read in conjunction with his article, 'The Authorship of the Pastoral Epistles' in the *Expository Times*, lxvii, 3, Dec. 1958.

2. The article is that mentioned in note 1 above.

3. For example, O. Cullmann, *The Christology of the New Testament*, translated by S. C. Guthrie and C. A. M. Hall, S.C.M. Press, 1959, p. 83 ff.; H. Kosmala, *Hebräer-Essener-Christen*, Brill, Leiden, 1959. J. Gnilka, 'Die Erwartung des Messianischen Hohenpriesters in den Schriften von Qumran und im Neuen Testament', in *Revue de Qumrân*, 7, 2, June 1960, p. 395, gives further references. All the above were written before the discovery of the fragment about Melchizedek (n. 4).

4. From Cave 11, officially designated 11 Q Melch. Published for example in *Christian News from Israel*, xvii, 7, April 1966, p. 23, and studied by M. de Jonge and A. S. van der Woude in '11Q Melchizedek and the New Testament', in *N.T.S.*, 12, 4, July 1966, p. 301, and by Joseph A. Fitzmeyer, S. J. in 'Further Light on Melchizedek from Cave 11', in the *Journal of Biblical Literature*, lxxvi, 1, March 1967, p. 25. The still more recently discovered 'Temple Scroll' may perhaps when fully studied throw further light on the background of Hebrews. For this scroll see Y. Yadin in The *Biblical Archaeologist*, xxx, 4, December 1967.

5. The inference is uncertain, however. 'Those from Italy' may be companions of the author in Italy, or in Rome but belonging to elsewhere in Italy, or anywhere else in the Mediterranean world, but originating from Italy.

6. The loose ascription of *The Testaments of the Twelve Patriarchs* to this period is designed to leave open the complicated questions of date (perhaps varying for each *Testament*), manner of composition, possible

Notes

interpolation and other problems connected with this book, on which scholars have given and still give very different anwers. See for example D. S. Russell, *The Method and Message of Jewish Apocalyptic*, S.C.M. Press, 1964, pp. 55 ff. and F. H. Borsch, *The Son of Man in Myth and History*, S.C.M. Press, 1967, p. 162, n. 1.

7. J. B. Mayor, *The Epistle of St James*, Macmillan, 1897.
8. Docetism was a general tendency rather than a characteristic of a particular school of gnostics, but Cerinthus (fl. c. 100) was specially associated with this error by early church writers (e.g. Irenaeus and Eusebius).
9. E. Käsemann, 'Ketzer und Zeuge', in *Zeitschrift für Theologie und Kirche*, Vol. 48, 1951, pp. 292 ff.
10. Dacre Press, Westminster, 1949.

CHAPTER FIFTEEN

1. R. Bultmann, *Theology of the New Testament*, translated by K. Grobel, (2 vols.), S.C.M. Press, Vol. 1, 1952, p. 228.
2. *Jesus of Nazareth*, first written in modern Hebrew, translated by H. Danby and published by G. Allen & Unwin, London, in 1925.
3. *The Messiah Jesus and John the Baptist* (*According to Flavius Josephus' recently discovered 'Capture of Jerusalem' and other Jewish and Christian sources*), English edition by A. H. Krappe, Methuen, 1931.
4. *The Fall of Jerusalem and the Christian Church*, S.P.C.K., first edition 1951, second edition 1957.
5. In *Die Zeloten*, Brill, Leiden, 1961.
6. *Jesus and the Zealots*, Manchester University Press, 1967.
7. *Martyrdom and Persecution in the Early Church*, Blackwell, 1965.

General Index

General Index

General Index

Brooke, A. E., 108
Brooklyn Museum Aramaic Papyri, ed. E. G. Kennedy, 68
Brown, R. E., 275–6
Buber, M., 155
Bultmann, R.; 157–62, 246–7, 251, 257–8, 270–1, 290, 331, 333–5
Burial customs, 34, 35; *see also* Tombs
Burkitt, F. C., 239, 245
Burney, C. F., 223

Cadbury, H. J., 298, 300
Caesarea (Maritima), excavations at, 190–91
Cairo *geniza*, 216
Cairo Geniza, The, Paul Kahle, 103, 109–10
Caius, Roman presbyter, 268
Calendars, 179–81
Call of Isaiah, The, I. Engnell, 130
Canaan:
  ancestor-worship, 34
  call of Abram to, 29
  cult prophets, 128
  dating of Israelite occupation, 29, 31–2, 38–9, 45–7
  dating of patriarchal narratives, 39–45
  fertility cult practices, 120, 132
  form criticism of literary evidence from, 81
  influence on wisdom literature, 99
  patriarchal period, 36, 39–45
  prior to Hebrew settlement, 33–9, 58
  worship of Baal, 47–50, 52–3
Capernaum, 192
Carchemish:
  archaeological evidence from, 37
  battle of, 65–6
Casuistic law, 76, 77–8
Catholic Bible Quarterly, 28

Caves at Qumran, 178–9
Census taking, 41
Cephas (Peter), meeting with Paul, 295
Cerinthus, 268, 358 note 8
Chadwick, H., 294
Chalcolithic period in Canaan, 34, 58
Chanukkah (Feast of Dedication) 273–4
Chariots:
  Ahab's use of, 56
  introduction by Hyksos, 37, 38
Charles, R. H., 174, 176
'Charisma', 336
Christ, titles of, 314; *see also* Jesus
Christian father, concept of Old Testament canon, 216
Christian Theology of the Old Testament, A, G. A. F. Knight, 155–6
Christianity, Christian Church:
  and Hellenistic cults, 287–8
  as a 'way' in Judaism, 199
  background to rise of, 287–9
  concept of, as Body of Christ, 290–91
  deviation from Judaism, 280–81, 285
  early anti-semitism, 203
  early beliefs about Holy Spirit, 264
  early expectation of second coming, 306–7
  emergence as institution, 307, 319
  influence of Jewish scriptures, 212–20
  Jewish character, 203–11, 250–51
  merging of history and tradition, 264–5
  place of Old Testament in, 145–6, 158–9

362

General Index

General Index

General Index

Hakim, Khalif, 193
Halder, A., 133
Halakah, 198–9, 209
Hamor, 41
Hannah, Song of, 87
Hannibal, 170
Hanson, R. P. C., 304–5
Haphtorah, 209, 272–3
Haram, Jerusalem, 53, 54
Haran, North Mesopotamia, 40, 42–3
Harnack, A., 157, 160, 170, 300, 301, 302, 303
Harrison, P. N., 310–12
Harvard University, 42, 60
Hatch and Redpath, 110
Haustafeln, 317
Hawkin, John, 238–9
Hazor, 35, 36, 37, 38, 54–6
He that Cometh, S. Mowinckel, 125
Hebrew Bible, textual material, 102–7
Hebrew language:
  in apocryphal literature, 216
  in Dead Sea Scrolls, 175
  in Old Testament, 153–5
Hebrew poetry, 50–3
Hebrew script, 60
Hebrew seals, 61–2
Hebrew Thought Compared with Greek, T. Bowman, 153
Hebrew University of Jerusalem, 111–12, 201
Hebrews, Epistle to the:
  acceptance as canon, 229–30, 231
  authorship, 283, 313
  Christology in, 313–14
  nature and characteristics, 309, 313–15
  relation to Ephesians, 1 Peter, James, 310
Heidegger, M., 333
Heilsgeschichte, 141–2 149, 153

Heitmüller, W., 288
Hellenism, 206–7, 277, 287–8, 322
Hellenosemitica, M. C. Astour, 39
Hengel, M., 338
Heracleon, 189
Hermas, *Shepherd* of, 230, 231
Hermeneutics, 153–65, 258–60
Herod the Great, 190, 191, 195, 197
Herod Agrippa, 281, 302
Herschel, A., 155
Hesse, F., 163
Hexateuch, 149
Hezekiah's prayer, 87
High priesthood, defilement of, 171, 176
Hippolytus of Rome, 268, 270
Historical Tradition in the Fourth Gospel, C. H. Dodd, 274
History and Interpretation in the Gospels, R. H. Lightfoot, 257
History of Israel, A., J, Bright, 82
History of Israel, The, M. Noth, 81
History of the Synoptic Tradition, R. Bultmann, 247
Hittite kingdom, archaeological evidence of, 37, 48
Hittite treaty documents, 78–9
Hobart, W. K., 300
Holtzmann, H. J., 237–8
Holy Spirit:
  Christian concept of, 177
  in beliefs of early Church, 264
  in modern theology, 333
Holy war, Hebrew traditions of, 127
Holy week, problems of dating and sequence, 180–28
Honest to God, J. A. T. Robinson, 291
Hooke, S. H., 117–18
Horae Synopticae, 238–9
Hort, L. J. A., 236
Hosea, Book of, 97–8
Hoseabuch, H. S. Nyberg, 107

368

General Index

Jeremiah, confessions of, 92, 94, 136

Jericho:
  archaeological evidence from, 33–4, 35, 36, 37, 38, 39, 46–7
  capture by Joshua, 46

Jeroboam, 57–8

Jerusalem:
  accounts of 'Council' at, 301–2
  archaeological evidence of pre-exilic site, 53–4
  capture by David, 53
  capture by Moslems, 193
  city boundaries, 53
  conquest by Babylon, 65–6
  cult traditions, 123, 124, 128–9, 132
  destruction, 70 A.D., 161, 251–2
  Dome of the Rock, 53
  early settlement, 35
  Fortress Antonia, 195–6
  Paul's visits to, 279
  sacred sites, 192–5
  site of ancient temples, 53
  see also Temple

Jesus:
  agony in the garden, 337
  as healer, 274
  comparison with Teacher of Righteousness, 183–5
  concept of, as Jewish martyr, 337–8
  concept of place in history of Israel, 160
  concept of the Last Supper, 182
  evangelists' view of, 213
  messianic claims, 258
  ministry, 274
  movement from Galilee to Jerusalem, 269
  quest for the historical, 238, 252–65, 330, 336–9
  quotations from scripture, 198
  rabbinic parallels in teaching of, 201

  relation of teaching to quest for historical, 261–2
  responsibility for creation of own traditions, 263–4
  resurrection, 255, 257, 262–3, 331, 332, 339
  site of birth, 195
  site of death and burial, 192–5
  site of trial, 195–6
  titles of, 314
  use of Aramaic and Greek, 217
  see also Christology

Jesus of Nazareth, G. Bornkamm, 260

Jesus of Nazareth, J. Klausner, 337

Jewish martyrs, 171, 220, 313, 337

Jewish scholarship and New Testament studies, 201–2

Job, Book of:
  concept of Wisdom, 136
  place in Old Testament theology, 150, 152, 164

Joel, Book of, 97, 132

Joel Studies, A. S. Kapelrud, 132

Johanan ben Zakkai, 199

Johannine epistles, 323–6; *see also under each epistle*

John, Gospel according to:
  acceptance as canon, 265, 268
  account of Jesus' ministry, 269, 274
  account of Palestinian topography, 274
  account of trial of Jesus, 196
  authorship, 266, 267–8
  concept of Holy Spirit, 264
  concept of Jesus, 266–7
  early association with Revelation, 268
  elements of Judaism, 271–4
  evidence of liturgical orientation, 272–4
  historicity, 234–6
  nature and characteristics, 265, 269–71, 274–5, 330–31

370

General Index

Kidron valley, 192

Kingdom of God, concept of, in Old Testament, 159

Kingship, concepts of, 88, 90, 91, 99, 100, 116, 117, 121–5, 132, 133, 185

Kingship and the Gods, H. Frankfort, 121–2

Kirkbride, Diana, 34

Kirkuk (Arrapkha), excavations at, 42–4

Kittel, *Biblia Hebraica*, 103, 104, 107, 111

Klausner, J., 289, 337

Knight, G. A. F., 155–6

Koine see Greek Language

Kommentar zum Neuen Testament aus Talmud und Midrash, 200

Konyahu, son of Elnathon, 102–3

Kraeling, E. G., 68

Kramer, S. N., 99

Kraus, H. J., 91, 116

Kyrios-Christos, W., Bousset, 289

Labyrinth, The, S. H. Hooke, 117

Lachish:
    dating of destruction, 45–6
    identification of site, 31–2
    literary evidence from, 62–4
    seal from, 61
    settlement at, 35
    threat from Babylon, 63

Lachmann, K., 226, 237, 243

Lady Wisdom, concept of, 134–6

Lake, Kirsopp, 204, 288

Lamentations, acceptance as canon, 216, 219–20

Laments:
    communal, 86
    individual, 86, 87, 88, 124–5

'Laodiceans', 230

Lapp, Paul, 31

Last Supper:
    problems of date, 180–82
    relation to Eucharist, 181–2

Late Bronze Age in Canaan, 38–9, 46

Latin Church in Jerusalem, 193

Latin version of the New Testament, 225

Law, oral (*halakah*), 198–9, 209

Law and Covenant in Israel and the Ancient Near East, G. E. Mendenhall, 78–9

Law codes, 100

Law suits in prophetic literature, 94

Laws in the Pentateuch, 76–8

Lazarus, raising of, 273–4

Learned societies, journals, 27

Leben Jesu, D. F. Strauss, 269

Lectionary, Jewish, 108–9, 272–4

Legend of Keret, 50

Lessing, G. E., 237

Letter of Adon, 64–5

Levi, and the priesthood, 185

Levitical priests, 77

Lexicographical information in Ugaritic and Hebrew texts, 51

Life of Constantine, Eusebius, 193

Life of Jesus, D. F. Strauss, 233–4

Lightfoot, J. B., 170, 235, 236, 287

Lightfoot, R. H., 257

Lindars, B., 212

Literary criticism:
    of the New Testament, 233–42
    of the Old Testament, 72–5, 82–4, 96–7, 101

'Literary structure of Israel's oracles', R. B. Y. Scott, 93–4

Liturgies in the Old Testament, 87

Logos:
    concept of, in Fourth Gospel, 268
    identification with Wisdom, 136

Love, concept of, in Deuteronomy, 161

Loewe, H., 200

General Index

General Index

Rahlfs, A., 108

Ras Shamra, texts from 84, 115, 119, 120, 129–30, 132

Rawlinson, A. E. J., 245

Rebekah, 42–3

Rebirth of Images, A, A. Farrer, 326

Redaction criticism, 330–31

Rediscovering the Teaching of Jesus, N. Perrin, 261–2

Re-enthronement themes, 53, 89, 117–18, 122, 126–7, 132

Rehoboam, 56

Reitzenstein, R., 288, 290

Religion of Ancient Israel, The, Th. C. Vriezen, 116, 138

Religion in the Old Testament, R. H. Pfeiffer, 140

Religion of the Old Testament, The, K. Marti, 131

Religionsgeschichte, 138–9

'Religionsgeschichte und alttestamentliche theologie', O. Eissfeldt, 140

Religious language, problems of meaning, 119–20

Resurrection, The, 255, 257, 262–3, 331, 332, 339

Revelation, Book of:
acceptance as canon, 229–30
authorship and characteristics, 324, 326–8
early association with Fourth Gospel, 268
Greek language, 207
texts of, 224

Revelation discourses, 270–71

Revue du Qumrân, 27

Richter, W., 100

Riesenfeld, Harald, 263

Ringgren, H., 116

Ritual humiliation of the king, concept of, 121, 123, 124–5

Rkb brbt, interpretation of, 52

Rkb rpt, interpretation of, 52

Roberts, B. J., 103

Robinson, J. A. T., 291

Robinson, J. M., 260–61

Roman Catholics:
concept of Fourth Gospel, 275–6
concept of Old Testament canon, 214–15
modern critical scholarship, 27–8

Romans, Epistle to the:
acceptance as canon, 230
authorship, 235–5, 283, 285
nature and characteristics, 280, 291, 292–3, 355 note 6
texts of, 292

Rothenberg, B., 56

Rowley, H. H., 116

Royal psalms, 86, 122–3, 124–5

Rule of Qumran, 175, 176–7, 179, 182–3, 184, 198

Rule of the Congregation, 182–3

Sabbath, abandonment by early church, 250–51

Sacral Kingship in Ancient Israel, A. R. Johnson, 122

Sacred marriage themes, 118, 121

SA-Gaz, cuneiform ideograph from Ugarit, 44

Sages, emergence in Israel, 99, 100

Samaria:
collapse of, 59
fortifications, 59
ostraca from, 60–61
papyri from 68–70
period as capital of northern kingdom, 57–9
revolt against Alexander the Great, 69

Samuel, 95, 128

Samuel, Books of, scrolls versions, 105

Sanballat, governor of Samaria, 69

Sanday, William, 238–9

Saqqara (Memphis), excavations at, 64

General Index

General Index

Index of References

Index of References

Index of References

Index of References

Index of References

The Study of Religions

H. D. Lewis and Robert Lawson Slater

'To maintain that all religions are paths leading to the same goal, as is so frequently done today, is to maintain something that is not true. Not only on the dogmatic, but on the mystical plane, too, there is no agreement.'

These forthright words from an expert on oriental religion reflect the modern, realistic approach to the comparative study of religions. The results of western re-appraisal of three great living traditions – Hinduism, Buddhism, and Islam – are outlined in the first part of this Pelican by Professor Slater, who discusses the history, literature, beliefs and practices of these religions and comments on their internal diversity and their attitudes to divinity. In the second part Professor H. D. Lewis relates trends in philosophy to the study of religions, examines the Hindu and Buddhist concepts of God and questions whether such Christians as Paul Tillich have done well, in the high-minded cause of fraternity, to generalize their faith to the point at which it loses its essential Christianity. This book was originally published under the title *World Religions*.

The Pelican New Testament Commentaries

Paul's Letters from Prison

Philippians, Colossians, Philemon and Ephesians

J. H. Houlden

Paul was a Jew of the dispersion, familiar with Greek
ideas and culture. An exotic style, the corruption of texts
handed down to us, and a thick layer of pietistic
interpretation produced by 2000 years of Christianity,
have obscured his work for us. The purpose of this book,
which includes Paul's letters to the Philippians, Colossians,
Ephesians, and to Philemon, is to let Paul speak for
himself, without the assumptions imposed by many
modern readers.
Paul's main concern was to reconcile the two dominant
principles of his work: the omnipotence of God as Lord
of the Universe, and the alienation of man. This
reconciliation Paul saw typified in the person of Jesus; but
in one very clear direction – the direction which landed
him in jail. Man's alienation could be cured not merely
by coming to a better 'moral state', but by coming into a
new status, a new pattern of social relationships.

The 'captivity epistles' are of dubious authorship and
from different times, but together they form a valuable
introduction to the apostle's work.

Also available
Paul's First Letter to Corinth   *John Ruef*

The Pelican History of the Church

1. The Early Church
Henry Chadwick

The story of the early Christian church from the death of Christ to the Papacy of Gregory the Great. Professor Henry Chadwick makes use of the latest research to explain the astonishing expansion of Christianity throughout the Roman Empire.

2. Western Society and the Church in the Middle Ages
R. W. Southern

In the period between the eighth and the sixteenth centuries the Church and State were more nearly one than ever before or after. In this new book Professor Southern discusses how this was achieved and what stresses it caused.

3. The Reformation
Owen Chadwick

In this volume Professor Owen Chadwick deals with the formative work of Erasmus, Luther, Zwingli, Calvin, with the special circumstances of the English Reformation, and with the Counter-Reformation.

4. The Church and the Age of Reason
G. R. Cragg

This span in the history of the Christian church stretches from the age of religious and civil strife before the middle of the seventeenth century to the age of industrialism and republicanism which followed the French Revolution.

5. The Church in an Age of Revolution
Alec R. Vidler

'A most readable and provocative volume and a notable addition to this promising and distinguished series' – *Guardian*

6. A History of Christian Missions
Stephen Neill

This volume of *The Pelican History of the Church* represents the first attempt in English to provide a readable history of the worldwide expansion of all the Christian denominations – Roman Catholic, Orthodox, Anglican, and Protestant.

The Pelican Guide to Modern Theology

Volume 1
Systematic and Philosophical Theology

William Nicholls

In modern times theology has run into that same crisis
which has been induced in the whole of civilized culture
by the advance of science. This first volume outlines the
directions of thought adopted by such modern theologians
as Barth, Bultmann, Bonhoeffer and Tillich in the face of
the scientific challenge. Though concerned in the main
with what must be recognized as a German Protestant
tradition, Professor Nicholls's study does much to clarify
the latest developments in Catholic theology as well.
It reveals a liveliness and openness in modern religious
thought which suggest that, whatever it may become in
the future, theology is not dying.

Volume 2
Historical Theology

J. Daniélou, A. H. Couratin and John Kent

Christianity is not simply enshrined in the Bible; nor is it
merely doctrine, nor merely worship. It has formed and
been formed by history. In this second volume Cardinal
Daniélou provides a modern commentary on patristic
literature (in which can be found the genesis of the classic
dogmas of the Christian Church); Canon Couratin
outlines the development of Church liturgy and the
manner of Christian worship, particularly for baptism
and communion; and, in his discussion of ecclesiastical
history written in the last forty years, Professor Kent
clearly reveals the modern trends in one aspect of
theology. The whole volume evidences the weight of
tradition which necessarily influences the modern
Christian theologian.